The Technology
M&A Guidebook

The Technology M&A Guidebook

Ed Paulson
with Court Huber

John Wiley & Sons, Inc.

New York • Chichester • Weinheim • Brisbane • Singapore • Toronto

Library of Congress Cataloging-in-Publication Data

Paulson, Ed.
    The technology M&A guidebook / Ed Paulson with Court Huber.
      p. cm
    Includes bibliographical references and index.
    ISBN 0-471-36010-4 (cloth : alk. paper)
      1. Consolidation and merger of corporations. 2. High technology industries–Mergers.
    I. Huber, Court. II. Title

    HD2746.5 .P38 2000
    620'.0068'1–dc21

                                                                00-026152

Table of Contents

Preface

Companies today must deal with rapidly changing marketplaces and technologies on both a domestic and international level. This dynamic situation requires rapid responses by the companies that intend to remain viable, growing competitors. Some startup companies capitalize on the needs created by rapid change and design their corporate strategy specifically to become attractive acquisition candidates for larger industry players. Companies like Cisco Systems realize that developing technology using internal resources may not be the least expensive or least risky course when compared to acquiring a company with an already established market share, technology, or product set.

Knowing that an acquisition is a desirable business direction is one thing. Finding that right acquisition candidate and effectively executing the acquisition process in such a way that initial objectives are later achieved is a demanding and risky process. Analyzing a company for its legal and financial merits is an important exercise for any company, but this process only goes part of the way when a technology company is involved. Much of the value of a technology company may not even appear on the financial statements. The value may lie with key personnel, specialized manufacturing processes, intellectual property agreements, or other aspects of company operation that are not readily discernible from publicly available information. The target's current and strategic value opportunity must be assessed in light of specific technology industry norms. These values might be uncovered during the due diligence process or simply through extensive industry experience on the part of the buyer.

Adding to this complexity is the very real possibility that the target company may not be publicly traded or even show a profit. Placing a value on a publicly traded stock is risky enough, but justifying the placement of a multimillion dollar value on a company with no positive earnings requires specialized analysis and solid forward-looking assessments that are in many ways unique to technology fields.

Many excellent books are available to readers that cover M&A (Merger & Aquisition) tactics, strategies, and valuation procedures for firms. My intention with this book is not to duplicate existing efforts. Instead, I intend to add a technology focus to a distillation of this existing body of knowledge while balancing the needs of the experienced manager who may be a financial novice and those of the financial expert who may be a technology or M&A novice. It is not uncommon to have a technology manager involved in, or even managing, the search for and investigation of an acquisition candidate. That same manager might be chartered with the sale of a specific technology division of a larger company. Quite often, this manager has excellent technical and management skills but little to no financial or M&A management background. The financial and other overview chapters of this book are designed to help managers in this position understand the demands of the M&A process and how they can be managed. Financial managers who are new to technology and/or M&A activities will find the financial chapters a review but will likely find value in the M&A, marketing, sales, and technology chapters. Experienced technology managers may also find the technology chapters interesting; they are designed to present the accepted realities of a particular industry which will likely differ greatly from the reader's own industry's realities. The intention with these technology chapters (Chapters 11 to 15) is to present enough information so that the reader can effectively understand the nuances of another technology industry while evaluating a company in that segment. A complete glossary of terms, along with additional M&A information, is located at my Web site, www.edpaulson.com, as is an email link (author@edpaulson.com) for those who wish to recommend additional terms or who wish to contact me directly.

In a world of change, globalization, and uncertainty, of one thing you can be sure: M&A is a powerful tool in today's technology business environment, and this tool can be used to your benefit or against you. Reading this book and applying its recommendations to your particular situation is an excellent first step making M&A work for you. Thank you for keeping technology the incredible economic engine plus source of wonder that it is, and thank you for purchasing this book. Your feedback on ways that it can be improved as a tool for its readers is greatly appreciated.

Ed Paulson, Chicago, IL

The Technology
M&A Guidebook

Stages of the M&A Process

For both the buyer and the seller, the M&A process is an exciting and stressful experience. Like any experience that is full of uncertainty, different personalities, and risk, the more realistic your expectations, the more likely you are to weather the process successfully. You might even become one of those people who are addicted to "the deal." The intent of this chapter is to introduce you to the overall M&A process from beginning to end. The beginning of the process might not be where you expect it to be, and the end certainly extends past the final signing of agreements. Taking a few minutes to work your way through this chapter will help you to gauge your timing, activities, and expectations, and will make the entire process more productive and profitable.

The Differences between Buying and Selling

For every transaction there must be a buyer and a seller. One cannot succeed without the other, and both are dependent upon each other for a successful transaction outcome. Successful negotiators and salespeople are experts at understanding the other person's perspective. Even though both may have opposing viewpoints with respect to the specific final process and outcome objectives, both also have a vested interest in making the process proceed to a productive and profitable conclusion. Understanding that an M&A transaction cannot be consummated without the other person's agreement provides some motivation for your understanding of their perspective.

The basic difference between buying and selling can be summed up in this way:

- The buyer is looking for future value to be derived from the purchase. Toward this end, the buyer is looking to purchase the maximum amount of company for lowest possible price.

- The seller wants to sell for the highest possible price combined with the fewest number of future entanglements.

- Buyers and sellers in a strategic merger are looking for a lasting partnership relationship that benefits both buyer, seller, and their respective shareholders.

It is naive to assume that both parties are working toward the complete mutual satisfaction of all parties concerned, especially when the dollar amounts involved become large. But it is also naive to assume that everyone is a business mercenary out for his own particular self-interest to the exclusion or sacrifice of the other party. For example, a seller who sets too high an asking price will likely meet with a longer sale process and much frustration. And a buyer who offers too low a purchase price (low enough to be insulting to the seller) will hurt his own credibility and undermine his ability to negotiate with that seller in the future.

There is a "good faith" aspect to any large-ticket sale process that forms the foundation of any solid business transaction. If you have ever done business with someone you do not completely trust, you know that good faith is often the element that brings an otherwise stalled transaction back to life. Conversely, a lack of good faith can undermine any possibility of creating a solid transaction between parties who would otherwise be excellent buyer and seller candidates. A balance must be found between watching out for your self-interest while ensuring that the other party doesn't feel cheated or completely insulted in a transaction.

In reality, some people succeed by being completely ruthless, but I have found that these people exist on television more than in real life. Anyone who practices business in this way is often a "one deal wonder" who might excel on a single transaction but generally cannot repeat the performance. Word gets out, and everyone now expects that person to be the shark that he has shown himself to be and to handle the negotiations accordingly. My experience has been that most people will naturally and jealously protect their own company's best interests. Most are people of integrity who want some level of reward for both parties, but who are hoping to tip the reward factor more in their company's favor. Approaching a negotiation within this context of integrity is almost always an excellent starting point.

Something else to consider about M&A is that the buyers and sellers are much like responsible yet divorced parents. They are happy to have made the major transition involved, but they also have an ongoing interest in the well-being of the child. A seller, especially a founder-seller, will often want a voice in the future operation of the sold entity. The buyer might well want the founder-seller involved in the future operation of the entity as it embarks on its new life. The transferred business becomes the child that both parents choose to nurture as a future project. This point may look as though it applies to only very small businesses, but many large companies are run by original founders who have created a solid internal following over previous years of success. Alienating the seller may also alienate many key employees who may transfer with the purchase, and buyers should be wary of this possibility and its ramifications.

If bad blood exists between buyer and seller, just as with two divorced parents, the final result generally will be hardest felt by the children. In the case of an acquisition, the negative impact will be borne by the sold company in the form of impeded future performance and unfulfilled objectives. If the seller has a portion of the sale price tied to future financial performance and that performance is below projections, then the seller loses. If the future financial performance does not meet initial expectations, then the buyer certainly loses. It is in the interest of both parties to have the negotiations proceed from a perspective of self-interest, but not at the expense of future cooperation. The more that you understand about the other parties in the negotiations, the more likely you are to achieve your transaction goals and create a post-purchase entity that meets or exceeds expectations.

Preparing to Sell or Buy

A common misconception is that a business manager can decide to buy or sell a company today, and simply close the deal within a few weeks. That might be the case on rare occasions, but an M&A transaction is usually complicated and may take months, or even years in some rare cases, to finalize. Large company transactions requiring regulatory or antitrust approval may not be approved at all, but may tie up both companies for extended periods of time in dealing with the involved regulatory bodies. If you are selling, you must prepare your company to look as appealing as possible to a potential buyer. If you are buying, you must do some homework to determine the proper selection criteria for determining the optimal acquisition target company. These points may seem obvious but you will find that implementing the details associated with achieving these "obvious" points requires direction and commitment. Chapter 16, "Preparing to Buy and Sell," outlines the details associated with presale preparations, but here are a few items to whet your appetite:

- Your legal structure should be in order so that there are no unexpected legal, tax, or litigation issues that will catch you or a prospective buyer by surprise.

- Your financial reports should be auditable with a minimal number of red flags (problems) coming to the surface.

- Your operational plans should be standardized so that another uninitiated party can understand the value intrinsic to what you do.

- Your personnel and management should be stable and experienced, because a prospective buyer will often want the management team to transfer with the company when purchased.

Just as you would put a new coat of paint on your house before selling, you should make your company look as attractive as possible. This takes time, effort, money, and foresight. Sellers might find that their company runs better with all of these value-enhancing factors in place which makes their implementation a good idea for all parties involved. Buyers will find that preparatory work enables them to recognize the right acquisition fit when it comes across their desks. Buyers are well served by giving advance consideration to a number of important aspects of the transaction, such as:

- What is the desired strategic fit between your company and the proposed acquisition target?

- What are the financial parameters within which the acquisition must conform? These parameters may include annual sales, expected purchase price, financial structure, ownership, and others.

- What are the desired personnel requirements between the acquired management and that of your company?

- Are there intrinsic economy of scale parameters that qualify or disqualify a potential acquisition target?

- What levels of technology and engineering are required to enable the acquired company to meet the buyer's technology goals?

There are many different aspects of an acquisition target that must be considered before you can determine if a proposed company is right for you. See Chapter 16, "Preparing to Buy and Sell," for a more detailed discussion of the important advance actions that optimize your likelihood of success. Of one thing you can be sure: The more that a buyer understands his or her motivations for acquiring another company, the more effective the buyer will be at separating the unlikely candidates from those that present the highest likelihood of a successful transaction.

Both buyer and seller should form an M&A team of professionals and managers who will work with you throughout the process. The team should include:

- An accountant for assistance on the financial side of the transaction.

- An M&A attorney who is experienced with transactions of your type, whether a privately held, publicly held, or nonprofit organization.

- A tax attorney (who might be the same person as the M&A attorney, but does not necessarily have to be).

- Key members of your management team who understand the business aspects of the transaction. Don't skimp on selecting these people. If the deal doesn't make business sense, it is really no deal at all, even if it does make financial and legal sense. Select these personnel based on previously determined strategic business goals for the M&A transaction.

- You might want to investigate business brokers who can assist you with finding either a buyer or a seller, depending on your side of the transaction.

- Finally, you must ensure secrecy on the part of all people involved. This point cannot be too heavily stressed, especially if you are the seller. More on the need for seller secrecy is presented in Chapter 16.

In summary, buyers should not expect to find the right deal unless they have done the homework needed to recognize that deal. Sellers must make themselves as attractive as possible and must understand their most likely buyer, if they plan to get the highest possible price for their company. The more you know about what you are looking for, the more likely you are to find it. Companies will find that time spent preparing for a transaction will better ensure a smooth and profitable transaction.

Finding the Candidate

Think back to the last time you purchased a house. Unless you were one of the lucky people who simply stumbled on the right house, you probably spent a lot of time looking at all types of houses before you found the one that was right for you. Your Realtor asked you questions about bedrooms, baths, garage size, and square footage, and so on. From this information your Realtor narrows down the field of possible houses from the unmanageable thousands available to the manageable few that present the best possible fit. The same is true for a business acquisition. There are thousands of businesses that could be potential candidates, but only a few that will ultimately meet your desired criteria. Finding them from the thousands of candidates is a tricky and usually time-consuming process.

Just as the search for a house can be narrowed down by defining basic selection criteria, so can the search for the "short list" of possible acquisition candidates. Here are a few items to consider as you start refining your initial filtering criteria:

- The maximum and minimum revenue range
- Geographic location
- Years in business
- Market share
- Reputation (either good or poor)
- Distribution channels
- Technology provided
- Corporate culture
- Specific business strengths, such as R&D, sales/marketing, or production
- Low-cost as opposed to high-price provider
- Services or products provider

- Industry

- Publicly traded or privately held

- Reputation of the management team

This list can continue to a high level of detail, which will help in refining the search. Don't be surprised if a very detailed list reveals no companies at all; at this time, you start dropping "nice-to-have" items from the list and search based on "must-have" items. Don't be fooled into thinking that a highly refined list will find exactly the right target. Much of the successful M&A process is derived from the interaction of management, owners, shareholders, and financial backers, all of which cannot be effectively quantified. All you are trying to do at this point is distill down the list of possible companies to a short list of the (roughly 10 or so) companies on which a more detailed investigation can be performed.

Some people employ the services of a business broker at this initial qualification stage. These companies take a percentage of the transaction total (usually five to fifteen percent) for assisting with the initial search and with the consummation of the final deal. Using a broker usually speeds up the filtering stage of the acquisition process, but it is not cost-free. Remember that their fees must be paid at some point and are embedded into the purchase price. The more that buyer and seller know about each other, the more accurately they can assess the likelihood of a successful future business relationship. Plan for this process to take time. Spend the required time in the due diligence stage and thoroughly understand what you are committing to with the sale or purchase.

Buying and/or selling a business is one of the most important decisions a business owner or manager will make. The seller sees the sale as a payoff for years of work. Handling the sale improperly can shortchange those years of effort and attention. Purchasing the wrong company draws valuable resources from the parent company, causing both the parent and target company to go into financial distress, seriously hurting both the buying company and often the career of the person responsible for the acquisition. The sell/buy decision is best made rationally, without haste, to best ensure a successful postsale result. Overzealous emotion and enthusiasm should be saved for the postsale environment, in which the consummated deal must perform according to expectations.

The Meetings

The M&A process usually becomes quite complicated unless the transaction value is small and the number of parties involved are few. The buyer has a team of experts, as does the seller. If there is any antitrust exposure, there will be added complexity. Even small companies may have antitrust exposure under very specific market situations. See Chapter 17, "Competitor Transactions," for additional information on antitrust issues. Should either party be a publicly traded company, the complexity increases again. Should either party be involved in litigation of any kind, the complexity increases yet again. Be aware that unexpected and often unwelcome surprises come up during the M&A process. These surprises might stem not from deceit on anyone's part, but simply from oversight.

The seller and buyer will have a number of internal meetings early in their respective processes that help define the various objectives of the purchase/sale. Notice that none of these meetings involve anyone outside of the immediate company. This is the planning stage for both buyer and seller. The next meetings often involve a business broker who will assist in either marketing the firm if you are the seller or finding viable acquisition targets for the buyer. Once the target companies are determined, initial meetings will be set up to investigate the willingness of the parties to either buy or sell.

After these initial meetings, a letter of intent (or letter of understanding) is often prepared stating both parties' desires to proceed to the next step. Important items are outlined in this letter, along with the contingencies associated with each item. There are people who contend that a letter of intent is a waste of time because it is not legally binding, except with very specific conditions attached. These conditions are usually highly focused in scope and not general in nature. There are others who contend that this letter is critically important because it represents a written understanding between the parties involved. I fall into the second camp of people.

A letter of intent can be effectively used as a communication tool that ensures that both parties are working in the same direction and with the same overall intentions. Its creation forces the discussion of many important and specific items that might have been initially overlooked but would have ultimately been encountered later in the process. Assume, for example, that you intend to purchase a company with the expressed intention of breaking it up into smaller entities which will then be resold. Assume also that the seller specifically will not allow that to happen. This discord, which is a deal-stopper, is best discovered at the early stages instead of later after the expensive due diligence stage is completed.

The seller and buyer both have a vested interest in finding deal-stoppers at an early stage. Sellers will ultimately have to reveal detailed, potentially confidential information in the later due diligence process. Buyers will invest time and money in performing this due diligence. Eliminating candidates at an early stage saves money, time, and aggravation, while also reducing risk for all involved parties.

The Due Diligence Stage

Due diligence is usually the most time-consuming, nerve-wracking, and expensive stage of the M&A process. The intent of this stage is to help the buyer understand the inner workings of the seller's company. The better the understanding, the more realistic the expectations and price. It requires that the buyer be given a high degree of access to the selling company's customers, financial records, legal records, and operations, sales, and marketing functions. Investigators are looking for items that either validate the offered price or items that diminish the company's value and its purchase price.

The seller is torn between two conflicting desires during this stage. On one hand, the seller wants the buyer to learn what is needed to feel comfortable with both the seller's asking price and quality of offering. On the other hand, the seller does not want to reveal unnecessary information to the buyer, should the deal not consummate in a final purchase. This fear of disclosure is particularly acute when the buyer is the seller's direct competitor, and for very good reason. Every company would love to know the detailed financial, marketing, and sales aspects of its competition, and due diligence requires that this information be disclosed. Should the transaction fall apart, the seller is placed at a decided disadvantage compared to the buyer, who disclosed little or no confidential information about its own internal processes during due diligence.

Once again, this is where the letter of intent comes into play. Sellers should make their secrecy boundaries clearly known in the letter of intent, especially if those secrecy boundaries are immutable. The buyer can either accept or reject those boundaries at this earlier stage instead of being caught by surprise later. Nondisclosure agreements (NDAs) are also executed early in the process specifically with the intent of protecting the secrecy needs of the parties involved. The NDA is often executed before the parties ever meet for the first time, especially when a broker is involved.

As an alternative approach to immediate full disclosure to the buyer by the seller, an interim stage can be defined. Here, the buyer gains access to certain information with the intention of deciding on a purchase price and set of acceptance conditions. The buyer then commits to the purchase, in advance, contingent on these conditions being met. This approach provides both the seller and buyer with some level of protection.

There is risk on both sides with the revealing of confidential information. The seller who is constantly worried about giving away secret information should remember that each piece of confidential information revealed to a buyer also represents another potential area for litigation should the transaction not consummate as intended. Assume that the seller, during due diligence, reveals specific information about a major customer that is not currently a customer of the buyer. Assume also that the purchase by that buyer does not occur and that due diligence was completed. Should the buyer just happen to gain a major portion of that major customer's business within a short time after due diligence, the seller may contend that information gained during due diligence enabled the buyer to obtain that business, which will likely be in violation of the nondisclosure agreements. A buyer incensed enough about the situation might turn to litigation as a possible remedy. If the buyer had never been exposed to this confidential information in the first place, it would not have been put in the position of having to defend itself. For this reason alone, many large companies shield themselves from the confidential information of smaller companies as a standard business practice. Due diligence, by its very nature, pushes the threshold of confidential information disclosure and should be treated with the respect it deserves. Chapter 18, "Performing Due Diligence," presents the due diligence stage in great detail.

Here are a few minimum items that should be included in any due diligence effort:

- A legal structure review, including tax liabilities, employee disagreements, class action suits, or other pending litigation.

- A review of ownership and capitalization structure.

- A general breakdown of the customer base, with a more detailed analysis required to make an effective assessment. See Chapter 9, "Detailed Marketing and Sales Evaluation," for more discussion of marketing and sales due diligence topics.

- A review of intellectual property rights, including trademarks, patents, and other areas of unique and intrinsic value. This is particularly true for technology companies.

- Outstanding liens that are guaranteed by the company and/or its owners.

- Technology evaluation that includes development tools, cycles, processes, and personnel. Key value areas should be highlighted and evaluated in light of acquisition goals.

- Financial statement review for the prior three to five years, including the minutes of board meetings and so on.

- Annual reports and required Securities and Exchange Commission (SEC) filings for any publicly traded company. This action was probably already taken during the prequalification screening stages.

Due diligence is a complicated process which should be given major emphasis. It is that stage where the buyer determines whether the target company is really everything that the seller claims it is. The buyer's acquisition team is critical at this stage. Communication within the team ensures that nothing gets overlooked and helps to consolidate the vast amounts of information collected.

Due diligence works both ways, especially if the buyer expects the seller to take stock or future promises as part of the transaction. The buyer should also be willing to open his own company records to the seller so that the seller can determine his level of risk in taking future promises in lieu of today's dollars. Sellers also get a chance to learn more about the internal workings at the buyer's company, which also enables them to determine for themselves if a cultural fit between the two exists. After all, sellers will likely become employees of the buying company once the transaction is finalized.

A willing seller is critical during due diligence. The integrity of all parties must be intact or the seller could fight the buyer's information requests at every step, making it a tough and stressful process for all concerned. For this reason alone, many buyers shy away from a hostile purchase involving an unwilling seller or competitive situations that require extensive disclosure of confidential information that sellers are simply not comfortable providing. Due diligence is an integral and critical part of the M&A process. The way it is handled tells a lot about the buyer and seller while providing the foundation upon which a final purchase price is based.

Special Technology Comments

If you purchase a specific company with the intention of acquiring its technology or its technical personnel, the process gets more complicated. A detailed engineering analysis that assesses the reality of integrating and effectively using the technologies involved must be performed. More than one company has acquired technology assuming that their own engineers were good enough to make it work as desired, only to later discover that the reality of the situation was frustrating and expensive. Anything is possible with both time and money, and the shorter the time, the greater the money required. Unfortunately, some technology projects simply cannot be time-compressed beyond a certain point, no matter how extensive the resources thrown at them.

Integrating technology should not be assumed an easy process; unfortunately, this integration assessment is often made by nontechnical M&A managers. As with any complicated process, you are best served by first outlining a process for technology evaluation and then walking through the process one step at a time. Make sure that you include the input of engineers that are familiar with the technologies involved when performing the technology area evaluation to minimize unfortunate and expensive future surprises.

Arranging Financing

As the due diligence stage comes to an end, the buyer and seller should be closing in on a specific price for the acquisition, including associated stipulations. The capacity to fund the purchase is required of the buyer, and the seller is well advised to ensure that the buyer can come up with the required financing. Just as a house buyer is prequalified for the required financing, so should a business buyer be prequalified. This financing will depend heavily on the financial condition of the acquired company, but the end result is the same. The buying and/or selling company must be creditworthy or the deal will simply not go through.

Buyers have usually lined up financing when the letter of intent is signed, and sellers are completely in line to ask early on about the buyer's ability to fund the purchase. A meeting to discuss methods of financing is warranted earlier in the process once a general price range is established to ensure that both parties are not wasting time. Sellers may seriously consider stalling the due diligence stage until the buyer has shown itself to be creditworthy. Chapter 6, "Deal Types and Their Funding," presents a number of different acquisition purchase funding methods.

Negotiating and Signing the Agreements

Once the due diligence stage is finished, the lawyers begin negotiating the specific terms and conditions of the deal. As a business manager, it is important that you walk that fine line between overcontrolling the negotiations and making sure that the overall business intentions are met. The detailed legal discussions are usually best left to the lawyers who negotiate these types of transactions on a regular basis.

Remember that lawyers are great at creating a legally binding agreement, but they are not always great at making sure that the agreement makes business sense. That is where the management team plays a critical role. Signing a legally binding agreement that makes little business sense is obviously counterproductive. Signing a solid business agreement that is not legally binding on the parties involved is nothing but a future breeding ground for discord and litigation. See Chapter 21, "Legal Considerations," for additional information regarding the legal aspects of M&A transactions.

Operating the Ventures

Many people think that the merger and acquisition process stops at the signing of the agreement, and these people are in for a rude awakening. The buyer must now make the acquired company perform up to its purchased expectations. If you think about it, a good marriage starts when the bride and groom say "I do" and the creation of a solid marriage happens based on what is done from that point forward. It is no different with an M&A transaction. The contract simply defines the parameters for the future relationship. Only people can make that future relationship work so that the planned expectations are met or exceeded. This is where buyers and sellers find out if all that they thought true during the due diligence stage is really true. This is when the buyers meet the employees, customers, vendors, and financial partners on a daily, operational basis. This is when the sellers get to work with the buyers on a regular basis. This is when transaction-generated agreements are met or avoided. Personalities, cultures, and technologies must merge at this stage or future performance problems (which may undermine profitability) will likely arise.

Underestimating the pitfalls associated with this stage is a serious mistake. More than one acquisition that looked great on paper has fallen apart in the postacquisition reality of personalities, cultures, and mismatched goals. Chapter 22, "After The Deal Closes," takes a detailed look at postsale integration issues. Whatever you do, don't ignore this important topic. All the due diligence and financial negotiating in the world won't stand up to a poorly executed integration plan.

Moving on to the Next One

When the current transaction is finished and the postsale integration is underway, your acquisition team should be in a position to move on to the next one. Before moving on to the next transaction, it is a good idea to assess the effectiveness of your current team in light of the last transaction. What could be done to improve the next acquisition? Sellers can only sell once in a while, where buyers can buy as often as their financing and operation will support.

Chapter Summary

The M&A process is more often than not a long process full of details, personalities, and decisions. The larger the target company, the more complicated the process. If you are purchasing a company strictly as a financial venture, the M&A process is complicated enough. Adding specific personnel, technological or strategic objectives to the transaction goals simply complicates the process even more.

Buyers and sellers should understand their specific motivations and goals as they pertain to the purchase under investigation. Clearly defined goals help greatly in evaluating the impact of subsequently uncovered details. Developing these goals requires advance preparation and evaluation on the part of both buyer and seller and greatly enhances the likelihood of postacquisition success.

It is important that buyer and seller understand the perspective of the other party involved in the negotiation. The M&A process takes an extended period of time, during which the buyers and sellers are constantly learning more about each other. Maintaining an environment of trust and integrity helps greatly in dealing with numerous issues. Should trust or integrity be called into question, the entire transaction could be placed in jeopardy, even though on the surface all the operational and financial pieces seem to fit.

Care should be exercised by both buyer and seller before moving into the due diligence stage, as this stage requires extensive disclosure of confidential information and a substantial time commitment for both parties. A letter of intent should be signed prior to moving to the due diligence stage to ensure that both buyer and seller are working toward the same goals with the same set of assumptions. Make sure that both buyer and seller keep a close eye on the postacquisition environment so that future areas of enhancement or trouble can be discussed before the actual transaction is finalized. Performing the steps associated with the purchase of a company may take several months, but the combined companies have to coexist and operate into the future for years to come.

2

Motivations for Buying or Selling a Business

Any stock market investor knows that predicting the right time to buy and sell publicly traded stock is equal parts art, analysis, luck, and experience. For every person who sells a share of stock there must be another buyer, and so each investor will evaluate an investment opportunity from his or her own perspective in determining the timing and value of that particular investment. The same set of market conditions will present a sell signal to one buyer while simultaneously presenting a buy signal to another.

There are several common motivations for buying and selling a business. Some motivations deal with strict opportunism in that a specific opportunity is worth pursuing at this particular time. Others deal with a methodical search for the right strategic fit between the buyer and the seller. Others are driven by personal seller motivations or circumstances that are simply beyond any person's control. Determining the right time to buy or sell a business depends on doing your homework before the actual buying or selling act is initiated. The emphasis of that homework depends on the motivations of buyer or seller. This chapter takes a look at the most common motivations for buying and selling a business, as these motivations lay the foundation for later M&A actions.

Buying, Selling, and the Economy

Buying a business usually involves more money than the buyer can obtain on his or her own, whether the buyer is a company or an individual. The price of an item is intimately linked with the financing costs involved with the item, whether it be a house, a car, or a company. The more favorable the financial climate, the easier it is to obtain outside funding for a specific purchase. The lower the financing costs, the lower the overall cost of ownership. The less expensive the cost of ownership, the more a buyer can spend to obtain a given company. In light of these points, it would be a natural and correct assumption that a more robust economy creates lower finance costs and allows buyers to pay more for a company without putting the buying or selling company in a precarious financial postpurchase position.

In later chapters, we will see that the current value of a company is heavily based on the expected market-determined interest rates and inflation. Both of these parameters are based on the state of the economy in that the Federal Reserve will attempt to control inflation by raising interest rates. A quick summary is that as inflation rates start to increase, interest rates will also start to increase. These increases in interest rates further increase the discount factor which is used for financial analysis and thus drive down the present value of any future expected income. This reduction of the present value of future cash flows also causes the viable purchase price a company to decrease. Discount factors and present value analysis are presented in detail in chapter 5, "Financial Analysis Concepts."

From this simplified discussion, it can be understood that an economy with low inflation and interest rates creates increased company market values while, conversely, higher inflation and interest rates drive down the current value of a company. (Matrices 2.1 and 2.2 demonstrate this visually.) Does this mean that you should never sell or buy in a down economy? The answer to this question is "It depends." Assume that a given target company has certain loans that must be either paid off or refinanced at a given point in time. Assume also that the current interest rates are high enough to keep the company from qualifying for enough funding to cover the debt. The company management chooses to address this problem by raising funding through the sale of the company. This selling company may now be an excellent purchase target since a buyer with cash might be able to purchase this company for a highly reduced price. In fact, the company purchase

Matrix 2.1 Selling Company Performance Matrix

Selling Company Performance Compared to Market Conditions		Company Performance	
		Weak	Strong
Market Conditions	Weak	Probable bankruptcy or bargain purchase.	Commands a higher selling price due to higher returns based on current market options.
	Strong	Usually poor management and could present excellent purchase.	Commands a reasonable market valuation and price.

Matrix 2.2 Purchasing Company Performance Matrix

Purchasing Company Performance Compared to Market Conditions		Company Performance	
		Weak	Strong
Market Conditions	Weak	Will likely not have the resources to finance a purchase.	Excellent position to purchase companies while giving up minimal shareholder wealth.
	Strong	Might become a takeover target itself. Should consider purchasing a stronger management team.	Will pay reasonable market valuation and price for a company and likely obtain required financing.

might be fundable by a creditworthy buyer at a specific reduced purchase price simply due to the increased interest rates. The lower price is prompted to offset the increased financing costs. Sure, the buying company pays more finance charges, but the reduced selling company purchase price should off-set the increased financing charges in such a way that the purchase makes financial sense. The higher that interest rates become, the more it becomes a cash-rich buyer's market since the cash-rich buyer does not need to qualify for as much borrowed money as do other cash-poor buyers.

As a seller, you might be forced into selling your company simply to meet your financial demands. This situation should not be treated as a negative reflection on the company's intrinsic value. An astute buyer will look for well-run companies that fall on difficult financial times due to changes in the external financial environment and not consider this as a direct negative reflection on the management team. This type of company could present a great financial opportunity for the right buyer. In general, it is best to avoid selling in a down market or in one filled with uncertainty. Uncertainty translates into risk, which also decreases the present value of a future event, which inevitably drives down the perceived current value of a company.

A company with publicly traded stock might want to use its own stock to finance the purchase of the another company. If the stock market places a high value on the purchasing company's stock, then the purchasing company must sell fewer shares to fund the purchase. If the market valuation drops, then more shares must be sold, which often dilutes the purchasing company's stock enough to create shareholder dissension.

Once again, notice that a down market presents financial complications for all parties concerned. On the other hand, if the purchasing company has a strong financial performance history and strong market valuation while the rest of the market is in a slump, this buyer has a unique opportunity to purchase struggling companies for lower prices while exchanging fewer of its own shares.

It is clear from Matrices 2.1 and 2.2 that running a strong company is a no-lose proposition whether you are a buyer or a seller. If your company shows poor financial returns in a strong market, then you might yourself become the target of a takeover offer or contest.

Technology as a Motivator

Changes in technology can cause a company to either sell or buy, depending on its position with respect to the technological changes in effect. This section takes a closer look at ways in which technology can motivate the purchase or sale of a company.

Technology Creates or Eliminates Markets

At the risk of stating the obvious, few industries are more radically affected by a technology shift than today's high technology fields. The impact of the IBM PC introduction was completely underestimated at the time of its introduction. The incredible impact of the Internet and its wide and rapid market acceptance took more than one executive and industry expert by surprise. Some people, myself included, believe that the ultimate impact of the Internet has not even begun to show itself. More detailed information about the Internet is presented in Chapter 15, "Internet-Related Businesses."

Technology occasionally changes entire industries. Look at the impact of the first integrated circuits, the ability to transport high speed data connections over twisted pair wiring, the introduction of fiber optics, and improved microprocessor design and production advancements as examples of technology changes that caused dramatic business paradigm shifts. Looking back to the late 1880s and the introduction of the telephone we see proof that markets, omnipresent today, were often dismissed at their introduction. Alexander Graham Bell resorted to paid admission performances of his new telephone device to support his family while his initial phone designs began to generate revenue. Western Union turned down an 1876 offer to purchase the telephone patent from Bell for $100,000 in the belief that it could never replace the telegraph. They tried to correct their judgment error in 1877 when they tried to purchase the patent, an offer Bell refused. How would you like to be the executive who decided to turn down Bell's first offer to sell?

This story illustrates an important point. It might be difficult to recognize industry-changing technology when it comes across your desk. But ignoring it will put you and your company at great risk. In fact, Western Union decided to create its own telephone products and network after Bell refused their purchase offer, and a court decision forced Western Union to sell all of its telephone operations to Bell once it was determined that Western Union had infringed upon his patent. The current power of the telephone industry needs no explanation. The integrated circuit, the microprocessor, and the Internet are similar technologies that truly changed the way we do business and live our daily lives and many of us can honestly state that we missed the potential implication of their introduction .

Technology can be a motivator to both the buyer and the seller. Buyers with strong, established market positions can help greatly with validating a new technology and capitalizing on its initial success. IBM did this with their introduction of the original PC and the PC XT products. It basically legitimized the concept of a desktop computer product, even though Apple, Radio Shack, Atari, and others had products on the market for years prior to the initial IBM PC introduction.

A smaller company is motivated to sell its technology to another company in an attempt to more rapidly acquire market acceptance and presence. Or the smaller company might simply need money to help fund its expansion. This money might be obtained through an *initial public offering* (IPO), in which shares of stock are sold to the general public. An alternative approach is to find a larger, more financially capable company to purchase the smaller company, with the hope that the purchasing company will recognize the intrinsic worth of the technology even if the financial picture is less than optimal.

The incredible rise of the Internet's popularity has created its own set of M&A opportunities that many feel are still in their infancy. The Internet truly represents a technology that is transforming the way the globe transacts business and people live their lives. A July 28, 1999 *Investor's Business Daily* article (page A7) quotes some Internet M&A facts as presented by Broadview International LLC. Here are a few facts that pretty much speak for themselves:

- The number of Internet-related mergers tripled from 150 in 1998 to 447 in 1999.

- The value of these deals also increased from $4.9 billion in 1998 to $37.5 billion in 1999.

- Microsoft, Lucent, and Cisco all averaged a deal a month for the first half of 1999, with most of these deals being Internet-related.

A larger company might decide to purchase technology instead of developing it internally. Such motivations are discussed later in this chapter.

Regulatory and Legal Changes as a Motivator

Many business restructuring binges have been triggered by changes in the regulatory environment as dictated by local or federal regulatory bodies. The Justice Department is involved in any changes in regulation that occur at the federal level. These changes usually affect the larger technology entities that control a large enough portion of their respective industry and marketplace that the company can manipulate the industry to its specific advantage and to the disadvantage of its competitors—and ultimately the consumer.

Microsoft was under scrutiny for this type of practice in the Justice Department trials of 1999 and 2000 dealing with, among other things, Microsoft's incorporation of Internet Explorer as an integral feature of its Windows operating system. In this particular case, the Justice Department claims that Microsoft used its Internet Explorer product to eliminate competition from products such as Netscape's Navigator and Communicator. The claim and concern was that the ready availability of Internet Explorer, being a standard part of the Windows 98 operating system, would cause the consumer to simply install Internet Explorer and not even consider an alternate product such as Navigator. As Netscape's market threat disappeared, Microsoft's hold on not only the operating system but also the standardized Internet access desktop utility would increase to such dominant proportions that consumers, and Microsoft's competitors, would have no other option other than simply cooperating with Microsoft's demands.

The Justice Department's claim is that this type of strong business position by any company presents a substantial hurdle to a fully competitive marketplace, one that typically reduces consumer options and eventually leads to increased prices. The Justice Department's mandate is primarily concerned, from an antitrust perspective, with ensuring enough competition in any industry to present consumers with genuine options and low prices. The underlying assumptions are that any company obtaining such a dominant market position that it can manipulate an entire industry will eventually lead to reduced industry competition, which reduces the number of options available to consumers, which eventually leads to increased prices. Whether the Justice Department serves its own agenda or that of the marketplace is a hotly debated topic at the time of this writing, and I will not take a stand one way or the other. What is clear, however, is that M&A activity that involves a substantial market share must consider Justice Department approval. Even smaller firms may be impacted by antitrust scrutiny, if that particular small firm has a strategic position in a market such that its acquisition by one company could put other companies (those who compete with the purchasing company) at a pronounced market disadvantage.

The principal laws that affect antitrust in the United States are the Sherman Act, the Clayton Act, the Federal Trade Commission Act, and the Robinson-Patman Act. Each of these laws proscribe specific activities that are not sanctioned because they are assumed to reduce competition. The Clayton Act is probably the most important when dealing with mergers and acquisitions. Companies must operate on a daily basis within the constraints of these laws. M&A activity between market leaders and organizations of any substantial size must consider the Justice Department's likely reaction to the proposed purchase. Take a look at the 1999 merger proposal between MCI/WorldCom and Sprint as an example of an M&A transaction that suffered many ups and downs as a result of Justice Department scrutiny. It is worth noting that competitors to those companies involved in the acquisition are usually the first ones to complain to the Justice Department and request that the acquisition be denied on antitrust grounds.

Changes in the regulatory environment can dramatically create or reduce opportunities for M&A activity. For illustration purposes, I refer you to the Carterfone decision of 1968. In this case, a small telephone products company named Carter Electronics Corporation sued for, and won, the right to connect one of its products to the AT&T network. Winning this case opened up the public telephone network to end consumer products provided by non-AT&T sources, which had previously not been possible. The adjunct telephone product market resulting from Carterfone's win spawned a vast number of new companies and extensive resulting M&A activity. This single legal shift caused a ripple effect that eventually allowed smaller manufacturers to design and market telephone products that anyone can purchase through a local retail outlet instead of having to lease them through AT&T, which was the case prior to the Carterfone decision. For another example, in 1969 Microwave Communications, Inc. (MCI) filed a successful suit to allow for connection to the existing network with the intention of transporting long distance calls through a non-AT&T network. This winning suit also spawned an entirely new industry of companies and subsequent M&A activities.

Large and small companies alike must keep an eye on the regulatory and legal environment of their particular industry. A recent, nontechnical, regulatory issue occurred when Barnes & Noble attempted to purchase Ingram, a major distributor of book products to both chain and independent stores. The independent book stores were concerned that the proposed Barnes & Noble/Ingram company would no longer provide them with books, which would put them in a serious competitive disadvantage. They caused such a legal and public relations uproar that Barnes & Noble withdrew its offer. If the purchase had been allowed, the smaller independents might have been driven out of business due to higher product prices and more limited product availability, making them excellent acquisition targets for Barnes & Noble. I am not saying that this was indeed Barnes & Noble's intention, but it did raise enough antitrust questions that the proposed acquisition was dropped.

Motivations for Buying a Company

The most common reasons for purchasing a company are listed in this section, with recommendations about applying each reason to your particular situation. The intent of this list (Table 2.1) is to assist you in determining your purchase motivations, which will assist later with finding the most likely target acquisition candidates.

A company presented with a market or financial opportunity must act to take full advantage of the opportunity. An ongoing business is continually presented with opportunities for expanding its business scope. Selecting the right opportunity for the right time is a matter of corporate vision that comes from planning and a deep understanding of the needs of a business. Deciding that a company needs enhancement, the buyer's management team must then determine the optimal route for performing this enhancement. It can be done either through internal development or through acquisition. The right approach depends on the purchasing company's culture, the available acquisition target opportunities, available financing, and the general market conditions, among other things.

Some company cultures simply do not allow for the introduction of an external company's products or culture. This was much the case with the old IBM, where the culture revolved largely around the belief that something that was "not invented here" must be bad or, at best, deficient. IBM has changed substantially since those days and now uses acquisition as an integral part of its business strategic processes. The "not invented here" (or NIH) factor is still present in some corporate cultures around the world, although its prevalence is rapidly diminishing.

External circumstances might also dictate whether technology should be purchased or developed as an internal company project. Western Union, after missing its initial opportunity to purchase the telephone patent in the late 1880s, went on to develop its own telephone products. The legal protection provided by the telephone patent kept Western Union from growing this

Table 2.1 Buyer Types and Motivations

Buyer Type	Attributes and Motivations
Financial buyer	Primarily interested in the target company as a financial investment. May purchase the company to split it into smaller units or to bundle with other owned companies for resale.
Bottom fisher	The buyer who looks for highly undervalued companies so that the target can be purchased at a reduced price which translates into reduced risk. Companies that grow too quickly and develop financial problems are excellent bottom fisher acquisition target companies.
Strategic buyer	One looking for an important technology, marketing or other benefit that the buyer does not yet have. By adding this strategy through purchase, the buyer hopes to acquire synergies that make the new combined company stronger and more valuable than the sum of the parts.
Product line or Market share expansion buyer	One interested in purchasing a company that provides a product line or market presence that expands the buyer's. Buying the products or market presence is often cheaper and faster than the buyer's developing it from scratch.
Tire kicker	One that looks around for acquisition deals, takes up the seller's time, and then never makes a purchase.
Employee Stock Ownership Plan (ESOP), Management Buyout (MBO), or Leveraged Buyout (LBO)	Related to the financial buyer except that the buyers might be the current company management or employees themselves. This is sometimes called "taking a company private," when publicly traded shares are involved.

business, which it eventually had to either close or sell. If Western Union were to decide that being in the telephone business was a corporate priority, it would have to either develop products that provided similar services which did not infringe on the patent or simply buy the patent rights. External circumstances in this case dictated Western Union's available options.

The larger the scope of the desired enhanced capabilities, the more complicated the procedure will be for procuring them. For this reason alone, a clearly defined set of objectives is required to ensure that time is spent on the best possible fit between the purchasing company and potential acquisition targets. Spending the time up front to clearly define simple answers to the following questions is a buyer's minimal first step.

1. What is currently deficient within the purchasing company that would be enhanced by an acquisition of some type? This deficiency might come from personnel, engineering, production, finance, marketing, or a combination of any or all of these areas. The simpler you make the deficiency definition, the easier it will be for you to find a viable acquisition target.

2. Could the purchasing company develop the capability itself without having to pursue the purchase of an outside company? If so, what would be the time frame and cost associated with this development? What would your competition be doing during this time frame with respect to introducing a comparable technology?

3. Can the purchasing company's culture weather the introduction of another culture, and if so, what are the cultural criteria needed for the purchased culture that will make cultural integration most likely successful? The importance of this factor should not be underestimated. See Chapter 22, "After the Deal Closes," for more information relating to merging of corporate cultures.

4. How much money does the purchasing company have to spend, and how will the balance of the purchase price be financed? There is usually an upper price limit that can be spent on a particular purchase, and price levels may vary based on the financing methods used.

5. What are the top five required results from the proposed acquisition? These results might include financial gain, integration of personnel, addition of new technology, enhanced production capacity, and reduced manufacturing costs, among others. Make sure that you have agreement within the management team regarding the value of these five points. Additional results will present themselves as you work your way through the process, but avoid diffusing the intent with too many secondary results.

6. What technological requirements must be met by the acquisition target's products, services, and internal operational technologies? Do you want established technology with a proven reliability record, or do you want cutting-edge technology that might open new market areas?

7. What geographical criteria must be met for the acquired company? You might want the company to be local if the intention is to enhance production capabilities, but you might need it to be international if the intention is to open international markets.

8. Must the target meet certain regulatory requirements to avoid antitrust violations or scrutiny? The larger the market share of the purchasing and/or target companies, the more advanced scrutiny should be applied to this point. It will help the buyer avoid spending large amounts of money on an acquisition that had little chance of regulatory approval in the first place.

Remember that no discussions with a proposed acquisition target have taken place at this point. You are simply determining the internal issues driving the need and interest in performing an acquisition search in the first place. Spending the time at this stage will make the later stages of the acquisition process more fruitful and less time-consuming.

Adding Capability

Assume that you are a circuit board manufacturer whose production plant running at 90 percent capacity, with increased future orders projected by your sales department. Assume also that you are located in the midwest and expect future orders to come from the Silicon Valley area. You know that your midwest location places your products at a pricing disadvantage with respect to your West coast competition, and that you currently use 20 percent of your midwest capacity manufacturing boards for Silicon Valley companies. Acquiring an existing circuit board manufacturing concern in the Silicon Valley area would serve a number of important corporate strategic and tactical goals.

1. Transferring the Silicon Valley customer production needs from the midwest production plant to Silicon Valley drops your mid-west usage to 70 percent, allowing room for midwest sales/production growth without the immediate need for a new midwest facility.

2. Opening a Silicon Valley plant reduces your shipping and sales costs to Silicon Valley customers, making your products more competitively priced in that region.

3. The anticipated future midwest orders that might have forced a major plant expansion can now be accepted with less corporate disruption and at a lower internal corporate cost.

Given this simple scenario, it makes sense for this midwest manufacturer to actively look for an acquisition target in the Silicon Valley area. The target company will also have its own customer base, which typically reduces the financial risk to the purchasing company. The internal analysis was needed on the buyer's part to determine that substantial surplus capacity and Silicon Valley area location were two important selection criteria for any proposed acquisition target. The more clearly defined these criteria are, the easier it is to narrow the scope of proposed acquisition targets. If the initial search turns up no candidates, then the buyer can relax the criteria until they find a target that meets their needs. If none are available, then the buyer might end up developing the capability themselves, which is the topic of the next section.

Buying versus Internal Development

Once a company determines its required capability enhancements, it must then decide whether its interests are better served by developing the enhancements using internal capabilities or by purchasing the enhancements outright. A number of factors should be considered when making this determination, especially when dealing with a technology-related issue.

One such factor is the speed of the technology market window. If the technology is rapidly evolving in a quickly expanding marketplace, then purchasing the required capability might be the quickest approach, as well as the most financially appealing one. Assume, for example, that you can develop the technology in 18 months for a cost of $3.5 million, after which time you will begin to acquire market share related to that particular technology. It will take you six months to purchase a company with a 15 percent market share and established technology for around $5 million, which also happens to be one times its sales numbers of $5 million. The company has a net income of 15 percent, or $750,000 (15% of $5 million). This company's overall market has sales assumed at around $33.3 million ($5 million/.15).

On the surface, the $3.5 million is less than the $5 million, which might make it a more attractive option. But the decision to purchase saves you 12 months in bringing your products to the marketplace, and also makes you $750,000 in net income that would otherwise have been lost. Instead of dealing with a $1.5 million spread between the two options, you are now only dealing with $750,000 ($1.5 million − $750,000 [net income]). If your 18-month development schedule actually requires another six-month period (which is not uncommon), then the differential is reduced to only $375,000. The strategic benefits of getting into the industry more quickly and gaining a 15 percent market share early in a growing market might easily offset this $375,000 additional cost and might even turn it into a profit. If the marketplace itself is growing at a 15 percent annual rate, then the market will grow to $38.3 million in a single year, and the target company's sales revenues (remaining at a 15 percent market share) will grow to $5.75 million. If the net income remains at 15 percent, it now also climbs to $860,000, whittling the $375,000 differential found with the extended development schedule to only $210,000 ($1.5 million − $860,000 − $860,000/2). This $210,000 differential might be easily justified on a strategic basis or might be accounted for in the financial activities associated with the company purchase. Companies are often purchased with combinations of debt, stock, and other financial techniques. The way that R&D is treated from an accounting standpoint within the purchasing company may sway this decision away from internal R&D and toward acquisition, depending on the buyer's overall financial goals.

This is a simplified example, using a specially created set of circumstances to keep the math simple, but the general concept is sound with respect to illustrating the major reasons to purchase a specific technology instead of developing it. Just because internal development looks less expensive from an accounting standpoint, it might not be less expensive when reviewed from a business perspective that includes opportunity and market exposure costs.

Market Window Considerations

Technology markets change quickly, and today's hottest technology can become obsolete in a few months or a few years. Many of the technology advancements of today simply would not have been possible as few as five years ago, and they certainly would not have been possible at today's lower prices. This rapidly changing technological pace destroys older markets and generates new ones, also creating M&A opportunities in its wake.

Gordon E. Moore, cofounder of Intel and key developer of the microprocessor, created "Moore's Law" which contends that a new microprocessor chip is introduced every 18 to 24 months, and each chip has roughly twice the capacity of it immediate predecessor. This translates into an exponential increase in processing capacity when plotted over a number of years. According to the Intel Web site (www.intel.com), "In 26 years the number of transistors on a chip has increased more than 3,200 times, from 2,300 on the 4004 in 1971 to 7.5 million on the Pentium® II processor." Putting this increased processing capacity on a single processor chip enables huge increases in processing power while also substantially decreasing manufacturing cost. The fact that we can purchase the processing power of today at a price that is a fraction of initial IBM PC prices is truly one of today's business and technology miracles.

Each increase in processing power and decrease in cost spawns secondary markets that take advantage of that processing power in the form of embedded controllers, dedicated processors, real-time processing, and monitoring activities. Software applications are also developed to support the application needs of these smaller, more powerful hardware devices.

Moore's Law presents a market window, or time frame, within which existing technologies can be applied on the leading edge. If you add to this time frame the staged introduction of Microsoft's operating systems and Office products, which have an undisputed dominance in their respective market segments, you find a frequently changing technological landscape.

The incredible dominance of the consumer software marketplace by Microsoft has caused M&A activity. One notable example is that of Novell's early 1990s purchase (merge) of WordPerfect in an attempt to provide its customers with not only a network but also applications to run on that network. It didn't work out as planned, and the WordPerfect application suite was sold to Corel Corporation so that Corel could round out its graphic design product offerings with a comprehensive desktop office suite. Novell went back to working on its networking products and Corel started working to turn WordPerfect back into a desktop application powerhouse.

WordPerfect Corporation was not a company in need of repair. It was doing well prior to its acquisition by Novell, although only conjecture can determine what would have happened to WordPerfect had Novell not purchased it. While WordPerfect was once the standard for PC-based word processing, it now has a very small market share and has been almost completely replaced by Microsoft Word as the industry standard. The IBM purchase of Lotus Development was a similar defensive move by IBM against Microsoft's dominance of the desktop. Lotus Development was clearly a pioneer in the technology industry and brought strong resources to IBM when purchased. While the desktop application arena was once dominated by WordPerfect for word processing and Lotus 1-2-3 for spreadsheets with Microsoft being an operating system provider, we now find Microsoft the powerhouse (at 92 percent market share for office suite products) with WordPerfect and Lotus Development in an also-ran position. Microsoft did many things right during this period of time, while WordPerfect and Lotus business managers took some unfortunate missteps. Things can change quickly and dramatically for technology industries.

Strategic versus Financial Considerations

Motivations for purchasing a company fall into two basic categories: those motivated by simple financial analysis returns and those motivated by the need to add capabilities or even to create a business entity that, when combined, is stronger than the two individual companies were on their own.

The May 2000 merger between Viacom and CBS falls into the second category. The $37 billion merging of CBS stock into Viacom (1.085 shares of Viacom Class B stock for each share of CBS stock) not only creates a company with a prominent share of the broadcast industry (CBS), but also gives CBS access to Viacom's cable television outlets, provides wider household broadcast channels for Viacom's Paramount Studios products, and allows CBS access to Viacom's original content creation resources. These two entities, on their own, were major players in their industry. Combined, they are a powerful media conglomerate that sizes up well against the Time/Warner and Disney/Capital Cities/ABC media conglomerates. The markets responded favorably to this proposed combination by raising Viacom's stock $1.87 to $46.94 and CBS's stock $1.75 to $50.69 (September 7, 1999 closing numbers).

It is also attractive for a company to purchase another simply to improve its own financial condition and stock performance. Most executive managers are heavily rewarded on the performance of company stock under their leadership. If the stock price increases, then the manager earns more income. If it drops, bonuses and other compensation will likely be reduced or lost completely (along with the manager's job if the drop is precipitous). Managers have a fiduciary responsibility to act in the best interests of the shareholders. If the company is privately held by a single person or a few family members, then the legal implications of this responsibility are minimal. But if the company is publicly held with many shareholders, then any manager who is found to not be acting in the overall best interests of the shareholders could be put at risk of a class-action suit by the affected shareholders. As a consequence of this responsibility, managers are continually on the lookout for ways of increasing shareholder wealth by increasing stock prices.

Chapter 4, "Effectively Using Financial Ratios," takes a close look at the use of financial ratios as analysis tools. For purposes of this discussion, I need to introduce the price/earnings (P/E) ratio. This ratio is calculated by simply dividing the current company share market price by the company's reported earnings over the past 12 months. A company with a share price of $36.00

Table 2.2 Price/Earnings Ratio Illustration

	Purchasing Company	Purchased Company	Combined
Sales	$20,000,000	$1,000,000	$21,000,000
Earnings Rate	7%	15%	7.38%
$ Earnings	$1,400,000	$150,000	$1,550,000
P/E Ratio	20	30	20
Share Outstanding	1,200,000	1,200,000	1,200,000
Earning/share	$1.167	$0.125	$1.292
Share Price	$23.33	$3.75	$25.83[1]

[1] Share price increase: 11%.

with reported 12-month earnings of $2.00 has a P/E of 18 ($36/$2). The P/E ratio is listed for any publicly traded stock, and is used as a monitor for that stock's performance with respect to the rest of the market in general and its particular industry segment in particular.

Assume that a publicly traded company (purchasing company) chooses to purchase, using all cash for example purposes, another publicly traded company (purchased company) with the earnings and P/E ratios listed in Table 2.2. All purchased company shares are retired as part of the purchase and no new purchasing company shares are issued.

Notice from this example that by simply purchasing the company and putting its higher earnings percentage (15 percent as opposed to 7 percent) under the financial auspices of the purchasing company, and by keeping the P/E ratio constant at 20 (that of the larger purchasing company), the per-share market price jumps from $23.33 to $25.83, or $2.50 (11 percent). Notice that the purchased company would command a purchase price of at least its market valuation determined as $3.75 × 1,200,000 shares = $4.5 million. How this amount is financed might make this transaction financially unattractive, even with the expected increased share price, but you can see from this simple example that this type of financial transaction would appear attractive to an executive compensated by increased share prices.

Integral to this analysis is that the P/E ratio for the purchasing company remains constant and independent of the transaction itself. This may be the case when a well-run company is purchased and the total dollars of the transaction are small compared to the size of the purchasing company, which is true in this example, but there are no guarantees.

A company purchase might be pursued for either strategic or financial reasons. Some analysts contend that a purchase that dilutes earnings per share should only be pursued when a strategic fit and its resulting synergy are strongly expected. When you can find both strategic and financial motivations for making the purchase, you have a sweet deal that should probably be aggressively pursued.

Acquiring Proprietary Technology

Imagine that you are a major technology products vendor who just found out about a smaller company with a new technology that could obsolete a major portion of your product line. To add to the excitement, this smaller company has solid legal protection in the form of a patent that cannot be easily circumvented. Would you want one of your competitors to get hold of this technology instead of you? Probably not. Think about the strategic advantage your company would have if this technology and the engineers who created it were placed under your corporate umbrella.

This type of scenario plays itself out daily in the Silicon Valleys, Austins, and other technology hotbeds around the country. Smaller companies are always looking for entrepreneurial methods of solving major technology problems that have usually been created by, and often ignored by, the major providers. Once that technology is brought to a reasonable state of readiness, the smaller companies often become acquisition targets so that the larger companies can purchase the technology rights, personnel, or both. The smaller company is often happy to be bought, because it usually does not have the marketing or financial muscle to fully capitalize on its idea without outside help. Existing patent protection has a limited life, after which others can copy the idea and infringe on what was previously an exclusive market. As an alternative approach, many new companies in this situation fund their next stage of growth with a public stock offering instead of by being acquired. This has been the case with companies such as Yahoo!, Cisco, Seagate, Dell, Microsoft, and countless others.

There are other companies, such as Net Guru Technologies (NGT), which created the industry standard Certified Internet Webmaster (CIW) certification, which chose to sell to Prosoft as a way of more rapidly expanding the influence of its certification process. Yahoo!'s purchase of Broadcast.com (1999) is another example of a smaller company's technology being purchased by a larger one with a more established means of marketing that technology. Broadcast.com had a leadership position in providing "streaming media," which is the ability to provide audio and video content over the Internet. Yahoo! is continually looking for ways to enhance the value of its site to its users, which increases usage, thus making Yahoo!'s site more valuable. Yahoo! had to either purchase the technology, as it did with Broadcast.com, or develop it internally. The transaction trades 0.7722 shares of Yahoo! stock for each share of the outstanding 36 million shares and 7 million stock options of Broadcast.com stock. Both companies were traded on the NASDAQ. The marketplace seems to have approved the move, because the announcement caused Yahoo! share prices to increase $11.37 (7 percent) to $179.75 and Broadcast.com share prices to increase $11.81 (10 percent) to $130 (April 1, 1999).

When the underlying technology or proprietary content is the motivation for purchase, the selling company is in a unique position with respect to the buyer in that there is really no comparable competitor. This often means that the smaller company can negotiate pricing from a position of strength and hopefully command a higher price than it could get in a nonproprietary situation. There is no existing market valuation upon which the sale price must be based because there is really nothing else comparable. This might present an excellent purchasing opportunity for the buyer if the seller is motivated to sell, but might present an excellent opportunity for the seller if a bidding war between larger competitors can be started, causing them to bid up the price of the purchased company simply to keep the other competitor from obtaining the underlying technology and its associated competitive advantage. Remember that, from a buyer's perspective, this type of purchase usually has a strategic component to it that might completely dominate the financial aspects of the transaction. This is usually good news for the selling company since purchase price ceilings now take a back seat to the perceived value associated with strategic components of the acquisition.

Buying Market Share and Presence

Purchasing a company is a quick way to gain market presence in a new or emerging marketplace. Once again, a company can invest the time and money in creating that market presence itself, but might be able to accomplish the same goals with less money and risk by purchasing an existing company in that marketplace.

The April 1999 purchase of Livebid.com by Amazon.com falls into this category. Amazon.com is well known as a major Internet retailer that started out offering books online and is now leveraging its high name recognition into other Internet retail marketing areas. Livebid.com offers both the technology and the Internet presence to enable live Internet-based auctions. Livebid.com handled the auction of O. J. Simpson's memorabilia and, separately, the only known completely intact passenger ticket for the *Titanic*. Through its purchase of Livebid.com, Amazon.com quickly moved into the live Internet auction business, which helped it compete more favorably with companies such as eBay.com.

Cisco Systems' 1999 purchase of Cerent Corporation and Monterey Networks is another example of a major company purchasing technology instead of developing it internally. Cisco, a company that actively pursues the acquisition of other companies, understands that it must move into optical fiber technology to remain ahead of its competition and justifies the purchase as being attractive for its shareholders, according to Cisco chief executive John Chambers. In an interview in the *Chicago Tribune,* Chambers said, "We who understood our market understood that optical transport was going to explode and so our shareholders as well as industry analysts have been asking us for a while what we're going to do" (Reuters, 27 August 1999). It looks like Cisco just answered that question with this $7.36 billion stock transfer transaction.

These types of purchases only make sense when the purchasing company understands its marketplace and its strategic position within that marketplace. In addition, the purchasing company has a much easier time funding the purchase if its own core operations are intact and profitable. The higher the market valuation of the purchasing company's stock, the more purchasing power that stock commands on the M&A market. Most major companies have a staff of people who are continually on the lookout for attractive acquisition targets and for companies that might be potential acquirers. The most likely candidates are determined and monitored so that, when the right circumstances are present, the preliminary leg work has already been done and productive conversations can be started from the beginning.

Buying People with the Purchase

It is common for an acquisition to become attractive due in large part to the executive management team also being acquired. Many companies do not have an obvious heir apparent to the top management slots. An acquisition presents a technique not only for rounding out the company's operation and financial condition, but also for acquiring the personnel needed to fill key personnel slots. Don't ever forget that corporations are legal shells within which people work, and the personalities of the people involved are key to success of failure.

Once again looking at the Viacom/CBS merger, one finds that the acquisition of Mel Karmazin appears to have been an important consideration associated with the transaction. Sumner Redstone, CEO of Viacom, was 76 years old in 1999 when the transaction occurred, while Karmazin was 55. Karmazin will act as president and chief operating officer with an agreement to take over as CEO when Redstone leaves at some undetermined future date.

Larger companies may acquire smaller companies not only in an attempt to capture innovative technologies, but also with the intention of instilling an entrepreneurial spirit into the much larger organization. Although the intent might be noble, my experience has shown that entrepreneurs don't work well within the highly bureaucratic environments which usually accompany larger organizations. I know of several examples where companies were sold to larger firms only to have dissatisfaction and irritation result from the way the company was subsequently run. This dissatisfaction often increases to the point that the founders who sold their companies found that leaving was more attractive than staying under the new ownership.

If a major intention of the acquisition is to also acquire the management talent, then a careful evaluation of the fit between the acquired management team and the existing culture of the purchasing company must be made. In essence, the acquired management team should be interviewed just as though they were being evaluated for a job because that is the basic intent for the purchasing company. How this is handled during negotiations is a matter of individual personalities and circumstances, but the importance of taking this step slowly and with open eyes is critical if the transaction is to produce the intended final results. It is a lot easier to integrate technology into a company than it is to mesh the strong personalities that exist at executive levels in successful larger corporations and highly entrepreneurial smaller ones.

Motivations for Selling a Company

Sellers have various motivations for putting their companies up for sale, and the more you as the buyer appreciate these motivations the better you will be able to tailor a transaction to meet that particular seller's needs. This section outlines some of the major seller motivations for putting a company on the market.

Remember that companies, and their management, often have an emotional attachment that might supersede the financial aspects of a transaction. This is particularly true for privately held companies that are still run by the founders. This management team might have years or even decades invested in making their company what it is today, and being insensitive to this aspect of the transaction can eliminate a potential buyer before he or she even gets a chance to talk details.

Selling when on Top

Just as cashing in your chips while winning at gambling is a good idea, so is selling your company when it is running in top form. If your company is a top performer in a desirable market during an up economy, you have the best possible conditions under which to sell your company and obtain top dollar. If you have ever considered selling your company, this might very well be the right time. Remember that the present value of a company is dependent on its future earning power. When a company is running at its best its projected future earning power looks its brightest, which means that sellers will likely get top dollar. This situation is heavily dependent on the compensation structure in place for the executive management team. If you are the owner/manager of a company, then you will have a strong incentive to sell under these conditions.

If, on the other hand, you are the executive manager of a firm but not a shareholder, you might have a disincentive to sell. Selling will put minimal money in your pocket and might very well cost you your job as the purchasing company puts its own people into key executive slots. For this reason alone, most executive compensation schemes provide some type of incentive to the current management for considering attractive sale opportunities.

It is tempting to think that the world will remain bright when everything seems to be going perfectly, but business environments are cyclical with both highs and lows. If you are a business manager under 30 years old, you really never have seen a down market with high inflation rates (8 percent +), high interest rates (17 percent +) and high unemployment (6 percent +). These circumstances have happened in the past and will likely, unfortunately, happen again in the future. Business runs in cycles and an understanding that at some point a hot market cools and a cool market heats up again is important. Recognizing the signs of each takes a lifetime of experience, and accurately estimating the precise highs and lows is unlikely except when viewed from the future. If you are running a company that is performing well but could be negatively impacted by a market downturn, then selling while the market and the company are on top is a viable consideration. As an executive manager, you get paid to make these assessments and to take the right initiative at the right time. Only history can determine if you made the right call, but remember that history has the benefit of 20/20 hindsight.

Selling when the Market Drops Off

As stated earlier in this chapter, sellers are best served by selling a company when the market and the company's particular industry are in a hot state. But sometimes life is not kind enough to present this set of ideal circumstances, and you might be forced into selling the company when the market is taking a downswing.

If you plan to sell your company and anticipate a market decline, then sell before the market starts to decline because you will get a higher price and better financing in an up market instead of a down market. Selecting the optimal time is easier said than done. The best recommendation on this point is to simply sell your company when it is performing well and the general market conditions are favorable, assuming that you have intentions to sell at all. A declining market actually can be good news for you and your shareholders if you have a well-run company; conversely, it can be really bad news if your company is on a downswing itself.

Investors look at companies as investments which are compared against other available investments. If your particular investment looks good when compared to the others, it will command a fair price and might even command a premium since its expected return may be higher than that of comparable investments. Assume for a moment that the general market is dropping off but your particular industry is holding its own and not showing a comparable decline. If your company is profitable it might look better to an investor than other possible investment options in other declining markets.

Selling when Technology Changes

Selling when spurred by technology changes requires brutal honesty. It takes raw courage to admit that the technology that you have invested money and time into is going to become obsolete due to technology changes elsewhere. Few people saw the incredible impact that the Internet would have on the way we used to run our business lives, whether it be standard mail, fax, or overnight delivery technologies. The increasing number of people using email and the Internet has caused people to email files that previously would have been copied onto a floppy disk and shipped via overnight express. I know that is definitely true with my book writing. In prior books written before the accepted used of the Internet, my publisher and I would ship packages back and forth with both hard copy printout and floppy disks containing the electronic files. Now, we simply email the files back and forth, doing most of the editing online. A book of any substantial length could potentially entail hundreds of overnight packages that are now emailed.

Clearly, FedEx is not going out of business, and neither is UPS or Airborne Express. But they must recognize the shift within their industry and choose to capitalize on the changes by allowing customers to track packages using the Internet while heavily promoting their ability to ship products and packages overnight as well as the traditional overnight letters. Try shipping a bench tester through the Internet. Don't laugh. It might just happen in another 20 or 30 years and is already happening today for those products that are software-driven and involve no physical product transfer.

Assume that you are the CEO of a successful local courier service that primarily carries documents across town, and that only a small number of your packages are legal documents requiring original signatures. Along comes the Internet and the ready acceptance of email between different companies, and you start to see a decline in your business. If you determine that the funding required to shift your company's market focus from letters to packages is too large for your present situation, you would probably be better served by selling now and recouping as much as possible of the company's current value. Waiting a few years might undermine the excellent performance that you currently demonstrate and substantially reduce the obtainable sale price.

If you do not sell and instead try to shift the focus, and lose, then you might lose the majority of the company's value as a result of the gamble. If you successfully shift the focus, you are still in the game, but you have likely acquired debt to fund the expansion, which still potentially puts you at a competitive disadvantage. Selling early in the technology change process may present the best chance of receiving a fair price for the company, thus converting its value into cash that can be reinvested in another area.

Selling when Bored

This section is for the entrepreneurs in the group. You know who you are. You are the ones who like making quick decisions, can't stand it when something takes a long time to implement, always want to capture new markets, and want to shake up the status quo just to see what happens. Thank goodness for entrepreneurship, because it is the fuel for much of the innovation seen within technology industries.

While entrepreneurs are great at starting companies, they are often not great at running a company on a daily basis. A well-run company of any size will consist substantially of processes and procedures and likely have a small entrepreneurial development team. This might not be enough change for the entrepreneurial CEO and he or she might become bored with the business. This is a potentially dangerous time for a company, particularly if the company is privately held. The founder/manager must take the time to do an internal reality check to determine a current level of commitment to the company. If there is no way for you to satisfy your personality needs without jeopardizing the company's financial well-being, then I suggest that you polish your current company to a high luster and sell it before you start diffusing its focus and eroding its value.

Beware the inclination to simply decide that it is time to sell, and then sell. If you are lucky, you will get a reasonable price for your business. If you are not lucky, word might get out that you are selling, causing customers to flee to your competition which decreases the value of your company while also making it less attractive to potential buyers. This causes you to get a lower price for your company while placing much of your previously well-earned success in jeopardy.

Intellectual Property Considerations

Patents have a limited life span of 17 years, after which the underlying patented idea is no longer protected and can be copied and offered by other firms. This is a precarious time for a company that has made a living from a single patented idea. Selling the company is one of the various options available to a company in this position and purchasing a company with a pending patent expiration can be highly attractive to a company wanting a strong foothold in a market before the patent protection runs out.

Imagine that you are the CEO of a large avionics firm that provides a wide array of electronics equipment to the airline industry, but cannot provide the communication headset worn by the pilot because the headset design preferred by the pilots is patent protected by a third company. The patent for this headset is set to expire in five years. You could either set out today designing a comparable product so that you can jump on the market as soon as the patent expires, or you could approach the company that holds the patent about purchasing either the rights to the patent or the entire company.

The patent holder knows that competition will heat up substantially when the patent expires and might not have the needed resources to protect its market share. Joining forces with another firm that offers complementary products is a natural evolution for a firm holding a patent that is close to expiration.

This is one technique for finding possible acquisition candidates. By reviewing the currently patented ideas for synergy with your company's business plan and determining which ideas are close to expiration, you might be able to offer the company that currently holds the patent an alternate, attractive option that they might not have thought available. Patent databases are available that make this search process a quicker and less tedious process.

Selling to Improve Business Synergy

Business alliances are now a way of life, but it was once thought that going it alone was the optimal business approach. Many contend that the global marketplace and speed with which business changes mandated this transition to a cooperative business approach. Combine this cooperative need with the ready international availability of the Internet and you have the foundation for both domestic and international alliances. Business synergy can be obtained through a formal alliance in which the companies agree to a certain level of cooperation while remaining distinct legal entities. It can also be obtained through M&A activities where one company simply purchases another with the intention of integrating the two entities into a single operational organization. A third approach is for the two companies to create a third independent company that is jointly owned by alliance partners, such as is being considered at the time of this writing between Toshiba and IBM. The proposed new company name is T&I Solution. IBM will own 49 percent of shares and Toshiba will own 51 percent (www.madaily.com, 26 October 1999, "Toshiba, IBM Japan in talks to set up information system venture").

An alliance requires a high level of cooperation between the partners to remain functional within the scope of its limited agreement . A purchase, on the other hand, acquires the personnel, market position, technology, legal rights, obligations, and goodwill of the purchased organization for use as needed by the purchasing company to achieve the required return on the purchase price invested.

Selling could be attractive to the purchased company for any number of reasons.

1. Joining forces with a larger company instantly opens up new market channels for products and services.

2. The larger purchasing company is better able to fund the next stage of a purchased company's product or service evolution.

3. The purchased company might address a lower and middle tier of the market, while the larger company addresses the upper tier. Combining the two organizations enables a one-stop shopping approach to customer needs while providing technological consistency across product lines.

4. Many customer and administrative functions, such as technical support and field installation, might be better handled through the established network of the larger company making the smaller company's products more attractive to prospective purchasers.

The data and voice networking industry has gone through immense restructuring and change over the last 25 years or so. What started out as a single telephone network under the control of AT&T is now divided into thousands of individual companies that provide a wide array of products and services. But the fundamental needs of customers in many ways have not changed. They want high reliability, high quality, rapid service response times when something does go wrong, service flexibility, lower pricing, and consulting services.

If you are a small company trying to get a foothold into the data communication industry, having a highly reliable product is usually not enough. You must also convince the customer that your products can be reliably installed in the required geographic locations and that service can be provided within required time frames should something go wrong. Smaller companies address this situation through a service and installation agreement with a national or international provider. They pay for this service arrangement while having no direct control over the service organization's operation or activity. Should the service provider not perform in accordance with expectations, customers will avoid using the primary company's products and ignore the fact that the service company is really at fault. You can see from this example that both the parent company and the smaller company win when the smaller company merges with a larger company that has an already-established service and installation organization. Companies should always be on the lookout for synergy situations that enable two companies to combine resources to create a merged entity that is more capable that either of the two companies were on their own.

Selling when the Stakes Get Too High

A fact of business life that is little known to those who work for large corporations is that owners of smaller, privately held corporations are usually required to personally guarantee any major loans made to the company. This personal guarantee puts the owner's personal assets at risk in the event of a business failure. When the loan amounts are small, the owners generally don't give this too much thought. But as the company becomes more successful and the guaranteed amounts move into the millions of dollars, the levels of personal risk and angst increase. This reason alone is enough for many small business owners to pursue a public offering or to simply sell the company. Buyers are well-served to understand the personal implications that these loan guarantees have on the owners of a privately held company. Relieving the owners of this obligation may be enough to prompt a sale that otherwise may not have been noticed or possible.

Assume, for example, that a five-year-old company has sales of $5 million, and that 90 percent ($4.5 million) of the company's revenues are offered with net 30 day terms. Assume also that accounts payable are obtained with net 30 day terms. There is a delay between the time when the accounts payable liability is incurred and when it turns into an actual sale, which in turn means that the company needs cash to pay its debts before the customers have actually paid their debts. A line of credit, secured by the accounts receivable, is usually obtained to handle this shortfall. This line of credit must be personally guaranteed by the owners. The line of credit could easily grow into hundreds of thousands of dollars or more depending on customer payment history. A default by a major customer could put the owner's personal assets in jeopardy if a line of credit had been secured using that particular customer's payment as collateral.

More than one privately held company has sold simply to avoid this higher level of liability, and a purchaser must understand that the emotional aspects of this situation might far outweigh the financial aspects of the transaction when dealing with this type of closely held company purchase. This spells opportunity for the buyer and debt relief for the seller, which is a powerful business combination.

Using a Business Broker

Just as selling or buying your home is easier when you use the services of a licensed real estate broker, so typically is the sale or purchase of a business process aided by the assistance of a professional business broker. The broker can represent either the buyer or seller, with full disclosure required to both parties about who is required to pay which fees. If the broker is retained by the seller, that the seller will determine the actions taken by the broker. Similarly, if the broker is retained by the buyer, then the buyer ultimately controls the broker's actions.

A business broker is also called an intermediary when the expected transactions are over $1 million. A business broker will typically receive compensation upon final closing of the deal, whereas the intermediary will receive some portion of the fees in the form of an up-front, nonrefundable retainer. We will use the term "broker" to refer to both intermediaries as well as brokers in this section unless otherwise noted.

One of the major benefits of working with a broker is anonymity. Sellers want to keep the fact that they are on the market a secret for as long as possible to protect their relationships with customers, vendors, and employees. A broker can represent the company to prospective buyers in a way that allows for initial evaluations while not revealing the company's identity. Naturally, if a company is unique within its industry it is easy for everyone involved to figure out the company's name. Even then, the identity remains conjecture instead of fact, because the name has not yet been actually revealed. This confidentiality can also work to benefit of the buyer because sellers can be approached without revealing the identity of the actual buyer, which might favorably, or unfavorably, affect the seller's initial reactions. Another major benefit of using a broker is his or her experience. Brokers buy and sell companies routinely, while your organization probably performs this function less frequently. Look for a broker who has been in business for a long period of time and who has impressive references.

Fees for brokers and intermediaries are typically based on the Lehman formula, which owes its name to the Lehman Brothers investment banking firm. The Lehman formula looks like this:

- 5% of the first million dollars of sale price
- 4% of the second million dollars
- 3% of the third million dollars
- 2% of the fourth million dollars
- 1% of all sale dollars over $4 million

Fees, if not based directly on the Lehman formula, are often referred to as a function of the formula, such as "double Lehman," which means that fees are two times the Lehman formula for the dollar level involved. An intermediary will typically want between 10 to 20 percent of the expected final transaction fees up front as a nonrefundable retainer.

The broker will provide services throughout the transaction process and can help a transaction move forward should the buyer and seller have some type of disagreement or problem during the M&A process. The broker will act as a personnel resource if needed to find accountants, attorneys, business appraisers, or other professionals who can move the transaction process forward. Should the deal fall through, the broker typically receives no compensation other than that agreed to as part of the retainer.

Just as a professional Realtor will want an exclusive arrangement for some length of time with any house seller, so will any broker want an exclusive arrangement with any represented business buyer or seller. The agreement typically compensates the broker when the seller sells to anyone or the buyer buys any business. This is where these types of arrangements can get sticky, and working with an attorney to ensure that you err on the side of overclarification of the agreements is a good idea. Whether you want to agree to these terms is a matter of personal style and preference, but if you are working with a broker that you trust, and one you believe will aid your transaction goals, then an exclusive arrangement should not be a major hurdle. If you have concerns about the person, deal with those concerns first before you worry about the agreement.

Here are a few points that should be considered in every broker/intermediary agreement:

1. Is this an exclusive arrangement, and what time frame will apply to the arrangement?

2. What restrictions do you want placed on the broker's additional activities as they relate to your agency agreement?

3. What happens at the end of the agreement time frame? For what period of time is the broker's previous work "grandfathered," in that prior contacts generated by the broker that later result in a successful purchase, will cause fees to be paid to the broker? What actions on the part of the broker will you require at that point to earn the fees?

4. What are the minimum and maximum commission ranges, and how is the money to be paid?

5. Are there any special incentives included with the agreement, such as having the broker find not only a viable acquisition candidate but also one that has a management team that could take over the operation of the parent company?

Choose a broker with care and patience. This is an important relationship that will dramatically impact the rest of the M&A process. The best way to select a broker is to receive a referral from a colleague who has used that broker's services and, ideally, for a sale or purchase similar in industry and scope to yours. Lacking a useful referral, try the following organizations for a listing of possible brokers that would fit your needs. Before you use any broker, get a listing of references and take the time to talk to each one in detail.

- International Merger and Acquisition Professionals, 60 Revere Drive, Northbrook, IL, 60062, (708) 480-9037.

- M&A International, 530 Oak Court Drive, Memphis, TN, 38117, (901) 684-1274.

- International Association of Business Brokers, 11250 Roger Bacon Drive, Festoon, VA, 22090, (703) 437-4377.

Special Small Business Considerations

Small, closely held corporations are subject to various influences that usually do not affect larger corporations. Selecting an heir in a publicly held corporation is a difficult process but one done every day in corporate America.

Selecting an heir for the founder/president of a closely held corporation is another matter altogether. Many personalities are involved in a large corporation's shareholder mix, while all shares of a closely held corporation might reside in the hands of a single individual or family group. The founder/owner might want a family member to take his or her place, but may have realized that there really is nobody within the family interested, or capable, of assuming that responsibility. Under these circumstances, a closely held corporation is sold to recoup its value before the founder/owner passes away. Such an organization is heavily reliant upon the expertise and personality of a single person. Losing that one person might also drain the company of much of its value.

Buyers interested in purchasing a smaller business, must not ignore the heavy impact of the personalities involved. This impact might be either positive or negative, but it must be investigated. It is also important that all owners be contacted early in the process to verify their willingness to sell their portion of the company. A few people will hold a very large percentage of the company's shares and one holdout with a majority of shares can make the entire exercise a futile process.

Hostile Takeovers

Any company that is publicly traded is a possible target of a hostile takeover. This is where an unsolicited and unwanted buyer attempts to purchase a major percentage of the target company's stock against the target company's management's own wishes. There is much argument about whether hostile takeovers are beneficial or detrimental to the business climate and I will not enter that debate at this point. It is sufficient to say that a hostile takeover is a viable business tactic that can force a target company to sell or merge even when it doesn't want to. The target company is not without its own methods of defense both before and during the takeover attempt. Poison pills, corporate charter amendments, and golden parachutes are three antitakeover techniques used by companies looking to dissuade a hostile takeover attempt.

Poison pill—shares of stock that are made available for issue by the target company should a hostile takeover be attempted. The intent of the poison pill is to make the target company less attractive to a prospective buyer. A typical poison pill might enable existing shareholders to purchase shares of stock at a substantial discount under the current market price should a predefined triggering event occur. A typical trigger event might be the acquisition of greater than 20 percent of outstanding shares by a single entity.

Corporate charter amendments—the corporate charter dictates the operational procedures for a corporation's board of directors. Amendments to the charter that make it more difficult to achieve board of director consensus, or the replacement of a majority percentage of the board, are effective tools against unwanted takeovers, and are called "shark repellent." A typical charter amendment might stagger the election of board members so that no single majority voting block of board members can be changed at one time.

Golden parachutes—Management votes itself highly lucrative severance packages which become available upon the transfer of company ownership. The disincentive to the hostile bidder is that a small group of individuals might make exorbitant profits from the transaction, but a dedicated suitor will likely not be dissuaded by the golden parachutes. Although these get a lot of media coverage, a golden parachute is not a truly effective antitakeover strategy unless coupled with a poison pill and corporate charter amendments.

A hostile takeover will usually come in the form of a bear hug, a tender offer, or a proxy fight. The bear hug is the most friendly of the options, the tender offer is probably the most common in recent business times, and the proxy fight is the most protracted.

Bear hug—The suitors approach the board of directors with an offer to purchase the company and do not go directly to the shareholders. The suitors might or might not announce their purchase intention to the general public at this time but the intention to the board of directors is clear. The board can either accept the offer or it might find itself in a contentious battle for control of the company.

Tender offer—The Williams Act dictates the legal process required for a tender offer. The buyer offers to purchase a certain percentage of the target company's stock for a given price, usually a premium price compared to the existing market price. Specific stipulations, such as the offer applying only for a fixed number of shares, within a certain time frame, with fixed terms and public announcement of intention to purchase, are typical of a tender offer. See Chapter 21, "Legal Considerations," for more information regarding the filings required for a tender offer.

Proxy fight—This technique is an attempt to take over a corporation by controlling its board of directors and its associated proxy voting rights. Shareholders are often apathetic in the exercise of specific voting rights with respect to their investments, the justification for which will not be debated here. Shareholders often vote by proxy instead of in person. Proxy empowers a board member to vote on the shareholder's behalf in the absence of that particular shareholder's cast ballot to the contrary. Maneuvering to take over board seats and their associated proxy voting rights is a proxy fight.

Some contend that the pending threat of a hostile takeover forces management of publicly held companies to more carefully monitor the financial performance of the organization, which translates into higher shareholder wealth. Others contend that the cost of taking antitakeover measures draws needed resources away from daily operations and wastes them on legal and financial actions that would not be needed in a nonhostile environment. Academics argue both sides of this topic with much intensity. Simply know that a hostile takeover is a very real option available in today's M&A environment whether you are a buyer or a seller.

Chapter Summary

There are various classes of buyers who will look for particular target company types based on their particular business investment objectives. Sellers, on the other hand, will have their own sets of motivations for selling the company. If it is privately held, the motivations might be highly personal. If the company is publicly traded, the motivations will typically be those driven by a desire for increasing shareholder value. Understanding your motivations as a buyer or seller helps determine the set of filtering criteria that selects target or buyer candidates with the highest likelihood of meeting your M&A needs.

The overall economy will strongly influence the ability and willingness of both buyers and sellers, with a strong, robust economy experiencing low inflation and interest rates providing a more enticing M&A environment. Down markets can also present buying opportunities for cash-rich buyers, with many potential target companies becoming bargain purchases as the economy and target company revenue stream slow down. Regulatory or technology changes may drive M&A activity independent of the existing financial environment. Any transaction that attempts to consolidate the operation of two major market share holders will almost always draw the scrutiny of the Justice Department, with the intention of ensuring that consumer interests are not jeopardized by the new, combined business entity.

Ultimately it is up to the buyer to determine if acquiring a company with the desired technology and/or business attributes is a less expensive, more reasonable route than simply developing the capability using internal resources. Technology companies are particularly prone to M&A activity simply as a result of the rapid rate at which technology changes. Two years might well mean the difference between the prominence or obsolescence of one technology, or company, and another. Choosing to develop capabilities using internal resources might not only cost more money, but it might also result in a failed development effort and late or disrupted market entry. The reality of these risks prompt technology companies to acquire existing technology with the intention of gaining early leadership in a given market.

3

Financial Statement Overview

Every business manager encounters accounting terminology and procedures at some point in his career. These terms and accounting procedures used to strike me as a nuisance until, as a manager, I had to depend on the accounting reports generated by those procedures. At that point I came to appreciate the consistency and reliability that they represented. The M&A process involves the analysis of financial statements. The more you understand these statements, the better prepared you will be to manage the professionals performing the detailed analysis.

This chapter is designed to help the nonfinancial manager understand the most important aspects of accounting financial statements as they specifically pertain to M&A activities. You will not qualify to take the CPA exam after reading this chapter but you will know your way around the standard financial statements, making you better able to assess the financial condition of a prospective acquisition target.

General Accounting Terminology and Assumptions

Accounting has its own terminology and language which have specific meanings within the financial industry. A clear understanding of this terminology will greatly aid you in the business implications associated with the various financial statements.

Accounting Information Is Historical in Nature

Information reported on a set of financial statements represents transactions that have already happened. This is a very important underlying concept; past performance is certainly no guarantee of future performance but it can be used as an indicator of what has happened in the past. As the business manager, your job is to determine the likelihood of the past performance being either met or exceeded in the future.

The good news is that this historical information, if presented in accordance with *generally accepted accounting principles* (GAAP), should provide an accurate picture of what did actually happen, within certain restrictions. Chapter 5, "Financial Analysis Concepts," is dedicated specifically to understanding the financial implications of the information presented.

It should be noted here that a set of well presented financial statements is not a guarantee that the information presented is financially accurate and prepared in accordance with GAAP. It is not uncommon for smaller firms to skimp on professional accounting guidance until absolutely necessary. Questions should be asked regarding who actually prepared the statements, where they obtained their bookkeeping data, and what assumptions were used in their preparation. The answers to these questions tell you a lot about the target company.

If the statements were prepared by a trained third-party accountant who also handles the company's bookkeeping records, then the statements reflect some type of objectivity, although they should not be assumed rigorously accurate without more investigation. If the statements were prepared by an internal staff member with minimal accounting background using internally recorded bookkeeping numbers, then the financial statements may be fiction as much as fact, and should be treated as such. The first approach may imply that the target company management is not averse to using outside professional services on important matters, which is generally a sign of management that can differentiate between critical and nominal issues. The second approach may imply that the management wants to keep everything pertaining to the company private and may have sacrificed financial management accuracy in the interest of privacy or cost saving. This situation should raise questions about other areas within the target company, such as its legal department, in which a similar approach might later cause problems for the buyer. If the target company is publicly traded, then the accounting data should be easily accessible and audited by a public accounting firm. Historical company performance is important to understanding both current performance and future performance claims. Verifying the reliability of the historical performance information presented is crucial.

Accounting Information Represents Levels and Flows

A company's financial status is constantly changing. When customer payments are received (inflow), the level of cash in the company bank account increases. When the company makes a vendor payment (outflow), the level of cash in its bank account decreases. Notice that the amount of cash on hand varies dependent upon the time of day at which the level is checked.

Cash flows into and out of the company over a given period of time. Accounting information is stored in accounts and accounts fall into four basic categories: asset, liability, income, and expense accounts. *Asset* accounts keep track of things of value that are owned by the company. Typical asset accounts include cash, accounts receivable, inventory, buildings, machinery, and furnishings. *Liability* accounts track money owed by the company to third parties. Typical liability accounts include lines of credit, vendor debts, credit cards, payroll taxes due, and loans. Asset and liability accounts are used to create a *balance sheet* which shows the status of all accounts for a given point in time. The difference obtained by subtracting the total liability accounts from the total asset accounts provides the amount of *shareholders' equity* contained within the company. Stated another way, total assets equals the total liabilities plus shareholders' equity.

Income (revenue) accounts track the amounts earned by the company while selling its various products or services. *Expense* accounts track the amount of cost for the company to earn the income shown in the income accounts. An *income statement* subtracts the total expenses from the total revenues for a given period and reflects the difference as the *net income.*

It is important to note that the income statement represents financial inflow and outflow for a given period of time (analogous to a videotape that demonstrates information and change over a period of time) whereas the balance sheet reflects the balances of asset and liability accounts at a given point in time (similar to a snapshot which captures a particular moment in time.) Notice that all of this information is historical in nature. Another statement, called the *statement of cash flows,* is used to track cash expenditures when using the accrual basis of accounting. Both the statement of cash flows and accrual method are covered later in this chapter.

Accounting Periods

Accounting periods are used to provide comparability between the information presented in the various financial statements. Comparable financial reporting periods enable investors to more easily and effectively compare the financial performance of different companies.

Companies manage their financial activities on a *fiscal year* basis. This is a twelve-month period that usually corresponds with the calendar year, but does not have to. A company can elect to have a fiscal year that does not correspond with the calendar year but must indicate its fiscal year in its financial reports. Each fiscal year is then divided into four fiscal quarters of three months each. Publicly available financial reports are usually generated and published for each quarter, with an annual report representing the fiscal year performance of the company throughout the entire twelve month period.

Assuming that a company uses a fiscal year that corresponds to the standard calendar year, the first quarter results would be reported as of March 31st of the year. The income statement would include information from January 1st through March 31st; the balance sheet would reflect account values effective at the close of the last business day on or before March 31st. Second quarter results are provided as of June 30th. Third quarter results are provided as of September 30th and fourth quarter results are provided as of December 31st. Company management might and usually will request interim financial reports that reflect performance on a monthly or even daily basis. These reports are not usually made public. In fact, most privately held companies never reveal their financial statements at all except to close financial partners such as financiers or other company owners. When first looking at a set of financial statements, always immediately verify the accounting period for which the information pertains and whether the information is presented using the cash or accrual method of accounting.

Matching

The entire intention of financial reporting is to provide the reader/investor with an idea about the company's net income, the amount of shareholders' equity and changes in this equity. An investor will look for the net income to remain positive or hopefully increase while also seeing the shareholders' equity increase from one accounting period to the next. A negative shareholders' equity means that the company's liabilities are greater than its assets. A company in this situation owes more than it owns, which is rarely a financially healthy situation.

It is important to make sure that expenses incurred while earning revenues during a given accounting period be tracked on that same period's financial statements. This matching of expenses and revenues is fundamental to the preparation of a useful and GAAP compliant set of financial statements.

Cash Basis of Accounting

Most households work on a cash basis of accounting. This means that you report income to your household when you receive your paycheck and record an expense when you write a check or pay a bill in cash. This approach enables the tracking of income and expenses for a given period by simply comparing when cash was received and when bills were paid. Matching requires that these two sets of figures be correlated to the same time period to prepare the cash basis income statement for the period in question. Your household does not typically make loans to people that require future collection within a 30-day period. Except for your credit card, you do not typically take out loans that require repayment within a 30 day period.

Businesses, on the other hand, do offer credit terms to their customers. And a business's vendors will usually offer credit terms to the business. Tracking this relationship between the amount of money owed to a business by its customers and the amount of money that the business owes its vendors is a critical part of a business's financial activities. Ratio analysis, which is presented in Chapter 4, "Effectively Using Financial Ratios," provides techniques for evaluating the effectiveness with which a company manages this short term collection/expense relationship.

Accrual Basis of Accounting

A business must track the amount it owes from the moment it makes a commitment to accept the vendor's parts or services, even though no cash may have actually changed hands. The business must also track the customer commitment to pay invoiced amounts from the moment that the company provided its parts or services to the customer even though, once again, no cash may have actually changed hands. Think of the business as accruing, or periodically adding as an increase, customer repayment obligations while it is also accruing vendor payment debts. This type of credit management and operation is an integral part of business. Effective tracking of these accrued customer receivable amounts and accrued company debts is critical to business operation and is called accrual accounting.

Accrual accounting records a transaction as a real event from the moment of obligation commitment as opposed to when cash actually changes hands, as is the case with cash basis accounting. A company can provide services to customers, accepting the customer's commitment to repay while at the same time using its own credit to obtain products or services from vendors. No actual cash has changed hands yet the company is transacting business. Eventually debts must be repaid with cash, but much business can be transacted without the immediate use of cash.

Revenue Recognition

Once accrual accounting is adopted for the preparation of financial statements, an interesting problem develops that does not arise with cash accounting. Revenues are fairly easily tracked with cash accounting since the revenue is typically recognized when the cash is received, and the time when the cash is received is easy to determine. Revenue recognition is more complicated with accrual accounting, making it more open to interpretation. This can present opportunities for creative financial accounting.

To recognize revenue, two basic criteria must be met: the earnings process must have been completed, and the expected payment must be reasonably assured. This seems pretty straightforward until you start to look at the huge array of situations that occur in everyday business life.

Assume that a customer signs up for a three-year Internet access account and chooses to pay the entire amount in advance. The account can be canceled by the customer with only 30 days notice; the customer is only required to pay for the month's time actually used, and the balance will be refunded. Should the company receiving the payment treat this total three-year payment as revenue?

Looking at the previous criteria, we see that complete compliance for revenue recognition has not been achieved. It is only accurate to record the revenue after the month of service has been provided. A company might be tempted to declare the total three years as revenue to inflate its sales growth figures, but a problem two years in the future could require that the company refund payments for months or years worth of service.

In fact, the company could record this payment as partially revenue receipt and partially a debt (liability). In reality, the company is actually liable for an obligation to refund to the customer, at the point of cancellation, the fees for any remaining unused months of the initially contracted and paid-for 36 months. If you were planning to purchase this company, knowledge about their particular revenue recognition procedures would make a dramatic difference on how you interpreted the company's financial statements.

Expense Recognition

How a company recognizes its expenses under accrual accounting is just as important as how it recognizes its revenue. Assume that the company has a vendor agreement that extends over a 6-month period, ending January of next year, with total payment due at the end of January. Assume also that the company uses a calendar fiscal year and reports its year-end results on December 31st.

Once again the company might be tempted not to include the expense in this year's financial statements so that expenses look smaller, which in turn increases net income as reported for this fiscal year. In fact, revenue and expense matching requires that the expense be reported for the period this year in which the obligation was incurred. In this way, expenses and revenues are matched for the time period reported and not skewed simply due to attractive vendor agreements.

Assume that you are looking at a company that uses aggressive revenue recognition accounting procedures, like those outlined in the last section, while simultaneously delaying the reporting of expenses, as outlined in this section. This company's income statement could show a profit, not because the company is actually profitable, but simply because it specifically used accrual accounting to its own benefit, in violation of GAAP. A set of audited financial statements should identify this situation ahead of time.

Financial statements contain narrative notes which usually include detailed information regarding revenue and expense recognition among other topics pertinent to the statements. It is often tempting to simply review the numbers and to skim the notes, but you may well find that the real meat of a financial statement is in its notes. In fact, you might find them amusing as you begin to appreciate the creative ways in which financial statements can be modified without breaking the rules, done specifically to present a specific business financial image.

There is nothing amusing, however, in being a company shareholder who later finds out that the previously stated financial information was incorrect. Pacific Gateway Exchange, Inc. (PGEX) announced on March 31, 2000 that it was adjusting its quarterly results for 1999 fiscal year as a result of "the timing of the recording of certain expense items, the expensing of certain items that had been capitalized and expensing the costs of preparing for a high yield debt offering that are over 90 days old. In conjunction with these adjustments Pacific Gateway is revising its quarterly results for 1999, resulting in earnings per share of 18c, 9c, 15c and (2c), compared to 22c, 13c, 18c and (4c) previously reported. There is no impact on revenue or cash flow" (PR Newswire, 31 March 2000: "Pacific Gateway Exchange Announces Audited Financial Results for 1999 and Amends Bank Debt Agreement"). The market did not respond well to this news, especially combined with the news that the CFO had also resigned. The next day share prices dropped to $10.25 per share (a 75% decline) from its Class Period high of $44-5/8 per share. A number of class action lawsuits were subsequently filed, which Pacific Gateway management must now deal with (Business Wire, 10 April 2000: "Spector, Roseman & Kodroff, P.C. Announces Securities Fraud Class Action Against Pacific Gateway Exchange, Inc.").

This story is not relayed to specifically single out Pacific Gateway or its management in any specific light, but simply to illustrate that incorrect reporting of financial information can have a direct and usually negative impact on the incorrectly reporting company.

Interpreting Audit Results

It is common to see a set of financial statements, recognize that they were audited by a reputable accounting firm, and assume that the numbers accurately reflect the financial condition of the company. In reality, this assumption cannot be reliably made until you have read the auditor's report, or opinion, regarding the information presented in the financial reports.

The auditor is an independent certified public accountant (CPA) who is hired by the company to confirm that the financial statements were prepared in accordance with GAAP. Here are a few items verified by an independent auditor:

1. Auditor agrees with the management application of accounting principles.

2. Any accounting estimates are considered reasonable by the auditor.

3. Assets and liabilities have been confirmed.

4. No *material* (substantial) errors exist in the reports.

5. Internal accounting systems and procedures have been evaluated as reliable.

Should an auditor have any problems with the areas indicated, the auditor will include an exception statement in the auditor's report, possibly further explained by an additional note.

It is common to find some statement to the effect that "the auditor verifies that the financial reports were created in accordance with GAAP but using numbers provided by the client company." When you see this type of statement you should immediately wonder where the underlying numbers came from and take the time to determine their level of accuracy. CPAs can issue statements that are not audited in accordance with the five points outlined earlier in this section.

The Income Statement

Income is a concept most of us can understand. With income, we acquire the ability to buy things. Without it, we have to use credit to purchase the things we need. The same applies to companies, and the income statement gives us an idea of how profitably a company is performing.

The basic income statement format is not rigidly defined, but there is a general sequence in which income statement information is presented. Table 3.1 is a sample income statement for a fictitious manufacturer of project management software named Proja Technologies, Inc. This information in no way relates to any existing company and is presented here simply for illustration purposes.

The format presented in Table 3.1 is similar to that used in most income statements. It begins with a breakdown of revenues, by source, and then subtracts the costs associated with generating those sales revenues, or *cost of sales*. *Cost of goods sold* (COGS) is sometimes used in place of the cost of sales nomenclature. Some income statements would include interest income as a separate section of the statement since it is not directly related to the major emphasis of this software development business. It is included here as part of revenues for simplification purposes.

Cost of sales includes some variable costs in that such costs vary in relation to the revenues. If more units are sold, then the variable cost will increase proportionately. If sales revenues decrease, then cost of sales will also decrease proportionately. It is worth noting that many fixed expenses can be included in COGS unless the business is a typical retail operation. The *gross profit,* or gross margin number, represents the amount of sales revenue left over to pay other bills after the direct costs associated with generating those revenues are paid. *Fixed expenses* are costs that the business incurs which are independent of sales fluctuations. These numbers remain constant with respect to changes in sales revenues.

Pretax income is the amount of sales revenue left over after all expenses except income taxes and dividends are paid. Subtracting applicable income taxes leaves the final *net income* value which can be either positive if the company is making money or negative for one losing money. Notice that shareholder *dividends* are paid from after-tax dollars. Owners of closely held corporations try to avoid paying dividends to themselves and instead try to

Table 3.1 Income Statement for Proja Technologies, Inc. For Fiscal Period January 1, 20xx to December 31, 20xx (All numbers in $US thousands)

		FY 20xx
Revenues		
Net Sales	$4,250	
Interest Income	$350	
Total Revenues		$4,600
Cost of Sales (COS)		$1,840
Gross Margin (Gross Profit)		$2,760
Fixed Expenses		
Salaries	$1,275	
Rent	$468	
Utilities	$211	
Depreciation	$85	
Research and Development (R&D)	$213	
Promotion and Advertising	$213	
Total Fixed Expenses		$2,465
Pre-Tax Income		$295
Less: Federal Tax	<$13>	
Less: State Tax	<$9>	
Net Income		$275
Retained Earnings (Beginning)		$504
Dividends Paid	<$125>	
Retained Earnings (Ending)		**$654**

take out benefits in the form of business expenses such as salaries, bonuses, or other deductible expenses. Dividends received by shareholders are subject to double taxation because the corporation first pays tax before paying out the dividend to the shareholder. The shareholder's dividend income is subject to tax at the shareholder's own applicable rate. The dividend payment is subtracted from the *retained earnings* number, which is part of shareholders' equity, a balance sheet item. Retained earnings are discussed in more detail in the balance sheet section that follows.

The Balance Sheet

While the income statement represents income and expense flows over a given fiscal period, the balance sheet represents the status of asset and liability accounts at the end of that fiscal period. The balance sheet is sometimes more difficult for people to understand since it does not directly relate to income but really reflects the net book value, or worth of a company as represented by the accounting figures.

Asset items have an initial value that was determined at the moment of the asset's purchase. If you purchase a machine for $50,000, then that asset has a *book value* of $50,000 at the moment of purchase. Its value is decreased over its useful life by the application of a *depreciation* expense that annually reduces the asset's value to its final, or salvage value. Depreciation is an expense item that appears on the income statement but accumulates annually as a negative asset, *accumulated depreciation,* a balance sheet number. The total accumulated depreciation decreases the initial purchase price of acquired assets to provide the remaining asset book values at any future point. Specific asset depreciation schedules which record the amount of depreciation applied to each corporate asset are tracked within the company's accounting system and may be reviewed as part of the due diligence process. Think of depreciation as an accounting technique for decreasing the value of an asset based on the wear-and-tear derived from normal operation over its useful life. An asset may actually be useful for longer than its depreciable lifetime but it will be reduced to a $0 book value from an accounting perspective.

Assets are divided into *short-term* and *long-term* categories based on the amount of time it takes to convert that asset into cash. Assets that are assumed to be convertible to cash in 12 months or less are called short-term assets, or *current assets.* All others are long-term assets. Typical current assets include cash, accounts receivable, and inventory. Typical long-term assets include machinery, buildings, goodwill, patents, and major tangible items.

Liabilities are also divided into short-term and long-term based on whether or not the liability is payable within a 12-month period. Short-term, or *current liabilities,* are required payable within a 12-month period. Long term liabilities require payment over a period longer than 12 months. Typical current liabilities include accounts payable, payroll taxes payable, and credit card debt. Long-term liabilities include items such as mortgage notes, vehicle loans, and equipment loans. It is also common to represent the cur-

Table 3.2 Balance Sheet for Proja Technologies, Inc.
Period Ending December 31, 20xx
(Thousands of $US)

Assets	
Current Assets	
Cash	$139
Inventory	$168
Accounts Receivable	$438
Total Current Assets	$745
Other Assets	
Buildings	$1,232
Equipment	$649
Less: Accumulated Depreciation	$457
Goodwill	$185
Total Other Assets	$1,609
Total Assets	$2,354
Liabilities and Shareholders' Equity	
Current Liabilities	
Notes Payable	$74
Accounts Payable	$192
Income Taxes Payable	$64
Other Current Liabilities	$37
Total Current Liabilities	$367
Long Term Liabilities	$875
Total Liabilities	$1,242
Shareholders' Equity	
Common Stock (458,000 shares at $1 par)	$458
Retained Earnings	$654
Total Shareholders' Equity	$1,112
Total Liabilities and Shareholders' Equity	$2,354

rent portion of a long-term debt as a separate line item if material to the financial analysis.

The layout of a balance sheet as shown in Table 3.2 enables the reviewer to easily see what portion of the company's assets and liabilities is current and what portion is longer-term. This information becomes important when doing a ratio analysis which is the subject of Chapter 4.

The shareholders' equity portion of the balance sheet is of great importance to shareholders, and you as a potential purchaser should think of yourself as a shareholder. This simplified balance sheet includes *common stock* and *retained earnings*. The common stock number reflects the *paid-in capital* (money or services) provided to the company in exchange for the listed number of shares of stock at the *par value* shown. Par value is an accounting tool used for tracking stock transfers and has little to do with actual market valuation of a share of company stock. The *retained earnings* indicate the amount of net income that has been retained by the corporation and not distributed to shareholders as dividends.

My hope at this point is that you are starting to get an understanding of the relationship between the income statement and the balance sheet. Net income not distributed to shareholders as dividends is added to retained earnings as displayed on the balance sheet, increasing shareholder's equity. None of this has any direct bearing on what might be the publicly traded value of Proja's stock. The market determines the stock value based, in part, on the information shown on these financial statements. The data shown on the financial statements are book values for the company and have little to do with market-set stock valuation. A company with a positive shareholders' equity is one that owns more than it owes. One with a negative shareholders' equity is one that owes more than it owns. A negative shareholders' equity value is usually the sign of a company in financial trouble and likely on its way to a financial collapse. One with a large shareholders' equity might indicate a company that is not putting enough of its earnings back into building the company's own operations.

Oddly enough, a company with a large current asset value along with high shareholders' equity and a low stock price may become a prime takeover candidate. The acquiring company gets large current assets as part of the purchase, which might then be put to more financially efficient use in other parts of the acquiring company's business. Chapter 6, "Deal Types and Their Funding," takes a closer look at techniques for using the target company's assets to assist in funding the purchase itself.

The Statement of Cash Flows

Once a company adopts an accrual basis of accounting, it must have a mechanism for tracking the changes in the company's actual cash position. The company management will want to know how cash was received and spent during the fiscal period under investigation. Such data bridges an information gap that would otherwise exist between the balance sheet and income statement. This is the purpose of the *statement of cash flows,* which is part of any full set of financial statements.

Referring to the Internet service provider revenue recognition issue example presented earlier provides a way of illustrating the difference between cash flow and income. Assume that the company claims revenue for the entire three-year contract period but only collects payments on a monthly basis. Over a fiscal year period, the company would have only collected 12 payments, but is showing 36 payments in its revenue statement. This situation should create a large disparity between the income statement revenue number and the statement of cash flows section dealing with operating activities. Under these circumstances one would expect the income statement revenues number to be substantially larger than those shown on the statement of cash flows. It is important to remember that revenue and expense items shown on the income statement may not, and likely will not, directly correlate to actual cash transactions for a company using the accrual basis.

Projecting the Future with Pro Forma Statements

So far we have looked at the historical aspects of financial statements. If these statements were useful only for looking at the past, their use would be limited from an M&A perspective. You purchase a company primarily expecting future benefits and not to benefit from something that has financially already happened. Predicting that level of future performance is the purpose of the pro forma financial statements. Pro forma statements use historical performance data as a starting point for predicting the future. Integrated into the statement are anticipated future performance expectations such as percentage increases in sales, decreases in cost of sales, and increases in

**Table 3.3 Income Statement for Proja Technologies, Inc.
(All numbers in $US thousands)**

		FY 20xx	FY 20x1	FY 20x2	FY 20x3	FY 20x4
Revenues						
Net Sales	$4,250					
Interest Income	$350					
Total Revenues		$4,600	$4,876	$5,1685	$5,4786	$5,8073
COS		$1,840	$1,821	$1,8033	$1,7853	$1,7674
Gross Margin (Gross Profit)		$2,760	$3,054	$3,365	$3,693	$4,040
Fixed Expenses						
Salaries	$1,275					
Rent	$468					
Utilities	$211					
Depreciation	$85					
R&D	$213					
Promotion and Advertising	$213					
Total Fixed Expenses		$2,465	$2,732	$2,8413	$2,9550	$3,0732
Pretax Income		$295	$322	$524	$738	$967
Less: Federal Tax	<$13>		<$110>	<$178>	<$251>	<$329>
Less: State Tax	<$5>		<$10>	<$16 >	<$22>	<$29>
Net Income		$275	$203	$330	$465	$609
Retained Earnings (Beginning)		$504	$654	$732	$937	$1,277
Dividends Paid	<$125>		<$125>	<$125>	<$125>	<$125>
Retained Earnings (Ending)		$654	$732	$937	$1,277	$1,761
Estimated Annual Sales Revenue Growth	6%					
Estimated Annual Fixed Expenses Growth	4%					
Estimated Annual Decrease in COS	1%					

fixed expenses. Naturally these future performance estimates are just that—estimates. However, you have to start somewhere in determining future financial performance. Table 3.3 shows future performance estimates for Proja Technologies.

Some pro forma analyses allow parametric analysis, in which financial performance is estimated based on varying a given parameter such as inflation, market share increase, or another important parameter. You are well served by placing your pro forma statements in a spreadsheet format so that parametric analysis can be easily performed.

A person looking at the pro forma income statement for Proja Technologies, Inc. might not agree with the assumptions, but he could clearly see the basis for the calculations. At the very least, this type of predictive representation of the future provides a starting point for determining the expected future benefit that would be derived from purchasing this company.

Chapter Summary

Investors, managers, and financial analysts make decisions and future predictions based on financial reports which include the income statement, the balance sheet, and the statement of cash flows. These data are reported on a quarterly and annual fiscal basis with the matching of revenue and expenses being an integral part of their creation. The assessments made by these professionals are only as accurate as the information contained within the reports. GAAP procedures are an attempt to standardize the creation of financial reports, but there is still much left open to the interpretive, and creative, eye of the financial manager. It is important to read all of a financial report, including statements made by the auditors and the notes, to get a clear picture of a company's financial condition. This information, combined with a comprehensive ratio analysis, should give you a clear financial understanding of a target company's historical and expected future financial performance.

The statement of cash flows provides an important look at the ways in which the company used cash during the accounting period (which is not obvious from the income statement). Reviewing the statement of cash flows with the income statement is an important part of any financial analysis. Looking at trends in reported financial performance over a three- to five-year historical period provides important insight on the company's performance. Increasing shareholder's equity, revenue, and net income from one year to the next is usually a positive sign, while decreases usually indicate financial changes that deserve more investigation.

Effectively Using Financial Ratios

Having financial data at your fingertips is helpful, but converting that raw data into useful information is an additional necessary process. Evaluating a set of financial statements to the extent that you get a somewhat intuitive understanding of the company's operations is as much a skill as an art. Financial due diligence is a process in which the various financial tools are used to highlight areas that require additional investigation. *Ratio analysis* is an important tool in performing that evaluation and one worthy of your understanding. Reading this chapter, along with Chapter 5, will provide you with the needed basic skills to be conversational with any financial analyst or accountant encountered in your technology M&A activities.

Ratio Analysis Overview

Comparing companies within the same industry is a good idea when performing any acquisition target analysis. But this process is easier said than done, especially when the two companies being compared are of substantially different sizes. If one company has annual revenues of $5 million where the comparative one has annual revenues of $75 million, the process of comparing the financial details is cumbersome at best. Comparing the financial information presented to a benchmark reference allows you to compare the companies on a more even basis, and is the purpose of ratio analysis. Engineers refer to this process as *normalizing* the data to a common reference point. Ratio analysis normalizes the financial data to a financial statement common reference, such as revenues, so that a relative comparative reference can be made.

Calculating the ratio itself might not be as valuable as noting how the ratio changes over time. Some analysts calculate ratios differently than others, and unless you are intimately familiar with the source of the numbers and the formulas used, the raw ratio number itself might be useless. But if the number is calculated the same way over time and those time calculations present you with a trend, you will have a basis for further investigation. This last sentence brings up a very important point with respect to ratio analysis: It is not an end in itself, but simply a pointer to areas for further investigation. Evaluating a company is like solving a mystery in that a number of individual clues all add up to a total picture, and finding the place to look for those clues is an important part of the process. Ratio analysis is a useful tool for finding places to look and the rest of this chapter will highlight its application in that regard.

As the manager of the M&A process or a member of an M&A team, you will not be called upon to perform a ratio analysis, but you might very well have a seasoned financial professional or accountant perform that analysis for you. I believe that you should be able to interpret their results in a way that provides insight to the financial operation of the target company while also providing guidance to other M&A team members. Finally, be cautious about accepting a ratio without also seeing the underlying values used to create that ratio. Computers are used to generate much of the analysis we use on a daily basis. Trusting the computer-generated numbers without verifying the underlying data is a mistake in any technical industry and also a mistake in financial analysis. Make sure that you apply the human interpretive aspect to any ratio analysis.

Percentage Analysis

It is particularly helpful to understand the breakdown of a business's financial performance as a percentage of a common factor. Knowing, for example, the percentage of total sales that finally winds up as net income is vitally important information. Comparing the net income number to the total sales fig-

**Table 4.1 Income Statement for Proja Technologies, Inc.
(All numbers in $US thousands)**

	FY 20xx	Percent
Revenues		
Net Sales	$4,250	92.39%
Interest Income	$350	7.61%
Total Revenues	$4,600	100.00%
COS	$1,840	40.00%
Gross Margin (Gross Profit)	$2,760	60.00%
Fixed Expenses		
Salaries	$1,275	27.72%
Rent	$468	10.16%
Utilities	$211	4.59%
Depreciation	$85	1.85%
R&D	$213	4.63%
Promotion and Advertising	$213	4.63%
Total Fixed Expenses	$2,465	53.59%
Pretax Income	$295	6.41%
Less: Federal Tax	<$12>	
Less: State Tax	<$9>	
Net Income	$275	5.98%
Retained Earnings (Beginning)	$504	
Dividends Paid	<$125>	2.72%
Retained Earnings (Ending)	$654	

ure provides this information as a ratio that can then easily be converted into a percentage.

It is common to use total sales revenue as the base amount (denominator) to which all other numbers on the income statement are compared. It is also common to use the total assets number as the base amount for balance sheet comparisons.

You can see from the Table 4.1 that much additional information pertaining to Proja Technologies is revealed with the percentage representation of the presented data. For example, we now see that 5.98 cents of every sales revenue dollar shows up as net income. We also see that 40 cents of every sales revenue dollar pays for cost of sales (COS). Decreasing COS by 5 percent (to 35 percent) would theoretically increase pre-tax income by 5 percent (to 10.98 percent) assuming all other fixed expenses remained the same. We also see that Proja's single largest percentage fixed expense is salaries, which is typical for a software development company but might be atypical for Proja's particular industry. The primary point here is that additional useful analysis information is provided by this percentage display of the financial data rather than simply by the raw numbers. Comparing Proja's percentage breakdowns to its competitors' provides an interesting basis for comparing Proja's performance to its industry.

Assume that Proja's next closest competitor shows a COS of 35 percent and salaries of 24 percent, yet this competitor has sales revenues that are comparable to Proja's. In this case you know that further investigation is required in the COS and salary areas of Proja's financial operation since its competitor is generating comparable sales revenue with lower salary expenses. It is still too early to claim that Proja's salaries are too high, but it certainly warrants further investigation, after which time the buyers can make their own assessment with more complete information. Once again, the ratio does not by itself mean much, but it acts as a pointer to other areas deserving of investigation.

Evaluating Ratio Meanings

Ratio analysis is primarily used to evaluate a company's operation in one of several areas.

1. *Liquidity analysis*—evaluates a company's ability to pay its short-term debt with available short term (current) asset items.

2. *Activity analysis*—evaluates the efficiency with which a company converts its assets into revenue and products or services.

3. *Solvency and long term indebtedness analysis*—evaluates the company's status as pertains to longer-term financial viability.

4. *Profitability analysis*—evaluates the incomes obtained from the revenues generated along with total capital invested.

This section takes a detailed look at the most popular ratios used to evaluate these various financial areas of interest.

Liquidity Analysis

Cash availability is critical to a company's ongoing financial survival. Without cash to pay employees, they quickly leave to find another job. Without cash to pay vendors, they quickly stop providing their products or services. Without cash to pay loans, creditors usually force the company into default or complete dissolution.

Liquidity analysis evaluates the company's ability to pay its short-term obligations. After all, if the company cannot make it through the next few months, its longer-term strategic prospects look bleak indeed. Liquidity analysis is particularly important when determining the amount of cash that might be needed by an acquired company in the time frame just after its acquisition. If the acquiring company has its own cash shortage problems it should be very careful about acquiring another company with serious liquidity problems. On the other hand, acquiring a company that is flush from a liquidity perspective might make sense for an acquiring company experiencing its own liquidity shortage.

The current ratio provides a good first step in any liquidity analysis.

$$\frac{\text{current assets}}{\text{current liabilities}}$$

The current ratio compares the company's ability to pay its liabilities that are due in the next twelve months with the assets that the company can convert into cash within the next twelve months. If the current ratio is less than one, the company does not have sufficient cash to meet its existing obligations. This is rarely a good sign. A current ratio that is too high for the industry might indicate that the company is hoarding cash, has account receivable collection problems or is simply not reinvesting or expanding the company operation.

Current assets includes inventory, which is typically not easily convertible into cash and likely not convertible on a dollar-to-dollar basis because only a fraction of every dollar of inventory could feasibly be converted to cash. This is particularly true for a company that might be carrying a substantial amount of obsolete inventory on its financial statements. For this reason, some feel that the *quick ratio* provides a more accurate assessment of liquidity status.

$$\text{quick ratio} = \frac{(\text{cash} + \text{marketable securities} + \text{accounts receivable})}{\text{current liabilities}}$$

This ratio only includes items that are generally easily converted into cash which could be used to pay current liabilities. Any going concern that is in business with the intention of staying in business into the future will require some level of accounts receivable as well as cash to function. For this reason the liquidity tests are simply a measure of the level of safety the company has with respect to meeting its current obligations.

The current ratio and quick ratio provide insight into the relative levels of cash available to meet the company's obligations but does not tell us anything about the number of days that the company could remain financially viable in the event of a serious revenue drop. The *defensive interval* lets you know, in a very conservative way, the answer to this question.

$$\text{defensive interval} = 365 \times \frac{(\text{cash} + \text{marketable securities} + \text{accounts receivable})}{\text{projected expenditures}}$$

$$\text{where: projected expenditures} = \text{COS} + \text{other operating expenses}$$

The result of this ratio calculation reveals the number of days that the current assets would sustain the company based on the projected expenditures. A completely accurate assessment of the projected expenditures requires access to inside company information, but an estimate can be made by applying the historical expense percentages to pro forma revenue projections. This is obviously only a guess of future requirements, but it enables the calculation of the defensive interval, which gives you an idea of how many days the company can last from a cash perspective given the current assets and expected expenses.

Activity Analysis

The success of any company is based on its successful daily management activities, and tracking the financial management of those activities is the purpose of the ratios presented in this section. Three particular and critical operational areas will be investigated: inventory management, accounts receivable, and accounts payable.

The *inventory turnover* ratio provides insight into the efficiency with which the company manages its inventory. Particular types of organizations, such as manufacturing and retail, must efficiently manage their inventory since it represents a major expense and asset item on the company's financial statements.

$$\text{inventory turnover} = \frac{\text{COGS}}{\text{average inventory}}$$

COGS is also called cost of sales (COS) and is an income statement value that accounts for items actually sold during the period. Average inventory represents all inventory items and is obtained by averaging the period's beginning and ending inventory values from the balance sheet.

The inventory turnover ratio value will vary between industries and a higher turnover value is generally considered a good indicator of effective inventory management. A higher number means that the existing inventory is being replaced with new inventory on a more frequent basis with the result being that this disappearing inventory is showing up as sales revenue and COGS. This type of inventory turnover is critical for retail organizations and can make the difference between a PC supplier that remains on business and one that disappears, as is discussed in Chapter 12, "Evaluating PC/Workstation and Related Hardware Businesses."

If the inventory turnover ratio is one, then the inventory turned over (was replaced) one time during the period under investigation. An inventory turnover ratio of four for an annual analysis indicates that the inventory turned over four times during the course of the year. This number should be compared to other companies in the same industry to accurately assess the inventory management practices of the target company.

$$\text{average number days inventory in stock} = \frac{365}{\text{inventory turnover}}$$

This calculation tells you the number of days, on average, that items remain in inventory before being converted into revenue.

Items that remain in inventory for a long period of time indicate potentially obsolete products or inventory tracking systems that cannot accurately monitor or predict the optimal inventory levels needed for the company's level of operations. Inventory turnover ratios that are too low for an industry might indicate lost sales due to the lack of inventory availability to meet customer demands. Once again, the norms for an industry combined with trends over time provide pointers into whether or not inventory management is a potential problem for the company under investigation.

Manufacturing firms have a more complicated inventory management process than a retailer or distributor which simply purchases finished goods for resale. A manufacturer purchases raw materials which are run through some type of manufacturing process. These raw materials are converted into finished goods that are then sold to customers. The data required for some portions of this section of the analysis are typically not publicly available and must be obtained from the target company, usually during the due diligence process. Think of manufacturing inventory as really being divided into three stages:

1. *Raw materials* inventory that is purchased from vendors, usually with some type of credit terms such as net 30 days.

2. *Work in process* (WIP), inventory at various stages of the manufacturing process, which may take only a few hours to a few weeks depending on the goods being manufactured.

3. *Finished goods* inventory, items ready for sale whether they have been manufactured from raw materials or simply purchased for resale. This stage is similar to that of a retailer which simply sells finished goods.

Companies with production problems often experience a high inventory level in the WIP stage when compared to efficiently run manufacturing organizations. It is wise to evaluate inventory in all three stages of production when looking at a manufacturing organization as your target acquisition.

Consider the following ratio for cost of goods manufactured:

cost of goods manufactured = COGS

+ ending finished goods inventory − beginning finished goods inventory

This value represents the cost of all goods manufactured during the time frame under investigation. The cost of goods sold represents the cost of all items sold during the period. The difference of ending finished goods inventory (at the end of the period) minus beginning finished goods inventory (at the start of the period) represents the increase (decrease) in the cost of manufactured inventoried items that were not sold. If the cost of goods manufactured increases during a period of decreasing revenue, there may be a problem with sales forecasting or the cost of raw materials may have substantially increased. In either case, further investigation is warranted.

The following inventory-related ratios apply to activity analysis as well:

$$\text{days WIP inventory} = 365 \times \frac{\text{average WIP inventory}}{\text{cost of goods manufactured}}$$

The ratio for *days WIP inventory* provides an average of how long it takes to convert raw materials into finished goods, providing an estimate of the average manufacturing cycle. For the average amount of time that raw materials remain in inventory before entering the manufacturing process, use the *raw material inventory days* ratio.

$$\text{raw material inventory days} = 365 \times \frac{\text{average raw materials inventory}}{\text{raw materials used}}$$

A company practicing "just in time" production processes should show a continuing decrease in this value with the intention of minimizing the number of days to its reasonable minimum.

To figure the total number of days it takes for raw material purchases to be converted into finished inventory, use the following ratio:

$$\text{production inventory days} =$$

$$365 \times \frac{\text{average (WIP inventory + raw materials inventory)}}{\text{cost of goods manufactured}}$$

This number, along with the other inventory ratios presented, should be in alignment with the rest of the company's industry competition. Otherwise, the acquiring company will inherit paying the higher inventory carrying finance charges associated with the time frame between when the vendor payments are due and when the customer payments for sold finished goods are received. This difference represents a cash deficit that the company must compensate for either through cash expenditures, lines of credit, or factoring of accounts receivable, all of which cost money.

The effectiveness with which a company manages its accounts receivable operation is also critical. Accounts receivable represent credit that the company has offered to its customers. Should a customer not repay that credit in a timely manner, or worse not at all, the company has to make up the shortfall from sales to other customers. The *receivables turnover* ratio provides information about a company's receivables management activities.

$$\text{receivables turnover} = \frac{\text{credit sales}}{\text{average trade receivables}}$$

This ratio only considers sales made on credit since these are the only sales that generate an accounts receivable entry. The numbers are further restricted to those sales from *trade receivables* (those received from normal operations) as opposed to those generated from nonoperational activities such as financing or securities exchanges. An exception to this restriction would apply if these financial activities are a normal part of the company's operation as seen with finance companies. A high receivables turnover ratio indicates a company that collects its customer receivables in a timely manner. A low number may indicate a company with problem customers who do not pay their bills on time, or at all. For further analysis, use this ratio:

$$\text{average number of days receivables outstanding} = \frac{365}{\text{receivables turnover}}$$

This ratio tells you the average number of days that an average customer takes to pay his debt to the company. This number should ideally match the credit policy of the company, meaning that if customers receive thirty-day credit terms, this ratio should closely match thirty days. A number that is substantially longer than the company's credit terms indicates that a collection problem may exist with the company. Notice that an increase in the receivables turnover ratio decreases the average number of days receivables outstanding value.

Solvency and Long Term Indebtedness Analysis

The liquidity analysis looks at a company's short-term financial health, but it is not a valid indication of a company's longer-term financial prospects. As with the other ratios presented, it is important to look not only at the ratio for a given point in time but also at how that ratio has changed over time. Keep in mind that the intention, wherever possible, is to work with ratios that can be calculated from most publicly available financial reports.

The following ratio provides an assessment of the company's ability to pay off its existing debts using its existing intrinsic value as represented by shareholders' equity. If this ratio is greater than one, then the company owes more than its "net book value," which is calculated as assets minus liabilities. This ratio, for most companies, is two or larger because companies make extensive use of debt to purchase items like buildings, equipment, and other large-dollar items. The right value for a particular company will vary between industries. If this ratio is greater than one, then the company owes more than it is worth. This ratio, for most companies, is two or larger and varies between industries.

$$\text{debt-to-equity} = \frac{\text{total debt}}{\text{total equity}}$$

where: total debt = current + long-term liabilities and total equity
= all shareholders' equity

Both total debt and total equity are calculated using balance sheet values.

An increase in the debt-to-equity ratio normally indicates that the company has recently taken on more debt. A decrease in the debt-to-equity ratio normally indicates that the company has decreased its use of debt either out of choice or because it could not obtain the desired credit. Once again, this ratio simply indicates additional areas for investigation.

Profitability Analysis

Ultimately a business remains in business by remaining profitable over a sustained period of time. Ratio analysis provides us with an objective measure of a business's profitability. A brief introduction to some of these ratios was presented in the prior section on percentage analysis. Many of the ratios presented in this section are nothing more than a mathematical representation of the percentages shown in that section.

The gross margin ratio indicates the portion of every sales dollar that is left over after direct costs (cost of sales) are accounted for. There are very specific value ranges within which the Gross Margin should fall for a specific industry, and this range will vary widely between industries.

$$\text{gross margin} = \frac{\text{gross profit}}{\text{sales revenue}}$$

A gross margin calculation, followed by a comparison to the industry as a whole, should be one of the first calculations performed when analyzing a target company. If this number is low when compared to the industry as a whole, then this particular company's cost of sales are higher than average and further investigation is required. If they are much lower than the rest of the industry, then this company is either doing something very right or is cutting its costs with a potential negative longer term effect being the probable result. For example, assume that a national communications network equipment provider recently changed service organization contractors, with an associated substantial decrease in service costs which in turn decreased the cost of sales. You would then be well advised to learn more about that service organization since you, as the acquiring company, will inherit any negative impact resulting from this change. If the cost reduction move does not materially affect customer service, this could be interpreted as a solid move by the existing management team.

$$\text{profit margin} = \frac{\text{net income}}{\text{sales}}$$

The profit margin indicates the amount of each sales dollar that is left over, after income taxes are paid, for company profit. Once again, you will find that acceptable ranges for the profit margin will vary between industries, with the one constant being that this number must remain positive or the company is losing money.

$$\text{margin before interest and tax} = \frac{\text{earnings before interest and tax (EBIT)}}{\text{sales}}$$

This ratio calculates a company's earnings before tax and interest expenses are deducted from the sales revenues numbers.

$$\text{EBIT} = \text{net income} + \text{interest expense} + \text{Income tax expense}$$

Notice that interest expense and income tax expense must be added to the net income number to compensate for their having been subtracted in the initial calculation of the net income figure. This calculation is valuable to a company considering a merger of the target company into its existing operations, because the target company's loans will likely adopt the financing rates of the acquiring company along with its tax rate. This situation makes the EBIT number a more accurate assessment of expected income as it relates to the acquiring company.

Should the acquiring company not intend to refinance the target company's existing loans, the pretax margin might present a valuable alternate analysis ratio.

$$\text{pretax margin} = \frac{\text{earnings before tax (EBT)}}{\text{sales}}$$

where: EBT = net income + Income tax expense

Notice that interest is not removed from the analysis since the existing interest payments would simply be assumed by the acquiring company.

Investors are continually looking for the best possible return on their investments. In the case of a company, the assets represent the investments being used by the company to generate revenues and ultimately net income. The return on assets (ROA) ratio provides a measure of this return.

$$\text{ROA} = \frac{\text{EBIT}}{\text{average total assets}}$$

Using EBIT instead of net income for this calculation provides a level measure of return for this investment when compared to other investments on a pretax and prefinance charge basis. This approach is valuable when comparing various firms that have differing levels of financial leverage and creditworthiness because the tax and interest expenses are removed from the analysis.

$$\text{return on equity (ROE)} = \frac{\text{pretax income}}{\text{average shareholders' equity}}$$

The ROE calculation provides the stockholder or investor with an assessment of how efficiently the company's equity is being used to generate pretax income. Making this a pretax calculation, once again, puts this investment on a more level evaluation basis when compared to other pretax investments. Notice that this calculation includes interest costs required to generate this income and does not account for the amount of debt to which the company is legally obligated. If the ROE calculation shows that the company is generating a lower return on equity than would be provided from other investments, then equity investment in this company looks less attractive.

$$\text{return on total capital} \ (\text{ROTC}) = \frac{\text{EBIT}}{\text{average (total liabilities + total Stockholders' equity)}}$$

The ROTC ratio provides the return experienced by the company when all provided capital is included in the analysis. All liabilities represent money given, by lenders, to the company for its use as does all shareholders' equity, even though interest is being paid only on the liabilities. The ROTC value represents the total return for all capital to which the company, and its shareholders, have committed. Removing interest expenses from the equation treats the borrowed money as though it represented cash assets being used by the company without any interest penalty applied. This presents a more accurate picture of how efficiently the total capital is being used, whether borrowed or not.

Mixing Balance Sheet and Income Statement Values

These ratios compare values obtained from the various financial statements. Remember that income statement values are calculated over a period of time where the balance sheet values are determined for a given date. This timing difference can create problems when performing the calculations, and therefore care should be taken to minimize any mismatch of data. Taking a look at the defensive interval ratio, we see that the numerator is composed of balance sheet items while the denominator is composed of income statement items. If accounts receivable and cash are low at the end of the accounting period but high at the start, using numbers obtained only at the end of the period would make the numerator unrealistically low, especially when the projected expenses value (denominator) represents an entire accounting period's accumulated buildup.

You can see from the Matrix 4.1 that averaging provides a more accurate assessment of the company's ability to pay its bills than simply using the End/Total value by itself. The beginning values are really the ending values from the prior accounting period. Most analysts feel that using averaged bal-

Matrix 4.1 Using Averages when Computing Values for Ratios

Item	Beginning	End/Total	Average
Cash + Marketable Securities + Accounts Receivable (B/S)	$1.85 million	$1.1 million	$1.475 million
Projected Expenditures (I/S)	—	$6.2 million	—
Defensive Interval using Total Projected Expenditures	108 days	64 days	87 days

ance sheet numbers provides a more accurate assessment of the company's financial condition than comparing income statement and ending-only balance sheet items in the same ratio.

Investment Ratios

Working with or managing a publicly traded company requires some understanding of the processes followed by shareholders and investors. This section presents several of the most commonly used ratios for determining shareholder returns.

$$\text{earnings per share} = \frac{\text{net income}}{\text{average number of common stock shares outstanding}}$$

This number is reported in most financial publications for any publicly traded stock and is reported on a periodic basis, usually a fiscal quarter or fiscal year.

Just because these earnings are available to stockholders does not mean that stockholders will receive these earnings. Stockholders receive their portion of the earnings when the board of directors votes to issue a dividend to shareholders. Current year earnings or losses are added to or subtracted from the retained earnings account on the balance sheet, from which dividends are subtracted.

The earning per share number is valuable when looking at the price of a share of stock as compared to the company's ability to generate earnings. This calculation is performed using the P/E ratio.

$$\frac{P}{E} = \frac{\text{current share market price}}{\text{prior twelve months earnings}}$$

The P/E ratio represents the number of years that a stock's earnings would have to be completely returned to the shareholders, at the current earnings rate, to pay an amount equal to the current stock market price paid by stock purchasers. The denominator of this ratio is fixed until the next set of earnings reports are released, so changes in the P/E are most frequently caused by changes in stock price. The P/E ratio increases as investors become more optimistic about a company's future financial performance and are willing to pay more for the stock. A pessimistic future view by investors will tend to reduce stock prices which decreases the P/E ratio. This ratio is only useful if the company being investigated has positive earnings, which is not always the case in today's technology environment. Other valuation/comparison techniques must be used when looking at companies with negative earnings, and these techniques are covered in Chapter 5, "Financial Analysis Concepts."

Some companies pay dividends to stockholders, and the reasons for paying these dividends can be diverse and heavily company-culture related. A measure of the dividends paid is the *dividend payout* ratio.

$$\text{dividend payout} = \frac{\text{dividends}}{\text{net income}}$$

This ratio is usually calculated using dividend and net income figures calculated for the prior twelve-month period. A firm in heavy growth mode will use its financial resources to fund its growth and pay little to no dividends to stockholders, which in turn shows up as a very small dividend payout ratio. More mature firms with a history of paying consistent dividends try to maintain their dividend payment policy and tend to have a higher dividend payout ratio when compared to smaller, higher-growth companies.

Chapter Summary

The investigation of financial statements and reports is an important first step in evaluating a possible acquisition target company. Using ratio analysis in conjunction with publicly available financial reports enables the financial analyst to get a more in-depth picture of the company's financial operation. A complete ratio analysis looks at liquidity, operations activity, solvency/long-term indebtedness, and profitability in developing a complete financial picture.

It is important to look at ratio trends over time instead of taking a specific ratio at a given point in time as an immutable positive or negative indicator. This is particularly true when considering that different analysts might calculate the same ratio using different financial report components.

Only by performing the required financial ratio analysis over a period of time and for the primary areas of interest can you acquire an intuitive understanding of the financial opportunity presented by the acquisition target. Great care should always be used to investigate and verify the underlying numbers used to generate the derived ratios. Comparing the ratio results of the target company to others in the target's industry group and to other investment opportunities enables the buyer to determine the investment opportunity presented by the target company.

5

Financial Analysis Concepts

Money is always at work in our economy. This money might simply be invested in government treasury notes or invested in the riskiest stock on the market, but the money is being used for some financial purpose which earns additional money. Investors are continually looking for the optimal way to invest their money so that they reap the maximum return on that money over a given period of time. If the investment options are risky (they have a high possibility of not being repaid), then the investor naturally expects to be compensated for that risk in the form of a higher rate of return. The less risky the investment, the lower the expected return, which is why FDIC bank accounts and government treasury notes pay such low interest rates. These investments are basically protected as long as the federal government remains in business, which means that money invested will eventually be returned.

Investing in a risky company's stock is another matter altogether, because shareholders are the very last people to get paid should the company be financially dissolved. This means that lenders, employees, and vendors are paid before the shareholders see any return of invested money. Buyers of companies are looking to become the primary owner of that company's stock. They compare the total purchase investment with available alternative investment actions for that same money. Only purchases that can be reliably shown to enhance the buyer's own share value to stockholders will typically be considered if the buyer is a publicly traded company. Value enhancement can be in the form of a dividend issue, increased share market price, or both.

This chapter leads you through an understanding of important financial principles and illustrates their use in financial investment decision making.

Integrating this information into decision making places any purchase or sale on a more solid financial foundation, which increases the likelihood of future financial returns from the acquisition.

The Time Value of Money

The value of money changes over time. *Inflation* decreases the purchasing power of next year's money while interest paid enables today's investment amounts to grow over time. The 1990s experienced very low inflation rates of under three percent, which is excellent for business in particular and the overall economy in general. Some foreign countries, on the other hand, are experiencing 100 percent inflation or more per year, which means that an item costing $100 this year will cost $200 at the same time next year, effectively cutting the purchasing power of money (or its value) in half over a 12-month period.

Expected interest income affects investment decisions in that a dollar invested today can reasonably be expected to provide the expected return within a 12-month period. Assume that the government 30-year treasury bill interest return rate is six percent. This means that a $100 investment today will, with all reasonable likelihood short of the liquidation of the United States, be worth $106 in 12 months. If I have an alternative investment for that $100 which yields only four percent and has some risk of nonpayment, then I would choose the treasury bill investment since it is a less risky option and provides a two percent ($2) higher return. What if that alternate investment projected, but did not guarantee, a 12 percent return rate? Now the decision is less clearly defined and a more detailed analysis of the risk of nonpayment is required. This is where financial analysis becomes an important tool for assisting us in the making of more complicated financial decisions.

Naturally you could always choose to invest in the risk-free option and simply accept the lower return, but you might be losing money on those riskier investments that actually make good on their promise of higher returns. Publicly traded companies that continue with this conservative investment approach eventually become asset-rich. At the same time, their stock price often drops due to poorer investment returns to shareholders when compared to the rest of the industry. The poorer returns result from less aggressive investments which provide lower-than-average market returns. Risk and reward are always at work in financial situations.

A company with a low stock price combined with large liquid assets can easily become an acquisition target itself. The buyer obtains access to the assets with the intention of putting them to more efficient financial use, yielding a higher return. Or so the theory goes. Understand that asset, stock, loan, and bond values are constantly changing based on the current market conditions and the specifics of the item under consideration. Time changes the value of financial items and the value of these items is often based on their expected future potential for generating income.

Discounted Cash Flow Analysis

A *discounted cash flow* (DCF) analysis is a formalized mathematical procedure for calculating the overall effect of money's value changes over time. It can even assist in determining the amount of additional income that an investment must provide to compensate for its added risk when compared to a risk-free investment such as the government treasury bill. Most spreadsheet programs can perform the DCF calculations for you if you understand the parameters being entered. Remember that no spreadsheet calculation can compensate for your own inability to enter the correct data and to properly evaluate the results.

Three items must be used to perform the DCF calculation:

1. the future expected cash flow expressed as a positive value if cash is received, and a negative value if cash is spent.

2. the number of periods (usually years) between the present time and when the cash flows occur.

3. the discount rate applied to the timing analysis to determine the value of that future cash flow as expressed in today's dollars.

The DCF converts any future cash received or spent into the equivalent of a dollar amount if spent today. This process enables the analysis of various sized financial transactions occurring at different times by converting them into a single number expressed in today's dollars, called the *present value*.

The present value of the future cash flow is calculated using the following formula:

$$PV = \frac{CFn}{(1 + k)^n}$$

where PV = Present value of the future cash flow; CFn = Cash flow occurring at the end of Period n; n = the period number in which the cash flow occurs as counted from today, with today being Period zero; and k = the *discount factor* applied to the analysis. The most commonly accepted discount factor (or rate) used is determined by the *capital asset pricing model* (CAPM), which is presented later in the chapter.

To obtain the total present value for a series of transactions you simply calculate the PV for each individual expected transaction and then add all of the individual present value calculations together to form a single number. This single number represents the total present value of all expected future transactions when discounted back to the present time zero.

Assume that you are presented with two different options for your $100,000 stock purchase investment. Company A plans to pay dividends of $3,500 per year for each of five years, and the stock is expected to be sellable for $125,000 at the end of Year 5. Total cash return (not present value) for Option A over the five years is $142,500. Option B plans to pay no dividends over the five years and the stock is expected to be sellable for $160,000 at the end of Year 5. Total cash return (not present value) for Option B is $160,000. Option B company is considered the riskier of the two investments and has a discount rate associated with it of 14 percent, while Option A has a discount rate of 11 percent because it is deemed a less risky company. Which is the better investment option? On the surface, Option B returns more cash over the five years and appears to be the better investment option, but look at Table 5.1 for what happens when a discounted cash flow analysis is performed that takes into account Company B's additional risk and time value of money as represented by the respective discount rates.

Notice that the summation of each year's cash flow discounted back to Year 0 (today) for Option A is around $4,000 more than the discounted cash flow for Option B even though Option B actually returns more cash. This result is not intuitive for most nonfinancial managers. It results from the sooner payments associated with Option A instead of waiting for the entire five years

Table 5.1 Discounted Cash Flow Analysis

Year	Option A Cash Returned	PV Option A with k=11%	Option B Cash Returned	PV Option B with k=14%
5	$128,500	$76,258.50	$160,000	$83,098.99
4	$3,500	$2,305.56	$0	$0.00
3	$3,500	$2,559.17	$0	$0.00
2	$3,500	$2,840.68	$0	$0.00
1	$3,500	$3,153.15	$0	$0.00
0	$142,500	$87,117.06	$160,000	$83,098.99

to get paid as seen with Option B. This simple example illustrates the importance of considering risk in conjunction with the timing and magnitude of money received and spent when considering any major financial investment.

DCF analysis becomes more precise as the degree of certainty with respect to the future cash flow projections increases, and predicting the future is educated conjecture at best. Analysts attempt to predict the future revenue streams of companies based on publicly available information combined with personal industry experience. The actual internal workings of a particular company remain relatively private and can only be extrapolated from the publicly available information unless specifically revealed by the acquisition target company, which is unlikely in the early stages of the M&A process and usually only comes to the surface during due diligence. Analysts may start with the initially assumed discount rate and then raise or lower it to adjust for higher or lower risk associated with the assumptions made.

An important characteristic of a DCF is that the results are heavily dependent on the discount rate assumed with the higher discount rate more dramatically decreasing the present value of any future received payments. For example, changing the discount rate on Option B to 12 percent (a two percentage point decrease) increases the present value from $83,099 to $90,788, making it the more attractive option and thus completely changing the investment analysis results and subsequent investment decision. Understanding the process used for determining discount rate values is of critical importance and is the subject of the next section.

The Capital Asset Pricing Model and the Discount Rate

Determining the right discount rate (k) for a given company's DCF analysis is another area where art and science converge. Any subjective aspects of the discount rate determination can be swayed to make the analysis support one intended result or another, which is why an objective approach to the determination of the discount rate is appreciated. The CAPM provides an accepted objective framework within which to determine the discount rate for a given company's stock. The analysis can still be performed with other discount rates, but the CAPM analysis provides a readily recognized and accepted method for discount rate determination.

Remember from previous discussion that investing in a government-backed product, such as the treasury bill, provides a basically risk-free investment for a smaller interest return rate. Any investment other than this risk-free option must return a higher rate and, consequently, have a higher discount rate, which is the basic CAPM premise. The equation symbol used for the risk-free investment return rate is Rf.

The next most secure investment option involving stocks would be one that matches the overall market as a whole as determined by a marketwide parameter, such as the S&P 500 overall annual return rate. Any other stock purchases must provide either a higher or lower return relative to this marketwide parameter. This return depends on the stock's risk as related to the market as a whole. The equation symbol used to represent the expected overall market return is Rm.

Stock volatility adds another level of risk to the analysis. Volatility is a measure of a stock's price changes in comparison to the overall market. If the market value increases, the stock should increase with and in proportion to the stock. But some volatile stocks will vary more than the overall market. For example, a 1 percent increase in the overall market value will cause a 2 percent increase in a specific volatile stock's price. Conversely, a 1 percent decrease in the overall market value will cause a 2 percent decrease in this particular volatile stock's price. Volatile stocks are considered riskier investments than those that track the market and a measure of this volatility should be included in any discount rate. The equation symbol used to represent a particular stock's volatility is β (beta).

Using these equation parameters we are now in a position to define k with respect to these other parameters:

$$k = Rf + \beta * (Rm - Rf)$$

where k = the discount factor being calculated using CAPM; Rf = the interest rate obtained from a risk-free investment, such as the United States government treasury bill; Rm = expected stockholder/investor rate of return as demonstrated by an overall market measure, such as the return rate of the S&P 500; and β = a measure of a particular stock's volatility as compared to Rm. Most stocks have a positive value, meaning that their price changes positively with respect to a change in the overall market. A negative value means that the stock value changes in the opposite direction of the overall market. A value of greater than one means that the stock price experiences greater fluctuations with respect to overall market changes. A value of less than one means that the stock price fluctuates less than the overall market value index, which for this book is assumed the S&P 500.

Assume that a particular company has a beta of 1. This means that a 1 percent change in the overall market value index causes a 1 percent change in the stock price. A company with a beta of 1.5 will experience a 1.5 percent change in stock price for a 1 percent overall market value change. A company with a β of .8 will experience a 0.8 percent change in stock price for a 1 percent change in the overall market value. Beta values are calculated using a statistical process and are readily obtained for any publicly traded stock through a number of sources including your stock broker, the financial press, or Standard and Poors company reports, among others.

Looking at the example from Table 5.1, we found that the discount rate for Option A was 11 percent and for Option B it was 14 percent. If we assume that Rf = 6 percent and Rm = 10 percent, a simple calculation using the following β values verifies that discount rate (remember that you will obtain β and don't have to calculate it):

Option A β = 1.25 calculates as: k = 6% + 1.25 * (10% − 6%) = 11%

Option B β = 2.0 calculates as: k = 6% + 2.0 * (10% − 6%) = 14%

These two beta values reflect the perception that Option B (β = 2.0) is a higher-risk investment than Option A (β = 1.25) giving B the higher discount rate (14 percent). This higher discount rate causes a lower present value to Option B's cash flows when compared to Option A.

Share Price Determination Processes

Now that we have seen the basic principles behind the DCF analysis and calculations, we can take another look at the determination of a stock's share price. It is important to remember that a share's price is determined by prices people are willing to buy and sell for in the marketplace, not directly by these formulas. These calculation techniques provide a theoretical framework from which those market negotiations can proceed. No one analysis technique is the ultimately accurate one, but all contribute insight in determining a fair price at which shares should be bought and sold.

Constant Dividend Growth Share Pricing

A share of stock is an asset to the investor who owns the share. A DCF contends that the value of the share today is a representation of its expected future returns discounted back to the present. The Gordon valuation model uses DCF as its basis to relate share price to the expected future dividends. This model assumes that ending first year dividend amounts are estimated and future dividend amounts are expected to maintain a constant growth rate indefinitely into the future. This assumption is generally unrealistic for a new or rapidly growing firm, but might apply to a more established firm with a consistent dividends track record.

$$P = Div0 * \frac{(1 + g)}{(k - g)}$$

where P = calculated current stock value estimate; k = discount rate, such as 11 percent (0.11); g = expected constant annual dividend growth rate, such as 4 percent (0.04); and Div0 = the currently paid dividend. This pricing model assumes all future dividends are included in the stock price and also assumes that the investor does not sell the stock at a future date. The next section discusses present valuation procedures when a future selling of the share is anticipated.

As an example, assume that a firm offers a current dividend of $2.00, has a historical annual dividend growth rate of 4 percent and must support a discount rate, from CAPM, of 11 percent. Its current share price is calculated as follows:

$$P = 2.00 * \frac{(1 + .04)}{(0.11 - 0.04)} = \frac{2.08}{0.07} = 29.71$$

Will future dividends always be consistently 4 percent greater than the year before? Probably not. Will the entire marketplace agree with your particular calculation of the discount rate? Will the entire market calculate the same price for a stock given the same information? Not likely. The Gordon valuation model provides a starting point for evaluating a company with a solid dividend payout history combined with the expectation that this historical dividend policy will continue indefinitely. Estimates of growth (g) can be obtained from online and paper financial sources such as First Call or Value Line. A brokerage house should be able to provide current and future growth estimates for publicly traded companies.

Market valuation for the target company, along with a reasonable starting point for a total company purchase price, is determined by multiplying the DCF-calculated stock price by the total number of outstanding shares. If the sample company has 1,000,000 outstanding shares of stock, and all the stock is of a single class, then the potential market valuation for this company, based on the earlier simple Gordon Valuation Model analysis, is $29.71 million ($29.71 per share × 1,000,000 shares). If the current market share price is less than $29.71, such as $25.00 each, then the target company may be a bargain in that it was valued by analysis at $29.71 and has a current market capitalization of $25 million. There is a lot more involved with the determination of the final offering price, as outlined in Chapter 19, "Determining the Right Price," and the final price will likely be much more than $25 million, but the calculations let you know that the company has a justifiable market valuation based on the Gordon analysis assumptions. This simplified analysis provides a general conceptual framework within which you can relate the various share pricing models and the value of a company.

Valuing Inconsistent Dividends and Future Stock Sale

Taking a look at another situation should help solidify some of these important present value concepts. This analysis would apply to a company that you plan to purchase today and hold for a five-year period, at which time the

Table 5.2 Present Value Analysis

Year	Dividends	Sale Price	Total	Present Value
5	$2.10	$35.00	$37.10	$22.02
4	$1.50		$1.50	$0.99
3	$0.63		$0.63	$0.46
2	$0.87		$0.87	$0.71
1	$0.65		$0.65	$0.59
			Share Price	$24.76
			PV Determined	

shares will be sold. Assume that a targeted company has a varying dividend payment projection. The intention is to sell the purchased company's shares at the end of a five-year period for $35 each. The $35 goal figure is assumed as a realistic future share price target based on the current stock price of a competitive company, from the same industry, of comparable revenues to that expected for the target company in Year five. Assume also that an 11 percent discount factor is applied to future cash flows.

Table 5.2 indicates that paying more than $24.76 as a current share price would be too much, given the set of assumptions used in the analysis. Are the assumptions correct? Only history will answer that question accurately, but you need to make the decision today based on some level of future assumption. Determining an accurate set of assumptions is probably the most difficult part of any analysis, but it is well worth the effort. It should now be clear that incorrect assumptions will create inaccurate calculation results, which may well lead decision makers to make decisions that will ultimately decrease shareholder wealth.

Weighted Averaging of Projections

Ask most business people to project a future revenue stream and they will give you some type of statistical answer such as "the most likely revenue levels will be $2 million per month." Implicit in this statement is that other revenue levels might occur and that the $2 million figure provided is the one most likely to occur in that manager's opinion. Opinions are heavily skewed by personalities, business experience, and other intangible factors that

Table 5.3 Future Revenue Value Estimations

Revenue Stream	Likelihood of Occurrence	Weighted Revenue Average
$1,500,000	5%	$ 75,000.00
$1,700,000	30%	$ 510,000.00
$1,900,000	40%	$ 760,000.00
$2,100,000	15%	$ 315,000.00
$2,300,000	10%	$ 230,000.00
	100%	$1,890,000.00

simply defy numerical analysis. Putting a dollar value on a "gut feel" is a challenging but fairly important process, especially when dealing with future revenue projections which define all other financial statement results. Using a weighted average approach to this situation provides some level of confidence that the other possible outcomes have been considered as part of the analysis. It is more productive to present a weighted average calculation than it is to explain it. Understanding comes from the calculations themselves.

Assume that discussions with managers indicate a range for different expected revenue values for the target company under investigation. The likelihood estimates of various future revenue values is presented in Table 5.3 along with the weighted average revenues based on that likelihood of occurrence.

Table 5.3 takes into account the possibility of different revenue streams. It assumes that there is a 5 percent chance that company may perform at the $1.5 million level, a 30 percent chance that it will perform at the $1.7 million, a 10 percent likelihood of a $2.3 million performance level, and so forth. Each of these percentage weights is then multiplied by its associated revenue level to provide the weighted revenue levels. The weighted revenue average levels are then summed to create a weighted average expected revenue level of $1,890,000.

Is this number accurate? Once again, only history can determine the answer to that question. But this weighted average provides an excellent assessment that includes the best "guesstimates" of the people making the revenue projection estimates.

The weighting is more heavily skewed toward assuming that company revenues will be under the $1.9 million mark, with 75 percent of the weighting falling in that revenue range. This tells you that the revenue es-

Table 5.4 Future Revenue Value Estimation Ranges

Revenue (millions)	Optimistic		Pessimistic	
	Likelihood	Average	Likelihood	Average
$1.5	5%	$75,000	15%	$225,000
$1.7	10%	$170,000	25%	$425,000
$1.9	35%	$665,000	40%	$760,000
$2.1	40%	$840,000	15%	$315,000
$2.3	10%	$230,000	5%	$115,000
	100%	$1,980,000	100%	$1,840,000

timators predict revenues more on the lower side than the upper side of $1.9 million.

Here are a few things to remember when doing a weighted average analysis:

1. Make the ranges as realistic as possible but not biased toward one number or another. If all range numbers were under $1.9 million in the example, you would limit the choices and have excluded the higher revenue possibilities skewing the analysis toward a lower dollar level.

2. All percentages must add up to 100 percent or the analysis just won't work.

3. Try to get feedback from several people who reasonably stand a chance of accurately projecting the number in question, revenues in this case. An optimistic and pessimistic scenario can be calculated using the highest and lowest weighted average results as shown in the table. A "realistic" scenario can be determined by averaging the higher and lower results to provide a mid-range assessment, as shown in Table 5.4. That result would be $1,910,000 for the results shown in the following table.

It is always important to remember and respect the fact that you are trying to predict the future and the future is always open to interpretation and change. Using this weighted average process helps you account for this inherent uncertainty. This same process can be applied to the various operational parameters, such as cost of sales, but gaining consensus on operational numbers is usually an easier process since operating costs are usually well-documented. Predicting future sales is always an exercise in wishful thinking tempered by a dose of historical and market reality.

Evaluating Important Financial Ratios

It is difficult in practice to find a common, easily calculated reference that accurately reflects the operational performance of the companies being compared. The net income of a firm represents a number that already has interest, depreciation, amortization, and tax expenses deducted. Once acquired, a parent company might refinance the debt of the acquired company to reduce the interest expenses. In addition, the acquired company's tax rate will now be that of the purchasing company, which once again changes the company's overall financial performance. The parent company might also redefine the amortization and depreciation schedules of the acquired assets once purchased.

This section takes a closer look at a few accounting and financial items that affect a company's financial statements. Once better understood, we will show how the effect of these items can be removed to present a more accurate and comparable basis of comparison between companies.

Interest Payments and Amortization

When a company makes a loan payment, both the balance sheet and the income statement are affected. A loan payment includes a portion for payment of interest expense (an income statement item), and a portion for payment of principal on the loan (liability) itself (a balance sheet item).

A highly leveraged company is one that makes substantial use of debt to fund its operations in comparison to the company's size. The interest rate on this debt increases, along with associated interest payments, as the perceived risk associated with providing these loans increases. Companies use debt as a way of magnifying their net income during periods of robust sales, but this net income magnification process has just as dramatic a negative effect should sale revenues take a serious downturn. Investors closely monitor the debt levels of a company because of this positive or negative leverage impact on net income.

The sales, marketing, and production activities of the company operate somewhat independent of the financing activities. Removing these financing activities from any comparative analysis of different companies provides a clearer picture of its operational performance. It is also wise to evaluate the debt obligations of a company before purchasing it, because those debt obligations will become those of the buyer and affect the buyer's own debtworthiness.

Interest expense is an easily obtained value since it is presented as a separate line item on the income statement. Depreciation and amortization are a little more complicated to understand but important to any financial analysis. As mentioned in Chapter 3, depreciation is an expense taken to account for the wear and tear on equipment over its useful life. Depreciation appears as an expense on the income statement. The total of all depreciation expenses taken to date is provided in the accumulated depreciation figure listed on the balance sheet.

When a company is purchased, the difference between the purchase price of the company and its book value is tracked as goodwill. Goodwill is then amortized over a period of time, just like an equipment asset would be. This amortization appears as an expense on the income statement. The cumulative amount of this amortization expense annually decreases the value of the goodwill asset as listed on the balance sheet. The depreciation and amortization expenses decrease net income, and both of these figures are dependent upon the accounting practices of the company. Aggressive depreciation and amortization accounting increases expenses and depresses net income while nonaggressive practices have the opposite effect.

Depreciation and amortization expenses are also listed as a separate line item on publicly available financial statements. Because this is another area of accounting discretion that can vary between companies, it is often advisable to remove these items from any financial analysis that compares two different companies.

EBIT and EBITDA

Because a company's loan and tax expenses will change after purchase, and indeed will vary between different companies, investors often use the EBIT value as a basis of real company performance. Interest expense is related to the amount of debt used by the company, and varying expense levels will vary tax payments. Trying to get a somewhat objective measure of company performance would require the elimination of these two components (interest and taxes) from analysis. EBIT does just that.

Looking at EBIT also helps when evaluating divisions of a larger corporation. The parent company (the company that owns the division's shares) will show its long-term debt and tax payments on the parent company's financial statements. Operational numbers associated with the division itself, such as accounts payable, inventory, sales, and other division-specific expenses will show up on the subsidiary's financial report. If this division is compared to another independently owned company which must account for its own interest and tax expenses, then calculating EBIT for the independent company provides a more valid basis of comparison to the division instead of simply using net income. Calculating EBIT is a pretty simple process:

$$EBIT = net income + interest + income taxes$$

All of these items are obtained from the income statement, and should show EBIT to be a larger value that net income alone.

Earnings before interest, taxes, depreciation, and amortization (EBITDA) is another common calculation employed when performing a comparative financial analysis. This calculation removes the effect of depreciation and amortization expense items along with the previously discussed interest and taxes deductions.

$$EBITDA = net income + interest + income taxes + depreciation + amortization$$

EBIT and EBITDA are then compared to another figure, such as the *enterprise value,* defined as:

$$enterprise value = market value of company equity + total debt - cash on hand$$

The market value of company equity is calculated by multiplying the company market share price by the number of outstanding shares. Total debt is simply the total of the company liabilities. Cash on hand is obtained from the balance sheet as the cash asset figure. The EBIT ratio is defined as:

$$EBIT \ ratio = \frac{enterprise \ value}{EBIT}$$

The EBITDA ratio is obtained by simply substituting EBITDA for EBIT in the prior EBIT ratio equation.

Making sense of the EBIT/EBITDA ratio is a little more complicated, but useful once understood. You can think of it as a pretax, interest, depreciation, and amortization analog for the P/E ratio, which compares a share's market price to its earnings. The EBIT/EBITDA ratio compares the total investment in a company to its basic income before financial or accounting policy-related expenses have been subtracted. Debt is treated as an investment in a company, because that is just what debt is when viewed from the perspective of the lender who holds the liability note. The lender gave the company money to use for generating operating income and expects that the company is earning a higher rate of return on the use of that money than the interest rate being paid to the lender by the company. Debts represent money that was retained by the company for its own use instead of being paid to the lender or vendor. Subtracting cash on hand from the debts provides a net outstanding debt figure since that money could be used to immediately pay down the debt.

The total equity value currently invested in the company is not the book value of share equity but the shares' market value. It represents the total shares' value if converted today into another asset form such as cash. In essence, investors are letting other investment opportunities pass them by because they are keeping their investment, at market share prices, in the company.

Dividing the total enterprise value by the EBIT or EBITDA provides a number that represents the number of times that EBIT/EBITDA value would need to be earned to equal the total enterprise value. Just as the P/E ratio represents the number of years that the company must create the current earnings figure to equal the current share market price investment, so does the EBIT/EBITDA ratio represent the number of years that this earnings level must be maintained to equal the total enterprise value. A higher EBIT/EBITDA ratio value means that a higher market valuation has been placed on the company, making its interpretation very similar to the P/E ratio. While P/E compares a single share price to the earnings per share, the EBIT/EBITDA ratio compares operational earnings levels to the total amount of external investment in the company as a whole.

Tying It All Together

This section provides an example of the presented financial analysis as applied to the valuation of two separate companies, A and B. The income statement and balance sheet for the two companies are shown in Table 5.5.

Table 5.5 Valuation Financial Analysis
For January 1, 20xx to December 31, 20xx
(All revenues in thousands except share data)

Income Statements	Company A	Company B
Revenues	$1,200	$3,400
COS	$480	$1,190
Gross Profit	$720	$2,210
Selling, G&A	$240	$645
Depreciation and Amortization	$322	$1,021
Interest Expense	$16	$136
Total Costs and Expenses	$552	$1,802
Income Before Tax	$168	$408
Tax on Income	$59	$143
Net Income	$109	$265
Total Outstanding Shares	600,000	1,200,000
Earnings Per Share	$0.18	$0.22
P/E Ratio	23	16
Share Market Price	$4.19	$3.54

Balance Sheets December 31, 20xx	Company A	Company B
Assets		
Cash	$115	$80
Accounts Receivable	$269	$550
Other Current Assets	$66	$201
Total Current Assets	$450	$831
Other Assets	$1,897	$3,478
Less: Accumulated Depreciation	$879	$1,800
Total Assets	$1,468	$2,509
Liabilities		
Current Liabilities	$250	$831
Long Term Liabilities	$82	$82
Total Liabilities	$332	$913
Shareholders' Equity	$1,136	$1,596
Total Liabilities + Equity	$1,468	$2,509

Table 5.6 Financial Ratios

	Company A	Company B
Current Ratio	1.80	1.00
Quick Ratio	1.54	0.76
Debt-Equity Ratio	1.25	2.20
Book Value Per Share	1.89	1.33
Return on Owners' Equity	10%	17%

The financial figures indicate that B has the larger sales numbers by far when compared to A. B also has a larger asset base. It even appears that B is the better run company since it has a net income that is twice that of A. The picture starts to change a little when the financial ratios and EBIT/EBITDA ratios are calculated.

Ratio analysis indicates that B is making more use of debt than A, as is indicated by the higher debt-to-equity ratio (see Table 5.6). The ratio value for B is not unreasonably high, but it is higher than A's value. It also appears that this use of debt is increasing the return on owners' equity for B when compared to A. This use of debt does not come without a price, which shows up in the current and quick ratios, Both ratios indicate that A is far better prepared to handle a downturn in sales, and a drop in revenue, than B.

The market must also feel a little concerned about B's level of financial leverage, as shown with its P/E ratio at only 16 while A's ratio is at 23. Although B has higher net income, its larger number of shares causes its earnings per share to drop down to A's range which, when multiplied by the P/E ratio provides A with a higher market share price.

The EBIT and EBITDA values are higher for B, which would be expected with its much larger revenue values (see Table 5.7). Looking at the EBIT/EBITDA ratios we see that A is valued more highly than B, as shown by the higher ratio numbers. This analysis does not mean that B is a bad investment. It simply provides a framework for evaluating B to determine a reasonable purchase price.

A discounted cash flow analysis can be run to confirm whether our analysis is in the right ballpark. To simplify the calculation, the Gordon model was used based on the assumption that the earnings per share would be completely returned to the corporation, which is the case in a company purchase (see Table 5.8). There are zero public shareholder dividends paid and all earnings are returned to the buying company as a type of internal dividend.

Table 5.7 EBIT/EBITDA Ratios

	Company A	Company B
Enterprise Value	$2,512	$4,244
EBIT	$184	$544
EBIT Ratio	14	8
EBITDA	$506	$1,565
EBITDA Ratio	5	3

Table 5.8 Discounted Cash Flow Analysis

	Company A	Company B
Risk-free interest rate (Rf)	6%	6%
S&P 500 Return % (Rm)	9%	9%
β	0.85	1.50
Discount Factor (k)	9%	11%
Annual Growth Rate (g)	4%	4%
Earnings Per Share (D)	$0.18	$0.22
DCF Share Price Calculation	$4.00	$3.40

We see from the DCF that the β for B is higher than for A, which would be expected from its higher use of debt to leverage income. This affects the discount factor used for the calculations. We find that the Gordon model-calculated share price does not exactly match that found from the income statement calculations, but it is reasonably enough within the ballpark for each company to indicate that our analysis is not completely out of touch with financial reality.

Comparing Companies of Similar Size

The prior example showed a technique for evaluating two companies of substantially different sizes. This section illustrates the value of these analysis techniques on two companies with very similar sales but very different methods of funding operations.

**Table 5.9 Income Statement Summary
(All revenues in thousands except share data.)**

	Company A	Company B
Revenues	$1,200	$1,200
COS	$480	$420
Gross Profit	$720	$780
Depreciation and Amortization	$296	$378
Interest Expense	$16	$48
Total Other Expenses	$552	$636
Income Before Tax	$168	$144
Tax on Income	$59	$50
Net Income	$109	$94

Table 5.10 Balance Sheet Summary

	Company A	Company B
Total Current Assets	$ 450	$497
Total Assets	$1,468	$1,417
Current Liabilities	$250	$497
Total Liabilities	$332	$579
Stockholders' Equity	$1,136	$838
Total Liabilities + Equity	$1,468	$1,417

Tables 5.9 and 5.10 show that B is substantially more aggressive in its use of depreciation and pays much higher interest expenses than A. The higher interest expenses would be expected from the much higher debt-equity ratio shown in the next table. The higher usage of interest and aggressive depreciation has also caused a decrease in the net income when compared to A. In Table 5.11, a valuation and DCF analysis are illustrated.

Looking at the EBIT/EBITDA calculations in Table 5.12 really provides insight into the way that the use of interest and depreciation can affect the financial performance of a company as reflected on the financial statements.

Notice that the EBIT and EBITDA values in Table 5.12 for B are higher than for A, but ratios are lower. The higher EBIT/EBITDA values indicate

Table 5.11 Valuation and DCF Analysis

Valuation Analysis	Company A	Company B
Outstanding Shares	600,000	600,000
P/E Ratio	23	14
Earnings Per Share	$0.18	$0.16
Current Market Share Price	$4.14	$2.24
Current Ratio	1.80	1.00
Quick Ratio	1.54	0.80
Debt-Equity Ratio	1.25	2.20
Book Value Per Share	1.89	1.40
Return on Owners' Equity	10%	11%
Discounted Cash Flow Analysis	**Company A**	**Company B**
Risk-Free Interest Rate (Rf)	6%	6%
S&P 500 Return %	9%	9%
β	0.85	1.50
Discount Factor (k)	9%	11%
Annual Growth Rate (g)	4%	4%
DCF Share Price Calculation	$4.00	$2.40

Table 5.12 EBIT/EBITDA Ratios

	Company A	Company B
Enterprise Value	$2,512	$1,311
EBIT	$184	$192
EBIT Ratio	14	7
EBITDA	$480	$570
EBITDA Ratio	5.24	2.30

that B is actually running more efficiently than A from an operational perspective in that more EBIT is returned for B than A for the same level of sales. The ratios also indicate that the use of debt causes great enough concern in the mind of investors that they are willing to purchase the shares only at a share price that represents a much lower P/E ratio. This lower share price drops the market value of stockholders' equity which, when added to the higher loan amounts, substantially decreases the enterprise value of B as compared to A.

This analysis might in fact indicate that B is a bargain purchase for a buyer with the ability to refinance or reduce the debt. The company appears operationally sound with returns on equity and EBIT/EBITDA returns that are higher than A. Detailed analysis of B's financial condition with restructured financing might indicate an increase in buyer earnings because B is market-valued at almost 50 percent of A's value for the same revenue levels yet shows a more efficient operation as indicated by the higher EBIT numbers. If B is a private company without a market-determined share price, then this analysis would provide you with a better ballpark range of B's purchase price. If the seller is asking for a purchase price that shows an EBIT ratio of less than 7, then B could represent an excellent bargain. If the asking price is higher than 7 then it might simply be too high.

Chapter Summary

A lot of work goes into the application of financial principles to get a clear financial understanding of a company's operation. It is important to remember the assumptions associated with each of the analysis techniques used and to keep a clear picture of the analysis objectives. It is also important to remember that any future estimates are no better than educated guesses based on experience and calculations flavored with a lot of instinct.

A computer programmer who creates a software program with a limited set of logical options and constraints can predict the program's actions with a high level of certainty. Unfortunately, financial analysis is not a hard science in which your calculations become reality. There are simply too many unknown variables to consider, many of which you cannot control such as the weather, the economy, future management decisions, or international incidents. Financial analysis can provide you with valuable insight as to the financial operation of a company which will lead you into additional areas of investigation. The intent of this investigation is to provide you with the information needed to assess future risks as accurately as possible while also presenting some initial valuation techniques that assist in determining the companies worthy of additional scrutiny as acquisition candidates. No single technique is the one that works flawlessly for every circumstance, but the combining of analysis techniques provides various ranges within which a reasonable purchase price should fall.

Ultimately, you will have to place a value on the target company and make an offer to purchase or walk away. The assumptions used will affect the value calculations and your ultimate purchase offer. Analysis of the type presented here will help you to determine reasonable pricing levels that are more than a hunch.

6

Deal Types and Their Funding

The M&A field has its own language and methods of funding large company purchases. Understanding these terms and funding techniques is important to understanding the objectives of the deals themselves along with their specific transaction arrangements. The type of transaction, such as a reverse or forward merger, may be determined more by strategic marketing objectives than by financial considerations. Funding levels and techniques must be considered when either buying or selling.

Acquisition Types

When speaking of acquisitions, one must be careful about the type of acquisition being proposed. All are not created equal and each can have a dramatic legal and financial impact on the transaction. A *merger*, for example, means that two companies intend to combine into one with only one set of corporation shares being in existence after the merger. An *asset acquisition* implies that both companies retain their respective corporate shares but that corporate assets transfer from one company to another. This section introduces you to the various types of acquisitions, their characteristics, and general implications. Throughout this chapter I will refer to the purchasing company as BuyerCo and the target (purchased) company as SellerCo.

Merger Types

Mergers involve the retiring of either the buyer's or seller's stock, or both. Chapter 8, "Special Accounting and Tax Considerations," takes a detailed look at the various implications of transaction funding arrangements.

FORWARD MERGER

Perhaps the most familiar merger type is the *forward merger.* The buying company of a forward merger retains its stock in the post merger time frame and the purchased company's stock is retired. Purchased company shareholders are compensated for their retired shares with some combination of cash, stock, and other tangible assets. The value of the assets exchanged is set at the time of purchase agreement.

For example purposes, assume that BuyerCo purchases SellerCo and all shares of SellerCo are retired, leaving only shares of BuyerCo. Often, shares in BuyerCo are exchanged for shares in SellerCo with some exchange rate established at the time of purchase. Assume that BuyerCo shares have a market value of $20 and SellerCo shares trade at $10 each. This means that the market value of two shares of SellerCo equal one share of BuyerCo, so SellerCo shareholders are adequately compensated if one share of BuyerCo is traded for two shares of SellerCo. The actual traded shares ratio is rarely this simple, but the share valuation and trade concept applies to all transactions involving a stock transfer between buyer and seller.

The buyer might leave the seller's name intact and even treat it as a completely separate business unit after merger completion. This decision has little to do with the financial aspects of the merger and more to do with marketing and sales considerations and the reason for the purchase in the first place. A forward merger leaves only the buyer's shares after the transaction is completed.

Assume that BuyerCo has an excellent market reputation. Assume also that SellerCo has recently suffered highly negative media coverage but its products and services remain outstanding. Putting BuyerCo's name on SellerCo's products and services would make sense since an excellent offering would now be purchased from an excellent company. Sometimes SellerCo is represented as a division of BuyerCo as, "SellerCo, a BuyerCo company." This approach retains a distinct identity for SellerCo after its purchase, and is useful if there is a possible future intention of once again selling SellerCo as a separate entity and retaining its brand awareness will increase SellerCo's value upon resale.

REVERSE MERGER

A *reverse merger* is the reverse of a forward merger in that the shares of the buying company are retired and the shares of the seller are left intact. In this situation BuyerCo shareholders receive shares in SellerCo based on some type of valuation ratio between the two shares. Referring to the example in the prior section, each BuyerCo shareholder would receive two shares of SellerCo stock leaving only SellerCo stock behind after merger completion.

Assume that BuyerCo is financially solvent but has recently suffered very negative media coverage, while SellerCo has an excellent reputation. Merging so that SellerCo remains the operations arm of the merged companies allows BuyerCo's products and services to be offered under the SellerCo name. SellerCo management often becomes subordinate to, or is replaced by, BuyerCo management under these circumstances.

TRIANGULAR MERGERS

A triangular merger is one that involves a subsidiary of one company as part of the transaction. It may be either a forward or reverse triangular merger, depending on whether shares in the subsidiary or the other merger partner remain after the transaction. A company is considered a *subsidiary* when the parent company (BuyerCo) owns more than 50 percent (controlling interest) of the outstanding voting stock of the subsidiary (Sub1).[1] A subsidiary might retain its own corporate identity and stock, enabling it to merge with SellerCo. Shares or other BuyerCo assets can be traded with SellerCo shareholders in exchange for SellerCo shares.

A *forward triangular merger* involves a subsidiary (Sub1) of BuyerCo and another company (SellerCo) with shares in Sub1 surviving the merge and SellerCo shares being retired. Assume that BuyerCoSub1 decides to merge with SellerCo. SellerCo shareholders receive some form of compensation for their shares and only BuyerCoSub1 shares remain after the merger.

A *reverse triangular merger* transfers shares of the subsidiary (BuyerCoSub1) to the seller (SellerCo) with assets or SellerCo shares transferring to BuyerCoSub1 shareholders in exchange for retiring BuyerCoSub1 stock. Only SellerCo shares remain after the merger. This does not mean that Sub1 cannot become a subsidiary of SellerCo upon completion of the transaction. This choice is more dependent on marketing and sales than financial considerations.

---

[1] See Glen A. Welsch, D. Paul Newman, and Charles T. Zlatkovich, *Intermediate Accounting* (Homewood, IL: Irwin, 1996), 932.

Table 6.1 ConsolCo Shares Transferred For BuyerCo and SellerCo Shares

	BuyerCo	SellerCo	ConsolCo
Market Valuation (millions)	$200	$100	$300
Outstanding Shares (millions)	10.0	10.0	10.0
Value Per Share	$20	$10	$30
Shares/ConsolCo Share	1.5	3	—
ConsolCo Shares/Share	2/3	1/3	—

CONSOLIDATION

Two companies are said to have "consolidated" if the two merge into a new entity with new stock issued, and if the stock of both previous companies is retired. Assume that BuyerCo purchases SellerCo. The intention of both companies is to create a new company, ConsolCo, that becomes the consolidation of both SellerCo and BuyerCo. Both BuyerCo and SellerCo shares being retired in exchange for new ConsolCo shares. This represents a consolidation.

Whether BuyerCo and SellerCo retain their names is more dependent on marketing and sales than financial considerations. The number of shares of ConsolCo that transfer to shareholders of BuyerCo and SellerCo is dependent upon the relative values of the three companies at the time of consolidation.

Assume the valuation information in Table 6.1 as it pertains to the proposed consolidation to understand a typical valuation and stock transfer scenario.

Notice that SellerCo shareholders receive fewer ConsolCo shares, but the total value of ConsolCo shares transferred equal the total amount of SellerCo value contributed to the new consolidated ConsolCo company.

Asset Purchase

Asset purchases are relatively straightforward in that the buyer purchases the ownership right to an asset. Ownership typically includes obligation to repay any associated debts or other liabilities. When the asset transfers to the buyer it transfers at an agreed-upon price, which has depreciation and tax implications. Some states may impose a transfer tax on the sale of the asset. Asset purchases do not transfer any corporate liabilities to the buyer other than those specifically negotiated at the time of the transaction. Asset acquisition can frequently limit the buyer's legal exposure associated with the purchase to those specifically purchased assets and liabilities enumerated in the contract. Conversely, purchasing the stock of a company transfers all company liabilities (including contingent and unknown) to the buyer along with all assets. Anything legally associated with the purchased company transfers to the buyer with a company purchase through stock acquisition.

Divestiture

The seller of a subsidiary company is said to have divested itself of the sold division or subsidiary. There are a number of reasons that a company would divest itself of a subsidiary division.

1. The subsidiary might be a very well-run company that can be sold for a cash profit that can be used to finance the parent company's own operation.

2. The subsidiary might not fit with the parent company's strategic direction. Selling the subsidiary keeps precious business resources from being diverted to the subsidiary, which better ensures the success of the parent.

3. The subsidiary is not performing up to expectations. The parent might sell the subsidiary to avoid having to take a larger loss at a later time or incur the expenses associated with a complete liquidation.

4. Regulations might change causing the parent to divest itself of its subsidiaries, as happened with the breakup of AT&T in the 1980s and as might, at the time of this writing, be in the future for Microsoft as a result of its Department of Justice litigation.

Number 2 above might well provide cash to fund the parent's operation, which is a double win for the parent company.

The parent is the seller and receives some type of compensation for the divested subsidiary. This compensation is negotiated between the buyer and seller/parent just like any buy/sell transaction.

Types of Funding

The buyer must come up with a way to pay for the purchased company. There are any number of ways that the purchase can be funded, such as simply paying cash as with Chase Manhattan Corporation's purchase of the investment banking firm of Hambrecht & Quist Group for $1.35 billion. Or it might be an all-stock transaction, as with the Cisco Systems purchase of Monterey Networks, when Cisco transferred 7.3 million shares to Monterey Network's shareholders, a deal valued at $501 million. This section presents various purchase arrangements along with their respective important characteristics.

Cash Purchase

Perhaps the easiest scenario to understand is that of a full cash purchase. The buyer simply pays the seller the agreed-upon purchase price in cash at the time of sale. The implications of a cash sale may cause its simple attraction to become less appealing.

1. Cash sales must be recorded as income to the seller at the time of the sale. Whether the cash is recorded as ordinary, short-term, or long-term capital gains income is dependent upon how long the seller held the sold shares of stock and the corporation (business) structure of the seller. If the sold company is a sole proprietorship, then all received cash is treated as ordinary income at the time of sale except for various property or investments that transfer with the sale.

2. Cash sales degrade the cash holdings of the buyer company, which might adversely affect its liquidity ratios, such as the quick and current ratios.

3. Cash sales are simpler than stock transactions, meaning that they can be accomplished in a shorter period of time with fewer public filings, particularly if the seller is a privately held company.

4. Cash sales do not require the distribution of additional shares. This means that earnings are not diluted over more outstanding shares. The earnings per share value and book value per share is not directly affected by the company purchase. If the market perceives BuyerCo's action as putting the company in an adverse cash position as a result of this all-cash purchase, then there may be downward pressure on BuyerCo's share market price.

Debt Funding

Just as you and I would take out a loan to make a major purchase, a company can take out a loan to finance the purchase of a company. The collateral used for the loan might be simply the purchased company itself, or the borrowing power of the buyer might be needed to secure the loan.

Debt financing requires the payment of loan interest and principal over

Table 6.2 Collateral Types and Loan Amounts

Collateral Type	Percentage Loan Amount To Value	Comments
Real Estate	50%-60% of appraised value	If the existing real estate loan-to-value is greater than this percentage, then this collateral is useless.
Inventory	60%	Banks don't want to sell your inventory.
Accounts Receivable	80%	Dependent on the quality of your receivables and collection track record. Consider factoring if you have a lot of faith in receivable quality.
Equipment	50%	Banks don't want to sell your equipment. Computers may be worth less due to rapid depreciation.
Other Debt	Dependent on BuyerCo's creditworthiness and relationship with commercial lender.	May require a 1% to 3% higher interest rate to compensate lender for subordinate position.

the life of the loan. Debt financing also includes covenants that the borrower must adhere to or possibly cause the loan to become due-in-full. Each covenant adds another restriction to the financial parameters within which the borrower must operate, which in turn reduces business options. Finally, the borrower might have to use its own borrowing power to secure the loan which changes its own equity ratios such as the debt-equity ratio and coverage ratio.

Banks will make loans accepting various assets as collateral and always loan only when they fully expect repayment. Counting on a bank to loan money on speculation is naive thinking that will only set up all parties involved for disappointment and potentially hard feelings. Table 6.2 indicates various percentage loan amounts you can expect for different types of collateral.

Loans tend to have the effect of reducing net income, because the interest paid on the loans is an expense. A reduction in net income is rarely good news to a publicly traded company, making debt an often undesirable purchasing method. The leveraged buyout (LBO) is a specific type of debt funding that is covered in Chapter 7, "Strategic Synergy and Transaction Structure."

Equity Funding

Equity funding is a very popular purchase price funding method, especially in the high-valued stock market of the 1990s. Equity funding requires that the buyer transfer shares to the seller in exchange for part or all of the purchase price. These shares must come from somewhere, however, and the buyer usually issues new shares in adequate supply to cover the purchase, based on an agreed-upon valuation.

Assume that BuyerCo trades at $49 per share and has 10 million issued shares of stock. Assume also that BuyerCo wants to purchase SellerCo for $4.9 million, which equates to 100,000 shares at $49 per share. For simplification purposes, assume that the market takes this issuance in stride and does not decrease or increase the BuyerCo share market price. (The details relating to the reality of this type of transaction are discussed in Chapter 7, "Strategic Synergy and Transaction Structures," and Chapter 19, "Determining The Right Price.") SellerCo shareholders receive BuyerCo shares in exchange for their SellerCo shares based on the relative value of a BuyerCo-to-SellerCo share as presented earlier. BuyerCo might even create a special stock class with special privileges that have been agreed to as part of the sale transaction negotiations.

An equity purchase transaction has no implications on income because no interest is paid on the purchase price. The sellers receive stock instead of cash, which allows the sellers a higher level of control over when the gain associated with the sale is realized. Any future gain recognized upon selling the shares might well be treated as a capital gain instead of ordinary income.

BuyerCo does not inherit any additional loan covenants. Its earnings are not negatively affected by increased interest payments. Earnings per share may be affected when the additional 100,000 shares are added to the already outstanding 10 million, creating 10,100,000 outstanding shares. The earnings are now divided by the higher number (10,100,000) to calculate the diluted earnings per share. This number must be lower than the earnings per share number would have been at the initial 10 million share level prior to issuing the additional 100,000 shares. Existing shareholders might be upset by this level of dilution and BuyerCo's management must prepare a valid financial story justifying the purchase of SellerCo.

Sellers can become large BuyerCo shareholders depending on the size of equity transactions. Some sellers require a seat on the board of directors to take any substantial portion of BuyerCo stock as part of the sale price. Why?

Simply because the seller's future compensation is heavily dependent upon BuyerCo's future performance and a voting seat on the board provides the seller with some level of control over future operations. BuyerCo management might not think this a good thing, or perhaps they might want SellerCo management involved in BuyerCo's daily operations. These types of questions are heavily dependent upon the specifics of the business situation and the personalities involved.

Seller Financing

In some cases the seller might be willing to provide BuyerCo with a loan that covers a portion of the purchase price. This option is usually only available when the purchased company is a closely held or private company.

Assume that BuyerCo is willing to pay $3 million of a $4.9 million purchase price in cash. BuyerCo might ask the seller to provide a loan for the remaining $1.9 million to be paid off over a certain number of years at a higher-than-market interest rate. In this way, the seller is compensated for assuming a subordinate repayment position than one which is usually required by the existing lenders, and BuyerCo does not have to come up with all $4.9 million at once. In addition, the seller sees income over a number of years, instead of all at once, which might favorably affect his tax situation.

Sellers are sometimes reticent to provide financing, especially if they will not have any managerial control over BuyerCo's operation because the financed portion of the purchase price is put at risk. Funding BuyerCo also keeps the seller involved with the company, which is sometimes not in the best interest of either the seller or buyer. Seller financing is not atypical and remains a viable method for funding a company's purchase price, providing potential financial and strategic benefits to both buyer and seller.

Creative Financing

There is no restriction stating that purchase transactions must be all one type of funding or another. Transactions can be a creative combination of any or all of the above funding options with risk and reward being negotiated with each funding type.

Assume that a company with attributes like those listed in the table is being acquired for a purchase price of $6 million. Table 6.3 is a possible financing breakdown for this particular purchase given the reported financial statement values.

This example is not meant to be the only way in which a creatively financed

Table 6.3 Creative Financing

Item	Value	Percent LTV	Loan Amount	Amount toward Purchase
Cash	$750,000	50%	$375,000	
Accounts Receivable	$1,350,000	80%	$1,080,000	
Short-Term Cash Available				$1,455,000
Inventory	$1,450,000	60%	$870,000	
Equipment	$1,100,000	50%	$550,000	
Secured Loan Amount				$1,420,000
Maximum Debt Service Ability	$3,000,000	80%	$2,400,000	
Additional Available Debt Financing Capability	$980,000	—		$980,000
Total Available from Cash and Debt Financing				$3,855,000
Seller provided Subordinate Financing	—	—		$2,145,000
Total Amount Available for Purchase				$6,000,000

purchase can be accomplished. It is meant only as an example to illustrate how the various funding methods can be applied toward a purchase. It assumes that only 50 percent ($375,000) of available cash ($750,000) will be applied to the purchase payment. It also assumes that 80 percent of the available accounts receivable will be applied toward payment. The total of cash and accounts receivable applied toward payment is $1,455,000. The maximum debt service value that the selling company's cash flow can support is $3,000,000, of which 80 percent ($2,400,000) is used to pay for the purchase. Sixty percent of inventory ($870,000) and 50 percent of equipment ($550,000) is used as collateral for a commercial loan with a maximum value of $2,400,000. Subtracting the inventory and equipment values from the $2,400,000 leaves $980,000 from the maximum loan amount to apply toward the purchase. Totaling all amounts provided from short-term assets and debt equals $3,855,000.

The balance of the purchase price ($6,000,000 − $3,855,000 = $2,145,000) is provided by the seller to the company in the form of a note subordinate to the other lender debt. This debt could take the form of a standard loan, convertible debt, an agreement to purchase stock in the buying company at an attractive price, or a combination of the above. This method of financing uses the resources of the purchased company and does not directly tap the credit power of the buying company. Any default on loans by the seller will likely put the buying company on the line for repayment, especially if a merger is performed instead of a stock purchase, which keeps the buying company as a separate distinct legal entity. This type of transaction structure works best when SellerCo is a closely held corporation with fewer shareholders. This is simply because the logistics of working with fewer sellers enables the process to proceed at a reasonable speed and with minimal additional complexity. If BuyerCo is a closely held corporation, its owners should expect to sign some type of personal guarantee for the loan amounts. This fact is usually a rude awakening for new business owners but should be old news to any owners able to consider the purchase of a six million dollar company.

Sources of Funding

Knowing how to structure the transaction is one thing. Actually getting the money is another thing altogether. This section takes a detailed look at the various sources of funding and the major items that must be considered when presenting your funding request.

Banking Institutions

Any buying company has a relationship with a bank. It is just a part of doing business. It makes sense to talk with your current banker about the proposed transaction to determine their particular levels of lending interest. Banks don't lend money on speculation. They do lend money based on a conservative analysis of the borrower's ability to repay the loan. Banks will only provide loans that they fully expect to be repaid and pass on loans with any substantial level of repayment risk. Bank loans will typically fall into the short-term (one year), revolving credit (one to three years), and intermediate-term (three to five years) categories. Typical short-term loan types include loans secured by accounts receivable and/or other current assets. Revolving credit lines may only require interest payments, without principal amortization payment, but do require that the entire loan amount be brought to a zero balance at some time during a specified time frame. Intermediate loans are generally secured by some asset, like equipment, and are usually provided only to a specified percentage of the asset's salvage value.

Discussions with a banker about a loan should not concentrate primarily on the creditworthiness of the borrower. They should concentrate on the value of assets. They should emphasize the quality of accounts receivable by showing historical aging reports and bad debt percentages. They should emphasize the ability of the company to make the payments on the debt and show that the required lending ratios have been met. Finally, they can emphasize that the borrowers have an excellent credit history as the final icing on the credit application cake. Reversing the order of emphasis simply frustrates the participants and decreases your likelihood of getting the loan.

Venture Capitalists

Venture capital is provided by those firms that are willing to make a higher risk investment with the expectation of getting much higher returns on that investment. Venture capital is provided to companies which cannot raise the needed funding through other usual methods due to a poor cash flow or smaller asset base. The venture capital firm may get its money from wealthy private investors or institutions who are looking for ways to generate higher returns with their money. Think of a venture capital firm as one representing a fund of investors who have all agreed to provide capital to higher-risk borrowers that meet specific criteria as outlined in the fund's charter. A venture capital funding arrangement usually requires that the borrower provide a board of director's seat to the firm along with specific covenants regarding future company operation.

Venture capital firms are also a source of what is called *mezzanine* financing. This type of financing provides funding to the borrowing company in exchange for a loan agreement and some type of equity participation. Required annual returns for mezzanine financing is in the 25 percent-or-more region, with a majority of the return obtained from the expected rapid increase in stock value. It is called mezzanine financing because it sits between common stock (at the bottom of the payoff list) and primary lenders (lenders who get paid first), just as the mezzanine level sits between the first floor and the upper balcony of a theater.

The likelihood of obtaining venture capital funding is very small unless you can effectively, and credibly, show that the company can generate enormous growth over a period of three to five years. In addition, there must be an exit strategy, or a way for the investor to recover the investment and expected returns.

Exit Strategies

An exit strategy is integral to any equity-related financing plan. Why should an investor provide you with money in exchange for shares of stock if those shares cannot reasonably be converted back into something of value, preferably money, at the end of the investment period? More than one employee has been excited by the prospect of stock ownership in a private company only to discover later that their stock cannot be sold to anyone other than the company owner. The owner basically has a corner on the market for that particular stock, which generally does not provide the employee with attractive redemption options when they choose to exercise their right to sell their acquired shares.

Venture capital investors must believe that a viable and reasonable exit strategy is planned or they also will not invest. This is why so many venture-funded companies eventually go public through an IPO. The IPO is part of the financial strategy and companies specifically work to financially optimize the company value, which in turn optimizes the value of the public offering. The intention is for all investors to be adequately compensated for their earlier investments while simultaneously enabling the company to acquire the needed funding to move it into its next level of growth.

Another exit strategy type might force the company to repurchase the venture firm's shares at a share price determined at the time of repurchase. The method for determining the purchase price is determined at the time of initial funding, often much to the later dismay of the hungry borrower who later learns the implications of the initial agreements. Should you pursue venture funding, make sure that you first approach firms with experience in your particular industry. In this way, the investor not only brings money to the table, but also brings industry experience, industry contacts, and possibly other firms with which additional synergy could be obtained.

Small Business Investment Corporations (SBIC)

The Small Business Administration (SBA) regulates the operation of privately owned small business investment corporations (SBICs). SBICs obtain low financial rates from the Federal Financing Bank, which is then made available as funding to small businesses in a very similar way as that provided by venture capital firms. Naturally, working with an SBIC is more complicated, because SBA guidelines must be followed. Funding can also be obtained directly from the SBA, without the use of an SBIC, but my experience has been that SBA funding is useful for funding real estate purchases but not viable for any type of speculative venture. Loan amounts from the SBA are usually fairly small and really only applicable to low dollar purchases of under $1.5 million.

Other Sources

The boom economy of recent times has created enormous wealth for large numbers of people and companies. This money can be tapped for the financing of M&A activities. A few of these alternate funding sources are presented in this section.

INSURANCE FUNDS

Insurance companies receive money in the form of payments and pay insurance claims as they become due. Life insurance is a possible longer-term funding source in that actuarial tables outline the average time frame within which claims will be filed and the revenue stream from payments is also well-defined.

PENSION FUNDS

Pension funds also have mass amounts of money that is invested in various ways with the intention of creating optimal return on the invested money while still having adequate funds to pay pensioner benefits. Once again, a high degree of certainty can be applied to when pension claims will become due since the age and retirement time frame of most pensioners can be well determined. This certainty enables fund managers to invest in ways that do not compromise future benefits while providing a reasonable return on investment loans made.

COMMERCIAL CREDIT COMPANIES

Commercial credit companies provide money in the form of loans just as a bank would, but usually with much higher fees and interest rates attached. They will also want a high level of collateral security in return for any loans made.

Working with Intermediaries

If the complexity of this process is starting to sound a little daunting, take heart. There are companies who specialize in finding funding for M&A activities, and charge a fee for the providing of this expertise. These people are called intermediaries and perform any number of different functions depending on the type of intermediary used.

Investment Bankers

The role of an investment banker is often misunderstood, resulting in large part from the use of the term *banker*. Investment bankers act on behalf of those who need money to obtain money from those who have money. They arrange the funding needed to facilitate a transaction and take a fee for their services. Fees were historically based on the Lehman Formula which charges fees based on the transaction's dollar size. The Lehman Formula is explained in Chapter 2.

It is becoming more customary for a firm to not use the Lehman Formula and instead request a nonrefundable retainer in exchange for the use of their services and expertise. This retainer is paid in advance and might fall in the $50,000 to $100,000 range (plus expenses), with additional fees tacked on for special circumstances or particularly large or difficult transactions.

The investment banking firm should be looked at as more than a conduit to money. It can also provide a wide array of services and expertise that both buyer and seller will find valuable. Remember that these companies work M&A transactions on a regular basis, while you and the other company involved might buy/sell infrequently. An investment banking firm will have contacts directly applicable to the M&A process. Fees are often negotiable, even though the firms say otherwise, and the best way to get a lower fee is to have various investment banking firms compete for your business. It is important that the firm's expertise is not treated like a commodity, but bidding between professional organizations happens on a regular basis. This is particularly true for buyers with an excellent credit record and a solid transaction to present.

The larger investment banking firms handle deals in the $50 million or higher range. Smaller firms will handle deals in the $5 million or higher range; business brokers typically handle the smaller deals. Few investment bankers are willing to handle deals under $1 million since the fees received do not adequately compensate for the work performed, which is relatively consistent between deals. It is reasonable to expect percentages to increase to the 7% or higher range for deals under $1 million.

Some well known investment banking firms include Lehman Brothers; Morgan Stanley; Salomon Smith Barney; and Donaldson, Lufkin, & Jenrette. As always, the best initial contact to one of these firms is through the personal referral of someone who has already used their services.

Business Finders

There are companies that specialize in finding other companies that meet the specific criteria of their client, and these will be referred to as "finders" for this discussion. These finder companies may not be investment bankers but do perform the valuable service of putting the buyer client in contact with a viable target company. The finder might put a viable buyer in contact with a selling client. In either case, the finder works for a commission-type fee that is paid once the deal is closed.

It is important that you not indiscriminately enter into an arrangement with a finder, since the finder might be legally due a fee even if you feel that he did not really find the company. The agreement should clearly define the requirements for fee payment but also ensure that the finder is motivated to locate the right company for your purposes. Fees are negotiable and should be lower than a broker's for the same dollar range. The finder simply acts as a "matchmaker" who introduces the two companies and then lets the deal take its own course, only expecting payment upon closing of the deal.

Business Brokers

A business broker serves a very similar function to that of a real estate broker, and indeed might need a real estate license to function in this capacity depending on the specific state involved. In exchange for a fee, usually based somewhat on that used by investment bankers, the broker will typically work with a seller to find a buyer for his business. Just as a qualified buyer is a necessary criteria for any house sale, so must a broker find a qualified buyer for the business in question. It is the broker's job to perform the pre-screening of potential buyers so that only those qualified to perform the purchase are brought to the seller's attention, unless the seller specifically wants it otherwise. The seller makes the ultimate determination of whether the business is sold to a particular buyer or not. It is important that a written agreement be used to outline the terms and conditions of the brokerage arrangement, including a clear definition of when payment is earned and due the broker.

The broker acts in a similar capacity to that of an investment banker in that the broker might have funding and legal contacts that make the transaction process proceed smoothly. A broker might even have access to companies that are not officially looking to buy or sell simply due to his active awareness of industry activities and wide contact network. Smaller companies, and their resulting smaller dollar value transactions, are often handled by brokers once the "for sale by owner" process turns out unsuccessful. Once again, the best source for finding a business broker is through personal referral from someone who had used the broker in his or her own business sale. Never forget that secrecy is critical when selling for all of the reasons outlined in Chapter 19, "Preparing To Buy and Sell."

Chapter Summary

The buying and selling of businesses happens on a regular basis. The large dollar volumes and strategic importance of these deals requires specialized expertise that is provided by any number of sources. The type of transaction, such as a forward or reverse merger, may be determined by marketing and sales objectives, with financial aspects of the transaction designed to support these objectives. The M&A teams should ensure that the deal structure and type support the ultimate business goals of the acquisition to lay the foundation for a higher postacquisition likelihood of success.

Access to funding is provided by numerous sources, such as business brokers, investment bankers, and possibly the sellers themselves. The right funding sources for a specific transaction will be heavily based on the dollar levels involved and the creditworthiness of both the buyer and seller. Care should be taken to avoid burdening the postacquisition entity with such high debt obligations that it cannot realistically survive failing to meet some of its projected financial objectives. This heavy debt service could financially jeopardize both buyer and seller.

Deals will involve debt, equity, cash, or some combination thereof. The right funding combination is the topic of Chapter 7, "Strategic Synergy and Transaction Structures." The accounting and tax implications of the various transactions, whether a merger or an asset acquisition, are covered in Chapter 8, "Special Accounting and Tax Considerations."

Merger and acquisition transaction funding can often become very complicated, which is when the expertise of an experienced professional will be appreciated. Investment bankers and business brokers provide that expertise—for a fee. Whether that fee is reasonable or not depends on your particular situation and specific resource availability. Fees are usually paid by the seller. Under the right circumstances (particularly for private companies), a shrewd seller may build the fee into the minimum acceptable selling price, effectively making the buyer pay the fee.

7

Strategic Synergy and Transaction Structures

One wonderful potential associated with a merger or acquisition is the ability to create a stronger single business entity than either company previously was on its own. This additional strength may arise from the addition of products, services, geographical coverage, intellectual property, or simply capacity. In any case, placing a value on this additional strength is an important aspect of the M&A process. Simply purchasing a company for a set price may present an excellent business plan. But purchasing a company to exploit the purchased company's unique attributes to improve the overall financial performance of both buyer and seller borders on a form of alchemy. This chapter takes a detailed look at various technical and financial aspects of the transaction that can present opportunities to make one plus one equal three. In addition, it presents ways in which transactions can be structured to capitalize on these synergistic opportunities.

Differentiating Strategic and Synergistic Issues

I have heard people interchangeably use *strategic* and *synergistic* when referring to a particular business situation. It is important to differentiate between the two because one can exist without the other, which will be clear by the end of this chapter.

A strategic purchase is one that defines a specific company direction and often has a radical impact on the company as a whole. It can include the decision to move into the global telecommunications industry, which subsequently prompts the company to purchase new technology that moves the buying company further in that direction. It might involve the purchase of a foreign telecommunications company to acquire a foothold in a foreign market. Strategy might include the decision to internally develop a technology instead of purchasing it from an outside firm, or vice versa. It might involve never acquiring a company at all but simply working on an alliance basis with other companies, or vice versa. In short, strategy can take on many forms, all of which might be right or wrong for the companies and industries involved. Only history ultimately knows which approaches worked and which did not meet expectations. It is fairly safe to assume that all strategic decisions have the potential for profound impact, either positive or negative, on the companies involved. It is possible to have a great strategy and poor execution and still survive. It is not, however, likely that excellent execution of a poor strategy will foster company growth and survival.

Synergy, on the other hand, allows two business entities to complement each other so that the strain on the combined companies is less than on each company acting independently. It may, for example, be possible to combine the accounting functions of both the buying and selling company and obtain a $1 million accounting expense reduction. The synergy between the two companies in this example enables a $1 million expense reduction which would not be possible with each company working as a separate entity. It might be possible for the buyer to use his own excess production capacity to meet much of the seller's production demands. This ability might eliminate the need for the seller to build another plant, possibly saving millions of dollars. The synergy between the buyer and seller create these opportunities. It might be a buyer company's strategic policy to acquire only companies that provide extensive synergistic opportunities. That synergy is then assessed and financially valued as part of the M&A process.

Cisco Systems is known for making a number of acquisitions in the course of a fiscal year. According to www.cisco.com, as of May 12, 2000 the company performed 11 acquisitions in 2000, 19 in 1999, 9 in 1998, and 20 others between 1993 and 1997, for a total of 59 over a 7-year period. This level of M&A activity requires a corporate commitment to acquisition as a basic company strategy. When asked if mergers and acquisitions now are just another form of outsourced R&D, Cisco CEO John Chambers said, "They (acquisitions) are a requirement, given how rapidly customer expectations change. . . . A horizontal business model always beats a vertical business model. So you've got to be able to provide that horizontal capability in your product line, either through your own R&D, or through acquisitions" (James Daly, "John Chambers: The Art of the Deal," *Business 2.0*, October, 1999).

This viewpoint is further reinforced in Cisco Systems' 1999 annual report: "Our strategy for technology excellence is to focus on internal product development and blend that with acquisition and partnerships. This strategy allows us to add more than 65 new products, acquire 11 companies and develop dozens of partnerships to help us pursue emerging markets and achieve market share leadership over the last year" (page 5); "We also continue to purchase technology in order to bring a broad range of products to the market in a timely fashion. If we believe that we are unable to enter a particular market in a timely manner, with internally developed products, we may license technology from other businesses or acquire other businesses as an alternative to internal research and development" (page 23).

Given these statements and the pace at which Cisco Systems acquires companies, it is clear that they treat acquisition as an integral part of their corporate strategy. Turning that strategy into specific targets and acquisition action plans is the art of the deal.

In summary, a company might make a decision to acquire one company instead of another based on specific strategic goals. The synergy between the two companies enables the combined buyer/seller entity to financially function more beneficially than the two entities operating separately.

Determining the Overall Impact of Synergy

Knowing that there is synergy and determining its value are two different things. Assume that BuyerCo is looking to purchase SellerCo and that a reasonable initial purchase price for SellerCo as a stand-alone company has been determined. The next steps for BuyerCo are to determine the areas of possible synergy, determine the value of that synergy, and evaluate the overall financial impact of the acquisition. Management typically wants to move directly to the last step so that the impact on earnings and share price can be determined, but step three cannot be done before steps one and two are completed, usually as part of the due diligence process.

DETERMINE AREAS OF SYNERGY

Finding areas of synergy is a lot like detective work and usually is accomplished by using due diligence process. Areas of possible synergy are:

1. Reduced general and administrative expenses in areas such as accounting, finance, personnel, and maintenance.

2. Reduced executive salaries because two tiers of executive management may not be required if the two organizations are to be completely merged, while keeping the acquired company as a separate operational unit may require the retention of executive and other administrative personnel.

3. Reduced sales and marketing costs, because a single sales force might effectively offer both BuyerCo's and SellerCo's products and services simultaneously.

4. Increased product or service sales due to attractive overlap between BuyerCo's and SellerCo's offerings. For example, SellerCo's customer base can now directly purchase BuyerCo's products and vice versa. A single sales call might generate more sales, which increases revenues while decreasing cost of sales.

5. Reduced purchasing costs resulting from larger purchasing power. Purchasing in larger quantities usually reduces prices.

6. Perhaps SellerCo was a major vendor to BuyerCo. The purchase might substantially reduce the intercompany price of offering SellerCo's products and services which in turn drives down BuyerCo's costs. This type of company purchase is called a *vertical acquisition.*

7. BuyerCo might be in a position to restructure SellerCo's debt with more attractive financing terms, which will reduce the interest expenses incurred on that debt.

8. Duplicate BuyerCo and SellerCo R&D facilities might serve the same engineering research function. Combining the two facilities into one would reduce overhead costs while perhaps fostering a higher level of interaction between the engineering groups.

9. BuyerCo's field service organization might be able to service SellerCo's products, possibly eliminating the need for redundant SellerCo field service expenses.

10. SellerCo might have an international manufacturing facility that can locally produce BuyerCo's products, reducing import duties and tariffs. These cost

reductions might increase profit margins on internationally sold products. The reduced costs might enable a decrease in price which increases revenues through increased sales volume.

11. The addition of the acquired products, developers, and technologies to the buyer's existing offerings hopefully will create opportunities for increased sales synergy. Increased synergistic revenue as a direct result of an acquisition is a recurring benefit. Finding revenue enhancement synergy should always be a top priority with any acquisition which, when combined with cost reduction synergy, provides an excellent base for a successful acquisition.

The variety of ways in which synergy can appear in a transaction are numerous and heavily dependent on the specific companies involved. The important thing is to know that synergy is likely there and you simply need to look for it to move on to determining the value of that synergy.

A word of caution is probably due here regarding the excessive use of cost-cutting during integration with the intent of making acquisition synergy appear more valuable. Although this might serve the short-term goal of justifying the purchase by making the acquisition look financially more viable, it might also make the overall postacquisition organization less healthy. This is particularly true if the cost-cutting involves the elimination of personnel who came with the acquisition. The company and its technology are static at the point that the transfer occurs, and without key people to make it work in the postacquisition environment, the buyers could be in for poor future results.

By analogy, you can lose weight by putting yourself on a starvation diet, and indeed might quickly get to your desired weight. Eventually you will need to increase your food intake to a level that sustains your life or very serious health consequences will arise. The same situation arises with companies that reduce costs to the extreme for an extended period of time, which puts the financial health of the overall organization in jeopardy.

DETERMINE THE VALUE OF SYNERGY

It takes time and analysis to place a financial value on synergy. Investigation and understanding of the financial and operational structure of both the buyer and seller are required. Revenue-generating synergy areas include improved sales call efficiency, cross-selling between the buyer's offerings and those acquired in the purchase, and the integration of acquired technologies into the buyer's to create an improved overall combined offering. This final approach is the one referred to by John Chambers in the earlier quotes regarding the development of a broad, horizontal product offering.

One example of sales force synergy is obtained by looking at the territories covered by the salespeople in each territory for both companies. This investigation would develop an understanding of the customers covered by each salesperson and whether the same customer is called on by salespeople from both BuyerCo and SellerCo. At this point you might be tempted to assume that the same salesperson could sell both companies' products, and this assumption might indeed be accurate. But an operational assessment requires a determination of whether or not the customer would accept the products sold from that same salesperson and whether the same salesperson would have the time, expertise, and incentive required to effectively sell both products.

A few commonly used and effective ways to increase sale revenue are to increase the number of sales calls that a salesperson makes, increase the percentage close rate for each sales call made, or increase the dollar value of each closed sale. Combining sales forces may help with the last two items from this list but it might also degrade effectiveness seriously enough in the first item to negate the gains obtained from the other two. Only a careful understanding of the sales and marketing operation of both companies enables you to determine if a number of sales positions can be combined, and to what degree. Buyers should also carefully consider the negative impact that personnel cuts have on remaining employees before deciding to reduce headcount to achieve a specific cost-cutting target. See Chapter 22, "After the Deal Closes," for a detailed discussion of various postacquisition personnel and cultural considerations.

Areas of synergy that are determined with a higher degree of accuracy are expense levels. Buyers and sellers have historical data upon which to base their projected synergy expectations, which makes this analysis far less open to conjecture than that related to estimating future sales force performance. Advertising expenses are used as the analysis example for purposes of this discussion, and readers are clearly advised that advertising is only one of many areas where expense synergy can be obtained. Analysis might show that SellerCo does not have the volume buying power of BuyerCo and the acquisition enables BuyerCo to reduce advertising expenses for SellerCo simply by combining SellerCo's advertising purchases under BuyerCo's blanket purchasing contracts. Notice that this synergy would not be possible if the two companies were not combined and might not even be possible between any two other companies with different structures. Synergy in various areas should be evaluated, if at least to see where the two organizations can combine operations to obtain some type of financial and/or operational gain.

Synergy can also have a negative effect, causing an increase in costs. Assume that two large companies within the same industry choose to merge operations. The larger combined organization might encounter a higher level of legal expense by handling regulatory litigation issues. Each by itself might not have experienced much of a regulatory threat but, combined, they might encounter substantial regulatory oversight. The recently approved merger between SBC and Ameritech may well be an example of this type of future negative synergy. A complete analysis must include both positive and negative synergy effects.

EVALUATE FINANCIAL IMPACT OF SYNERGY

Synergy can only be included as part of the M&A valuation process if a dollar value is attached to the synergy. This section expands on the advertising example presented in the last section. Assume that BuyerCo's advertising fees (not overall expenses) are 5 percent lower than SellerCo's, and SellerCo traditionally spends $1 million annually on advertising. Decreasing SellerCo's advertising costs by 5 percent by wrapping SellerCo's advertising under BuyerCo's blanket advertising rates would save $50,000 per year, or 5 percent of $1 million. Even better, you might find that adding SellerCo's advertising purchasing to BuyerCo's provides decreased rates for both companies because BuyerCo's overall buying power is increased by $1 million. The overall reduced rate provides much larger overall synergy savings.

Synergy effects can be tracked in a spreadsheet type of format so that the overall effect of the combination can be assessed. Table 7.1 shows the effect of expected synergy on earnings per share should the purchase be funded completely with equity from BuyerCo.

Notice from Table 7.1 that BuyerCo experiences an increase in earnings per share of $4.67 – $3.35 = $1.32. Even though stock dilution was involved with this transaction resulting from the issue of 50,000 additional BuyerCo shares, the increased earnings per share obtained from the expected synergy make this transaction attractive to BuyerCo shareholders. Table 7.2 shows the effect of synergy when the purchase is funded completely from debt instead of through the issuance of stock.

We notice that the earnings per share increases in both scenarios, making either equity or debt purchase an attractive prospect. Determining the best pur-

Table 7.1 Fund Purchase with Equity—BuyerCo Stock Issued to SellerCo Shareholders

	BuyerCo	SellerCo	Adjustment	Combined
Revenues	$15,000	$3,000	$900[1]	$18,900
COS	$6,000	$1,350	$(221)[2]	$7,130
G&A	$3,750	$900	$(500)[3]	$4,150
Interest	$169	$24		$193
Income Before Tax	$5,081	$726		$7,428
Tax @ 34% Federal Rate	$1,728	$247		$2,525
Net Income	$3,353	$479		$4,902
Outstanding Shares (000)	1,000	100		
Retirement of SellerCo Shares (000)			-100	
Issuance of BuyerCo Shares (000)			50[4]	1,050
Earnings Per Share	$3.35	$4.79		$4.67

All numbers in thousands except per share.

[1] Assumes that an overall 5 percent increase in sales revenue is obtained by the combination of both BuyerCo and SellerCo.

[2] Assumes that an overall 3 percent decrease in cost of sales is obtained by the greater volume buying power of the combined entity.

[3] Decreases obtained by combining overhead and administrative functions between the two companies.

[4] Assumes that two SellerCo shares are exchanged for one share of BuyerCo stock. 100,000 shares of SellerCo are exchanged for 50,000 newly issued BuyerCo shares.

chase option is really a matter of internal financial policy and management style. The equity purchase approach would be more attractive to a company with a preference toward reducing debt. Debt-funded purchase would be more attractive to a company intent on keeping its share base as small as possible.

Making the Sum More than the Parts

It can be seen from the examples in the prior section that synergy between buyer and seller can provide exceptional benefits to the combined entity. Simply purchasing SellerCo without obtaining the expected synergy would make the purchase far less attractive as is shown in the following figure which assumes an equity purchase. Table 7.3 shows how.

Although the purchase, without considering synergy, affects increases the earnings per share to BuyerCo shareholders, it does not favorably compare to future expectations when synergy affects are included with the analysis.

It is critical that company synergy be considered when performing M&A analysis, because it is arguably the key component that differentiates a successful from an unsuccessful acquisition. This simple example is designed to

Table 7.2 Fund Purchase with Loan, Keeping SellerCo Loans Intact

	BuyerCo	SellerCo	Adjustment	Combined
Revenues	$15,000	$3,000	$900[1]	$18,900
COS	$6,000	$1,350	$(221)[2]	$7,130
G&A	$3,750	$900	$(500)[3]	$4,150
Interest	$169	$24	$192[4]	$385
Income Before Tax	$5,081	$726		$7,236
Tax @ 34% Federal Rate	$1,728	$247		$2,460
Net Income	$3,353	$479		$4,775
Outstanding Shares (000)	1,000	100		
Retirement of SellerCo Shares (000)			−100	
Issuance of BuyerCo Shares (000)				1,000
Earnings Per Share	$3.35	$4.79		$4.78

All numbers in thousands except per share.
[1] Assumes that an overall 5 percent increase in sales revenue is obtained by the combination of both BuyerCo and SellerCo.
[2] Assumes that an overall 3 percent decrease in cost of sales is obtained by the greater buying power of the combined entity.
[3] Decrease obtained by combining overhead and administrative functions between the two companies.
[4] Interest on a $2,400,000 loan at an 8 percent annual rate. Assumes that SellerCo sold for one times revenue and 20 percent was provided to sellers in cash at time of sale.

Table 7.3 Fund Purchase with All Equity Stock Issued to SellerCo Shareholders

	BuyerCo	SellerCo	Adjustment	Combined
Revenues	$15,000	$3,000	$0	$18,000
COS	$6,000	$1,350	$0	$7,350
G&A	$3,750	$900	$0	$4,650
Interest	$169	$24		$193
Income Before Tax	$5,081	$726		$5,807
Tax @ 34% Federal Rate	$1,728	$247		$1,974
Net Income	$3,353	$479		$3,833
Outstanding Shares (000)	1,000	100		
Retirement of SellerCo Shares (000)			−100	
Issuance of BuyerCo Shares (000)			50[1]	1,050
Earnings Per Share	$3.35	$4.79		$3.65

All numbers in thousands except per share.
[1] Assumes that two SellerCo shares are exchanged for one share of BuyerCo stock. 100,000 shares of SellerCo are exchanged for 50,000 newly issued BuyerCo shares.

134

present a method for financially evaluating the impact of the synergy on the combined entity. Most of the work in the analysis involves the determination of synergy areas and the placing of financial values on them. Actually performing the financial analysis is really the simplest part of the process.

Martin Sikora, the editor of *Mergers and Acquisitions* magazine, states in the foreword to *Winning at Mergers and Acquisitions: The Guide to Market-Focused Planning and Integration* a sobering set of facts regarding the postacquisition success of businesses: "If commonly believed statistics are replicated, about a third of those (7000 M&A-type deals performed in 1997) will fail and another third won't measure up to performance projected when merger partners sealed their decision to combine. . . . Failure generally is equated with worst-case results at the target company. . . . Regardless of the specific manifestation, the underperformer generally falls under the broad rubric of falling short in creating shareholder value."[1]

It has been contended by Clemente and Greenspan that a major contributor to this lack of success is the heavy focus on financial synergy defined as cost reduction instead of as revenue enhancement opportunities. Their contention is that costs can only be reduced once and then become an integral part of the historical cost performance, while marketing and sales synergy can benefit and compound indefinitely into the future.

Making the sum of two companies equal more than the individual companies involved requires a hard look, but not only at cost reduction. It requires a hard search for the marketing and sales activities that can be exploited to increase the overall revenue stream of the two combined organizations. Ultimately the merged entity should have sales that exceed the sum of the two companies on their own.

Keeping the Founders around the Company

The purchase of a closely held company holds its own set of opportunities and risks. A closely held company is usually a strong reflection of the founder or owners who were instrumental in making the company a viable business entity. Entrepreneurs tend to be strong-willed, action-oriented people who have a hard time taking orders from others. This is a strength when starting a company from scratch but can present huge headaches for a larger com-

---

[1] See Mark N. Clemente and David S. Greenspan, *Winning at Mergers and Acquisitions: The Guide to Market-Focused Planning and Integration* (New York: Wiley, 1998), ix.

pany that attempts to integrate the purchased company and its entrepreneurial personnel into a more rigid structure.

Founders are, however, the people who made the target company successful enough to warrant its consideration as an acquisition target by the buyer. Cisco CEO Chambers provides some insight related to keeping target company employees around after an acquisition.

"When we acquire a company, we aren't simply acquiring its current products, we're acquiring the next generation of products through its people. If you pay between $500,000 and $3 million per employee, and all you are doing is buying the current research and the current market share, you're making a terrible investment. In the average acquisitions, 40 to 80 percent of the top management and key engineers are gone in two years. By those metrics, most acquisitions fail" (James Daly, "John Chambers: The Art of the Deal," *Business 2.0,* October, 1999).

There may be times when you are best served by getting the founders out of the merged picture and other times when it is beneficial to keep the founders around in the postmerger environment.

1. Founder/owners often have unique relationships with customers that might not carry over to the merged company without the founder's presence and endorsement.

2. Sold company personnel might be fiercely dedicated to the founder/owner who has paid their salaries for many of the past years. Losing the founder might also mean losing many of these key personnel or losing their dedication to the merged entity.

3. Founders understand their business, vendors, customers, and employees in a way that you will not understand until some time into the future. This qualitative information might prove valuable during the postmerger period.

4. Founders are used to calling the shots and might not march well to another leader's cadence. A dissatisfied founder can cause troubles for the new management, and a clear understanding up front is worth establishing.

5. Founders in technology companies are often the engineers who developed the products and services that made the company successful in the first place. Losing these technology resources may seriously undercut the company's ability to create future products that meet up to those developed in the past.

There are various ways to keep the founders interested and dedicated to the success of the merged venture. Several of these are presented later in this chapter. Here are a few thoughts for your consideration when determining the value associated with retaining the founders:

1. If you are familiar with the business and the industry, such as when purchasing a competitor, you might not need the founders around and are likely best served by severing the relationship at the point of ownership transfer.

2. If you are new to the industry and expect a learning curve delay before making confident decisions, then keeping the founders around in a mentoring capacity makes sense.

3. A technology purchase, in which the technology already functions without problems, makes founder retention optional. If the technology is complicated and proprietary, it makes sense to keep the technology developers around for a while after the purchase in both a development and engineering mentoring role.

4. When purchasing an international entity with the specific intention of expanding into a global market, you should keep the prior owners around in a mentoring capacity. This provides a smoother transition and minimizes the likelihood of a cultural difference undermining what would otherwise be a fruitful acquisition.

5. A financial acquisition with the intention of cost-cutting and/or selling of acquired business segments usually does not require the longer-term assistance of prior management. It might be beneficial to keep key members on in an advisory capacity immediately after acquisition, but this relationship should keep the prior management in a non–decision-making capacity. Their emotional attachment to the prior history may well cloud their current judgment with respect to breaking up the acquired entity to obtain maximum financial benefit.

6. Purchasing a closely held corporation where the founder/owners are an integral part of the business success almost mandates that the prior owner/founders transfer to the buyer in some management capacity. Otherwise much of the selling company value will walk out the door with the founder.

7. Larger companies often benefit by purchasing a smaller company with a creative and successful technical staff. They then put the acquired staff into an R&D unit where they can brainstorm and create using the higher funding levels provided by the larger buying company. This setup benefits the acquired entrepreneurs in that they get to create new technology, which is what they like to do and have proven that they do well. It benefits the buyer in that the entrepreneurs are around to assist with technology transfer issues while also not having to worry about them becoming management problems due to restless-

ness. In addition, this keeps these creative entrepreneurs within the buying company creating for the buyer and away from a competitor.

Let me provide a word of caution on this particular point. Companies that acquire personnel with the intention of capitalizing on their creativity must ensure that the postacquisition environment promotes creativity. A creative environment is often not one that matches the rest of the corporate culture; however, it is a requirement for such circumstances. I am not suggesting that there be no guidelines for this group, but I am asserting that restricting this group's environment simply to match some arbitrary corporate policy will likely also stifle the very creativity asset so highly valued during the acquisition process.

8. Many founder/owners are open to selling with the specific intent of letting someone else worry about the business aspects of company management. Many entrepreneurs create successful companies only to find themselves in management and no longer doing the technology-based work that made them successful in the first place. Buying their company and placing them in an R&D management/design capacity enables the entrepreneur to get back to the technology work that they initially loved. The buyer gets a motivated technology innovator and the entrepreneur gets to create, which was his initial passion.

The acquisition of a closely held corporation, or one intimately tied to the name or reputation of the founders, is based as much on emotion as it is finances. Make sure that you understand the seller/owner's personal motivation and take maximum advantage of these motivations to obtain maximum value from your purchase.

Transaction Structures To Support Strategic Goals

Once you have determined whether you want to keep the prior owners around or not, you can then determine the optimal transaction structure for your acquisition. This section takes a detailed look at the relationship between transaction structure and strategic transaction goals. The structure of the transaction must make business sense while also being financially viable. If the transaction's financial and legal structure undermines the business intention of the transaction, then the success of the acquisition is compromised from the start. First, know what you want from the acquisition and then structure the transaction to support those desires.

Purchase and Retain

Assume that the intention of the transaction is to integrate the purchased company into the buying company's existing operation. Personnel, equipment, goodwill, and other items are expected to be fully integrated into the buyer so that future examination shows a seamless integration. This type of transaction should be designed to promote future interest and positive motivation on the part of all involved personnel. In other words, the involved personnel must have a vested interest in the positive well being of the merged entity.

Presented here are two mechanisms for obtaining this motivation.

1. Stock transfers involve the transfer of BuyerCo stock to each SellerCo shareholder. The SellerCo shareholder immediately has a vested interest in the future financial performance of BuyerCo, because the value of the BuyerCo stock received as part of the purchase determines the price received by the seller. Transferring stock creates interest on the part of the SellerCo shareholders, and if those people are integral to the future success of the merged venture, you should have motivated and interested managers making future merged operation decisions. If a substantial portion of stock is passed to a single individual, that individual will likely want a seat on the board of the buying company. In this way the seller is ensured of some voting influence on the future operation of the buyer.

2. Some buyers negotiate employment agreements with key selling personnel to make sure that they work for the merged entity for some specific minimum future period. Sellers who enter into this type of agreement are advised to negotiate specific clauses that protect their interests should the buying company not be an acceptable employer. Otherwise the seller could find himself the employee of a company for which he would have never otherwise worked. He might be financially locked into staying until the end of the employment agreement or incur substantial penalties. The intention of this example transaction is to completely integrate the purchased assets and personnel into the buying company's existing operation.

Purchase and Separate

The buyer might acquire a company with the specific intention of subdividing the company and reselling the unwanted portions. These portions might be specific assets or entire divisions of the acquired company. This is called a *bustup transaction*. It makes sense to structure the bust-up transaction so that a minimal number of future encumbrances are encountered. For this reason many examples of this type of transaction involve no stock transfer from BuyerCo to SellerCo and instead involve an all-cash purchase. The cash might be obtained from a BuyerCo public stock offering or from BuyerCo debt, but SellerCo shareholders receive their compensation at the time of purchase and typically not at some time in the future.

Stock transfer transactions become particularly messy if the number of shares transferred to SellerCo shareholders represents a large voting block percentage and board representation. SellerCo shareholders with adequate voting power might interfere with the buyer's ability to subdivide the purchased company as needed to later maximize shareholder value.

Purchase and Eliminate

An asset deal is one in which the buyer purchases the seller with the expressed intention of eliminating the prior company altogether. In essence, the "going concern" aspect of the transaction is eliminated and the only value transferred from seller to buyer is the asset base. Goodwill and future earning potential are a nonissue in this type of transaction, which generally means that an asset deal commands a substantially lower price than other types of acquisitions. The present value of the company is the market value of transferred assets minus the market value of the debts. These transferred asset values are usually reduced by some percentage to provide the buyer with some financial breathing room when selling the assets.

An asset deal is usually only executed when the selling company is in substantial financial or operational trouble and simply should be put out of its misery. This type of transaction may involve stock, but it is more likely that the buying company would not want any of the SellerCo management on the board because their prior track records indicate minimal incremental value to BuyerCo would be derived from their board membership.

Risk and Leverage

Sellers want to obtain the highest possible price for their company, while buyers want to minimize purchase price. There may be times when the seller is not served by demanding an exceptionally high purchase price, because the additional debt incurred to pay that higher price might put the merged entity into financial distress. It is important to the seller for the merged entity to remain a viable business, especially when a portion of the seller's obtained value is based on postacquisition BuyerCo future performance. Some sellers choose higher stock transactions instead of higher cash transactions just for this reason. If the merged entity does not have adequate earnings to cover its existing and purchase-price-generated debt, then the entity's future financial prospects are degraded. Should the company become financially insolvent, that portion of the sale price obtained by the seller as future gain is placed in jeopardy.

Buyers and sellers should both ensure that an adequate margin of safety exists with respect to paying off acquisition debt. Acquiring too much debt might push the debt-equity ratio to a high enough level that BuyerCo's creditworthiness is jeopardized. Creditors will become less willing to extend credit if the coverage ratio increases beyond a certain value. In fact, BuyerCo might have existing lender covenants that preclude the obtaining of debt beyond agreed upon levels. All of these items are deal potential deal-stoppers and should be assessed early in the acquisition process to avoid unnecessary expense of time and money on a deal that cannot be properly funded.

Leveraged Buyouts

Purchasing a company using the value of the company alone to fund the deal is a *leveraged buyout* (LBO). The buyer attempts to invest as little of its own money as possible while executing the acquisition and purchase publicly traded shares of stock, essentially taking the company from "public" to "private." There are positive and negative evaluations of the effect of an LBO on a corporation.[2] The commonly highlighted positive aspects of an LBO are that managers own a high percentage of the company stock, that internal monitoring of expenses and performance increases in a post-LBO environment, and that postbuyout companies experience positive increases in operating income and margins in the first two years after the buyout while simultaneously decreasing inventories and capital expenditures relative to the industry median. The commonly highlighted negative aspects of an LBO are that LBO sponsors and dealmakers are simply looking for ways to gener-

[2] See Patrick A. Gaughan, *Mergers, Acquisitions, and Corporate Restructurings, Second Edition* (New York: Wiley, 1999), 312–317.

ate personal short-term gains and cash out of the LBO within five to seven years of the LBO, that around 45 percent of LBOs completed between 1979 and 1986 returned to public ownership before August of 1990, and that the post-LBO company is so highly leveraged that it has a much higher likelihood of falling into bankruptcy. The LBO is a viable acquisition tool that may be applicable to your particular situations.

A few key points contribute to a successful LBO:

1. Not paying too much for the acquisition of the target company, because every dollar of sale price adds more debt that must be serviced by the purchasing company.

2. The purchase is financed with debt instead of equity, which enables the LBO shareholders to experience a high financial upside with minimal financial downside other than the down payment. A typical financing target is 80 percent of purchase price.

3. The company must be ripe for a substantial increase in operational efficiency derived either from a change in management, a change in management incentives, a substantial reduction in costs, or a combination of changes. Increased efficiencies should create increased profits which help cover debt service and better ensure the LBO's future viability.

4. At some future point, the LBO must reduce the debt service. This is usually accomplished by a public stock offering (remember that the LBO took the company private) once the company is on a more solid financial footing. Another approach is to simply find a buyer who is willing to purchase the entire company, which is now performing within acceptable ranges. Proceeds from the stock offering or the sale are used to pay off the LBO lenders.

Technology companies may present LBO opportunities depending on the industry, lenders, and personnel involved. Startup companies are often founded by technical personnel who lack effective business skills. Although the technology and operation might be excellent, the lack of business management skills might seriously degrade the company's financial or marketing condition. An LBO that places experienced business management in key positions while leaving the successful technical team intact may provide a substantial increase in operational performance over a relatively short period of time. This combination might be enough to entice lenders to fund the LBO. Lenders might also be willing to invest in an underperforming technology firm, believing that the overall market for the company's technology is destined for a substantial increase but requires a change in key management personnel before making the investment. An LBO firm that has the needed personnel and contacts to coordinate this type of transaction could bring the company, lenders, and personnel together to turn a losing business venture into a top performer.

The more solid the financial track record of the company and the less volatile its market, the easier it is to obtain funding from lenders. Remember that lenders are by nature risk-averse and lend primarily on a high fixed asset base and high pro forma confidence in the firm's ability to service its required LBO debt.

The ultimate funding of an LBO is usually divided between three financial groups: senior lenders (50 to 60 percent of LBO price), subordinate lenders (20 to 30 percent of LBO price) and equity financing (20 percent of LBO price). Senior lenders are commercial banks and other lenders who are traditionally risk-averse. These lenders require that they be in first position to recover their funds should the company go into default. Senior lenders usually command an interest rate on their debt that is 2 percent or so above a low-risk interest rate such as Subordinate, or mezzanine, lenders are next in line to recover in the event of default. In return for their higher risk of non-recovery, subordinate lenders usually require an interest premium of 6 percent to 8 percent above a low-risk interest rate such as the 10-Year United States treasury bond.

Equity investors are usually the firm coordinating the LBO itself. They acquire a pool of capital from their own investors who understand that the money will be invested in LBO-type of activities. The LBO firm itself expects to obtain an overall 35 percent or higher internal rate of return (IRR) on the transaction. The future gains that provide the high IRR are obtained from the sale of stock and/or the eventual total sale of the company itself to another buyer. The overall intention is that the future share sale price be substantially higher than the LBO share price, because the company's operational performance should have substantially improved during the intervening time frame as a direct result of the LBO.

Sample LBO Pricing Analysis

A walk through the calculations associated with a simple LBO outlines the principles behind LBO valuation and pricing decisions. Assume that TargetA company is for sale and you believe it to be a solid LBO candidate. You must next determine the level of debt that could be reasonably serviced by TargetA and compare the resulting LBO sale price with existing share market prices. TargetA's current pertinent financial information is shown in Table 7.4.

With Table 7.4 as a starting point, you can now make some LBO pricing-related calculations which ultimately lead to a reasonable LBO fundable per-share price. Assume that lender discussions indicate that they are willing to loan to a company with a maximum EBIT/interest payment ratio of 1.3. Assume also that the 10-Year United States treasury bond interest rate is 6.5 percent and that lenders require a 2 percent premium over this rate for the LBO funding.

1. Dividing EBIT by 1.3 provides the maximum interest payments that TargetA can support, which results in a value of $14 million ($18.2 million divided by 1.3 = $14 million).

2. The maximum loan amount that can be paid by the $14 million in interest payments is $164.7 million ($14 million divided by 8.5 percent, 6.5 percent plus 2 percent risk premium).

3. Dividing $164.7 million by 80 percent provides the maximum LBO enterprise value of $205.9 million.

Table 7.4 TargetA Pertinent Current Financial Information

Income Statement	20xx
Net Revenue	$130,000
EBIT	$18,200
Net Earnings	$11,700
Outstanding Shares (000)	5,900
Earnings Per Share	$1.98
Balance Sheet Item	
Long Term Debt	$7,800

All numbers in thousands except per share.

Table 7.5 TargetA LBO Pricing Analysis Summary

EBIT/Interest Payments Max Ratio	1.3	
Maximum Loan Interest Payment Amount	$14,000	
Assumed Loan Interest Rate	8.50%	
Maximum Serviceable Loan Amount	$164,706	80%
Required Equity Amount	$41,176	20%
Total LBO Fundable Enterprise Value	$205,882	100%
Net LBO Enterprise Value	$198,082	
Outstanding Shares	5,900	
LBO Per Share Estimated Value	$33.57	

All numbers in thousands except per share.

4. Subtracting $164.7 million in debt funding from the total value of $205.9 indicates that $41.2 million in equity funding must be obtained (20 percent of 205.6 million).

5. Subtracting the long-term debt of $7.8 million from $205.6 million provides the net LBO enterprise value of $198.1 million.

6. Dividing $198.1 million by the total of 5.9 million outstanding shares provides a LBO maximum per share price of $33.57.

If TargetA's shares are publicly trading at under $33.47 each, then this LBO appears financially viable. The lower the market-traded share price is when compared to the calculated maximum LBO share price, the greater the safety margin on the calculations and purchase, and the more financially attractive the LBO appears. If the market share prices are higher than the $33.47 the LBO is more difficult to justify unless particular synergy is obtained between the LBO group and TargetA's operation. This is particularly true when you consider that publicly traded share prices often increase in price when intention to purchase the shares is publicly announced.

Using Table 7.5 for reference, any LBO group would want to perform a detailed due diligence process on TargetA to find any areas that would detract from or add to this calculated value. But this type of analysis provides a starting point for determining if a company is a viable LBO candidate worthy of further investigation. Notice that the total LBO fundable enterprise value is 11.3 times the EBIT value ($205.88 million divided by $18.2 million). If you assume that TargetA can be sold in five years for the same EBIT multiple and project that the EBIT in five years will be $33 million, then the following internal rate of return calculation can be performed:

1. The projected sale price for TargetA in five years is 11.3 times $33 million = $373.3 million.

2. Assume that $133.4 million is still due on the debt financing. Subtracting $133.4 million from $373.3 million leaves $239.9 million after the sale.

3. Subtracting the initial equity investment of $41.176 million from $239.9 million leaves $198.7 million as the net return on the investment over a five-year period.

4. Performing an internal rate of return calculation based on the initial equity investment of $41.176 million and the expected net receipt of $198.7 million in five years shows an IRR of around 37 percent. This number is greater than the required 35 percent IRR set by the LBO group which once again indicates that performing an LBO on TargetA is a marginally viable option.

Lenders will keep a close eye on ratios when lending to an LBO and rarely lend when the debt-to-equity ratio is greater than 4:1. LBOs represent a viable way of funding a company purchase; however, incurring the large percentage debt and resulting leverage associate with an LBO make this process risky if projections are not met and highly profitable if they are. Risk and reward are always involved when dealing with financial decision making.

Employee Stock Ownership Plans (ESOP)

The Employee Retirement Income Security Act (ERISA) of 1974 enabled the implementation of an Employee Stock Ownership Plan (ESOP). An ESOP is a way in which the company employees become stock owners of their own employer. When dealing with M&A activity an ESOP can be considered in two contexts. The first is as a mechanism for employees to finance the purchase of their own employer. The second is as an antitakeover technique that dissuades unwanted tender offers. Both approaches are discussed in this section.

An ESOP as a Purchasing Tool

An ESOP is a pension plan set up by a corporation that invests exclusively in the stock of the employer or its subsidiaries. While a 401(k) plan allows investment in stock other than that of the employer corporation, an ESOP is restricted to only investing in employer stock. The overall intention is that employees will work harder for the corporation knowing that their retirement income is based on company financial performance. There is a downside, however, in that bankruptcy of the corporation also bankrupts the ESOP stock and may leave employees without a job and possibly without a pension.

The company contributes a percentage of employee salaries to the ESOP program. The percentage contribution is typically in the 8 percent to 10 percent range. Employers benefit in that ESOP contributions are tax-deductible and employees are not taxed on contributions until funds are withdrawn from the ESOP. A high and consistent overall company salary level is usually required to support ESOP-related activities.

ESOPs are divided into two subcategories: leveraged and unleveraged. A leveraged ESOP borrows money to purchase its own company's stock. The company makes contributions to the ESOP, which are then used to repay the loan principal and interest. A company can contribute up to 25 percent of eligible employee compensation to a leveraged ESOP. The leveraged ESOP is the one most used with M&A activities because it provides a mechanism for acquiring the larger sums of money required for a company purchase. An unleveraged ESOP is not used to borrow money and enables the company to contribute up to 15 percent of eligible employee compensation to the ESOP plan.

Private companies are often purchased by employees from owners who want out of the business. There are ESOP-related tax incentives for the seller and incentives for the employees. Assume, for example, that a company falls on difficult financial times and might be forced into a shutdown. Employees, using an ESOP, might be able to talk the owners into a substantially reduced selling price and pay for the reduced price using a leveraged ESOP. In this scenario, the seller wins in that the corporation retains some of its value and the employees win in that their jobs continue while reserving the possibility of a large financial gain should the company turn around under employee ownership.

An ESOP is also an alternative to an IPO in that it can be used to raise capital amounts greater than that needed to purchase the company stock. This extra cash is available for company use and does not have the high offering costs associated with an IPO, but does come with a higher risk associated with the incremental debt and possible negative leverage effects.

An important tax benefit associated with a leveraged ESOP is that the corporate employer is contributing to the ESOP and taking a tax deduction; therefore, both principal and interest payments are effectively tax-deductible as opposed to simply the interest deduction normally allowed with most loans. This tax advantage decreases the cost of the loan, making a leveraged ESOP more financially attractive.

ESOP as an Antitakeover Step

Some companies use an ESOP as an antitakeover measure. This is accomplished by setting up an ESOP that owns a specific percentage block of company shares. This ownership percentage is not available for purchase by an outsider, which keeps an unwanted buyer from purchasing the required percentage of shares required by state law to consummate the takeover. Delaware sets the required percentage of purchased shares at 85 percent, which means that a Delaware corporation with an ESOP that owns 15 percent or more of company stock is immune to unwanted takeover attempts.

Chapter Summary

It is possible to focus on the financial aspects of an acquisition and place less importance on the strategic aspects of the transaction. This approach is short-sighted and ignores the aspects of an acquisition that may provide the most long-term value. Corporate strategy is the starting point that determines the overall direction of a corporation and usually dictates the parameters of a viable acquisition target. Synergy is determined by the revenue/expense-enhancing or -reducing aspects of the acquisition itself.

The acquisition must support company business goals or else no amount of financial maneuvering will turn a poor business fit into a strategically attractive purchase. The cultures of the two companies must be considered so that transaction details are structured to capitalize on cultural and employee strengths. It might be determined beneficial to retain key employees or founders after the purchase; conversely, the best course of action may dictate that the founders sever ties with the target company after its purchase.

It is important that the transaction be structured to not only be financially viable, but also to support the longer-term strategic goals of the purchase. One important goal of the transaction may be the retention of key managers and engineers as valuable, motivated employees in the postacquisition environment. This point is particularly true of high technology companies that may not as yet have a marketable product but have a unique enough technology to justify a buyer's interest. Making sure that these key engineers and managers remain motivated in a postpurchase environment is an important aspect of the transaction that should not be overlooked.

Positive marketing and sales synergy should be an important early consideration, because this synergy increases revenues which increases expected future company performance on a repeating basis. Areas of expense reduction synergy between buyer and seller should also be examined as possible ways of decreasing costs after purchase.

Sellers interested in providing themselves with a tax break while also providing their employees with substantial future investment gains might consider an ESOP instead of the outright sale of the company to an unrelated third party. ESOPs present exciting opportunities to employees who obtain the opportunity to create wealth for themselves through stock owners, but they must understand that financial failure of the company can also eliminate any ESOP values, bankrupting the employee pension plan as well. The leveraged buyout or management buyout enables employees and managers to obtain an equity stake in their own employer with the hope of decreasing costs, increasing efficiencies, and eventually providing higher returns to employee/owners.

8

Special Accounting and Tax Considerations

Obtaining as much value as possible from any M&A transaction is a primary goal of every buyer and seller. The specific structure of a transaction will have specific financial reporting and tax consequences for both the buyer and the seller. These consequences can have a resulting major impact on the net after-tax price seen by the seller and the net financial benefit experienced by the buyer. Structuring a transaction so that it meets certain requirements can increase the transaction value to both buyer and seller. Opinions vary as to whether the method of accounting for a transaction actually impacts its value. The Financial Accounting Standards Board (FASB) is considering, at the time of this writing, the elimination of the pooling of interests method of accounting, a method that is used in many of today's M&A transactions. In most situations, minimizing the tax paid as part of a transaction is desirable. There is controversy as to whether the method of accounting actually impacts the perceived performance of the transaction, because cash flows are ultimately unchanged by the accounting choice. Various tax and accounting topics are investigated in this chapter with the intention of educating you about their respective requirements. Armed with this information, you can then decide their importance to your particular transaction.

Differentiating Accounting and Taxation Requirements

Both buyer and seller must account for any M&A transaction. Accounting procedures that follow FASB guidelines are needed to ensure consistent shareholder and investor reporting of these transactions. The resulting financial statements will also form a basis for the determination of the tax impact of the transaction for both the buyer and seller.

The seller is the one receiving some form of compensation for the sale of the business and who must deal with the tax consequences of any gain or loss received from the sale. The buyer must report the purchase on his or her financial statements, and the accounting methods used to report this purchase will have a direct and possibly substantial impact on the overall reported financial performance of the buyer's business. Typical buyer areas of impact involve the reporting of asset values, acquired debt, issued shares, income or loss, earnings, and depreciation. Depending on the specific nature of the transaction, the buyer might show positive or negative impact on corporate earnings which may have short- and long-term impact on share prices for a publicly traded company.

Buyer-Related FASB Rules Relating to Acquisition

Buyers have two ways for reporting the complete acquisition of another company: pooling of interests or purchase. The acquisition must fall into one of these two categories; they are not alternative selections but more of a stipulation to which the transaction must conform. If the acquisition cannot be financially reported using the pooling of interests method then it must be reported using the purchase method. Each has its own set of implications that are presented here in summary form with details following later in the chapter. The general differences between the two reporting methods is their way of handing asset transfer value, the reporting of current income/loss, the creation of goodwill, and the future income impact of the current transaction.

POOLING OF INTERESTS

The pooling of interests method combines the buying and selling companies into a single financial entity that looks just like the two have been a single entity throughout the entire fiscal year. Once the pooling is accomplished, any financial division between the two entities disappears. A specific set of requirements must be met before pooling becomes an available option. Most acquisitions are reported using the purchase method instead of the pooling method simply because the specifics of the transaction do not meet the pooling requirements. These pooling requirements details are covered in a later section of this chapter.

It is important to understand that pooling of interests transfers balance sheet and income statement values from the seller to the buyer in an unchanged way. Any seller income or loss for the fiscal year is transferred to the buyer just as if the buyer experienced that income or loss. Asset values transfer to the buyer at their current book values as do the liabilities and retained earnings. No goodwill is created or transferred in the transaction, which is a major point of criticism for the use of pooling of interests. The extra goodwill paid by the buyer in purchasing a company at a premium over its market value is not directly accounted for or amortized over future years as is done with purchase accounting. This lack of amortization, according to critics, makes it more difficult for investors to track the future performance of an acquisition.

Bill Roberts' December 1999 article in *Electronic Business* magazine, "FASB Tries to Eliminate Pooling of Interests," presents the views from several perspectives. In the article, FASB chair Edmund L. Jenkins contends that "the purchase method gives investors better information about the initial cost of the acquisition and its performance over time." Dan Scheinman, senior vice president of legal and government affairs for Cisco Systems, a company that uses pooling in 60 percent of its acquisitions, states that "In technology's fast-changing business environment pooling allows companies like Cisco to take risks without absorbing any penalty to their market capitalization." George Van Gehr, managing partner of Alliant Partners, Inc. of Palo Alto, CA, tends to reinforce the stand taken by Jenkins. The purchase method "will require the buyer to account for the results of these acquisitions over time, something (that) can be conveniently neglected under the pooling method."

Results reported in a November-December 1999 *Harvard Business Review* article, "Stock or Cash? The Trade-Offs for Buyers and Sellers in Mergers and Acquisitions," imply that managers who concern themselves more with the manner of accounting and less with the value generation opportunity presented by the acquisition will be punished for thinking the market cannot tell the difference between the two methods of accounting and will myopically focus only on short-term earnings. "Studies consistently show that the market does not reward companies for using pooling of interest accounting. Nor do goodwill charges from purchase accounting adversely affect stock prices. In fact, the market reacts more favorably to purchase transactions than to pooling transactions. The message for management is clear: value acquisitions on the basis of their economic substances—their future cash flows—not on the basis of short-term earnings generated by accounting conventions."

Here are a few potential buyer benefits promoted by those in favor of the pooling of interests method:

1. Assets transferred at seller-based historical book values keeps the assets from being increased in value to current market values, as is done with the purchase method. Lower asset values translate into lower future depreciation expenses.

2. The transaction creates no goodwill that would decrease current and future expenses, because future goodwill amortization expense is not involved.

3. If the acquired company has a higher earnings level than the buyer, then the buyer benefits immediately and in the future from the acquisition by being able to report the purchased company's higher earnings as the buyer's own. Future earnings are also expected to be higher resulting from lower depreciation and amortization expenses when compared to the purchase method. Based on these sets of purported benefits, a publicly traded company would find pooling an attractive method of accounting for an acquisition and Scheinman's comments would tend to reinforce that contention. Once again, a discussion of pooling's merits or drawbacks may be moot by 2001 if FASB eliminates it as an acceptable method of accounting for acquisitions.

POOLING OF INTERESTS EXAMPLE

The following is an example of a simplified pooling of interests acquisition transaction between SellerCo and BuyerCo. Assume that the selling company has a market share price of $10 per share and has a total of 500,000 outstanding shares that must be retired for a total of $5 million (500,000 × $10) as part of the purchase. Assume that the seller shares have an accounting par value of $1 each. Assume also that the buyer shares trade for $40 each, that the buyer has 1,200,000 shares issued prior to the acquisition, and that 125,000 new shares will be issued to compensate the seller's shareholders for the retirement of their seller shares. This seller and buyer background information is summarized in Table 8.1.

Table 8.1 Pooling of Shareholders' Equity Interests Example

	SellerCo	BuyerCo	Adjustment	Pooled
Share Market Price	$10	$40		
Purchase Price	$5,000,000			
Share Par Value	$1	$1		
Outstanding Shares—Seller	500,000		–500,000	
Outstanding Shares—Buyer		1,200,000	125,000	1,325,000
Common Stock Value—Seller	$500,000		(500,000)	0
Common Stock Value—Buyer		$1,200,000	$125,000	$1,325,000
Additional Paid in Capital	$135,000	$245,000	$375,000	$755,000
Retained Earnings	$1,100,000	$7,500,000		$8,600,000
Totals	$1,735,000	$8,945,000		$10,680,000

Table 8.1 shows that $500,000 worth of SellerCo balance sheet share value must be retired as part of the transaction, but that the BuyerCo only issues $125,000 worth of balance sheet valued new stock. The difference in balance sheet value ($500,000 – $125,000 = $375,000) contributed by SellerCo is accounted for as an adjustment increasing *additional paid in capital*. This transaction requires that each SellerCo shareholder receive one BuyerCo share in return for four shares of SellerCo stock. No goodwill is required for this transaction, because the balance sheet items transfer at book value and because the market value of shares is not reflected as part of the pooling calculations other than in determining the number of seller-retired and buyer-issued shares.[1]

PURCHASE METHOD

This section assumes that the same transaction presented in Table 8.1 is performed using the purchase method instead of the pooling method. Cash deals transacted in the United States must be accounted for using the purchase method.

The purchase method treats SellerCo assets as though they were transferred to BuyerCo at fair market value. In the example in Table 8.2, using the same companies as in Table 8.1, goodwill is added to the transaction to account for the difference between the fair market value of the transferred as-

[1] See Joseph M. Morris et al., *Mergers and Acquisitions: Business Strategies for Accountants* (New York: Wiley, 1995).

Table 8.2 Acquisition Accounting Using the Purchase Method

	SellerCo	BuyerCo	Purchase Adjustment	Purchase Method Combined Results
Assets	$3,135,000	$15,445,000	$500,000[1]	$19,080,000
Goodwill			$1,365,000[2]	$1,365,000
Total Assets	$3,135,000	$15,445,000	$1,865,000	$20,445,000
Total Liabilities	$1,400,000	$6,500,000		$7,900,000
Common Stock Value — Seller	$500,000		$(500,000)[3]	0
Common Stock Value — Buyer		$1,200,000	$125,000[4]	$1,325,000
Additional Paid in Capital	$135,000	$245,000	$3,340,000	$3,720,000
Retained Earnings	$1,100,000	$7,500,000		$7,500,000
Total Shareholders' Equity	$1,735,000	$8,945,000		$12,545,000
Total of Liabilities and Equity	$3,135,000	$15,445,000		$20,445,000

Step up in asset values to fair market value.
Goodwill calculated as $5 million purchase price – FMV assets ($3 million + $.5 million FMV increase) = $1.5 million.
Retirement of SellerCo common shares.
BuyerCo shares issued to compensate SellerCo shareholders.

sets ($3.635 million) and the actual purchase price ($5 million.) The retained earnings of SellerCo are not transferred to BuyerCo. Liabilities are assumed to be transferred at their current values, which are further assumed to be at fair market value. Additional paid in capital is increased to compensate for the differences obtained between the increased asset values and the par value price of stock issued ($125,000) to maintain consistency between assets, liabilities, and shareholders' equity.

COMPARING POOLING AND PURCHASE METHODS

A major purported benefit associated with the pooling method as opposed to the purchase method is the ability to include the current year's earnings in the buyer's financial statements. Tables 8.1 and 8.2 compared the balance sheet impact of the two methods. This section takes a comparative look at the income statement effects of the two methods. In both cases the SellerCo shares are retired in exchange for 125,000 BuyerCo shares. No other consideration, such as cash, is involved with the transaction. Basically, all income statement items are added together to get the results associated with the

Table 8.3 Income Statement Calculations (Acquisition Date July 1, 20xx)

	SellerCo	BuyerCo	Pooled Results[1]	Purchase Results[2]
Sales	$5,000,000	$30,000,000	$35,000,000	$35,000,000
Net Income after Tax	$500,000	$2,400,000	$2,900,000	$2,650,000
Outstanding Shares	500,000[3]	1,200,000	1,325,000[4]	1,325,000[4]
Earnings per Share	$1.00	$2.00	$2.19[5]	$ 2.00[5]

[1] Represents the combination of SellerCo and BuyerCo income statement values for the entire year of the purchase, independent of the timing of the purchase within the year.
[2] Income of the purchase method combination is included in the combined results only after the acquisition takes place, which is for one-half of the year. Only 50% of the $500,000 net income value is included in the purchase results.
[3] This stock is retired in exchange for 125, 000 shares of BuyerCo stock.
[4] Represents the sum of the initial 1,200,000 shares of BuyerCo stock plus the additional 125,000 issued to purchase SellerCo.
[5] Calculated by dividing the postacquisition net income after tax by the number of postacquisition shares outstanding.

pooled results. Purchase results are assumed to have no synergistic effects of either a positive or negative nature which combines the income statement values for future years, but may not provide any income changes for the year of the acquisition.

You can see from the simple example in Table 8.3 that the ability to include the complete yearly earnings for the year of acquisition can make a large difference on the resulting reported earnings per share. In this case, the earnings per share value is increased by almost 10 percent using pooling instead of purchase method procedures. Some accounting professionals contend that this earnings increase created by the use of pooling instead of purchase accounting actually fools no one, and it indeed may even be detrimental, if the *Harvard Business Review* contentions are believed.

Future financial reports that use the pooling method for recording a transaction should show an increase in earnings because depreciation and amortization expenses will be lower when compared to the purchase-recorded transaction. Lower expenses translate into higher expected future overall earnings and the resulting higher reported earnings per share. The market will determine if the higher earnings reported by pooling warrant a higher share price with the understanding that the value of a company is determined by its ability to generate future positive cash flows, and not by its historical method of accounting for acquisition transactions.

Seller-Related IRS Rules Regarding Taxable Transactions

So far in this chapter we have looked at the transaction from the buyer's perspective while looking at the two accounting methods used for recording the acquisition's affect on the buyer's reported financial statements. The seller is also faced with his own set of concerns with respect to the handling of the transaction. A seller must be concerned with minimizing the taxes paid on the proceeds received from the sale. This section takes a look at the various types of sale transactions and their affect on the seller's tax situation.

TAXABLE TRANSACTION OVERVIEW

Transactions will either be taxable or nontaxable to the seller depending on the specific nature of the transaction. In general, only the seller is directly tax-impacted by the form of the acquisition. Acquisitions are performed by buying either stock or assets. A stock purchase is the easiest and generally less complex approach, because it deals with the entity as a whole instead of its individual pieces. By purchasing all of the stock in a company, the buyer assumes all assets and liabilities associated with the selling (purchased) company.

An asset purchase requires dealing with each individual asset, determining its fair market value and any associated asset-specific liabilities along the way. However, it is very possible to purchase an asset and not purchase any portion of the selling company. For example, a buyer could purchase a warehouse building from another company and not incur any other seller-related liability other than those associated with the building asset itself.

Seller taxes payable on the transaction differ based on the type of seller and the type of transaction. A buyer that purchases a company's stock really purchases the stock from the shareholder, bypassing the company completely in the transaction. Should the buyer pay cash for the stock, from a tax perspective, the cash is passed directly to the shareholder who is then liable for the applicable taxes. Should the buyer provide stock as payment for seller stock, then the stock is transferred to the selling shareholder, again bypassing the company. A buying company will deal with the selling company when the selling company is the shareholder of the entity being sold, such as is the case with the sale of a subsidiary. Special tax laws apply to this situation and are presented later in the chapter.

Here are some general guidelines that apply to seller transactions:

1. Stocks sold by individual shareholders that have been held for 12 months qualify for long-term capital gains tax treatment. Federal capital gains rates are currently 10 percent for those individuals in the 15 percent tax bracket and 20 percent for those in higher brackets. The federal capital gains reduced tax rate provides a 5 percent reduction for those in the 15 percent bracket and up to a 19.6 percent tax reduction on the sale for those in the highest personal tax bracket. State tax rates vary.

2. Stocks sold that were not held by the shareholder for the required long-term capital gains period are subject to personal income taxes payable at the individual shareholder's personal tax level.

3. Companies are not eligible for a capital gains tax reduction, making the holding period irrelevant for that purpose.

4. Sold assets are taxed on the gain obtained from the sale. The gain is calculated by subtracting the basis of the sold asset from the sale price. The basis is uniquely determined for each asset. The determination is reliant on the initial purchase price, capital additions to the asset, and allowed reductions in basis value, such as those obtained from depreciation expenses. If the asset sells for less than its basis value it is considered to be sold at a loss, and that loss will likely be deductible (possibly reducing the selling company's overall tax liability). However, special rules may limit the amount and timing of deductible losses.

5. When a company sells an asset it must record the gain or loss associated with the sale and either pay tax on the taxable gain or record a deduction, if allowable, associated with a loss.

6. Should the company liquidate after selling its assets, it must then distribute the remaining cash of the corporation (resulting from the liquidation) to the shareholders, who must then pay tax on any gain over their stock basis at their respective individual levels. This situation subjects asset sale proceeds to taxation at the corporate level and then again at the shareholder level (double taxation).

There are a number of cases in which a shareholder, receiving buying company shares in exchange for their selling company shares, will not be subject to tax on the received share value. Why? Because the IRS contends that the selling shareholders have not realized any tangible gain through an exchange of stock of comparable value and the seller still has a vested financial interest in the operation of the buying company. When the buying company pays for seller shares with cash, the selling shareholders are no longer involved or have any vested interest in the operation of the buying company. Purchasing selling company shares through the use of buying company shares retains the selling company shareholders as interested shareholders in the new merged entity.

NONTAXABLE TRANSACTION

The IRS allows certain types of corporate acquisition transactions to proceed without taxation as long as minimum requirements are met. These types of tax-free mergers and acquisitions are referred to as *reorganizations.* Reorganizations come in various forms, from type A to G, with types A to D being of the most interest from an acquisition perspective. A few basic requirements must be met for the transaction to be treated as nontaxable to the sellers:

1. Substantially, all seller assets must be transferred to the buyer. The types of assets involved and the minimum percentage transfer requirements affect whether or not the transaction will be treated as nontaxable.

2. Stock-related transactions require that the buyer acquire at least 80 percent of the voting and nonvoting stock of the seller. The IRS contends that this level of ownership enables the buyer to obtain *control* over the seller, which is one requirement of a nontaxable transaction.

3. The sold business entity must be assumed to continue as an operational entity into the future, and as such complies with the *continuity of interest* requirements of a nontaxable transaction. A stock purchase performed using buyer stock that is transferred to the sellers keeps the sellers interested in the combined buying entity's future performance because the future share values are dependent on future combined entity performance.

The IRS reserves the right to restructure a nontaxable transaction as taxable if the transaction appears questionable. For example, assume that a company is sold to a buyer in exchange for buyer shares of stock. Assume also that the buying company immediately liquidates the purchased assets after the transaction is completed. The IRS might look at the acquisition as a way of avoiding tax on the liquidation of the sold company and disallow the nontaxable nature of the transaction.

Remember that liquidated asset proceeds are taxed at shareholder personal tax levels (up to 39.6 percent), whereas transferred shares are not immediately subject to tax. When shares are later sold, they might only be subject to the lower (20 percent) capital gains tax. It is in the seller share-holder's best financial interest to have the buyer liquidate the sold company instead of the shareholders doing so. There is no intended continuity of in-terest in this transaction, and the IRS might well restructure this transaction as taxable should this type of circumstance be involved.

TYPE A REORGANIZATION

Type A reorganizations can occur as either a *statutory merger* or a *consoli-dation*. The statutory merger involves the transfer of all seller assets and lia-bilities to the buyer in exchange for stock in the buyer company. Only buyer stock remains after completion of the merger. A consolidation occurs when two companies transfer their assets to a third newly created company and re-ceive stock in the new company in exchange for the asset transfer. Stock in the two prior companies is retired and ceases to exist, and only the newly formed company stock remains. Here are a few salient points pertaining to Type A reorganizations:

1. State laws might narrow the restrictions that apply to a Type A reorganization and should be verified for the state(s) involved.

2. The continuity of interest requirements must be met. This means that the sell-ers must receive enough stock in the buying company to keep their interest and attention with respect to future performance and operation of the entity.

3. Stock and other securities, such as debt, can be used in a Type A reorgan-ization, but the continuity of interest requirement must be complied with or the reorganization might come into question.

TYPE B REORGANIZATION

The Type B reorganization essentially turns the acquired company into a subsidiary of the buying company. Seller stock is acquired by the buyer and the seller stock remains in existence with the buyer acquiring a controlling interest in the seller corporation. A few basic requirements must be met to qualify for a Type B reorganization:

1. The buying company must immediately obtain a controlling interest in the ac-quired company which, for IRS purposes, translates into 80 percent or more of acquired company stock voting and non-voting stock.

2. Only buying company voting stock may be traded for selling company stock.

3. Selling company shareholders may not be presented with a cash instead of stock sale option.

There is the possibility of the buyer acquiring *creeping control* in the seller. In this case, the seller stock is acquired in exchange for voting shares in the buyer over a 12-month or less period. The intention of the stock purchases must be for the buyer to obtain a controlling interest (80 percent or more) in the seller.

TYPE C REORGANIZATION

The Type C reorganization covers the transfer of *substantially all* assets to the buyer in exchange for buyer voting stock. Notice that seller stock is not involved in this transaction; only the seller assets are involved.

1. At least 70 percent of the seller's gross assets, or 90 percent of its net assets, must be transferred to the buyer.

2. Transferred assets must be critical to the continuation of the seller's business interests, so we once again see the continuity of interest requirement present itself.

3. All buyer stock involved in the transaction must be voting stock.

4. Eighty percent or more of the fair market value of transferred assets must be paid for with buyer voting stock. The remaining up to 20 percent fair market value can be paid in the form of seller liabilities assumed by the buyer, cash, or other buyer property that is transferred to the seller. This type of nonstock transfer to the seller is called *boot*. (Note: Boot is a term that applies to all types of reorganizations and is not exclusively related to the Type C.) The assumed liabilities can have a value of more than 20 percent of the asset consideration paid to the seller as long as no other form of boot is included in the transaction.

5. Sellers must pay tax on the received boot portion of the transaction, but the stock portion is nontaxable until the received shares are subsequently sold.

6. Buyers are typically not required to obtain shareholder approval to perform a Type C reorganization. Seller shareholders will have to approve the sale because the selling company is basically selling the assets needed to continue in existence.

The buyer must account for the acquired assets as a purchase which means transferring assets at fair market value which typically means incurring future depreciation expenses.

TYPE D REORGANIZATION

Type D reorganizations are divided into two major categories: *acquisitive* and *divisive,* with the divisive type having several subcategories under it. The breakup of AT&T was a Type D reorganization. The acquisitive type is commonly referred to as a *reverse merger* in that Company A transfers assets and stock to Company B in exchange for a controlling interest in the stock of Company B. In essence, Company A shareholders become the primary owners of Company B even though Company A usually ceases to exist after the transaction and Company B shares remain in existence.

1. Company A shareholders must receive enough shares in Company B to have a controlling interest in Company B operation. Controlling interest is assumed to mean at least 80 percent of Company B voting and nonvoting shares.

2. Any Company A shares or assets remaining after the reorganization are transferred to Company B shareholders.

3. If a company qualifies for both Type C and Type D reorganization, it should be considered a Type D.

Assume that Company A wants to transfer all of its assets to Company B and that the Company A shareholders want a controlling interest in Company B when the reorganization is finished. This is a Type D reorganization. If Company B has 10,000 outstanding shares and transfers 8,500 of them to Company A shareholders as part of the transaction, giving the prior Company A shareholders a controlling interest in Company B, then the basic requirements of the Type D acquisitive reorganization have been met.

Divisive Type D reorganizations separate the parts of a corporation into smaller business units which then become separate from the original corporation. Divisive reorganizations can be *spin-offs, split-offs,* or *split-ups.* For the purposes of this discussion, assume that Company A is the initial company pursuing a Type D divisive reorganization and that it has created a separate corporation, Company S, into which it has transferred the assets of the prior Company A business unit intended for separation. In exchange for this transfer of assets, Company A receives Company S shares of value equal to the assets transferred to Company S and retains a controlling interest in

Company S. The handling of the Company S shares determines the type of divisive reorganization—whether it is a spin-off, split-off, or split-up.

A divisive Type D reorganization must meet four basic criteria:

1. Both the initial entity (Company A) and the divided entity (Company S) must remain actively engaged in business activities after the division.

2. Company A must issue stocks to its shareholders so that the shareholders obtain a controlling interest in the divided entity(ies), Company S.

3. Company A can transfer only stock or securities of the new subsidiary(ies) to shareholders.

4. The intention of the division must not be to avoid tax payments from either Company A or the divided entity(ies).

A spin-off provides Company A shareholders with shares in Company S in adequate numbers and value to compensate Company A shareholders for the value spun off to Company S. Company A shareholders now own shares in both Company A and Company S.

A split-up divides the assets of Company A into two completely new corporations, Company S and Company T for example. Company A assets are transferred to both Company S and Company T, with shares in each company being provided to the prior Company A, which now owns a controlling interest in both companies. Company A then dissolves, transferring Company S and Company T stock to Company A shareholders, in proportion with their prior Company A investment, as part of the liquidation. Split-ups are typically used when a corporation has warring internal factions that just don't seem to get along and would be financially more successful without each other. One faction goes to Company S and the other goes to Company T.

A split-off is like a split-up, except that Company A remains in existence and a new Company S is created. Company A shareholders then either obtain shares in Company S in exchange for their existing Company A shares or simply retain their existing Company A shares. When completed, some shareholders remain Company A shareholders while others turn into Company S shareholders. A split-off is another effective way to separate internal factions that conflict more than cooperate.

For these and other transactions, any boot in the form of cash or other property will be subject to applicable shareholder taxes.

TYPE E REORGANIZATION

Type E reorganization involves the modification of the corporation's financial structure and does not involve the acquisition or division of the corporation undergoing the Type E reorganization. Exchanging one stock type for another would constitute a Type E restructuring. For example, exchanging common stock for preferred stock would involve financial restructuring but would not involve an acquisition of any type.

TYPE F REORGANIZATION

Companies that transfer their corporate jurisdiction from one location to another undergo a Type F reorganization. Transferring a corporation from one state to incorporate in another would constitute a Type F reorganization as would a name change.

TYPE G REORGANIZATION

Type G reorganizations are done in conjunction with some type of bankruptcy proceeding. This is a complicated process and is beyond the scope of this book.

Buyer Pooling of Interests: The Twelve Conditions

Not every buyer qualifies to take advantage of the pooling of interests method of accounting. Specific criteria must be met to qualify for pooling of interests, and sellers who are set up as viable candidates for pooling may find themselves more valuable at sale time. This section outlines the various requirements associated with pooling of interests.

There are twelve basic conditions that must be met for the buyer to be able to use pooling of interests accounting methods in recording an acquisition. You will see as you work your way through this listing that the two companies must be essentially independent for a period of two years prior to the transaction, that voting rights and stock must transfer from the seller to the buyer in a percentage consistent with SellerCo percentage ownership, and that BuyerCo must have the intention of continuing with SellerCo's essential operations.

Condition One: The Companies Must Be Autonomous

The two companies involved in the transaction must not have been a subsidiary of another corporation for a two-year period prior to the initiation of the acquisition plan. A subsidiary is defined as a company in which another corporation owns 90 percent or more of the company voting stock. Subsidiaries of new companies are exempted from this two-year ruling. The two-year period timing is dependent on the date of initiation of the transaction, which is determined by the date on which a irrevocable offer is made, subject to specific conditions which must later be met.

Condition Two: The Companies Must Be Independent of Each Other

There must be no more than a 10 percent voting stock ownership of any involved company with any of the other involved companies.

Condition Three: Transaction Completion in One Year

The entire transaction must be consummated (completed) within one year of the initiation date. The initiation date is defined in Condition One above.

Condition Four: Voting Common Stock Must Be Exchanged

The purchase must be funded with buyer common stock with voting rights identical to those of the majority of its already outstanding shares. Over 90 percent of the selling company's voting stock must be acquired as part of the transaction.

Condition Five: No Change in Common Equity Interest

The structure of equity interest in any involved companies cannot be changed for the two-year period prior to the initiation date, or during the period between the initiation date and transaction consummation. Changes in structure would include the issuance of new stock, the exchange of stock, or changing the terms associated with a stock option plan.

Condition Six: Limited Stock Reacquisition

Involved companies can purchase their own stock from shareholders, so-called *treasury stock*, during a two-year period prior to initiation as long as the acquisition was done for reasons other than to facilitate the acquisition. This limitation also applies to the period between the initiation and consummation dates of the transaction. If a publicly held company acquires stock with the intention of reissuing it in a way not related to the pending pooling of interests acquisition, then the stock should not be deemed *tainted* and should not disqualify the participants from pooling of interests.

Condition Seven: Static Ratio of Ownership Interest

SellerCo shareholders must hold the same ratio of ownership in the new entity as the other SellerCo shareholders participating in the transaction. Assume that two shareholders hold one percent and two percent, respectively, of SellerCo stock before the transaction. If the first shareholder eventually owns 0.5 percent of BuyerCo voting stock after the transaction then the shareholder must wind up owning twice that, or one percent, to keep the relative percentages in alignment. In addition, the same form or consideration must be provided to all SellerCo shareholders in exchange for their stock.

Condition Eight: Voting Rights Preservation

Shareholders must retain unrestricted voting rights in BuyerCo. These rights must transfer from SellerCo to BuyerCo shareholders on a prorated basis based on their percentage ownership of total outstanding shares in SellerCo. This condition is tied to Condition Seven outlined previously. BuyerCo voting stock can be issued to retire SellerCo restricted stock without negating pooling of interests availability.

Condition Nine: Consummation Represents 100 Percent Completion

The entire transaction must be completed upon the final consummation date and in no way be dependent on pending future issuance of shares, other securities, or additional consideration.

Condition Ten: Combined Stock Cannot Be Reacquired

There must be no agreement on behalf of the combined company (BuyerCo) to repurchase or retire any of the shares issued as part of the acquisition. SellerCo shareholders who received BuyerCo shares as part of the transaction can sell their shares to another company or person as long as that new buyer is not BuyerCo. This subsequent selling of shares by the new BuyerCo shareholder must be completely voluntary on their part and not a contingency of the transaction for the pooling of interests opportunity to be preserved.

Condition Eleven: Financial Arrangements Are Precluded

BuyerCo must be careful that it does not provide additional consideration to one SellerCo shareholder that is not also available to other SellerCo shareholders. Examples of special consideration could include special loan arrangements, employment, and consulting agreements secured by the issued BuyerCo shares, among others.

Condition Twelve: Period of Holding of Significant Assets

The combined company can have no plans to sell a substantial portion of the acquired assets within a two-year period of the consummation date. Disposal of prior SellerCo assets as part of the normal course of SellerCo business or with the intent of eliminating duplicate facilities of other operating capabilities does not negate the usage of the pooling of interests method.

Special Small Business Tax Benefits On Sale

Qualifying small business owners who sell their business may have a substantial tax benefit waiting for them thanks to the 1993 Tax Reform Act. The act enables a qualified small business stockholder to exclude 50 percent of any gain received on the sale or exchange of their stock. The tax savings to the selling owner with this type of tax break can be substantial. This section takes a look at the requirements needed to take advantage of what could be a very special opportunity for selling small business owners.

To qualify for the C-type small corporation special tax benefit, the selling company must be a qualified small business, which is one that meets the following criteria:

1. It must be a Subchapter C corporation, which is the bulk of corporations. Subchapter S corporations do not quality for the benefit.

2. Stock being sold must have been obtained upon its initial issuance in exchange for money, property, or services provided directly to the company by the shareholder. The shares can transfer from the company to the shareholder through an underwriter without disqualifying the benefit.

3. The company that issues the stock must meet specific qualifications at the time of stock issuance and for the substantial portion of all other times after. Those qualifications include not being any of the following:

    a. a Domestic International Sales Corporation (DISC) or former DISC

    b. a regulated investment company, such as a mutual fund

    c. a Real Estate Investment Trust (REIT)

    d. a cooperative

    e. a Real Estate Mortgage Investment Conduit (REMIC)

    f. a corporation that (directly or through a subsidiary) has a possessions credit election in effect.

4. The corporation cannot own real property with a value that exceeds 10 percent of the corporation's total asset value.

5. Stocks and securities owned by the corporation cannot have a value that exceeds 10 percent of the total corporation assets minus liabilities.

6. More than 80 percent of the corporation's assets must be used in actively conducting one or more qualified trades or businesses. Qualified trades or business include all businesses except the following:

    a. health care service

    b. law

    c. engineering

    d. architecture

    e. accounting

    f. actuarial science

    g. performing arts

    h. consulting

    i. athletics

    j. financial services and/or brokerage services

    k. businesses that rely on the reputation of one or more employees as its principal asset

    l. banking, financing, investing, or other similar firms

    m. insurance firms

    n. businesses involved with the operation of a restaurant, motel, hotel, or similar venture

o. farming

p. any business that involves the extraction or depletion of a specific resource

As you can see, there are some substantial restrictions involved with obtaining this investment tax break, but the break can be substantial if the seller qualifies. If you are the buyer, knowing that the seller qualifies for this break might provide some negotiating room with respect to price and deal structure if this tax break can fund as much as 50 percent of the tax impact.

ESOP Special Advantages for Selling Owners

This section is really aimed at those sellers who own their own companies. There is a substantial tax advantage received by sellers who sell their companies to ESOPs in that the sale may well be completely tax-free to you. Here are some of the basics from a seller's perspective. More ESOP establishment details are provided in chapter 7, "Strategic Synergy and Transaction Structures."

1. The seller must sell between 30 percent and 100 percent of the company to the ESOP.

2. You must have held the stock for more than three years prior to the ESOP sale.

3. You must invest the ESOP sale proceeds in other United States corporation securities.

4. Applicable income taxes will be due at the later date when you sell any securities purchased with the ESOP proceeds.

5. Your company cannot be publicly traded at the time of the ESOP.

6. Companies in which you invest cannot derive more than 25 percent of their revenues from passive investments, and at least 50 percent of company assets must be used in the conduct of trade or business. In essence, the invested-in company cannot simply be a financial holding company but must perform some type of operational function. Most major United States corporations, other than financial corporations, will qualify for this requirement.

The beauty of this approach from the seller's perspective is that the seller gets to invest the sale proceeds into a diversified investment portfolio which may include any number of different companies' stocks. If the company had been sold to a single entity, then the proceeds from the sale would likely include stock in the buying company, which puts a large portion of the purchase price in a single, nondiversified investment portfolio. To diversify the portfolio, the seller would have to sell acquisition-transferred shares, take the tax hit, and then reinvest in other stocks. The ESOP approach enables the seller to obtain a safer, more diversified portfolio without paying tax on the sale price. The employees get a vested interest in the performance of their employer, which often turns out to be the motivation needed to generate above-average returns.

The Tax Implications of Liquidating

A special note is warranted here regarding the tax implications to the selling company of first a sale of assets and then liquidation of the company, passing liquidation proceeds to the shareholders. The double taxation involved with this transaction can turn more of the sale proceeds over to the IRS than is retained by the shareholders.

1. When the corporation sells the asset, it must pay tax on the gain obtained from the sale. This may well impose a 35 percent federal tax fee on the asset sale proceeds. State tax rates vary.

2. When the corporation liquidates, it transfers the liquidated assets and/or money to the shareholders, who must then pay tax on the received money and/or assets. Depending on the holding period of the liquidated company shares, the proceeds from the liquidation may qualify for long-term capital gains tax treatment.

A special case exists when a corporate subsidiary liquidates, passing the proceeds from the liquidation to the parent company or a close corporation major shareholder who owns at least 80 percent of the voting stock. In this particular case, the transfer of assets to the holder of the 80 percent ownership (the 80 percent distributee) is tax-free, but the tax applicable at the later sale date will be payable when the received assets are subsequently sold. This clause is provided to avoid triple taxation in the liquidation of a controlled corporation subsidiary in that liquidated assets would otherwise be taxed at the subsidiary level, the parent corporation level, and then again at the shareholder level.

This clause does, however, present an interesting loophole for majority owners of closely held corporations. The closely held corporation can transfer its assets to the 80 percent distributee, who is likely the sole owner of the corporation, who then holds the assets for later sale, at which time the then-applicable tax is due. The corporation does not have to pay tax on the sale of the assets because the assets were passed to the shareholder on a tax-free basis. Personal tax is still due upon asset sale, but that is only one tax instead of two, which is always good news.

Chapter Summary

This chapter took a detailed look at the accounting methods used for recording an acquisition. It reviewed the financial statement and tax implications for a buyer and detailed the tax impact of the sale for the seller. The controversy surrounding the methods of accounting for an acquisition, pooling of interests and purchase accounting, was presented. The purported benefits of the pooling of interests method of accounting for the acquisition were presented in comparison to the alternative purchase method of accounting. FASB is considering the elimination of the pooling of interests method and readers are advised to verify the current status of the accepted procedures when determining the method right for their particular situation. The twelve specific criteria that must be met to qualify for pooling of interests were also presented.

Several tax-free reorganization plans, along with the required criteria for qualifying for tax-free transaction treatment, were presented. The tax and employee benefits of selling to an ESOP instead of a corporate buyer were also presented. The double taxation implications of selling assets and then liquidating the corporation, passing the remaining cash to shareholders, were investigated. It is important to remember that the structure of the transaction and the specific nature of the buyer and seller will also impact the tax status of the transaction. The tax laws might well create a tax premium, or benefit, that will be of value when placing a price on the purchased company.

Privately held buyers, who typically try to minimize income taxes paid by maximizing expenses to minimize income, might prefer the purchase method because it enables higher future depreciation expenses due to possibly higher asset fair market values and the inclusion of goodwill amortization. Public companies that intend to use the pooling of interests method in reporting a transaction are advised to remember that the form of accounting cannot make up for a poorly performing posttransaction environment. Emphasis should first be placed on the value of the acquisition to the organization as a whole, and only then should the method of accounting be determined. Believing that the method of accounting can artificially increase or decrease share prices does not seem to be validated by market reactions.

9

Detailed Marketing and Sales Evaluation

Prior chapters reviewed some of the major financial considerations involved with assessment of a target company. This type of financial analysis is a critical aspect of a company's valuation but it is one that provides a primarily historical perspective. Buyers purchase a company more for its expected future benefits to the firm than for what the purchased company has done in the past. Creating a credible version of this future perspective requires an extensive look at the marketing and sales aspects of the target company. After all, future target company revenues will come from the success of future sales and marketing programs. A historical look at the success of these programs helps to define strengths and weaknesses associated with the revenue generation aspects of the target company and provides a framework in which to assess future performance claims.

Future overall financial performance can be enhanced somewhat by financial manipulations and cost-cutting, but this type of financial fix is short lived. Reliable future financial enhancement comes from generating increased revenues while controlling costs. It is always easier and more fun to manage spending for a company experiencing annually increasing sales revenues. This chapter and Chapter 10, "Special Technology Marketing Considerations," lay the groundwork for understanding and evaluating the target company's sales and marketing programs during due diligence. This chapter deals primarily with the general aspects of a marketing and sales assessment that are applicable to most companies, whereas the next chapter adds important points that specifically relate to technology companies.

Many people feel that the marketing and sales aspects of due diligence are the most important, because sales must exist for a company to succeed. Understanding the topics presented in these two chapters will greatly improve the buyer's ability to assess a target's sales activities as they will relate to the future. These chapters also help sellers understand the sales and marketing fit between their company and that of the buyer. If a buyer highly values a marketing fit, the buyer will pay more to acquire a company with an ideal fit. Sellers may have to outline that fit for the buyer to obtain the highest possible selling price.

Defining the Market Condition

No matter how well a company is run it must exist within its market's macroenvironment. The overall health of that macroenvironment, combined with the target company's specific position in that market, directly impacts the expected future performance of the company. A company with poor operational performance might survive if its external macroenvironment is robust and growing, while this same company might end up bankrupt if the external macroenvironment takes a severe negative turn. This information is summarized graphically in Matrix 9.1.

A few items must be evaluated to complete a comprehensive assessment

Matrix 9.1 Company-to-Market Comparison Barometer

		Market Characteristics	
		Growing Market	Shrinking Market
Company Performance	Excellent	More company research required to determine source of positive growth.	Probably a well managed company or one with highly positive extenuating circumstances.
	Poor	Probably a poorly managed company or one with highly negative extenuating circumstances.	Poor performance in a shrinking market is not uncommon. This company may not present a viable acquisition target unless further due diligence reveals hidden value.

of an overall market's current health and future growth prospects. If you are already in the industry segment of the targeted company you may, and probably will, have many of these facts at your fingertips. If not, you will find it worth your time and expense to accurately define them. Remember that you are, fundamentally, trying to assess the target company's future sales revenue performance prospects and to determine if those revenue expectations are based on wishful thinking or based on viable marketing-based best-guesses. Here are a few questions that must be answered when performing a market assessment:

1. What is the current overall market size and is it growing, stagnant, or shrinking? The prospects for greater future revenues is always better within a growing market than in a shrinking one.

2. What is the target company's percentage market share of its industry segment and has its share been increasing or decreasing? The larger the target company's percentage market share, the better its position to capitalize on positive market growth. It is also more likely to suffer on a percentage basis should a market decline come to pass.

3. Are there any pending technology changes that would dramatically upset the status quo within the industry? Technology changes can make or break both industries and companies and you want to understand where the target company fits in this continuum.

4. Is there any pending legislation or litigation, such as a class action suit, that would dramatically upset the status quo for the industry? Major lawsuits and settlements, particularly those associated with a class action suit, can seriously distract a company at a minimum or even put the company out of business if it loses the case. Knowing what you are getting into in this area is always the best remedy.

5. What is the condition of the largest competitors? Does the target company currently command a sizable lead over its closest market competition or is the lead narrow and shrinking?

6. What will be the competitive reaction to your acquiring the target company and how will that affect the overall relative industry relationships? Some competitors will consolidate with other companies once your acquisition is public knowledge. Instead of dealing with only this market's competition, you might find yourself dealing with larger marketing gorillas from your own industry or others.

Chapter 18, "Performing Due Diligence," along with the Due Diligence Checklist appendix in this volume provide a more detailed listing of topics that should be considered during the evaluation stages of the process.

Much of this marketing and strategic information is readily available from trade publications except for the sales information related to privately held corporations. Don't necessarily expect to get irrefutable numbers, because much marketing data is based on projection, extrapolation, and derived information instead of from detailed surveys. Make sure to keep your eyes open for information that might appear from the most unlikely sources. An Army intelligence officer told me that most pieces of information, by themselves, mean nothing. But when used in conjunction with each other, all of these seemingly unrelated pieces of information can provide incredible intelligence insight.

An October 26, 1999 *Chicago Tribune* Business section article (page 3) provides some insight into the domestic U.S. computer market and the relative performance of Dell and Compaq.

> Dell, based in Round Rock, Texas, sold nearly 2 million PCs from July through September, grabbing a 17.1 percent share of the U.S. market, up from a 13.4 percent share in the year-earlier third quarter, according to research firm Dataquest. . . . Compaq, based in Houston, sold 1.78 million computers, giving it a 15.3 percent market share, up from 15 percent a year earlier. IDC (International Data Corporation) also said Dell finished ahead of Compaq in the July-September period. . . . Both noted that Compaq continued to hold the lead for global sales.

Taking a look at this information we can glean some overall industry facts.

1. 2 million units, totaling 17.1 percent of the United States market for unit sales, implies that the total third-quarter unit sales were 2,000,000 divided by 0.171 = 11,695,906.

2. Performing the same calculation on the Compaq percentage unit and total unit sales (1,780,000 units divided by 0.153 = 11,633,986 total unit sales) implies that some round off is involved in the calculations to provide the approximately 60,000-unit difference. The two numbers appear to be in the same ballpark indicating that they are consistent to each other, although they might not be exact.

3. Dell's market share increased over the prior twelve-month period from 13.4 percent to 17.1 percent, or 3.7 percent. Compaq's market share increased by 0.3 percent, from 15 percent to 15.3 percent over the same twelve-month period. The total market share owned by both Dell and Compaq increased by 4 percent and they did not take market share from each other since both increased, indicating that some other competitor(s) must have lost 4 percent market share over the same period.

4. Find another article that provides an average industry sale price per PC. This data might be directly or indirectly provided in the Dell annual report. Multiply the average price per PC by the total PC market calculated at 11,633,986 units using the more conservative Compaq figures.

5. Finding another article that outlines the percentage unit sales or dollar sales growth over prior or projected future years provides expected market revenues numbers.

6. Looking at Dell and Compaq's historical percentage market share figures might indicate who was gaining or losing market share in the past. These past figures provide some basis for future sales revenue projections for these two market leaders.

This information was obtained from public sources and should be readily available with a few hours of research either at the library or online. And this does not include any information from industry newspapers, but only general public information provided by the *Chicago Tribune*. This information provides a basis for evaluating the projected future performance of another, smaller player in Dell and Compaq's industry segment. If this smaller company made projected revenue claims that cannot be backed up with percentage market share required to meet those claims, then something is seriously amiss. Either your overall market projections are inaccurate (which is possible) or their projections are wildly optimistic (which is also very possible). It is up to you to determine which is the most likely culprit.

You must take action to determine answers to these important questions. You might have to purchase a privately funded report to get information you trust. You might need to send a team of people on a research mission to find the specific pieces of information you need to answer your questions. Simply keep your eye on your ultimate target, which is to provide a reasonable assessment of the target industry's growth prospects and to glean some understanding of the target company's likely share of that future growth.

Market Maturation Stages

Markets and products go through maturation stages and each stage of the maturation process comes with its own set of indicators. Much of this information is adapted from that presented by Michael Porter in his classic *Competitive Strategy: Techniques for Analyzing Industries and Competitors.*[1] I highly recommend this book for any of you who are interested in developing a solid understanding of competitive strategic planning concepts and tactics. Markets go through the stages listed in Matrix 9.2, with the conditions listed as indicators of that particular stage's existence.

There are dozens of other factors that indicate the overall status of a market. Any one factor by itself may not indicate the start of a market maturing phase, but a combination of factors consistent with a given market stage should be investigated as if possibly true to best ensure the catching of the stage onset at the earliest possible time. Assume, for example, that a detailed evaluation of a target company's customer buying patterns shows a decline in the number of repeat customers and a large increase in new customers. Couple this with the fact that the target company has not introduced a successful new product in the last three years. This combination might well indicate a product mix that is in the declining maturity stage with the new customers simply being those interested in purchasing this older technology at a bargain price.

Verifying the average price per order might show that the company is offering price reductions to get new business to keep it afloat while its products go into decline. Purchasing this company based on historical sales projections would be a huge mistake since expected future revenues cannot match historical levels if this example's declining market scenario outlined is accurate.

De Facto and International Standards

Rapidly changing markets also create standards that are accepted by the industry as a whole but not really sanctioned by some of the standards bodies, such as the International Standards Organization (ISO) or others. In many

---

[1] See Michael E. Porter, *Competitive Strategy: Techniques for Analyzing Industries and Competitors* (New York: Free Press, 1998).

Matrix 9.2 Market Maturity Stages

Characteristics	Market Maturity Stages		
	Emerging	Mature	Declining
Market Growth Rate	High	Low	Negative
Number of new competitive entries	Many unless held off specifically by legal constraints such as a patent.	Competition shifts to a service and price basis due to more experienced and numerous competitors and products.	Extensive consolidation or leaving the market.
Number of new customers	Many new customers	Many repeat customers	Shrinking customer base as they move to newer technologies.
Economic barriers to entry	Potentially high economic and legal barriers.	Lower economic and legal barriers	Companies looking for financially viable way to exit the market.
Rate of technology change	High change rate	Nominal change rate with changes coming in cost reduction technologies.	Technological stagnation as it is replaced by newer technology
Relative certainty of projections	Highly uncertain environment	Relatively certain environment	Uncertain environment resulting from unknowns such as rate of decline.

cases a technology becomes an officially sanctioned international standard long after it has already been adopted as an industry, or de facto, standard. Examples of accepted official standards would be the IEEE 802.3 specification that defines the local area networking technology currently referred to as Ethernet. This standard was hammered out by consensus of the membership of the Institute of Electrical and Electronic Engineers (IEEE) and was eventually adopted as the de facto standard for most local area network installations. Other standards competed for this revered market position, such as Token Ring, but Ethernet certainly was the historical winner, with other network technologies such as 100BaseT now enjoying general market acceptance, expanding on the conceptual framework accepted with the Ethernet-related standards.

A de facto standard that we all know about is the Microsoft Windows operating system. The only standards board that regulates the use of the various Windows products such as Windows 3.1, Windows 95, Windows NT, Windows 98, and Windows 2000 is Microsoft, with a little "help" from the Justice Department in recent years. Even though this operating system might not have been through any standards committee review process, it is clearly the standard upon which most current application developers base their software products. Why? Simply because the available market of PC users running a Windows operating system is huge and growing daily. If you are going to spend the time developing a software product it makes sense to develop it for the operating systems showing the largest installed base for potential future purchase.

There are a large number of de facto standards that exist in technology areas and many will be presented in later chapters, as applicable. My point here is to highlight the unique set of market conditions that exist in the technology areas that might not exist in other industries. Much of this de facto standards adoption evolves naturally from the fact that technological change and market acceptance happen quickly in technology fields. Often, this change happens faster than the standards committees can create the standards. There are other areas, however, where standardization created the basis for large market growth such as that seen with the Internet. Without the existence of the TCP/IP networking standards suite, I highly doubt that the Internet would have evolved as the incredible juggernaut it has become. Instead of enjoying the benefits of a consistent networking protocol standard, we would probably live in a world of mixed protocols, mixed vendor messages about who has the best products, and little network-wide consistency.

Standards are important to the technology industry, and understanding the types of standards adhered to by your target company's products is critical to understanding that company's relationship to the rest of the industry. A company that publicly promotes itself as being a technology leader while still using technology that is a few generations old is likely fooling itself regarding its level of market leadership. A progressive company that is unprofitably using new technology to address niche markets may simply need the redirection that a larger, more experienced buyer can provide to truly capitalize on its internal development expertise.

Defining the Company's Marketing Position

Focus is a critical aspect of business life and success. Without focus, energies are easily diverted into actions and steps that, although filling up the day with busy action, do not tend to directly move the company closer to its ultimate goals. Companies that are market-driven tend to define an overall marketing intention that is then supported by the company's other activities. How a company defines itself in the minds of consumers is critical to a prospective buyer because that consumer perception will be purchased with the company. Whether that perception will transfer to the buying company completely intact, or preferably with positive synergistic effects attached, is part of any effective due diligence process. Not understanding the market position of the purchased company and simply looking and the financial information could spell future failure.

Assume, for example, that the buying company is one specifically oriented toward the retail consumer of computer products. The targeted selling company is one with a high technology development team that is well-funded from a large R&D budget and rarely deals with a consumer market. Their products are sold to intermediate companies who then convert this advanced technology into viable consumer products. Consumer companies tend to be highly customer service-oriented, while R&D organizations work more like universities with longer, less immediate time frames. Although the selling company might have a very attractive financial picture to offer, it might not be the right purchase for this particular buyer. If the purchased company starts to distract the buyer from its core business, which is consumer sales, then the purchase could cost the buyer more than the agreed-upon purchase price. Future customer relations could suffer, future sales could suffer, and both the buyer and seller could find their combined operation less attractive than the two premerged separate entities.

In addition, the general marketplace might become confused when looking at the merged companies. The perception associated with the buyer is one of high service, reasonable price, and quick delivery of consumer products. The perception with the acquired R&D-oriented company is one of high technology, guru employees, and creative minds who rarely are seen in public. If the buyer is not careful, consumers could interpret this acquisition as a move by the buyer into the R&D area creating some doubt about its retail consumer commitment.

The buyer could specifically design a marketing program that capitalizes on the strengths of both companies creating a consumer perception that future products will be better from the acquisition. Assume that the buyer has decided to specifically target the advanced performance video design desktop market and the seller's products specifically address that market. The buyer could treat this acquisition as a vertical integration merger with the intention of creating a tighter link between the video technology of the acquired company and the rest of the desktop system. Serious video desktop workstations users might think this an excellent move and look favorably on the acquisition.

My point here is simply that a company must understand its market position from the consumer's perspective, and capitalize on that perception to its best benefit. When acquiring another firm, the integration of the two company's market positions must be evaluated for either positive or negative future impact. The acquisition of WordPerfect by Novell is an example of what turned out to be a mismatch that cost both companies. Novell is best known as a local area networking software company. It designs, sells, and supports networking software and equipment that acts as the backbone upon which applications function. WordPerfect produced application software for the office environment. Novell's intention appeared to be the integration of WordPerfect's application software on top of its networking backbone. This could have been a great move, except the move seemed to distract both teams such that both suffered as part of the purchase. WordPerfect was eventually sold to Corel Corporation, who put a lot of time and effort into bringing the WordPerfect products back up to expected contemporary technological standards while also providing some integration with its existing and successful graphics software products.

The Novell purchase (merger) of WordPerfect in 1994 was executed for 59 million shares of Novell stock and options for an estimated value of $1.4 billion. Corel later purchased WordPerfect from Novell in 1996 for $124 million. This is the type of acquisition-based return on investment nobody wants to see on their financial record. The WordPerfect suite of products appears to be a better fit for Corel, which already develops and sells desktop application products than for Novell, which is a networking company and a completely different business segment.

Could it have worked for Novell and WordPerfect? Possibly, but only with realistic assessments of the problems waiting in the wings when you take two companies with very different market positioning and attempt to present them with a common face. Always remember that predicting the future is as much conjecture as it is fact, often with more weight is on the conjecture side. Obtaining realistic assessments and understanding helps to sway the pendulum from away from conjecture and toward fact. Use this type of evaluation exercise to serve a variety of purposes: (1) to familiarize yourself more with the company, its customers, and its products; (2) to familiarize yourself with the markets into which the company sells its products; (3) it gives you a chance to work with the target company personnel on a specific project with a specific, well-defined purpose, a good way to test the viability of future projects in a postacquisition environment.

The Standard Industrial Code and the North American Industry Classification Standard

Talking about a market is one thing. Actually specifically defining that market is another thing altogether. If you are working with a one-product company the definition is relatively straightforward. How do you classify a company like Microsoft, with its business hands in so many different pies ranging from operating systems, networking software, databases, Internet products, and even equipment? The process gets complicated quickly and requires more definition and investigation.

A number of entities provide market information covering overall market growth, historical and projected information, sales by major competitors, and expected technology influences. Always remember when reading these reports that someone preparing the report had to make determinations along the way that affect the report outcomes. Understanding the basis for their determinations helps substantially when deciphering the published data.

Until recently, the most commonly used means of delineating business segments was using the Standard Industrial Code (SIC), which divided industry into a set of numeric classifications. SIC was created and managed by the United States Government Office of Management and Budget (OMB). Companies then reported themselves as belonging to a specific SIC and reports were created reporting the aggregate results by SIC. Assume that you wanted to verify industry information for Novell. You could reference Novell in any number of publications and find that its SICs are 7373 (local area network [LAN] systems integrator) and 7372 (prepackaged software). Using these two SICs you could then obtain SIC-specific information for these two Novell-related ones. This approach sounds good in theory, but it had some limitations in practice, especially when referring to technology fields that evolved faster than the SIC classifications were changed. In addition, the SIC classifications were often too general in nature, too arcane to follow, or sometimes so detailed that you had to consolidate different SICs to get a number representative of an industry.

Effective in 1997, the OMB, in conjunction with Canada and Mexico, produced the North American Industry Classification System (NAICS), which applies to not only the United States' businesses but also to Canadian and Mexican businesses as well. A special information sector (sector 51) was added to this classification system to account for rapidly growing business sectors. Companies included in this section transform information into a commodity that is produced and distributed, and activities that provide the means for distributing those products, other than through traditional whole-sale-retail channels. Database and directory publishing (subsector 514), software publishing (subsector 511), and online information services (subsector 511), among others, are included in this 51 sector. To give you an idea of the potential complexity of using this classification system, subsector 541511 is used to classify companies that design software to meet the needs of specific users, which differentiates them from the sector 511 companies that produce standardized software. Computer and electronic product manufacturing (subsector 334) was also added as a special section as were others that are not directly related to high technology fields.

Coming back to the beginning premise of this section, remember that the intent of segmentation is to create some way of investigating, or contacting, a specific group of people or companies with similar characteristics. The SIC and NAICS provide a first start at obtaining general market characteristics because these divisions are typically used by governmental and other research organizations.

Various Market Research Sources

Here is a partial listing of research companies and resources that will get you started if you are not already using a market research firm. All site links were checked at the time of the writing, but as we all know, Web links change.

- Frost & Sullivan, www.frost.com (old-line technology research firm that provides original research reports for a fee)

- GartnerGroup, gartner5.gartnerweb.com/public/static/home/home.html (provides original research reports that are frequently referenced in the public media for a fee)

- International Data Corporation (IDC), www.idc.com (an original research company often referenced in the public media)

- Sage Research, www.sageresearch.com/default.html (provides research reports for a fee)

- The Investext Group, www.investext.com (a central clearing house for reports from many other research firms for a fee)

- Market Search, www.marketsearch-dir.com (provides a listing of reports created by other marketing research companies)

- @Researchinfo.com, www.researchinfo.com/index.html (you can get a listing of various domestic and international research firms from this site)

- Barchart.com, www.barchart.com (provides stock analysis tools for investigating a publicly traded stock)

This listing is by no means extensive, but it will at least get you started in finding the firm that has researched the specific topic of interest to your particular situation.

Market Segmentation

Market segmentation is arguably the most powerful marketing tool in use today. It enables the detailed analysis of the primary buying candidates for a company's products and services. Segmentation can be done by any number of parameters, and the parameters used are usually based on some combination of available data and topic of interest. Demographic data is rapidly becoming one of the most sought-after parameters in today's Internet-driven economy. Knowing whether the buyer is male or female, advanced degreed or not, a parent or not, the owner of a credit card or not, and of a certain income bracket is rapidly becoming the legal tender of the modern information age.

The use of segmentation data in an M&A environment helps to determine the potential strategic fit between the buying company and its potential acquisition targets. Segmentation will likely be analyzed from several different perspectives, with a simple example usage presented here.

1. The buyer will perform an internal segmentation analysis to understand the buying characteristics (demographics) of its own existing customer base.

2. The results of this existing customer base analysis will then be compared against existing and projected market trends.

3. The buyer will then evaluate its current position against that of its competitors in determining its likelihood of gaining or losing market share in future years. Areas where future sales opportunities are in question are areas that require strengthening.

4. The buyer may then choose to acquire another firm to round out what are considered weaknesses in its current and anticipated future offerings.

5. An acquisition target search is undertaken to find possible acquisition target companies that already provide products, services, or market presence in the buyer's deficient segments. The SIC or NAICS for the desired market segment can be used as the first search criteria after which additional criteria such as total sales, location, years in business, and other filtering criteria can be applied.

This is a highly simplified procedure compared to what happens in reality, but one that highlights a relationship between market segmentation and the acquisition process. Without an understanding of the buying company's strengths and weaknesses within specific market segments, the buyer will have difficulty refining the acquisition target search criteria so that a manageable number of potential and viable target companies are uncovered.

The reason that I emphasize this filtering process is that a buyer will filter through potentially hundreds of potential candidates before limiting the search to only a few. The more accurate the early filtering procedures, the better the likelihood of finding a target that will ultimately meet your acquisition requirements. Denzel Rankine, in Chapter Four of his book *A Practical Guide to Acquisitions: How To Increase Your Chances of Success* provides incentive for buyers to perform a systematic analysis of target companies.[2]

1. Based on an AMR/ICME study, 32 percent of companies reported that at least 50 percent of their strategic objectives associated with an acquisition were achieved when the target company search procedure was left to pure opportunism or chance.

---

[2] See Denzel Rankine, *A Practical Guide to Acquisitions: How To Increase Your Chances of Success* (West Sussex, England: Wiley, 1998).

2. The same study states that 54 percent or higher of companies that performed a systematic search and analysis based on a strategic plan reported that over 50 percent of their strategic objectives were achieved.

3. Systematic buyers also tend to find more than one candidate, which provides them a little more flexibility and bargaining power when actually making the offer. Sellers may well become more negotiable if they know that the buyer has more than one viable option on the line.

4. Buyer regret is also assumed to be reduced because the buyers performed the required sorting before making the acquisition. The likelihood of finding another viable deal after committing to a purchase is greatly minimized when a formal search is performed.

Here is an example of the impact of a market segmentation analysis that I performed in the early 1980s when working as a marketing manager for a California high technology firm. I asked the simple question, "Who are our customers and what do they buy?" Much to my amazement, nobody could answer the question in a definitive way. They could provide anecdotal information and a lot of hunches, but nobody could provide specific numbers regarding which of our products sold best into the various customer markets. I ended up manually tabulating the information with a hand calculator, which took a week or so. PCs had not yet been invented at the time and getting customer reports from the MIS department was a glacial experience. The raw data I used came directly from shipment reports. By the way, this was a $30+ million company and a market leader in its specific industry.

When finished I had learned that 95 percent of the company revenues came from the sale of 3 percent of our products, and that the vast majority of our products were sold to a handful of customers. With deregulation of the telephone industry looming on the business horizon, the need to determine the impact of divestiture on these key customers became of paramount importance. Of particular note was the relationship between the models sold and the customers who bought them. Further research obtained from this analysis enabled us to better determine the next generation of product development projects with those development activities being funded by the savings obtained from eliminating development on product lines that generated little or no revenue. This analysis also resulted in the creation of marketing managers who concentrated on our major customers within their market segments.

This simple analysis not only created new products, but also decreased costs while causing a restructuring of the marketing department. Customer knowledge is very powerful and market segmentation is a key technique for accessing that power. The more you understand about both the buying and selling company market segmentation strengths and weaknesses, the more likely you are to find the right acquisition fit. This fit is one that not only makes financial sense but also shows the highest likelihood of providing the desired synergistic and strategic future revenue increases.

International Marketing Influences

The analysis of any technology company in today's business environment must include a look at the possible impact of international activities. These activities might include announcements by international technology companies regarding their marketing plans for the United States, anticipated new product releases, M&A activity that might provide an international company with a domestic United States foothold, or even the geopolitical situation. An Asian earthquake in mid-1990s seriously impacted the future projected import of memory chips from certain Asian supplies. This expected memory chip shortage impacted United States PC manufacturers, causing Dell to announce its intentions to start shipping systems with less RAM memory and apparently prompting Compaq to create a shipment commitment between Compaq and Micron, a chip manufacturer. Independent of how these particular business actions actually turned out for the companies involved, it is evidence that the international situation must be considered when performing a market analysis. A company with an established strategy for dealing with the possible chip shortage would likely be considered a safer investment than one that has not already considered the impact of the Asian earthquake on its suppliers or customers.

Evaluating Their Customer Base

It is very possible for a company to show excellent financial performance while retaining fundamental underlying flaws in its operation. One area where these flaws can appear is within the distribution of sales revenues over the existing customer base. This section takes a closer look at the customer base and methods of analysis that will reveal either the positive or negative aspects of the existing customer sales operation.

A Few Large Customers or a Broad Base?

It is not uncommon for a business, especially a smaller one, to develop a heavy dependence on orders from a single major customer. This initially looks like great news to the smaller company that finds itself in the position of having a major customer with large buying power. But this large customer relationship can distract the vendor from developing other customer relationships that can help the vendor weather the revenue drop associated with the chance of losing this major customer. A first place to start any customer base analysis is with the distribution of product revenues over the existing customer base. I have generally found that the 80/20 rule applies in this regard in that 80 percent of the sales revenue will come from sales to 20 percent of the customer base. The broader this base of customers, the more likely the company is to weather the loss of a few customers. The more narrow this customer base, the more exposure the company has to a serious revenue hit resulting from the loss of this major customer. I am not saying that acquiring major customers is a bad business situation. I am saying, however, that purchasing a company that is heavily dependent on a single major customer puts your and the company's future revenues squarely in that customer's revenue basket.

What if that customer has a downturn in its own business and needs to cut back on orders? What if the customer has an executive management change and the new executives decide to put everything out to competitive bid? What if your company should drop the ball on a few orders and the customer chooses to split its orders that previously exclusively went to your company over several vendors? What if technology changes drive the company to a new methodology that is not offered by your company? The preceding are just a few instances where a change in the customer's business climate could adversely, and dramatically, impact the target company's revenues. Notice that many of the presented instances are completely outside of your control.

Assume that the earlier presented simple revenue-to-customer analysis reveals several major customers who control the bulk of the company's sales revenue. You must now find out as much detailed information as possible about the customer and its history with the target company. Here are a few questions that, when answered, will get you pretty far along the way in evaluating their future potential:

1. Are they a long-standing customer, and what initially started the business relationship?

2. Has the relationship evolved from its early beginnings, or are they simply buying the same products today that they purchased years ago?

3. What is their sales history and has it increased or decreased over the years?

4. Is there a consistent purchase pattern or is it erratic, prompted by their internal business demands?

5. Is there another, informal or formal, relationship between the target company and the customers? This could be in the form of friends or relatives as executive managers in the target and customer companies. You might find that the customer is a partial owner in the target company. It might even be that the target company was once a division of the customer, who spun it off as its own division.

6. What would be the effect of your company's purchasing the target company on the relationship between the target company and its major customers? Is there any type of political, personal, business, or technical reason for these customers to change their historical buying patterns in a postacquisition environment?

7. How stable are these major customers within their own business environments? After all, if they show a drop in revenue you will likely see a drop in their purchases from the target company. Projected customer gross revenue increases could also be good news as long as you are confident that a portion of that increase would come toward the target company.

8. What type of payment history do these major customers have? Do they pay on time or have there been delinquencies?

9. Are there any special contractual arrangements between the target company and these major customers? Do they get special payment terms or highly discounted pricing? Are there any special contractual covenants that could put these contracts in jeopardy?

10. Is there any talk of M&A activity involving any of these major customers? If purchased, would you expect the customers to continue buying from your target company?

You should not consider this listing of ten questions to be the end of your analysis. More than likely, these questions will raise other questions, but you might find that you are comfortable with these customers after simply finding out some of this basic information. The important thing is that you ask the questions, all the time keeping an open mind and ear when listening to the answers. Companies with long-term clients often have tacit arrangements with their customers that they are not consciously aware of; this is particularly true for smaller companies. As an evaluator, you must learn to separate the internal perception of the target's personnel from the objective reality of the situation. This customer analysis process is an excellent first step in creating this understanding.

Product or License Sales Revenue

It is common for technology companies to supplement their products' sales revenues with the sale of technology licenses. This licensing revenue should be shown as a separate line item on the financial statements and is worthy of some investigation. Even if it does not appear on the financial statements, a few questions about possible technology licenses are warranted during any due diligence process. By the way, licensing agreements can be highly profitable. The cost of sales is minimal since it usually only requires some schematics, drawings and other documents, and training.

Anyone with a technology license could be a potential competitor depending on the terms of the licensing agreements. Asking about and understanding the nature of the licensing revenues and agreements is also a mandatory activity for any technology company. You might find out that the target company has a licensing agreement or contractual obligation to support manufacturing activities in a foreign country that is recently undergoing major upheaval. You might choose to purchase the company anyway, but you are better served by knowing this information in advance rather than after the purchase is final.

By Market and/or Technology

Breaking down sales revenue by market segment and/or technology is usually another valuable exercise. In this case you are treating an entire marketplace or technology segment as a major customer. Assume that it is 1988 and you are looking at a company that sells disk compression software that enables a hard disk drive to store more data than its original size. If this technology accounts for a substantial portion of the company's revenues, you would be well-served to evaluate market trends that would affect this revenue stream. When Microsoft added this capability to its standard operating system, the market for the target company's products would have dropped dramatically. My point here is that the customer analysis would not reveal any major customers, but the technology analysis would reveal a major technology segment that, when negatively impacted, would substantially impact target company revenue.

The same type of discussion can be applied to specific market segments. Assume that your target company sells services to the financial industry that enables different financially oriented firms to seamlessly work with each other, basically circumventing the restrictions placed on the industry by the Glass-Steagall Act. The recent repeal of the act by the 1999 Congress would completely change the landscape for the target company's products because financial firms could now simply combine on their own, negating the need for the target company's products.

Treating any technology or market segment as a major customer can keep you from being surprised by unexpected changes in those markets. Try this as a procedure to get you started with your analysis:

1. Start with the revenue by customer analysis you performed earlier in this chapter.

2. Overlay the SIC or NAISC for the customers on top of this analysis so that you now have a breakdown of revenue by classification category. If your information is detailed enough you can try to prorate the revenue by specific category. This is generally not possible, however, so I suggest applying the total revenue to all customer-applicable classifications at once. Remember that you are essentially looking for the classification categories that represent the majority of your customers and their potential future revenues.

3. Determine trends that might exist in these classification by using the market research resources presented earlier in this chapter. Are there major regulatory changes happening within any of the classifications? Is major M&A consolidation or divestiture happening within the industry? Are international companies buying into the industry?

4. How will these anticipated trends affect the salability of the target company's offerings?

By Geography

Depending on the buyer's goals, analyzing sales by geography may provide important information to the M&A process. Depending on the company, its sales may be geographically located simply by the nature of the business. Retail outlets, for example, tend to draw the majority of their business from the local community. Computer component manufacturers will likely show a widely dispersed geographic pattern to its revenue generation activities. Or, if you are component supplier in Austin, Texas, the majority of your sales might go to a single customer, like Dell Computer.

My point here is that understanding sales by geography is a handy exercise simply because the buyer will inherit these sales characteristics. If the buyer does not have a support or sales network that supports a national, or international, sales activity, then it must work within the network already in place by the target company. If this network is having problems, then the buyer must figure out a way to address these problems to obtain an optimal return on its purchase investment. In addition, no synergy is provided if the buyer and seller cover different networks but marketplace expansion can come from the varying geographical coverage.

This exercise may also show that certain geographies provide the majority of sales while others simply break even, or worse. It may be that savings can be obtained by closing or consolidating poorly performing target company geographies in which the buyer has a strong marketing presence. It might be better, however, to close or consolidate poorly performing buying company offices in areas where the target company has a well-performing marketing presence. Geographical distribution is particularly important if you are acquiring the target to gain access to international markets. Realistically understanding the sales, by product, in those areas, along with the specific distribution channels used to obtain those sales, might be the major item of value purchased as part of the acquisition.

By Distribution Channel

Getting the product sold and into the hands of customers is the intention of any distribution channel. Certain products lend themselves to being sold directly by the developer's own sales force, while other products are best sold through distributors. Understanding the specifics associated with selling and distributing a product is another important aspect of a company evaluation. A major factor in determining the right distribution channel is whether the product is a technical product or consumer-oriented product. The more technical the product, the more likely the company is to sell and market the product through its own direct sales force. The less technical the product, and the easier the product is to understand by the end buyer, the more likely it is that the company will sell through distribution.

There is always a tradeoff between control and reach when choosing a distribution channel. A product can obtain much faster and broader market exposure when sold through established distribution networks since the salespeople, support personnel, and customer base are already established. A new product is a nominal addition to those already in place. In exchange for this more rapid market exposure, the manufacturer usually loses some level of familiarity with its customers. The manufacturer is not the one talking directly to the customer—the distributor is. It is common for the manufacturer to be slow on understanding customer-driven market changes if the distributor is not rigorous about providing that feedback. The reality is that distributors handle many different products, of which the manufacturer's might be "just another" in the sales book. In addition, distributors try to "own" their customer base and often hoard customer data, to the dismay of the manufacturers whose products they represent. For these reasons alone, it is important to understand the relationship between the target company and its distribution channels.

1. If the product is relatively nontechnical and being sold directly to customers, you might find that the target company's management had a tight control philosophy that cost them money in the distribution and sales area.

2. If the product is highly technical and being sold through standard distribution channels, there is a high likelihood of friction between the customer base and the target company. Why? Simply because a highly technical product usually is sold to a highly technical customer who may well know more about the product than a relatively nontechnical salesperson who is also selling hundreds of other products. A detailed discussion about customer relations, return rates, complaints, reorder rates, and methods of monitoring end customer satisfaction (one that relies on something more than the distributor's assessment) should be high on any buying company's priority list.

3. How long has the distributor been selling the target company's products? How have sales been compared to their initial projections when the relationship was first established?

4. What particular services are provided by the distributor? Is it a full-service distributor, a licensee who purchased the rights to the technology (typical of an international distributor), or does the distributor plan a local contact role for sales and installation with all postsale support provided by the manufacturer?

5. Does the distributor sell any products that would be considered competitive with either the target or buying company's products? What would be the distributor's reaction to the merger? What would be the reaction of the buyer's existing distributors to the acquisition and its associated distribution network?

6. Is there a complementary synergy available by consolidating some buyer and target company products through one channel, such as the buyer's, and others through another channel, such as the target company's?

7. What types of services does the distributor provide to the manufacturer supplying its products? This point relates, among others, to the data-hoarding issue.

Never forget that the sales and distribution channel is the money funnel through which all sales revenue must flow. If the sales operation cannot sell the products, the company will quickly run out of operating funds. The surest way of increasing the future value of an acquisition is to increase its sales as a standalone business, or to use synergy between the buyer and seller to create increased sales for both companies. Only from a thorough investigation of the sales and distribution functions can a sound projection of future sales performance be obtained.

Evaluating the Sale Cycle

Every industry has its own sale cycle. This cycle extends from the point that the customer is first contacted about their interest in a product or service to the point where the product or service is actually put to use in the customer's environment. The sale cycle may only be a few minutes, such as that seen in a retail computer store when a customer purchases a software package. It can be months, or even years, when dealing with a highly technical product with a large dollar value and a high strategic importance. An entire organization will design its sales, marketing, manufacturing, and financial structure around the timing of this sale cycle. Two companies merging with the intention of combining the sales and marketing functions must consider the synergy, or lack thereof, of the two companies' sale cycles. If one has a 90-day cycle and the other has a 9-month cycle, there will likely be problems in successfully combining the two.

The temperament of the salespeople will be different. The level of sales support required will be different. The level of financial funding required for the longer sale cycle will be larger. Shorter sales cycles are usually associated with lower price ticket items where the longer sales cycle products will involve very large dollar amounts. The lower the price tag, the less strategic the sale. The higher the price tag, the more complex the sales process and the greater the need for a strategic selling approach.

Different sales forces have different skill sets. The incorrect mix of products and sales force skills can be a recipe for future sales disasters. For this reason alone, a careful assessment of the sale cycle of both the buying and target companies products and services is a mandatory requirement.

I have seen companies assume that they would simply hire the right people after the deal was completed only to find out that substantial sales force disruption almost never translates into a near-term increase in sales. Instead, significant disruption almost always translates into customer confusion, decreased morale, and a 90 to 180 day training period for the new salespeople. This type of fallout is fine if you already have it included as part of your acquisition expectations. Sometimes, however, the enthusiasm and energy of the transaction infects participants to the point that the future impact of major obstacles is minimized to the detriment of future success.

Marketing Approach and Strategy

Just as a smoker and nonsmoker will have a tough time coexisting in the same household, so will highly different types of organizations have a difficult time working in conjunction with each other. A more fundamental problem with the combining of two highly different types of organizations, from its products to its personnel, is the confusion that the combination can cause in the minds of company customers.

Assume that the target company is a low-price, high-volume producer and the buyer is a high-price, lower-volume producer. Although the two companies might sell to customers at same companies, it is highly likely that the actual persons making the purchase within the customer's company will be different people and even departments. This is simply because the purchasing procedures for lower price products is usually completely different from that of a higher ticket item. Now comes the problem. How does the combined entity present itself to the combined customer base? Or even more fundamentally, should a combined face be presented at all? Can a company be both a high-ticket, advanced technology products company while also providing the highest-volume, lowest-cost products on the market? Although it is possible to do both, it is highly suspect and many buyers will simply discount both stories to the point that neither will be effective.

In today's finance-oriented world, it is important that the buyer and seller have a good story to tell the investment community. It is also critical that the two companies give serious consideration to similarities, or dissimilarities, that might exist between the marketing message, approach, and strategy between the buying, target, and postacquisition combined entities. If not handled properly, a serious image problem can arise in the minds of customers and investors, putting unnecessary negative pressure on both sales revenues and stock prices. Here are a few ideas to get you strategically started on addressing this situation:

1. If both companies have the same general marketing message, then a message that presents the combined entity as more and better should be effective.

2. High-volume, lower-price producers might be able to position the acquisition as a portent of lower prices due to higher economy of scale.

3. High-ticket item producers might consider presenting the combined company as adding expertise and technology that will keep the combined company's products and services on the cutting edge.

4. Companies with disparate marketing messages might consider keeping the two companies separate for a while after the acquisition. Allowing customers to see that the two can effectively transact business after the acquisition is a solid first step in gaining confidence. The gradual elimination of the target company's identity from public announcements should allow for successful integration without causing distress in the customer's mind.

There are complete books written on effective brand management and choosing the right marketing strategy in association with a merger of acquisition. Just make sure that you do not treat this important topic as something that will "just work itself out" in the future. It can and will work itself out. You just want it to work itself out in your favor.

Evaluating the Competitive Situation

No successful business exists in a vacuum. It is a business certainty that success will breed competitors who want to take their portion of your success.

The buyer and seller of an acquisition transaction both have competitors who are always looking for weaknesses that can be exploited for business gain. In addition, competitors will want to interfere with any acquisition that will seriously impair their competitive position. An acquisition must be considered not only as a stand-alone event but also in the context of expected competitive reactions to the acquisition.

1. Buyer competitors might see the acquisition, think it is a good idea, and then pursue the purchase of another of the seller's competitors in the interest of staying competitive.

2. Buyer competitors might decide to enter into a bidding war with the buyer, driving up the price of the acquisition and possibly putting the target company into the position of having to select the initial buyer's competitor instead of the original buyer as the acquiring firm.

3. Competitors of either buyer or seller could file a lawsuit claiming some type of antitrust issue, which can tie up the acquisition in the courts for a long time and likely for a large legal expense.

4. More than one strategic alliance has been formed out of the merging of two other companies. As one company expands in size its competition will take steps to remain competitive through formal alliances that increase the market power of the combined companies. Some will merge and others will form consortiums that do not include the merged company which initially caused the alliances in the first place.

5. Sometimes the merging of companies creates a large, single entity that is now easy to target. Microsoft has created a love-hate relationship in the industry in that some people love their products but hate doing business with the company. I actually had a colleague ask me one day if I thought she was "dancing with the devil" in using and promoting Microsoft's products. Becoming the biggest guy on the block also makes you a bigger target and could turn other industry players against the larger merged entity for something more than business reasons. This is really pretty irrational, I admit, but not necessarily inaccurate.

6. Do either the buyer or target have strategic alliances with other companies that will require modification, or might be completely voided, in the event of a merger? If so, the impact must be assessed not only for its near-term but also for its longer-term effects on the combined entity.

7. Acquiring a competitor, called a horizontal acquisition, will almost surely raise some legal and governmental eyebrows if either company commands a sub-

stantial market share. The Department of Justice will likely use the Herfind-ahl-Hirshmann Index (HHI) to determine the competitive effects of the business combination. This index is a mathematical function based on the square and then sum of the relative markets share of all competitors. If this index, calculated using the combined market share of both companies, goes up by too much as the result of the merger, then the Department of Justice might get involved. More on this topic is covered in Chapter 17, "Franchised and Competitor Transactions."

There are a number of excellent books out that deal with competitive evaluation and strategy in great detail that is beyond the scope of this section. The book by Michael Porter referenced earlier provides an accepted, structured framework for the analysis of competition. Thinking in advance about potential competitor actions resulting from the merger or acquisition and then assessing the impact of their actions is a sound M&A practice and strategy.

Chapter Summary

Although a lot of emphasis is placed on the financial aspects of an acquisition transaction, it is the marketing and sales success in the postacquisition environment that will heavily determine the success or failure of the acquisition. This chapter took a look at a number of general marketing and sales issues that should be considered when analyzing a company for possible acquisition. Where applicable, the special nuances related to marketing and sales of technology companies was included, although much of the information presented applies equally to technical and nontechnical firms alike. It is recommended that a detailed assessment of the companies' marketing positions, product and customer mix, personnel requirements, and competitive situations be evaluated in both a pre- and postacquisition environment. Much of the information needed to gain insight into a company's marketing activities is publicly available and does not require proprietary information access. This initial public information assessment will raise questions that can later be answered during due diligence, if the acquisition gets to that stage.

It is naive to believe that competition will stand idly by and watch the acquisition take place. It is also equally naive to believe that customers of both the buying and selling companies will not have some level of concern about the acquisition. Your customers are watching the business activities of their major vendors. By the way, so are your major vendors watching your acquisition activities. Understanding the market position of both the buyer and seller in a preacquisition environment is a required first step. This background provides the needed foundation to develop the right postacquisition marketing position and sales organization that presents the combined entity in a positive light to all external parties and to employees alike.

10

Special Technology and Marketing Considerations

Technology is a vital part of any contemporary organization's operation and is of paramount importance when evaluating a technology company. More than one company has sold a product to its own customers and not realized that they do not apply the same approach to their own operation. Just as the cobbler's kids might have the worst shoes, a technology company might have a poor plan for implementing its own products within its own operation.

Technology firms must address a specific set of unique circumstances that are not present with other less technical firms such as rapid change, the impact of the Internet, constantly evolving development tools, intense pricing pressure, and a very sophisticated customer base. Evaluating a technology firm as one would a meat packing firm would be a mistake, just as evaluating a meat packing firm as though it were a data networking firm would be a mistake. This chapter takes a close look at the various aspects of the marketing and sales operation that pertain specifically to technology firms.

Technology Sector High Change Rates

One of the irrefutable characteristics of the technology industries is their high rate of change and evolution. Some companies thrive on this high change rate, while others led the pack in the early days only to become also-rans as the market moved into maturity and decline.

High change rates mean that technology fields often move from one emerging market to another without ever having a product remain in a mature market for very long. Faster, cheaper, more reliable, and smaller are the mandates of the technology industries. Any company that is not basing its strategic marketing and sales plans on meeting these mandates will likely find itself in a declining market phase within a three-year period. Remember Moore's Law? This is not to imply that all technology markets are constantly in flux or without opportunities for mature market operation. It is very possible that some portions of technology industries might be at a high degree of change while others are only nominally impacted by the changes.

For many years during the late 1980s and into the mid-1990s, COMDEX looked pretty much the same to me. Sure, the processor speeds and overall storage capabilities might improve, but there really wasn't much new happening on the hardware front. The computer designs looked very similar. The overall characteristics looked similar as well, and indeed adopted many of their characteristics from the same group of core original equipment manufacturers (OEMs.) This high degree of homogeneity forced the vendors to basically compete on price and service.

The feeling associated with the purchase of a PC is similar to that experienced when purchasing a car from a group of different reputable dealers. Once you pick out a make and model you want, the rest of the process comes down to the most convenient dealer that makes you the best price offer. This is a definite sign of a mature market, and the PC industry has been in that mature stage for a number of years. This PC marketplace maturity provided a stable platform on which other industries could develop. Peripheral devices and specific applications such as gaming have created niche markets dependent on the base PC. These developers use the PC as the base platform for delivering their product, which is a high-quality interactive gaming experience.

Oddly enough, these niche application industries may now drive new PC system purchases. The desire to run a low-priced gaming software package costing under $100 might drive a consumer to spend thousands of dollars on the latest PC hardware and 3-D surround sound speakers, thus providing the ultimate gaming performance and experience. This is an example of the tail wagging the dog in that this inexpensive application is prompting a multi-thousand-dollar purchase, but a true one nonetheless.

Vendors that understand this market dynamic can take advantage of it and thrive during market maturation stages. Those that don't will try to compete on price alone and eventually be listed as one of the casualties of market maturation. Unfortunately, much of this market-oriented wisdom is obtained from hindsight and is much more difficult to see when an industry is in the middle of the market change.

Product- or Market-Driven Technology Company Issues

Successfully running a technology business is a blending of engineering development, implementation, customer relations, and business management skills. Many technology companies are initially started by engineers who may or may not have business management experience. In more than one case, engineers have either managed the company like engineers expecting everything to be deterministic, or perhaps turned the company management over to slick marketing and sales management people believing that you have to be slick to succeed in business. In my experience, neither of these approaches is particularly successful. This section takes a look at the implications of these two different management styles, and the ways they must be assessed when considering the acquisition of a technology company.

Engineers as Managers

Contrary to popular belief, engineers have vision and creativity . It takes a highly creative person to think up an idea for a product, design the product, and then actually create it from nothing other than equations and a selection of raw materials. The engineering process requires a detailed vision of what the product should ultimately look like and perform, as well as the skills to make it a reality.

The engineering principles applied to the design and implementation process are quite clearly defined. The engineer has likely calculated the various possibilities associated with different decision options and chosen the ones that provided the optimal solution to the design dilemma presented. Engineering is a fairly deterministic science, meaning that if a device is calculated to perform in a certain way, it will likely perform just as designed. That is, unless there is a flaw in the design, which is not discussed in this section. It is miraculous to think that a few mathematical equations can accurately predict the specific actions of electrons, but it is true nonetheless.

Unfortunately for the engineering manager, and often for the company that he manages, the future of business is not as deterministic as engineering. I defy anyone to precisely predict the number of pending sales that will actually close, or the future of interest rates and their impacts on discount factors. The future of any business environment is just not that certain. Engineers, however, often like to analyze the problems associated with predicting the future to the point that they cannot make a decision, simply because enough data is not available. Enough data will never be available: That is the sad truth, which takes us to the "hunch and luck" aspect of business decision making.

The acquisition of Warner-Lambert by American Home Products was the hot topic of the business news in late 1999. According to news reports at the time, Pfizer was the first company to make a bid for Warner-Lambert and the bid appeared to be accepted by Warner-Lambert. American Home Products then came to Warner-Lambert with a lower purchase price and offered other incentives to make the transaction appear "more friendly" compared to the Pfizer proposal. Watching the news reports, and seeing the interviews with the CEO of Pfizer, there is little doubt that the events were not expected to unfold as they did. Litigation was threatened, and Saturday Night Live even performed skits on the subject! Only history knows with any confidence how things turn out for Warner-Lambert or any other business situation for that matter. Managers must manage using their best assessment of the future at the current time of decision making.

It is common for engineering-run companies to focus their attention on the company's technology activities, spending less time with the business aspect. Instead of performing marketing research studies to determine the products or services that consumers are looking for, engineering-driven firms often think that they simply know what the right product should be and then point the company in that direction. Engineering managers think that future product decisions and customer choices are deterministic, which they are not, and often make choices that later turn out to be inaccurate.

I have worked in the marketing and sales departments of companies that were engineering-driven only to have products thrust upon us with no marketing input. "Sell what you've got," would be the corporate marching orders. Marketing was in direct contact with the customers. We knew what the customers wanted and which modifications they wanted to our current product lines, and yet engineering would rarely ask for product specification input from marketing. Later, detailed discussions with the engineering department indicated that engineering did not think that marketing understood the technology involved with the products. From the engineering perspective, marketing could not really have a valid input to the design process.

This approach successfully created animosity between these two very important departments, to the detriment of everyone concerned, including the customers. The incredible downside for engineering derived from this approach was that they later ended up modifying the products once they had been released to the field sales force. Customers would see the products, understand their operations, and then tell us what needed to be done for us to win their business. Engineering was then chartered, under extreme time pressure, to make the design modification so that we could sell the products and maintain the required revenue stream.

Collaboration with marketing will not guarantee that the product will not need modification after release. However, asking customers what they want, and then giving them at least what they asked for and preferably a few additional positive surprises, seems like a much safer approach to product development than having several engineers, who never talk to customers, dictating product features. I tell this story to illustrate that the internal processes of a company are important to understand if you are to understand the culture within which products and services are developed.

From an M&A perspective, you are well served in understanding the details associated with new product or service definition, design, and implementation. If a successful company uses a product-driven approach, then there are likely a few individuals inside the company with accurate insight into the market and its customer needs. You must make sure that these people transfer with the acquisition. If the company is market-driven, then verifying the research methodology that led to past successes is also a worthy pursuit. A methodology is easier to reproduce than is a unique technical person with a special insight acquired over a professional lifetime. Smaller technology firms may have a blending of personnel in both engineering and marketing which contributed to the company's success with past product releases. Understand this past successful dynamic and you stand a much better chance of channeling it in the future with new, postpurchase product development.

Managers as Engineers

A popular comic strip (that I personally love) about a guy with a curved tie and a mercenary dog has taken the public image of corporation managers to an all-time low. Imaging this scenario: A salesperson meets with a client who says that he will place a big order only if the manufacturer will make specific design modifications. The salesperson agrees that the company will make those changes and takes the order. He then comes back and drops the changes, along with what is typically an unrealistic time frame, into the engineering department's lap. Engineers have seen this happen too many times.

Managers who play engineer are just as dangerous as untrained engineers playing manager. There are specific technological issues that must be addressed adequately before a product can reliably be put into service. Unrealistically shrinking the time frame or budget associated with those changes simply puts the final product, and the ultimate relationship with the customer, in jeopardy. All of the financial analysis in the world won't design and create a product or service that meets customer requirements and extends or opens new business markets. A team approach is the best way to get the right customer input for the creation of design specifications while also ensuring that the agreed upon design can be provided within the required time and budget constraints.

Companies that are market-driven while also being sensitive to technical constraints will thrive, which I contend is the reason for Microsoft's incredible success. They have figured out a business model that enables them to incorporate this customer feedback as an integral part of their product definition and development process. Companies that are not market-driven, and simply force engineering to design unrealistic products under unreasonable time and cost constraints, can create animosity between the two departments that any acquiring company must address. These internal squabbles might not be obvious unless you start looking far below the surface.

Assessing the Blend

There are liabilities associated with a company that is either too product-driven or too market-driven. There is an optimal blend that successful companies achieve, and that blend changes with the market conditions, involved personnel, technology shifts, regulatory changes, and company ownership.

From an M&A perspective, the buyer and seller both are advised to assess the primary driving forces within their respective companies and then evaluate the likelihood of a successful postacquisition blending of those forces. It may be possible that one company has a great market-driven focus with a proven track record, while the other has a solid technology driving force. If the two can work together, the acquisition might create the best of both worlds. If not, then there could be very real personnel problems that could cause the loss of better people from both the marketing and engineering groups. Here are a few points to consider as you evaluate the cultures of the companies involved:

1. Where do the final product definitions come from? Are they defined by one group that requires acceptance by the others?

2. Are final product and service definitions the result of a collaborative process between the affected departments? Is there a formal product definition process that is followed within the company?

3. Are employees motivated to present new product or service ideas, and is there a formal escalation process for new ideas that is well understood throughout the company?

4. What percentage of new products have met or exceeded financial expectations over the last three to five years? Are they at least succeeding with 50 percent? If not, why? If so, why?

5. Has the company made or lost money, based on gross margin, from new product lines introduced over the last three to five years? To what does the company attribute its successes and failures?

This is by no means an exhaustive listing of questions, but they are enough to elicit responses that will shine some light on the target company's processes and indicate other areas of investigation. These processes can then be compared with those of the buyer to determine if synergy exists, or if improvement is needed on the part of either buyer or seller.

Understanding Offered Products and Services

Companies sell products and/or services. From those sales they receive revenues. It is always possible to look back and determine the sales rate associated with a specific product or service. It is another entirely to determine the future viability of those historical levels or the likelihood of substantial future increases or decreases. Every industry has its own set of complexities that can dramatically impact the future marketing chances of a product or service. Technology fields, once again due to the incredibly high rate of change, are more prone to these changes than most markets and require that the problem be addressed on a number of different levels. In addition, different levels of technology require a completely different set of personnel, standards, support, and financing. The overall marketing, sales, distribution, installation, and service aspects of a product must be determined before a knowledgeable assessment of a company's sales and marketing program can be obtained.

Consumer Product Considerations

Consumer products are those aimed at the general mass marketplace and, as such, cannot be too technically demanding. This does not mean that a high degree of technology is not involved with the development and marketing of the products. It is to say that the intended user of these products cannot be asked to perform technically demanding actions without some form of additional training. Ask your friends and acquaintances whether, after decades of availability, they know how to program their VCR for delayed time recording. Check to see how many of them have a VCR that blinks 12:00, indicating that the correct time was never set.

This is not a slight against the general consumer, who annually becomes more technically sophisticated. But this lower level of consumer expertise is a reality that any vendor of consumer-oriented products must address responsibly and credibly, or they will be disappointed with poor sales, a high return rate from dissatisfied customers or both. Computers have moved the general public to a much higher level of sophistication than one that had existed just a few years ago. The wide acceptance of the Internet has moved telecommunication terms such as modem, ADSL, ISDN, and others from the realm of geeks onto the pages of the local newspaper. Things are changing, of that you can be sure. Properly gauging the rate of change and consumers' acceptance of the changes is a tricky business.

Notice what must be in place for a consumer product to succeed in the marketplace:

1. A marketing channel that easily enables the consumer to find out about the product and familiarize himself enough with its operation to make a purchase decision.

2. An easy way to purchase the product, whether online or from a standard store. Payment methods must meet the customer requirements, or else sales can be lost simply on the payment requirements.

3. A distribution channel that gets the product to the consumer in the time frame required for that particular industry. Most consumer products are purchased requiring a rapid (24-hour or so) delivery time. Specialized consumer products, such as high-end audio equipment, may have more tolerant customers who are willing to wait for delivery of the product so that they can receive exactly the product they want.

4. Some type of warranty period and service network must be in place to deal with installation and repair issues. Otherwise, customers might return products that they think are defective only to later discover that the product was fine but the customer's installation or use of the product was actually the defective component.

5. The more important the product is to the consumer, and the higher the consumer's level of discomfort during a product failure, the greater the need for an extensive and potentially lucrative maintenance network that provides prompt, knowledgeable, and professional service.

In summary, the minimum requirements for a consumer-oriented technology company's products are that it be easily purchased by consumers, heavily name-branded so that customers recognize the name when making the purchase decision, easily obtained by the customer, easily and quickly installed by the customer or chosen technicians, competitively priced, easily serviced after purchase, and reliable. This is a tall order, and one that any buyer of a consumer-oriented products company will inherit, so you are better served by qualifying the status of each of these items before purchasing the company.

Technical Product Considerations

Technical products are those that require a high level of technical expertise in their sale, installation, operation, and maintenance. The development, sales, and support expertise associated with these products is different from that required for the sale of a less technically demanding, consumer-oriented product. I have usually found that it takes a high level of design sophistication to provide a product that is simple to operate while also providing a rich set of features combined with high performance. Technical products do not usually enjoy the wide market exposure seen by consumer products simply because the market for technical products is usually more limited and specialized. Technical product buyers tend to be more sophisticated and, as a result, more demanding. Technical products often come with a very high price tag, which requires that internal authorization be obtained before the purchase can be completed. Quite often the buyer will want to test the product, under somewhat realistic conditions, to verify that the product performs to the published specifications. Producing a product that does not perform to published specifications is usually the first sign of a company in trouble and should always be given close scrutiny.

While a consumer-oriented sale might take only a few minutes, a technical sale might take months to move from the prospecting stage to the actual closing of the order. The level of sales and marketing interaction is much more demanding for a technical product, often requiring sales engineers to participate at various points in the sales cycle. Technical buyers may not need postsale service and support, preferring instead to train their own internal people on the installation and maintenance of the products. Technical buyers who do require postsale installation and maintenance support will expect that the people performing these functions be personally professional and technically competent. I have seen more than one technical sale unravel simply from the lack of customer confidence in the postsale personnel.

Consulting services are also an integral part of any technical products or services environment. The more complicated the products, the more complicated it will be to integrate the products with other existing customer products. A consulting staff that can assist customers with required technical integration problems will go a long way toward creating satisfied customers and keeping them on your side. On the other hand, an unsupported customer who went out on a limb to acquire funding to purchase your products only to be left nonfunctional and unsupported after the sale might become a person with a private mission to make sure that you never sell to their company again. This is clearly not the reputation that any professionally run, serious business-oriented company would like to create. If you are evaluating a highly technical company as a potential acquisition target, a detailed look at the various steps of the sales cycle, cross-checked with employee skill and customer success levels, will tell you much about the current company operation.

Service Company Requirements

Service companies have their own set of effective operational parameters that differ in many ways from those of a standard manufacturing company. A service company does not have a product, per se, that it sells. When you go to a doctor's office, you do not leave with a product as much as with the belief that your continued health is more certain because of the visit. Should that belief not be there when leaving the doctor's office, you would likely look for another doctor. So, in the case of the doctor's office, you are really being sold a belief that the services provided improved your situation.

Technology service companies are in much the same situation. If a company has outsourced its information technology department to a service company vendor, the company must believe that the vendor will provide an improved service value over what the company could have done on its own. A service company has minimal capital assets and inventory. Most of its resources will lie with its people, because it really sells the expertise of its employees as its primary means of generating revenue. As the president of a service company once told me, "My assets go home every night and I simply hope that they come back the next day." The balance sheet cannot accurately reflect the status of the assets of a service company. The personnel involved and their relationship with the company must receive an in-depth investigation.

1. Evaluate the revenue generated per employee and then compare that number to the industry as a basis of comparison. Higher revenues per employee usually represents a more efficient organization.

2. Look for proprietary services, methodologies, and techniques that are the intellectual property of the firm. Determine what percentage of its revenues are actually generated from the use of this methodology, or whether the methodology is used for market positioning purposes only.

3. Determine the employee turnover ratio for the firm while paying particularly close attention to strategic areas with hard-to-replace personnel. A high turnover ratio coupled with high projected growth represents a large personnel challenge that must be assessed against the existing labor markets. A high retention rate, indicated by low turnover, indicates that the working environment is attractive to employees.

4. Verify salary levels for the service firm against those of the rest of the industry. A low turnover rate might indicate that a higher-than-average salary tradition will need to be carried into the future by whoever purchases the company.

5. Verify stock option and other incentive plans that are currently in place with the company. A buyer must then assess the positive or negative impact on personnel morale and motivation that would result from any changes to these benefit plans.

In short, any buyer of a service company must spend the time to understand the employee working environment. A products company might be able to limp along for a while if employee morale suffered as the result of an acquisition. Someone might still purchase the product if it provides a high enough value, even if the experience of the purchase is hampered by a poorly motivated employee.

A service company, however, simply cannot afford the dip in morale since that particular company's employees' expertise, education, skills, and enthusiasm is the primary items being purchased by the company's customers. This is not to say that restructuring cannot be done or that benefits cannot be changed. But any decreases in benefits coupled with disruptions might have a long-lasting impact on personnel, and ultimately on customers, that might take an even longer time to repair.

The Product Mix

A well-tuned product and services mix will provide opportunities for one product or service to sell another. This cross-selling is the optimal method for increasing sales revenues while decreasing costs for technology firms. A classic arrangement that takes advantage of this cross-selling is the selling of a maintenance agreement in conjunction with the sale of the product itself. Suppose that a company sells a product for $500 with a 60 percent gross margin. This means that each sold product generates $300 in gross margin. Assume that this same product can also be sold with a maintenance agreement that costs $200 but provides the company with a gross margin of 85 percent due to the high reliability of the sold product. The maintenance agreement generates $170 in gross margin.

In summary, the product sold by itself generates $500 in sales revenue and $300 in gross margin. The product sold in conjunction with the maintenance agreement generates $700 in sales revenue and $470 in gross margin. Notice that sales revenue increased by $200 (40 percent) and gross margin increased by $170 (57 percent) simply by selling the maintenance agreement along with the product itself. Increasing sales by 40 percent, adding a higher gross margin product while adding minimal complexity to the sale process, is an excellent way to generate incremental revenues while improving operating margins.

The selling of supplies that support the primary product sold is another common way of increasing the sales revenues associated with a sale. Selling toner cartridges in conjunction with the sale of a laser printer is one common combination. Technology products are somewhat unique in that the sale of a particular product must first be closed before additional products can be sold. The base unit of a PC, including the chassis, motherboard, and power supply, must first be present before any peripheral components can be added. Quite often, these core components are sold at a nominal profit margin so that the additional higher margin peripheral products can be sold in higher quantities.

Vendors have been known to slightly modify some attribute of these common components so that only compatibly modified peripherals will function properly. This essentially locks the customer into purchasing peripheral products from the manufacturer of the base unit containing the common equipment. Some third-party vendors will market compatible products once the market size increases to the point that it is financially viable, but the initial vendor is always in the best position to capitalize on this uniqueness requirement. Customers typically dislike this approach and often feel that they have been had when they find out about these seemingly arbitrary technology compatibility requirements. More than one industry has been created for the specific purpose of getting around these "sole-sourced" vendor requirements. If, on the other hand, the company can successfully demonstrate that its proprietary requirements actually enable it to provide its customers with a higher level of performance and value than could be done otherwise, then the customers might enthusiastically welcome the sole-sourced nature of the product.

I believe that today's technology business environment requires that vendors walk this proprietary technology line very carefully. If walked properly, the profit margins can be enormous. But if not walked properly, a negative reputation that could take years to dispel could be the disastrous fallout.

Sales and Technical Marketing Personnel

Getting the products sold, installed, distributed, and supported is a complicated business that is heavily dependent on the products and services being provided. Using highly qualified technical people to sell a relatively non-technical product will drive up the cost of sales. Using nontechnical people in a technical sales process will lose sales to competition and keep sales revenues under their maximum potential.

Understanding the marketing and sales personnel mix of a target company helps to understand whether the products or services are being marketed in a technical or nontechnical way. Further investigation will reveal whether that process is optimal. The sale of any product or service will proceed through a relatively well-defined series of steps. Different skills sets are required for each step of the process, and different organizations will likely have responsibility for some of the steps.

Matrix 10.1 explains that the various stages of a highly technical, high-price-tag item requires a number of different skill sets. An example of a highly technical product sale that falls into this category would be a central office telephone switching system for a major metropolitan area. Because these various skill sets are rarely obtained within a single person, a successful sale process is the result of a team effort with the technical salesperson often acting as the overall coordinator. Some companies dispatch proposal teams specifically to handle the application, proposal, and finance stages. The account manager will likely handle the close. Another team may be brought in to handle the postsale transition phase, and yet another team could be brought in to manage the subsequent day-to-day activities. All teams but the final one may travel from one customer to another applying their particular expertise to that particular customer's sales situation. Once their portion of the sales process is finished, the team moves on to the next opportunity. These teams develop a high level of expertise in their specific areas but sometimes lose touch with the real working people who must implement the commitments made by these initial teams. This lack of understanding can create difficult situations for the people who finally inherit the implementation of negotiated items. It is usually far easier to commit than it is to implement.

A great company with a great product in an educated market might be able to successfully sell its products and services without a complicated sales support structure, but it is usually a short-lived situation that corrects itself as competition enters onto the scene. Many of these stages can be compressed into a single sales encounter. A consumer purchase of a PC is an excellent example of moving from the Suspect to Close stage in what might only be a matter of minutes. In this case a single salesperson can handle the entire transaction. Or, even better, an educated consumer can simply pick the one he wants from a Web or store shelf location and pay for it with a credit card, involving no salesperson at all.

An M&A evaluation should map the sales steps needed to sell the target

Matrix 10.1 The Typical Stages of a Technical Sale

Step	Description	Personnel Requirements	Comments
Suspect	Looking at anyone who could use the product or service.	Often done through direct mail, Internet referral, or telemarketing. Entry level telemarketing personnel.	Strictly a numbers game of calling as many reasonably qualified potential customers as possible.
Prospect	A potential customer with a verified interest.	Salesperson with the minimum required technical experience.	More a sales process at this stage than a technical process.
Entree	First in-depth contact with the prospect.	Salesperson with some technical knowledge or application engineer backup.	Somewhat technical salespeople can usually handle this stage on their own.
Application	Determining the right products or services for this customer.	Detailed technical analysis of the customer's situation and which products or services will meet their needs.	Usually a highly technical process requiring a very technical salesperson or an application engineer.
Proposal	Preparing and presenting the proposal.	Salesperson with some help from finance and application engineering.	Looking to get acceptance by the customer. A sales process with some technical involved.
Finance	Acquiring funding for the proposed products or services.	Often an internal process on the customer's side.	Sales process assisting customer with getting the money to fund the purchase.
Close	Getting a signature on the sale documents.	Salesperson assisted by attorneys in preparation of contracts.	May have several iterations before the final contract is signed.
Postsale	Installation, training, and follow-up.	Maintenance personnel and trainers.	Technical maintenance personnel and sustaining salesperson.

company's products or services against the skill set of the salespeople involved. If there is a skill-to-stage synergy present that is commensurate with the products involved, then minimal reason for concern is warranted. If, on the other hand, a mismatch is discovered, the buyer must include this mismatch in its valuation analysis and look for synergistic effects between the buyer and target firm with respect to marketing and sales operations.

In general, the marketing of a technology-oriented product or service requires a higher level of technical expertise than a nontechnical one. If the technical personnel are not present in the target firm, they must be added to sustain value, which becomes the responsibility of the combined firms. If, on the other hand, the target company has a product or service that requires minimal or nominal technical expertise, but has a higher level sales force in place, then a shuffling of personnel from target to buyer could create personnel opportunities in the new combined entity. Only further analysis will provide the information needed to confidently make this decision and the intent of this section is to get you started on obtaining that information.

Service Agreements

Postsale service agreements are often a major source of revenue for a technology firm. Customers who rely on the proper operation of a product will generally purchase a service agreement from the manufacturer as a type of insurance policy. If a company produces a high-quality product and sells it into a high-visibility, mission-critical market, it might find the profit margins on its maintenance contracts highly lucrative. If, on the other hand, the products are designed and produced with a lower quality standard, then the service agreement might be invoked more frequently by consumers, which in turn drives down profit margins. Eventually, a low quality product intended for mission critical usage will simply not be sellable because consumers will have alternative products to choose from that will likely provide higher quality and less chance for outage.

In some industries, such as telecommunications or online data processing, the service agreement, along with the organization that backs it up, may be a primary reason for using one company over another. If the operational losses associated with an outage are substantial, then paying a premium for a high-quality service agreement that minimizes the likelihood and duration of an expensive or politically damaging outage makes sound business sense. A business buyer who cuts back on that very desirable maintenance capability as a postacquisition cost-cutting measure could find himself losing not only customers, but revenues in the future—and suffering a negative marketing image situation in the process.

Internal Technology Use

Technology is a useful tool for everyone, including the companies that provide the technology products that the rest of us use. I worked with a data networking company that sold terminals to its customers using the sales pitch that a terminal on each employee's desk increased that employee's productivity. The assertion was that this increased productivity would easily repay the company for the capital equipment costs of the terminal. Oddly enough, this same data networking company did not provide a terminal for each of its own employees, citing that the return on investment was too long to justify the expense. It is one thing to present a sales and marketing message in the interest of selling products or services. It is another altogether to say the right things in a sales presentation and also implement these business practices in daily business operation. This section takes a look at several areas of technology operation that, when investigated, provide tangible insight into the company's perspective on the use of technology in its own operation.

Production

Technology has made huge strides in providing real-time data to manufacturing and production managers. Where hours of manpower were needed to obtain a valid estimate of production times and yields, this information can now be obtained with a few keystrokes with the implementation of the right technology. Any manufacturer of high-volume, low-cost products must keep tight control over its production costs. Inventory management, material and workmanship defects, production time, and in-process rejection rates are the lifeblood of every production manager's day. Without this detailed information provided on a regular (and preferably real-time) basis, it is impossible to make the adjustments required to keep production throughput high, which keeps costs low. While this tracking was once done manually, most of it can now be done electronically. Workstation reject rates, reasons for rejection, and work-in-process cost totals can be obtained with a few keystrokes.

This information becomes important when considering an acquisition candidate with high-volume production requirements. If the company has not yet implemented advanced technology that tracks production statistics, then there is likely room for improvement over the historical production performance record. If the systems are already in place, then you know that you have a company that considers its production requirements important. In addition, you will likely find detailed production records and statistics available during the due diligence stages.

It would be a wise move to investigate the in-process reject rates experienced on the production floor if the company does not already have these statistics readily available. High in-process reject rates indicate a company trying to inspect for quality instead of one intent on designing in that quality from the beginning. And high in-process rejection rates always mean that a substantial portion of the company's inventory is stored somewhere on the production floor as work-in-process. High WIP inventory levels mean increased costs, which could present a future opportunity for the buying firm, but could also mean design flaws that are inherited by the buyer.

Purchasing is usually considered an integral part of the production process. This integration is desirable because the smooth, timely, and uninterrupted flow of raw materials into production is an absolute requirement for reliable and cost-effective production. Automation opened the door for this integration to occur on a real-time basis, and just-in-time manufacturing was the natural result. Although the concepts of just-in-time manufacturing are easy to understand, the implementation is complex and borders almost on obsession. A company committed to lower-cost manufacturing, which is required of every high-volume producer, must take the steps needed to turn those concepts into reality.

Evaluating the automation used to determine purchasing requirements, purchasing time frames, production schedules, work-in-process, in-process quality levels, and shipping schedules is a highly recommended process for any would-be buyer of a manufacturing company. If that company produces a product that could be used internally to improve employee efficiency, it is also valuable to determine the level of corporate commitment to implementing that technology. If it is good enough for customers to use, it surely should be good enough for internal use also.

Marketing and Sales

Anyone with a home telephone has been hounded by the whopping success obtained with the implementation of technology in the sales and marketing areas. Auto/power dialers remove the mechanical aspects of dialing the telephone and even time when the call is placed based on when the last call was completed. Databases of information correlate to make sure that another customer call is transferred to the telemarketing representative as soon as he hangs up on his last call.

Customer histories are stored online. Payment histories are stored online, along with past purchases. Software can correlate upcoming promotions to those who, based on past purchases and demographics, are most likely to purchase the next generation of products. Technology areas have special requirements in that the customer interaction usually continues into the support areas once the sale is finished. Having multiple databases that deal with new sales, historical sales, and customer support data is a breeding ground for data mismatches.

Investigating the level of field sales force automation is another worthwhile activity. Does a salesperson have the ability to investigate inventory levels, or to prepare real-time quotations, while at the customer site? Does the company train its personnel or simply provide them with the computers and software and hope for the best? Are the applications developed internally or are they custom-developed? To what level has the sales process been reengineered so that technology can be more effectively used to increase sales force efficiency? No single question from this list is a show stopper in itself. But in totality, the answers to these questions provide you with insight into the level of automation implemented in the target company.

Engineering and Development

New automation tools come out every day designed to streamline the software, hardware, and other engineering design tasks associated with product development. Are these tools in place at the target company or is every project treated like a new work of art that exists independent of all others that came before? What is the typical time frame for development of a new software or hardware product? When new technology comes on the market, such as a new operating system or programming language, how long is it before the company begins seriously investigating, or implementing, this technology? Does the company have any type of special relationship with the major industry manufacturers such as Microsoft, Intel, AMD, or Novell? If so, what is the basis for this relationship and what must be done to preserve it? If not, does the lack of this relationship interfere with the company's capacity to bring products to the market earlier than its competition?

How well documented are the company's design and operation procedures? Could someone new to the company understand, in a relatively short period of time, the design of a product such that maintenance or upgrade activities could be performed? Does the design require that the original designer remain healthy because nobody else really understands how it all fits together or works? Does the company have special insurance on this particular individual?

How are the intellectual properties involved with products or services stored? Is there a backup stored in a location where, if the building burned down, the intellectual capital associated with the company does not burn up with it? What percentage of time is spent by intellectual workers in keeping their skills current? Does the company encourage this continuing education or is it the employee's responsibility from both a time and money perspective? What is the company's retention rate on employees who have received certification training, such as becoming a Microsoft Certified Solution Developer (MCSD) or Certified Internet Webmaster (CIW)? If it is high, then the company is doing something right. If it is low, then there might be a problem in the personnel areas of the company that warrant further investigation.

Spending time in the engineering and other technical areas of a target company is an absolute must for any M&A buyer. It is likely best that an engineer perform this analysis simply because the language is such that only someone trained in the language can completely understand the nuances. Sending in a nontechnical MBA to talk with engineers about the details associated with TCP/IP packet sniffing or hub design could leave a lot of stones uncovered. Just as you would likely send a French-speaking employee to evaluate a French firm, it makes sense to send an engineer to evaluate an engineering department. It just helps to speak the language.

Assessing Internet Interaction

No discussion of contemporary marketing activities would be complete without an evaluation of target company Internet strategy. Without question, the Internet must play some type of role for any technology company. That role can be simply an internal communication tool or a complete customer interaction process. This is a topic worthy of an entire book on its own merits, but here are a few points to get you started in the evaluation:

1. Does the company have an Internet strategy? Has any part of that strategy been implemented and by whom?

2. Is the company using Internet technology for internal use as at least an information dissemination tool, and at best as a fully interactive part of operations?

3. Has the company performed any operational reengineering specifically to take advantage of the electronic benefits associated with Internet technology?

4. Does the company have a publicly available Web site? Who owns the site and how is it hosted? Does the company host its own or does it use an external hosting company?

5. Has the company's firewall ever been penetrated, and how sensitive is the information stored on the publicly available segments of their internetwork?

6. Does the company provide information to its customers using its Web site? Has it seen any improvements in relations or tech support problem instances or resolution times since implementing its Web strategy?

7. Are Web statistics tracked at the company, and how are they used in making decisions?

8. Has e-commerce become an integral part of the company's marketing strategy? If so, who implements the technology? Is the implementation accomplished using proprietary tools or those readily available and actively used within the developer community?

9. What percentage of the company's revenues are generated using Web ordering? Is this percentage increasing or decreasing, and what is the order filling accuracy?

10. What are the company's future Web plans, and how will the buying company's and selling company's Web strategy meld in the postacquisition environment?

Purchasing a company without a Web strategy may not necessarily be a bad move, especially if the buying company has an advanced Web strategy. It is likely that the buying company can integrate and implement the target company's Web strategy without having to undo any poor designs created by the target company's personnel. It is also likely that the two sites can use some of the same technologies, development personnel, and hardware platforms, so that economies of scale can be obtained.

Be aware that brand recognition associated with some Web site names has an incredible, intrinsic value in its own right. Yahoo! purchased Broadcast.com and Broadcast.com states that its user base nearly doubled in a very short period of time. The Broadcast.com CEO was smiling during this report. It is difficult to mix store locations so that people going to one store can immediately be transported to the other. This is simply not a problem with the Internet, and combining Web sites so that they feed each other is a present trend that will undoubtedly become more popular in the future.

International Business Implications

The United States does not have a monopoly on innovative technological ideas or evolving marketplaces. Now, more than at any other time in history, we exist in a global marketplace. Most major companies have one or more of their business operations performed in a non-U.S. country. This function might be a production facility in Indonesia, a software development lab in India, or a final assembly plant in Mexico. The major customer for a product might be in Asia, Mexico, Canada, or South America. Making these international relationships function on a daily basis is a skill that is usually developed over a number of trial-and-error efforts. Making these often-complicated relationships work takes continued commitment and attention.

The government of either the United States or the destination country can often interfere in ways that completely disrupt the natural flow of business. A *U.S. News & World Report* article published in late 1999 outlined some of the problems facing satellite manufacturers wishing to sell their products internationally. The article (Richard J. Newman, "The Air Up There: If You Build Them, Will They Fly?" *U.S. News & World Report,* 8 November 1999, 38) outlines the problems encountered by Hughes Space and Communications here in the United States when it tried to sell a satellite to Société Européenne des Satellites (SES) from Luxembourg. According to the article, Hughes had already sold seven similar satellites to SES but in this particular case had to take almost three months to work through a new set of regulations implemented by the United States government to protect advanced technology secrets. If a U.S. manufacturer wants to release information that is more detailed than a simple brochure, it must first obtain clearance from the United States Commerce Department. At the current time, there are over 45,000 applications submitted to this department annually, which are reviewed by 15 officers which equates to 3,000 for each officer! The average turnaround time for approval is 90 days, which presents some very real problems when responding to foreign requests for a proposal requiring a two- to four-week response.

My intention here is not to take one side or the other in this important debate between commerce and national security. It is only to outline the very real issues that appear when dealing internationally. Knowing these issues and determining methods of handling them is an integral part of international success. Purchasing a company that has already achieved a proven, successful track record in this regard can greatly streamline the learning curve for an acquiring company. If, on the other hand, you intend to purchase a foreign company, you are well served to find a local representative who not only understands the particular culture but also understands the legal implications. Assuming that business is transacted in other countries as it is transacted in your own is a sure way to meet with international business disappointment.

International technology issues are another mixed bag of good and bad news. A positive aspect of the dominance of companies like Intel and Microsoft is that a de facto standard exists not only in North America but also in most areas around the world. Standards now exist that may enable a company to sell its products in a foreign country where it might otherwise be precluded simply due to basic technology differences.

I taught a group of Russians a detailed Windows NT administration class in 1998. The entire class was taught by me in English, which was then translated into Russian for the students. Although they did not understand me, they clearly understood the English titles to the icons displayed on the screen. A common international technology language is being created on a daily basis, and I fully expect that this rate of standardized adoption will increase as the Internet continues to permeate our daily lives and the lives of our international friends.

Any company of major size that is not already participating in international business from either the marketing or operations sides might find itself working at a disadvantage a few years from now. M&A activities, often preceded by some type of strategic alliance, provide an excellent way to establish a foothold in these foreign markets. The more you learn about these foreign markets, and the more they adopt these standardized technologies, the more you may find that your already-existing products can be ported to match your new customers' requirements.

Chapter Summary

Technology companies have their own unique set of business influences that differ from those of other industries. If you are investigating a target company in your own industry, you will understand the implications of the various technological nuances. But if you are approaching a company from another industry, it is important that you look at this company through the filters of its own industry and not through your own filters, which may or may not be applicable. Understanding the target's current level of technology, methods of product definition, and development, along with the skill levels of technical personnel, gives the reviewer an excellent initial picture of the company's strengths and weaknesses. Technology changes rapidly, and assessing the way that the company deals with this change tells you something about the company's management practices. Buyers should compare the target's methods with the buyer's own methodologies to determine whether there is a complementary fit between the two or irreconcilable differences exist. Excellent financial statements will be no guarantee of future performance if the cultures of the buyer and seller cannot meld as needed to perform in the postacquisition environment.

Investigating the target company's marketing and sales operation on its own merits provides a first impression of the company. Buyers can then overlay the target's strengths and weaknesses to their own companies, looking for and hopefully finding strategic synergy that creates additional future marketing and sales value. Increased sales revenue is always good news independent of whether it comes from domestic, foreign, or other legal sources. Understanding a technology firm's marketing strengths and weaknesses provides the best possible platform from which to find this future revenue gold mine.

Buyers should compare their own product and service offerings with those of the target and assess the level of overlap or disparity that exists between the requirements of the two. Overlap or disparity in itself is not good or bad until compared with the buyer's objectives for this particular acquisition. The target's situation must first be determined before suitability with the buyer can be ascertained.

In summary, buyers of technology companies must continue the due diligence investigation past the various legal and financial areas and into the technical aspects associated with the company's products and services. Engineering levels, personnel, and cultures must be evaluated. Sales and marketing procedures, sales cycles, and personnel must also be evaluated for skill levels and experience.

The target company's personnel and methods have gotten it this far, but the buyer is interested in how the target will perform in a postpurchase environment. Serious lack of congruence among the skill levels, technology levels, and customer expectations of the two companies may indicate a poor acquisition candidate, simply because the likelihood of making the two work in a cooperative, seamless manner in a postpurchase environment is small. Buyer resources would be better spent working with candidates possessing a higher level of compatibility. Finding the right fit and exploiting this fit is the art of the deal—and is good news for buyers, sellers, employees, vendors, and customers.

11

Semiconductor Equipment and Chip Manufacturers

Electronic technology starts with the ability to process bits and bytes, and that processing is done in silicon. The chips themselves are made by chip manufacturers using equipment and technology provided by the semiconductor equipment industry. This means that AMD, Intel, and their competing semiconductor chip manufacturing companies purchase the manufacturing equipment that makes their production possible from semiconductor equipment manufacturing firms such as Applied Materials or Silicon Valley Group. This chapter starts with a look at the special aspects of the semiconductor equipment manufacturer industry and then investigates the special aspects of being a chip manufacturer. An overview of the important unique aspects associated with each industry is presented so that companies in these segments can be evaluated in the light of their particular industry characteristics.

Each area of technology has its own nuances and standard methods of operation that must be considered when evaluating a specific company investment. The intent of the information presented in this chapter is to augment the standard due diligence and target selection procedures outlined elsewhere in this book with information that applies specifically to the semiconductor equipment and chip manufacturing industry segments.

Semiconductor Equipment Companies

Two trends have continued to drive chip manufacturing, smaller line widths and larger manufacturing wafer sizes. The smaller line widths enable higher data processing levels per square inch of chip, and larger wafer sizes enable more chips to be processed on a single wafer which drives down production costs. It is this combination of higher line density and larger wafer size that has enabled the incredible values seen in the electronics industry. The semiconductor manufacturing firms design and produce the equipment that makes smaller line widths, larger wafer sizes, and other advanced developments possible. Their technical capabilities must be production-ready far in advance of when needed by the chip manufacturers because the manufacturer's chip design is predicated on the available semiconductor equipment and associated technology.

Companies in this segment are listed by S&P in the Equipment (Semiconductors) industry. Standard & Poors produces an industry Survey report that covers this and other industries and is released approximately twice annually. I have found these reports to be available from many public libraries and are certainly available from S&P. Several companies from the semiconductor equipment industry segment include Applied Materials (AMAT), KLA-Tencor (KLAC), Novellus Systems (NVLS), Silicon Valley Group (SVGI), and Terradyne, Inc. (TER). These companies showed a beta of over 2.0 for the period ending January, 2000, which is indicative of the wide stock price fluctuations that companies in this segment experience. These fluctuations are representative of either positive or negative reactions from investors to future cash flow projections and stem in large part from the cyclical nature of the semiconductor industry in general.

Industry Realities

Perceived end-user consumption of silicon chips in the form of computers, embedded controllers, or other devices drives the production needs of the chip manufacturers. Chip manufacturer design and production needs create demand for new semiconductor manufacturing equipment. The chip manufacturer designs are based on the technology level of the available semiconductor manufacturing equipment. This puts the equipment manufacturers on both the driving and receiving ends of a volatile industry. They drive the industry with their new technological advancements but are driven by the semiconductor chip manufacturing industry and its anticipated future production demands. The demand experienced by these chip manufacturers is affected by any number of factors such as general economic conditions, changes in technology, interest rates, historical industry-wide over or under supply and international competition among others.

A piece of semiconductor manufacturing equipment will cost in the millions of dollars and chip manufacturers may build an entire manufacturing complex on the belief that this equipment will perform as expected. When a chip manufacturer expands production to a completely new facility (called a greenfield), the equipment manufacturers benefit because that plant must be outfitted with new equipment and may translate into tens of millions of dollars in new revenue. The equipment manufacturers must trust that the chip manufacturers will come through on their equipment ordering commitments. Because a smaller equipment manufacturer may ship only a few units per year, a single missed shipment can have a dramatic impact on revenues and earnings. For these reasons, industry relationships become very important. Postsale maintenance and support is critical. The larger an equipment manufacturer's installed base the better its likelihood of upgrades and the stronger its alliances with its customers. Ultimately new technology and chip manufacturing expansion drives this market, but service will determine the strength of relationships and may well determine who gets future orders for competitive new manufacturing equipment. There are a few major customers for this industry which, if lost as a customer by one of the semiconductor equipment manufacturing firms, could have dramatic, if not catastrophic, political and financial repercussions on the equipment manufacturer. Maintaining these relationships is important for both the equipment and chip manufacturer. The Silicon Valley Group, according to an S&P report dated May 27, 2000, shows Intel as accounting for 56% of the company's net sales with the five leading customers together accounting for 74% of net sales (Standard & Poors Stock Reports, Silicon Valley Group (SVGI), Business Summary dated 16-May-00).

A change of manufacturing technology may prompt the ordering of millions of dollars worth of new equipment. So the introduction of a new, working technology by an equipment manufacturer is great news to not only the equipment manufacturer who gets to sell a batch of new equipment, but also to the chip manufacturers who get to design and sell more powerful chips at a possibly lower price. The equipment companies will likely have many years of R&D invested in a new technology before it is released to production and the equipment may take six months or more to build once an order is received. As a result, the equipment company may not see substantial revenues from new technology for many years into the future after release.

The basic industry reality for an equipment provider is that high R&D levels must be maintained, capital equipment costs are high, and customer service expenses are required to maintain critical relationships. These companies must also maintain enough liquidity to remain solvent during the potentially long time frame between R&D expenses and revenues received. If future financial viability of the equipment company comes into question, this could seriously interfere with its ability to persuade chip manufacturers to take a chance on their equipment products. It is difficult to convince a customer to spend millions of dollars on your equipment if the customer has a real concern about its vendor being in business next year, which would put future customer support in jeopardy. It is common for companies in this segment to maintain a current ratio of between 2.0 and 6.0.

Big dollars are at stake with this industry. There is currently a transition to the larger 300 millimeter wafer sizes and a reduction in line widths from 0.35 micron to 0.25 micron and lower. SEMI reports expectations for worldwide capital equipment expenditures to read $33.4 billion in 2001, which is up from $21.5 billion in 1998. These revenues are split out by SEMI as wafer processing, assembly and packaging, and test with wafer processing equipment revenues accounting for the largest portion of the industry sales revenues.

Important Considerations

Given the strategic nature of equipment sales, here are a few items that must be investigated as part of any semiconductor equipment manufacturing company assessment:

1. What is the target company's level of equipment technology compared to those on the cutting edge?

2. If the company is not on the cutting edge with their released products, what is happening on their R&D front to address this technology? What is the time frame for new technology introduction?

3. Do they have any development programs focused on the next level of technology beyond that already in new-release status?

4. What is the installed base for their most popular products? What are the known plans for their major customers, and how does the equipment company intend

to address those plans? Does the target have a widely diversified customer base or is it heavily tied to the success of a few chip manufacturing companies?

5. Are their current major customers new or repeat customers? Have these customers historically or recently upgraded from one technology to another using the target company's products?

6. What is the company's postsale trouble and support track record? Have any orders been canceled, and were any cancellations the result of technology problems?

7. What is the financial situation of the company's major customers? Will those customers be able to pay its bills with respect to the committed future orders?

8. What is the company's book-to-bill ratio and how does it compare with the rest of the industry? The book-to-bill ratio compares new orders with actual shipments and is usually tracked on a monthly basis. If more orders ship than new orders were received, then the book-to-bill ratio is less than one. If more new orders are received than were shipped, then the book-to-bill ratio is greater than one. A book-to-bill ratio that is rising likely indicates that the industry is becoming more optimistic and that future orders should increase. A book-to-bill ratio that is falling likely indicates that future optimism is waning, which may indicate a future orders slowdown. (This information is obtained from the nonprofit Semiconductor Equipment and Materials Institute (SEMI), which can be contacted at (650) 940-6902 or http://www.semi.org.)

9. Key employee retention status and intellectual property issues should be investigated, because these companies exist on or near the cutting edge while intellectual property rights determine future value.

10. What have been and currently are the company's R&D expenditures? Decreases in R&D expense from year to year may indicate that this company's new technology releases could be impaired in the future.

11. What is the company's current cash position as shown on the balance sheet? How does this cash position compare with projected needs and the industry as a whole? Ratio analysis may be used in this comparison.

12. What is the company's historical new business forecast accuracy track record? An accurate forecast indicates a company with a solid understanding of its customers and industry, while an inaccurate forecast indicates areas of possible improvement.

In some ways, the semiconductor equipment industry companies are like the companies that supply equipment to the automobile industry. Their products are expensive and must be ordered far in advance of when they are actually put into service. When put into service, a longer-term relationship is established with the customer, the auto maker. The auto industry is not as dynamic as the semiconductor industry with respect to major technological changes, but there may be applicable analogies for those performing analyses.

Semiconductor Manufacturing Firms

The semiconductor manufacturing industry produces chips that are used in any of a variety of applications. The most talked about are the microprocessor and memory chips that are used in every PC. Less known, but very useful to engineers and in a wide variety of nondigital products, are analog chips that are used in amplifiers, power supplies, and other important applications. Finally, there are logic devices, which are digital devices designed to perform a specific set of functions. These devices are particularly valuable to engineers and product manufacturers because many of them can be programmed by the product manufacturer as required for specific product design needs.

The amazing part of this industry is that it has seen 30 percent annual declines in price since the 1970s but has seen such substantial unit shipment increases that the industry as a whole has experienced a 17 percent average annual increase in revenues since the 1970s. Although this industry is highly cyclical, it is also one fully expected to keep growing as the demand for semiconductor-based technology continues to increase.

S&P tracks this industry as Electronics (Semiconductor). Several of its companies include Intel (INTC), Siliconix, Inc. (SILI), Analog Devices (ADI), Vitesse Semiconductor (VTSS), Novellus Systems (NVLS), White Electronic Designs (WHT), Advanced Photonix (API), National Semiconductor (NSM), Advanced Micro Devices (AMD), Cypress Semiconductor (CY), and C-Cub Microsystems (CUBE). Beta for this group varies from around 0.25 up to over 2 indicating that stock price volatility is likely heavily dependent on the specific company and industry segment involved.

Industry Realities

Building a semiconductor fabrication facility is an expensive matter. Today it costs between $1.5 and $2 billion to build one and this cost is expected to rise into the future. This high expense level presents problems in that the building of these fabrication plants must be undertaken years before the consumer demand is actually there for the chips being produced. Future market planning is an integral part of running a semiconductor manufacturing company and these estimates like many future projections are often inaccurate.

Semiconductor prices are highly regulated by the economics of supply and demand. If the supply for a specific chip is low, as happened in recent years with earthquakes in Asia, and if demand remains the same, then prices will rise. Supply and demand always drives pricing. Increasing component prices also translate into higher end-product prices, which are passed on to the consumer. If the semiconductor manufacturer, on the other hand, guessed incorrectly about demand for a part and winds up with a large oversupply, then chip prices will drop along with the end user product prices.

We all know that predicting the future is a tricky business that is full of surprises. This fact, combined with the long advance planning lead times associated with semiconductor production, likely means that cyclical price/demand periods will continue into the distant future. The only factors that might decrease this cyclical activity are a stabilizing of equipment technology resulting from physical design limits coupled with a maturity of demand so that it becomes more predictable. Many analysts do not foresee either happening in the near future and fully expect to see the cyclical nature of product supply and demand continue as a way of life.

Competition also plays an important part, as we have all seen with the ongoing microprocessor battles between Intel, AMD, and Cyrix. AMD continues to produce its products that often have comparable or better performance to that of Intel, while selling for prices that are usually much lower than Intel's. This situation is always good for consumers in that it places a downward price pressure on chip prices, but places operational and financial pressures on the chip manufacturing companies involved.

A domestic U.S. company cannot ignore the actions of its international competitors. Domestic consumers show little preference toward whether a memory or other supporting chip was produced in the United States or by a foreign firm. An international entry can cause a global oversupply of chips, which happened to DRAM in the 1995 to 1997 time frame, and can cause manufacturer revenues and margins to drop precipitously.

Important Considerations

Given the cyclical nature of the industry, it is recommended that a semiconductor company's performance be evaluated over time instead of for a given point in time. It is also recommended that its performance be plotted against an industry backdrop in conjunction with that of the other industry players. If the industry goes through a sluggish period and the target company still outperforms the industry players' averages, then the management team appears to be doing something right. Finding out what that is will provide useful insight into the value of this company. These industry trends may be regionally, seasonally, technologically, or economically induced.

If the target company's performance is below that of the industry average, then this also provides useful information. Determining the reasons for the lower performance also provides insight into the company's management and operational decision making. Remember that these firms are continually projecting the distant future while making major capital expenditure decisions today.

Chips are also more than silicon. They are also the programs that are designed into these chips. The level of standardization and performance built into the chip determines its market attractiveness and may allow increased margins. If a company produces a proprietary chip that performs a certain function, and it receives legal protection on the software functions performed, then it can receive higher margins if the product meets with a high level of market acceptance. It is definite that some other manufacturer will try to take that lead away by introducing a comparable product that circumvents the legal protection, but the first manufacturer will likely enjoy higher margins until the competition arrives on the scene.

Intel and AMD play this game with their microprocessor products, with Intel usually being the first one to market with a product. AMD is rarely far behind with a compatible competitive product which forces Intel to reduce its prices within a short period of time after product introduction.

Verifying the legal status of important software is critical, along with verifying the present status of key employees involved with the development and maintenance of that software. People create technology advances, companies don't. Never forget to perform a detailed investigation into the backgrounds and status of key personnel on the financial, marketing, production, and engineering sides of the house.

It should be expected that these companies show a high depreciation expense, because they are capital-equipment intense companies. They also show a high fixed cost, which must be amortized over a high production volume. If the products sell at the expected volume levels, then the profit margins for these companies can be excellent. If product sales are sluggish and require price decreases to move volume, then profit margins can quickly erode.

A closer look at AMD's 1998 numbers (presented in Table 11.1) provides a little insight into this situation. You can see from these numbers that the costs associated with operations were large, leaving only $304 million in operating income from $2.54 billion in revenues. This would be typical of a company with a large fixed cost component associated with its production. Depreciation plus interest expense totaled $534 million (over 20 percent of revenues), which would also be typical of a heavily capital equipment-dependent company.

R&D expense must also be examined carefully. AMD spent $158 million on R&D in the quarter ending September 1999 out of quarterly revenues of $662 million, which amounts to almost 24 percent. This is not a trivial expenditure, and obviously it was one that AMD felt it must make to remain competitive. The Intel 1998 annual report shows R&D spending levels that are around 10 percent of total revenues. Clearly either AMD is spending a higher percentage on R&D, or else the way that Intel is reporting its R&D number is diluted over nonsemiconductor revenues. In either case, more research is required to confidently determine the reasons and returns on these large expenditures.

The evaluation of a semiconductor manufacturer requires a hard look at the long-term debt commitments of the company and its ability to meet those obligations. A ratio analysis that focuses on long-term financial health is a requirement with the clear understanding that the company must financially survive through the short-term to ever make it to the long-term.

Table 11.1 AMD Financial Information (1998)

Item	Value in $US Millions
Revenues	2,542
Operating Income	304
Depreciation Expense	468
Interest Expense	66.5
Net Income	−103

Chapter Summary

The rapid rate of computer technology change is due, in large part, to the incredible advancements that have been made by the silicon equipment manufacturers and the ability of the chip manufacturers to implement that technology. There is some talk about our having reached the physical limits of the technology, but I have heard this type of talk before and have seen it proven inaccurate time and again in my 25+ years of watching this technology evolve. Demand for silicon chips will continue to grow as more uses for the technology are discovered. The equipment manufacturers will continue to develop new and smaller technologies that will themselves open up new business opportunities.

It takes years to develop the semiconductor equipment technology, months to manufacture the equipment once an order is received and months to years, and potentially billions of dollars, for the chip manufacturers to build the chip plants themselves. This large lead time mandates that demand forecasting be as accurate as possible and the equipment manufacturers are highly susceptible to inaccuracies. International competition continues to complicate the supply-demand relationship causing either over or under supply of product that can radically affect chip prices.

As new chip plants are built, equipment orders increase. Changes in technology such as from 200 millimeter to 300 millimeter wafer sizes causes equipment order increases as either new plants are built to accommodate the new technology or old equipment is replaced. Highly successful chip products also stimulate the construction of expanded capacity to meet demand requirements on a timely basis. A breakdown in relationship between the equipment and chip manufacturer can have a negative effect on both companies. It could delay the chip manufacturer's implementation of new technology and/or could interfere with the equipment manufacturer's sales to the chip company. Equipment manufacturers must remain current with respect to the technology of their specific chip manufacturing customer segment, must retain adequate cash to cover the time period between R&D and final receipt of customer payments, and must maintain excellent customer relations. Chip manufacturers must forecast future demand, implement new technology and remain financially solid enough to create the plants needed to meet final customer demands. These industry realities along with standard company due diligence must be applied to the evaluation of a company semiconductor equipment or chip manufacturer.

12

Evaluating a PC/Workstation and Related Hardware Business

The PC created a new technology and business world in much the same way that the Internet is changing contemporary business practices. Although this industry has matured greatly since its inception in the early 1980s, it is still a huge industry with very large players and lots of future room for growth. Every PC sold also carries with it various peripheral products such as hard drives, monitors, video adapters, and keyboards. After-sale products include LAN cards, modems, scanners, printers, and a wide array of additional peripheral products that would simply have no market without the large installed PC base.

Companies like Dell have pioneered an Internet commerce model that is now becoming the standard for other industries. The lean margins and high volume associated with this industry have driven production and marketing efficiencies to much higher levels than those which existed only a little over a decade ago. Each area of technology has its own nuances and standard methods of operation that must be considered when evaluating a specific company investment. The intent of the information presented in this chapter is to augment the standard due diligence and target selection procedures outlined elsewhere in this book with information that applies specifically to the PC/workstation and peripheral device industry segment.

The PC/Workstation Companies

The profit margins are being squeezed within the PC hardware industry, but there are still opportunities within this industry as long as the companies understand that price is still the major purchasing criteria. The recent industry trends have focused on creative ways of reaching the consumer: more efficient inventory control through custom-configured, real-time ordering of systems; reduction in purchase price to the under $1,000 U.S. range; and more extensive integration of multimedia and networking capabilities, such as the Internet, directly into the system.

Industry Realities

There are a number of industry realities that apply across the board to personal computer manufacturers.

1. The introduction of a new processor almost immediately drops the price on the prior version and computers that contain it, and within a short period of time causes products using older version processors to become obsolete.

2. The release of a new operating system often prompts the need for more powerful processing capabilities, which in turn prompts a new computer purchase. The supposed Windows-Intel (WINTEL) coalition has caused speculation that operating systems upgrades are designed specifically to prompt a hardware upgrade, but as far as I know there has been no proof of a conspiracy on the part of Microsoft and Intel.

3. It usually takes around six months for a new microprocessor to become tested and accepted by corporate users. After that evaluation period the companies will typically start ordering new processor product in quantity. Consumers might order sooner because they do not need the extensive evaluation period of a corporate MIS department and also generally have less rigorous and complicated requirements.

4. R&D is a minimal expense for a PC manufacturer. Their gross margins are typically in the 15 percent to 25 percent range and they tend to only spend around one percent on R&D. They let their suppliers absorb the R&D expenses when developing the products that comprise the final PC product. Net incomes for PC/workstation manufacturers are in the one percent to eight percent range.

5. PC manufacturing companies tend to have lower margins on conventional desktop systems and show higher margins on notebook computers (which may be proprietary) and servers, which are more customized.

6. These companies tend to either sell direct to consumers through the Internet (Dell) or through retail outlets (Compaq). Some companies are now merging the two approaches, with Gateway opening retail locations and Compaq ramping up its Internet sales activities.

7. Price competition is an integral part of the industry and vendors must simply be willing to compete on price and service.

8. Annual percentage growth rates for the industry are shrinking but remain over 15 percent, with some estimating future growth rates at around 10 percent. This would be a natural by-product of a more mature market. New corporate installations are slowing since most employees already have a workstation. This means that it is more likely that new system purchases may require replacing an older system, which is often more difficult to financially justify than the initial purchase.

9. International markets provide excellent opportunities for new system sales but pose challenges regarding distribution and support within those countries.

10. Inventory management is critical to company profitability. Just-in-time inventory management is the goal of every PC manufacturer and those that perform closest to this level with minimal in-process rejection rates will show the highest returns. Dell and Compaq build their PCs to match the customer order which indicates a solid level of control over their inventory management systems. The inventory turn ratio should be high for a well-managed PC manufacturing process.

11. Essential components such as microprocessors, memory, hard disk drives, video cards, mice, keyboards, monitors, and printers must be readily available to the PC company or it is shut down until the problem is handled.

12. The home PC market accounted for 40 percent of sales in 1998 and is expected to continue at a robust rate. This makes sales cyclical with Christmas, back-to-school, and other typically strong retail sales periods critical for PC suppliers.

13. The direct-to-customers sale method provides more immediate control over inventory and pricing levels, while a company that must build for distribution must order, build, and stock far in advance of the actual purchase date. This raises inventory levels and associated costs.

14. Tight margins require tight inventory control. This is particularly true for an industry where technology changes quickly and hardware can rapidly become obsolete. Obsolete product left in inventory may be difficult to sell and might eventually turn into a write-down loss, which is always an expensive outcome for the company absorbing the loss.

15. Just as retail outlets such as Wal-Mart will jealously protect the operational strategies that provide for their efficient inventory management, so must and will a hardware manufacturer protect its confidential processes that provide for higher-than-industry-average efficiencies. Verifying the source of these efficiencies, or the lack thereof, is an important part of the due diligence process for these companies.

16. In 1998, the desktop market comprised 80 percent of units sold, portable systems comprised 17 percent of systems, and servers made up 2.6 percent. Around 90 million computer systems were sold for a total value of $170 million, according to International Data Corporation, a market research firm, as presented in an S&P Industry Survey report from June 3, 1999. This industry is tracked as Computers (Hardware) and includes companies such as Dell (DELL), Gateway (GTW), Micron Electronics (MUEI), Vitech America (VTCH), Sun Microsystems (SUNW), Merisel, Inc. (MSEL), Apple Computer (AAPL), and eMachines Inc. (EEEE). Betas for this group of companies vary from around 0.5 to 2.0 and are dependent upon the specific company in question.

All other standard due diligence should be applied to a PC manufacturer, but treating a PC company like any other turns a blind eye to the above-presented issues that can truly make or break a company.

Important Considerations

Trend and comparative analyses are the most effective ways to assess the performance of a PC manufacturing company. Trend analysis shows whether the company's position is improving or degrading over time, and ratio analysis provides an excellent standardized way of comparing one company to another within this rapidly changing industry.

1. Inventory turnover is critical to this industry and an in-depth analysis of inventory management is required. How does the target company's turnover ratio compare with the others in the industry? Has the ratio been improving (increasing) or getting worse (decreasing)? What is the reason for the change?

2. What is the company's Internet strategy, and what percentage of its sales come from Internet orders? What are the return rates for Internet orders compared with the rest of the Internet-enabled industry suppliers? How is website development managed? Is it outsourced or in-house? Has their site ever been hacked with a negative fallout?

3. What percentage of the target company's existing inventory is actually obsolete by today's technology standards? How has the company managed inventory with respect to other historical technology changes, like that from one processor type to another?

4. What is the company's bad-debt ratio and its collection period as compared to the industry average? Retail sales over the Internet can be riskier than traditional retail sales, although the profit margins are much better. However, not seeing the customer face-to-face does have its potential risks in the form of an increased bad debt.

5. What is the company's level of readiness with respect to upcoming new processor or other technology releases?

6. How successful was the company in the marketing and sales rollout of its last technologically upgraded systems?

7. How does the company do its marketing, and what is its percentage of revenues spent on sales and marketing compared to the rest of the industry?

8. What special relationships does the company have with critical suppliers such as Intel, AMD, Microsoft, and others? Does this special relationship provide the company with an edge or disadvantage with respect to its competition?

9. Does the company have a retail or corporate sales model? How long has this model been in effect and what has been its historical success?

10. How does the company service the products it sells? Does it outsource the service or use its own service network? How are the service segment's profit margins compared to other companies in the industry? What is the service reputation of the company?

11. Does the company OEM integrate industry standard products or does it perform its own design and manufacturing? How was the decision made to take the approach they currently take, and what would prompt them to change course?

12. What is the company's server and Internet-enabled device strategy? What is its historical track record of addressing these important industries, and why should the current server and Internet strategy succeed?

13. Has the company substantially committed its future success to the success of a speculative technology or does it provide mainstream products using conventional technologies?

Perform your standard due diligence analysis and then apply these special checks to a PC manufacturer to see if there may be other hidden areas that only show up when the company is analyzed in light of its own industry traits.

Computer Peripheral Companies

Computer peripheral companies produce products that attach to desktop or workstation computers. Some peripheral devices are mandatory, such as the hard drive, keyboard, mouse, and video monitor. Others are only needed by a specialized group of individuals. Typical additional peripheral components include the printer, modem, sound card, specialized storage devices, joystick, scanner, hand-held devices, video capture units, and a wide variety of others. The disk drive segment is presented next in detail. The same approach applied to the disk drive can be applied to other peripheral manufacturers and suppliers as well.

Industry Realities

The disk drive industry is highly price-competitive, with extensive distribution channels and strict adherence to standards being the minimum requirement for participation. Amazing as this might sound, disk storage capacity has increased at approximately 60, annually. This incredible rate translates into a continual stream of new technology developments and product introductions. Disk drives are an integral part of a computer system and the smaller the drives become, the smaller the resulting computer can be. Software programs continue to require more disk storage due to their added complexity. End consumer users require more mobility, which translates into smaller, more portable, powerful computing devices. This combination prescribes that the need for higher storage capacities in conjunction with smaller size, lower price, higher reliability, and less power consumption will continue to be the mantra driving this industry.

The need for increased hard disk data storage also increases the need for backing up larger amounts of data. Quantum and Seagate have actively pursued hardware and software products in this expanding area. Products are generally sold through a multipronged approach that includes retailers, OEMs, distributors, dealers, and system integrators, among others. The disk drive industry is highly dependent on the health of the overall desktop industry as a whole, because these products must be included with another computer system and do not perform any specific function on their own. New operating system introductions often prompt the need for more disk space, which prompts disk drive purchases. An oversupply of product translates into a substantial decrease in price as the various drive manufacturers compete with very similar products in a price- and performance-driven market.

Vertical integration is common with these manufacturers as a technique for reducing the component costs. Manufacturing plants are usually located in non-U.S. locations as a cost reduction technique. For example, all of Quantum's hard drives in 1998 were made in Japan, Western Digital's drives were made in Singapore and Malaysia, and the majority of Seagate's production is done in the Far East. Some companies produce components in non-U.S. locations and perform final assembly and test in the U.S.

This industry is tracked as Computers (Peripherals) in general and has various peer group subdivisions, such as one for disk drives. The peripherals category includes companies such as Seagate Technology (SEG), Exabyte Corp. (EXBT), Identix Incorporated (IDX), Cherry Corporation (CHER), Procom Technology, Inc. (PRCM), Iomega Corporation (IOM), Adaptec, Inc. (ADPT), Quantum Corp. (HDD), and Lexmark Corp. (LXK). Betas for this group also vary widely.

Important Considerations

Smaller, cheaper, faster, and more reliable is the credo of the hard disk drive industry. Any company that is not continually working toward these strategic goals will likely have problems in the future.

1. Take a look at the company's current level of technology and compare that to the evolving standards of the time. How has the company historically performed in keeping up with technology changes, and have any industry changes been prompted by designs instigated by the target company? Does the company have any patents on technology or processes that cannot be duplicated and which provide the company with a competitive advantage?

2. Does the company have a product on the market with the most current technology? Is one planned for the near future if not already released? Is the product internally designed or purchased from another OEM?

3. What is the company's philosophy regarding developing internally or purchasing other outside-designed components? Has the company made any acquisitions of its own as a way of adding technological or product enhancements to its offerings?

4. How does the company manage its inventory? As was seen with the PC manufacturers, effective inventory management is critical for any low-cost, high-volume producer, which applies to most peripheral suppliers. Confirm the company's inventory management performance using trend analysis in conjunction with standard inventory management ratios.

5. What percentage of the company's revenues are spent on R&D when compared to other companies within the industry?

    Seagate states in its 1998 annual report that it spent a total of $585 million on product development and another $223 million on in-process research and development for a total of $808 million (11.85 percent) on R&D-related activities on revenues of $6,819 million. Maxtor, for the period ending 12/31/1998 posting revenues of $2,408 million, spent $152 million (6.3 percent). Quantum, for the period ending March 31, 1998, showed that it spent $322 million (5.5 percent) of revenues of $5,805 million for the same period. It is clear that this industry believes that R&D spending is an industry requirement with Seagate spending almost twice that of two of its major competitors. Whether this is a correct or flawed move on Seagate's part requires further investigation by any due diligence team. Given the understanding that the PC manufacturers have minimal money budgeted for R&D and rely on their suppliers to perform that function, having a credible R&D program makes excellent financial sense for any peripheral supplier.

6. Does the company have a direct corporate sales strategy and how does the Internet fit in with that strategy? What has been its successes and failures to date? Is there an Internet-based customer services/tech support function already in place, and how has it performed? How frequently is it updated and how is its success monitored?

7. How are products currently sold to consumers? Are they sold only to OEMs? Retail? Internationally? System integrators?

8. What is the product return rate and was a design or process quality problem the reason for the return?

9. Is this a company that leads the industry in technology development, or does it wait for a competitor to develop new technology and then capitalize on its competitor's creativity?

10. Can international political problems disrupt product availability for this particular company due to its reliance on international manufacturing or supply chains?

11. What is the company's in-process production quality level? Does the company experience high levels of in-process rejection or are the levels low? Trend analysis of work in process ratios over time and by products should provide some insight as to whether the company is managing its in-process quality properly.

Chapter Summary

The PC and workstation marketplaces are similar in many ways, but it is important to understand the differences. PCs are usually aimed at a consumer with less demanding requirements than those of a workstation user, who is often a business user applying the product to advanced graphic applications. A workstation will consequently have less price sensitivity than that of a PC to be used for email in the home. This difference becomes less as time goes on and the overall power-performance characteristics of the PC continue to increase while prices decrease.

What is clear for both the workstation and PC marketplace is the need for high efficiency in the sale, manufacturing, shipping, and installation of these products. Customer service and product reliability, in conjunction with low price, drive the winners in this area. Successful financial performance is determined by the company that can delegate as much of its R&D as possible to its peripheral suppliers, the PC manufacturer that can streamline its inventory control to minimize the amount of inventory on hand at any time while still providing the customer with rapid delivery. Profit margins for this industry are low and will continue to feel pressure as new processor technologies are released, international players enter the arena, and improved production techniques become the norm.

The peripheral equipment marketplace is driven by the same types of low-margin, high-reliability, and service standards of the PC/workstation marketplaces, with the exception that R&D is absorbed by the peripheral manufacturer in the design of its products. Any company that stands still in either of these industries may well find itself out of business before it even finds out that it has a problem.

Buyers should clearly understand the high-volume production aspects of companies in this area, along with their time to market, for the design and implementation of new technology products. Intellectual property rights should be carefully reviewed, along with any agreements that have a material bearing on the company's operation and success. These two industries leave little margin for inefficiencies and due diligence should concentrate on the way in which the company optimizes efficiencies in critical marketing, sales, production, and design areas.

13

Software Businesses

The incredible success of the personal computer revolution would not have been possible without the complementary increase in the availability of software applications that run on the PC. After all, a computer without a software application is just an expensive paperweight. People purchase computers to run applications, and the customer's initial need to accomplish a specific task usually drives the initial computer hardware purchase and subsequent upgrades.

It is, however, inaccurate to say that hardware upgrades do not spawn expansion in the software industry as well. As processing power and storage capacity have increased, so has the complexity of the software applications that run on those processing platforms. Graphic file editing on a PC was not really possible with any level of reasonable patience until the advent of faster processors, larger RAM storage areas and faster, larger hard disk drives. As these hardware enhancements became a part of the normal PC computer landscape, the applications (such as CorelDRAW!) appeared that took advantage of the increased processing capabilities.

There has been, and likely always will be, a symbiotic relationship between computer hardware and software. The software industry is tiered along a number of different dividing lines. Each area of technology has its own nuances and standard methods of operation that must be considered when evaluating a specific company investment. The intent of the information presented in this chapter is to augment the standard due diligence and target selection procedures outlined elsewhere in this book with information that applies specifically to the software development industry segment.

Industry Realities

The realities of the software industry are numerous and somewhat dependent on the section of the industry under investigation.

1. A change in underlying hardware to a higher level of technology usually prompts a change in the operating system that runs on that hardware platform.

2. A change in operating system usually prompts a change in the applications that run on that operating system.

3. Microsoft Windows-type operating system is installed on over 90 percent of the personal computers in use today worldwide.

4. Applications are usually developed for a specific operating system platform and must be converted, or "ported," to another operating system. For example, applications developed for the Macintosh operating system cannot run on a Windows-based PC without modification.

5. The available market for an application is dependent upon the installed hardware base that can run that particular application.

6. PC-oriented software is usually quite standard and comes in a prepackaged form usually sold through retail or distribution outlets.

7. Prepackaged software is a thriving, growing business that accounted for $135 billion in 1998 sales and is expected to grow at between 11 percent and 14 percent annually through 2002. This translates into an expected $212 billion industry in 2002! An industry subsegment breakdown for 1998 follows for the prepackaged application software, application development tools, and utilities/operating systems.

   Prepackaged application software program sales in 1998 were $63 billion and are expected to grow at 14 percent to 15 percent through 2002. This area includes packages such as Microsoft Office, CorelDRAW!, Quicken, and others that address a specific standard application need. Prepackaged application tools that handle data access, manipulation, retrieval, and program design and development sold $31 billion in 1998. This segment is expected to grow by 11 percent annually through 2002. Prepackaged system software such as the operating system, virus checkers, utilities, and management tools sold $41 billion in 1998, and the segment expected to grow at a 13.5 percent annual rate through 2002.

8. Mainframe computers are here to stay and so are the software packages that make them run. This was a $12 billion industry in 1998 and is expected to grow at around 4 percent per year. The ability of a mainframe to handle the immense amount of data required for Internet-type applications guarantees the survival of the mainframe for years to come.

9. Mainframe software is sold in much lower volume and usually on a more customized basis. Mainframe software is often leased instead of purchased and may cost from tens of thousands of dollars into the millions.

10. Ongoing relationships are very important in the mainframe arena because the number of installed computers is substantially smaller than the PC marketplace.

11. IBM holds a substantial 76 percent market share based on MIPS (million of instructions per second) shipped in 1998.

12. Market growth in 1998 measured in hardware MIPS shipped grew by a whopping 55 percent! So much for the mainframe being a dinosaur from the past.

13. Database management software sales increases are being driven by the Internet's intense need for quick, efficient, and simple data access. This market grew 15 percent in 1998.

14. The Internet continues to permeate every aspect of modern life, with around 1 billion users expected by 2005, up from an estimated 131 million in 1999.

15. The Internet is also driving a need for operating system independent applications that can run on smaller, less powerful platforms such as personal data assistants (PDAs). This trend is the first step in eroding the Microsoft operating system monopoly, with the Internet becoming the great equalizer.

16. Internet technology is now becoming widely used in intranets, with 25 percent of all Internet-related technology dollars being spent on intranet.

17. The Internet is also driving a huge surge in e-commerce type applications that include the ability for consumers to sell to consumers (C-to-C), businesses to sell to businesses (B-to-B), and businesses to sell to consumers (B-to-C).

18. International Data Corporation (IDC) predicts that $40 billion in goods and services were sold online in 1999, and expects this number to jump to an amazing $900 billion by 2003.

19. Software development is a people-intensive, creative business. A skilled labor pool is needed to support these expected growth rates and labor shortages will inevitably drive up labor, development, and resulting product costs. If

product manufacturing costs remain relatively consistent, then profit margins will likely suffer as labor shortages become more acute. This is a primary motivation for software manufacturers to deliver software over the Internet and to put their user manuals online for Internet access by users. These two delivery methods cut costs and often provide consumers with a higher level of service. I also personally like that electronic user manuals are easier to carry, easier to reference by using electronic searches, and better for the environment in that paper is not used for manuals that become obsolete in a short period of time.

20. Consumers require that software comply with existing standards, either de facto standards like Microsoft Windows or industry standards like those associated with the TCP/IP protocols.

21. Consumers tend to stay with a specific software product from one generation to another because data conversion, retraining, and administration learning time cost productivity. Consumers usually change software packages and vendors only when the new application addresses a specific need not met by the previous vendor or when the prior product did not perform up to a satisfactory level.

22. If the overall economy drops off or the rate of hardware change slows, hardware upgrades will slow and will likely slow software sales along with them.

This segment is tracked as Computer (Software and Services) and contains smaller peer groups, such as System Software—Smaller, for closer tracking of like software development companies. The Software and Services segment includes a large number of companies such as Microsoft (MSFT), Red Hat Inc. (RHAT), Autodesk, Inc. (ADSK), Corel Corporation (CORL), Softlock.com, Inc. (SLCK), The Santa Cruz Operation (SCOC), Saga Systems, Inc. (AGS), and Phoenix Technologies, Ltd. (PTEC). Many of the smaller to mid-sized companies in this segment do not show a profit at all and betas for this group vary over a wide range.

When a software development company is profitable it is really a cash pump. This is a rare industry, one where you can find a Microsoft showing a 31 percent net income as a percent of 1998 revenues, or a Computer Associates showing a 24.7 percent net income for 1998. Part of the reason for these types of high returns are due to the financial operational model.

The cost of manufacturing the product actually delivered by a software development company may be as little as a few dollars because it consists of

Table 13.1 Microsoft Financial Information

Item	FY 1998 Reported Value (millions)	Percent of Revenue
Revenue	$15,262	100%
Cost of Revenue (COS)	$2,460	16%
R&D	$2,601	17%
Sales and Marketing	$2,828	18%

a CD or disk, a few manuals, and packaging, with the cost of the printed manuals being the largest single variable cost item. This is why so many developers are looking for ways to provide those manuals on CD or over the Internet using services such as FatBrain.com. The bulk of the cost expense shows up in research and development, because a software program is nothing more than the end result of a massive intellectual property creation project.

To illustrate an example of how this financial model can work for a successful software development company, Table 13.1 shows Microsoft's financial information for its 1998 fiscal year. It is clear from the table that the cost of sales is very low for Microsoft, but its research and development costs are high when compared to other industries, such as the PC/workstation industry. These high R&D expenses are typical of any company that relies heavily on the creation of intellectual property as an integral part of its business model. Microsoft can produce a software package such as Windows NT that sells for around $600 retail and nets 84 percent in gross margin, or $504. The same $600 retail revenue sale for Dell will provide a gross margin of 22.1 percent, or $133. In summary, the profit margins in the software industry are excellent compared to those of other industries, such as PC manufacturing. Remember that Dell, on the other hand, only invests around 1.6 percent of revenues on R&D.

Software companies also sell on an international basis, which subjects their accounts receivable values to the whims of currency conversion rates. Favorable moves will have the net effect of increasing the value of existing accounts receivable, where negative moves will decrease the value. Understanding the company's international sales, marketing, and financing specifics is also imortant.

Trying to evaluate Microsoft and Dell using the same financial modeling assumptions would clearly be a mistake. The companies must be evaluated with respect to the other companies within their same industry, and then the industry as a whole can be evaluated against others for attractiveness to the buyer.

Important Considerations

Here is a partial listing of items that specifically relate to software development companies for your consideration. Naturally, the other standard due diligence reviews should be performed in addition to those steps outlined here. The software development industry has many companies that might make excellent acquisition targets for a buyer in need of the provided creativity. More smaller firms are springing up all the time, mostly due to the low cost barrier to entry and the likelihood of being purchased once a viable technology can be shown to work.

1. Does the company have a copyright on any proprietary software code that provides a unique advantage in the marketplace? Does it have a trademark or other legal protection on a specific methodology or procedure that could be better leveraged through the buyer's strengths?

2. What is the source for the software packages that generate the majority of company revenues? Is this software internally developed or was it licensed or purchased from a third party? If so, what are the details associated with that relationship?

3. Who are the key development personnel involved with the creation, coding, and evaluation of software products? What is the company's relationship with these key persons, and what is their expected future contribution to the company's success?

4. How many patches (fixes) were required to make the last major software release stable and commercially viable? How does this number of patches compare with the rest of the industry, and what was the customer reaction?

5. Have any major customer accounts been lost either during upgrade to a new version of software or after their implementation of a new version release? Why did they choose not to use the product, and what has been done to ensure that this situation does not come up again?

6. What operating system platforms are the target for the company's software products? Is that platform prevalent? Is it in an increasing or declining market? How did the company handle the transition to Windows 2000?

7. What is the company's strategy for porting their applications across different operating system platforms? What has been their success in this area? What is their LINUX strategy?

8. What are the company's marketing and distribution channels, and what is its level of existing customer resale success in the different channels?

9. Does the company use structured programming techniques that allow for easy updating, maintenance, and enhancement by future programmers? If not, how does the company handle these issues in a reliable, repeatable way?

10. What is the company's Internet-related strategy? Areas of interest should include directions for new products specifically related to the Internet and also directions for using the Internet as a possible delivery/development tool. Has the company integrated any specific Internet features into its existing product family?

11. If the company is a customer software supplier, what are the percentage revenue breakdowns for product sale/lease, maintenance, and upgrade support? How do these percentages compare with the industry as a whole? What is the percentage of customers who subscribe to an upgrade and is the installed base growing or shrinking?

12. What is the company's strategy with respect to future development languages and tools? Where is it now and how does its position compare with its competition?

13. What is the company's strategy for dealing with Microsoft? Even if they are in a different industry segment, they must in some way understand and relate to Microsoft and its possible impact on their particular industry segment.

14. How does the company perform on an international basis, and is it subject to international trade and currency conversion changes?

Understanding the creative culture of a software development firm is critical to understanding its success. Developers are a unique breed of engineers who often don't fit well within a structured environment. Make sure that you understand the existing aspects of the company that have made it successful to date, and ensure the preservation of those aspects in the postacquisition environment. There is a high demand for successful, experienced program-mers, and a successful software company acquisition must ensure the reten-tion of these important personnel resources.

Chapter Summary

A software development company has a large, up-front development cost which must be amortized over the sale of subsequent copies of the developed software. For this reason, a large R&D expense appears on a software com-pany's income statement. There are low financial barriers to entry for smaller software projects, which allows for the creation of many new firms. Many of these firms develop a product or technology with the expressed intent of sell-ing the company to a larger, more established firm when the time comes for marketwide distribution of the product.

The good news for successful companies is that the profit margins for this industry are large as compared to other industries, with a large portion of the company's expenses being spent on R&D and marketing. Cost of sales is typ-ically very low for this industry, and the current trend of electronic software and manual delivery will maintain this high profit margin. I predict that ex-pected increases in bandwidth to the consumer's desktop machine, com-bined with increasing consumer sophistication, will make this electronic delivery mechanism the accepted norm in the future.

This is a very complicated industry with a number of vertical and horizon-tal markets. It is critical to understand the primary market within which the target company operates and then compare its performance to others in the same market. It is also a good idea to use trend analysis so that you can com-pare the company's historical performance to its competitors during both good and poor external economic climates. This provides some insight as to how it will react to future major industry changes, which inevitably occur in this industry. The software industry is heavily driven by external forces such as hardware sales, changes in operating system platform versions, interna-tional economic climates, and general consumer optimism. The good news for developers of successful products is that consumers do not generally change from one software vendor to another unless there is some overriding reason, such as specific product features or lack of confidence in the developer and its products. Tracking the upgrade levels from one version level to another is a great starting point when gauging customer satisfaction levels. Taking the time to evaluate a software development company as you would any other and investigating the topics mentioned in this chapter which are specifically related to software development firms provides you with a much clearer understanding of the target company in general and specifically its prospects within the context of its respective industry.

14

Data Networking and Telecommunications Businesses

As the number of computers presently on corporate desks and in consumer homes has increased, so has the need to tie these computers together. Networks do just that and have been an integral part of the computer landscape from nearly the beginning. Many of today's "hot" networking technologies have actually been around for many years but needed a high enough market acceptance level to drive prices down to the point that the technology become commercially viable.

Terminals were initially tied directly to the computer and then migrated out to the office desk, with proprietary networking technologies used to communicate from the desktop terminal to the computer. The PC changed this by providing a processing-type workstation at the desk which took the processing load off of the central computer. PCs now had little need to communicate with the mainframe computer but needed to communicate with each other for data and printer sharing, which gave rise to the local area network (LAN). As people started moving around with computers, the need for remote access to the company network increased and substantial modem advancements occurred.

The need for easy sharing of information from widespread geographic locations spawned the invention of the World Wide Web, using the existing Internet infrastructure as the backbone. As graphic file usage became more prevalent on the workstations, the need for a high-speed, low-cost connection to the desktop emerged, which gave rise to the twisted-pair networking technology used in the LAN.

People now needed to communicate with larger data files from their homes as well as offices, thus prompting the implementation of various technologies that enabled high-speed data access to the home. The personal data assistant (PDA) surge is now driving the need for data connections over wireless media. Voice telephone calls have been transmitted in digital format for decades, and attempts have been made over the years to integrate digital voice and data information over the same networks. Some of these efforts were successful, and others have fallen into business obscurity. It now appears as though the integration of data and voice over a single digital network, namely the Internet or Internet-like networks, is finally coming into a high level of acceptance. Technologies like Integrated Services Digital Network (ISDN) have been around since the mid-1980s, and it was still referred to facetiously as "I Still Don't Know" as late as the mid-1990s. The good news is that ISDN is now becoming an industry reality, but so are cable modems and other technologies that are able to transfer much higher data rates than ISDN for a comparable commercial cost.

My reason for introducing this brief historical perspective is to provide some type of framework within which to understand the current state of and anticipated future evolution of the telecommunications industry. It may seem like ancient history to some, but it is important to remember that voice telecommunications was under the auspices of a single, regulated AT&T company until the mid-1980s. A judge's ruling at that time forced AT&T to divest itself of the various Regional Bell Operating Companies (RBOCs) and other holdings. The RBOCs are still in control of the local telephone service and wiring plant and are consolidating their strengths through mergers like the recent one between Ameritech and Southwestern Bell Corporation (SBC). The divested Bell Labs eventually became Lucent Technologies.

Today's communications industry is really divided into three basic categories: wireline telecommunications, wireless telecommunications, and data communications. Wireline refers to those companies who provide telecommunications services to the subscriber using a physical wire connection, such as that used by the local RBOC. Wireless telecommunications companies provide services using a radio transmission technique of some type, which started out primarily as analog technology and is rapidly migrating to digital. Data communications companies are those which concentrate on the transfer of computer data from one point to another, with the data ideally remaining in digital form from the beginning to the end of the transmission.

It has always intrigued me that the data and telecommunications worlds did not meld into a single digitally networked entity years ago, because the ones and zeros can travel over the same digital pipelines whether they carry voice or computer data information. The division only made sense to me when I assumed that the chasm was not technologically prompted but caused more by business and political reasons. That brings us to today.

Industry Realities

There are a number of industry realities that permeate the entire data and telecommunications industries. These realities in many ways dictate the upcoming evolution and the relationships between the companies and technology they provide.

1. The Federal Communications Commission (FCC) is charged with the regulation of telecommunications services in the United States. Telecommunications companies, such as the RBOCs and AT&T, must generally obtain FCC approval before any services can be offered.

2. The transfer of data from one point to another requires either a physical cable connection or a radio connection of some type. Once again, if the data travels using radio waves, it must be in accordance with FCC regulations.

3. The RBOCs own the existing twisted pair wiring plant that runs from the telephone company central office to the consumer's premises. Over 95 percent of homes in the United States have a telephone line/wire connection, and the penetration level is expected to remain relatively constant into the near future.

4. This twisted pair wiring plant has certain physical and electrical limitations that restrict the possibility of transferring very high data rates over reasonable distances as defined by the current wiring plant design. If history repeats itself, the relatively high DSL (digital subscriber line) rates provided today may be considered slow in only a few years.

5. If the backbone data transfer infrastructure does not expand to meet the demands placed on it by higher consumer premise data transmission rates, the entire network will still run slowly.

6. Consumers are constantly pushing for higher and higher data transfer rates to their premises. As this data rate increases, a greater demand is placed on the data transmission speed capacities of the backbone network that carries the data.

7. This constant push-pull effect between consumer desire for higher data transfer speeds and the backbone network's ability to provide these speeds means that technology, products, and services will continue to evolve and change on a regular basis for years to come.

8. The advent of cellular and wireless digital communication opens a new avenue for data communications between the consumer and the network. As mobile devices become more powerful, the need for a fixed communications port at the home or office may decrease.

9. The lines between voice and data communications are becoming seriously blurred. Assume, for example, that you obtain both a voice message and an email message from the same digital cellular handset. Is this a telecommunications or data communications operation? Assume also that the handset converts the voice message to written text that can then be read on your cellular phone display so that you get the message but never hear the speaker's voice at all. Is this a voice or data operation?

10. Voice communication over the Internet (voice-over-IP or VOIP) is becoming a reality. As more people obtain access to the Internet via their computers, the economic reality of making a long distance call over the Internet instead of the standard phone line will move customers to voice-over-IP. Why pay long distance charges to Australia when you can call for free using your Internet connection? The Internet connection might even allow you to see them at the same time!

11. Bandwidth (the ability to move large blocks of data over communication links) hunger has been, and likely always will be, a driving force behind the communications industry. Whatever you think is fast today will be considered slow in a few years.

12. Reality concepts will continually be challenged, tested, and expanded. A common 1984 telecommunication design assumption was that the maximum bandwidth limitation of twisted pair wiring was 3.4 kHz. In today's world of 1 gigabit twisted pair connections, this may sound hard to believe but it is true.

13. The industry is moving toward a more digital world, with analog technology quickly becoming to communications what the oil lamp is to modern lighting.

14. Major technology transitions do not happen overnight, but they do happen, as is evident by the now-common availability of ISDN. Innovation is often driven by smaller companies, who are then acquired by larger players who give that technology a national platform, a credible service organization and more rapid customer acceptance.

15. The Internet, the Internet, and a little more Internet is the future. Whether the Internet's success spawns another technology that replaces it will only be seen as the future unfolds. You can be assured that Internet technology is the confluence point for future data and voice technological advance, with the understanding that the technology may be used on a private intranet.

16. The lines between a local and wide area network are also blurring. This line was traditionally drawn at the point where the fast local area network connected to the much slower wide area network. When the wide area network portion can transmit at speeds up to or greater than the local area network, the entire nation becomes a local area network. It may not happen in the next 24 months, but it is going to happen.

17. Adherence to standards drives this industry. A company that develops a great new technology that does not adhere to current standards always fights an up-hill battle in getting widespread consumer acceptance. Notice the battle between CDMA (code division multiple access) and TDMA (time division multiple access) cellular technology and its proponents. Incompatible technologies often create a dividing line that consumers must navigate (often to their surprise) after having purchased their cellular phones.

18. Customers like consistency in their networks and, for this reason, tend to migrate toward a single vendor solution as long as that vendor reasonably meets the customer's needs. Early market leaders tend to do well in the telecommunications/data communications industry.

19. The cost per unit of bandwidth provided continues to drop and is expected to decrease in price into the future. Higher bandwidth, smaller, transparent, and reliable are the mantras for the telecommunications/data communications industries.

20. Business consolidation is highly likely as the industry pares itself down to a few major players who provide a wide array of services. Single-source solutions are well accepted in the communications industry.

21. Market opportunities shift within the data communications world. While the initial market interest was in connecting to the local area network, the current focus has shifted to making connections from remote locations back to the

customer premise. The ultimate intention is the implementation of a seamless communication network that knows no geographical boundaries. Understanding the target company's product and service positioning within the network topology itself is important to accurately project the company's future market opportunities.

The Major Players and Financials

This section is approached a little differently from the manner in which major players are presented in other chapters, in that here the major players are presented in light of their specific industry segment. The three segments presented are for wireline companies, wireless companies, and data communications companies. Each industry is facing its own set of challenges and, as such, is addressed in its own subsection.

Wireline Companies

Wireline carriers have traditionally been viewed as those firmly entrenched, solid citizens who provide dial tone but never really do much that is very exciting. In fact, they did not need to be exciting because they had a vise grip on the local access connection to the customer's premises. That is changing with the expanded prevalence of cable television connections that can transmit not only television signals, but also telephone, fax, digital, and video without suffering any degradation of signal. This is a powerful force that must be reckoned with.

In addition, the RBOCs no longer have a monopoly on the ability to connect to the consumer premises to provide telephone service. This means that competition will appear on the consumer's door looking to move the local telephone service from the RBOC to the new provider, and probably at a lower rate. The RBOCs have figured out that the world has changed and these huge, cash-rich competitive entities will start throwing their financial weight around.

AT&T, once the owners of the RBOCs prior to the mid-1980s divestiture, is now the owner of Tele-Communications Inc. (TCI) cable television services and has a strong alliance with Time-Warner regarding the provision of media content. If anyone understands the local loop, it is AT&T and they are now knocking on the customer's back door offering a variety of connection services to the consumer with the intention of taking the business away from the very RBOC that AT&T once owned. Over 65 percent of U.S. households have a cable connection, which presents a very large access opportunity for anyone who can provide telephone service through that cable connection.

The RBOCs are not standing still, however. They are merging with each other and pushing for the right to offer their own set of enhanced services to consumers including Internet connections, long distance, and cellular. This ongoing battle will likely benefit consumers although it might be very confusing in the interim.

Wireline carriers are tracked as the Telecommunications (Wireline) segment. Companies included in this group are a select few including SBC Communications (SBC), BellSouth Corp. (BLS), Bell Atlantic (BEL), US West (USW), and GTE (GTE), along with many smaller companies. Betas for this group of companies are fairly low; many of them have a value of less than one.

The wireline companies have traditionally generated a net income of between 9 and 21 percent. Whether they can maintain these net income levels as they deal with the upcoming competition remains to be seen. These companies are heavily capital equipment-dependent with large fixed expenses, and a decrease in revenues can have a dramatic impact on the net income, as is the case with any industry with heavy fixed expenses. Notice also that this industry generates over $190 billion in revenues and $23 billion in net income. Growth for this industry is difficult to quantify because this mature industry has a telephone line already in place at most customer locations. Much of the growth experienced comes from customers adding additional lines at a connected location. As cellular technology continues its expansion into the consumer marketplace, the need for that second line will decrease, taking the wireline carriers' second-line increasing revenues with it. For this reason you find many of the wireline carriers heavily investing in cellular technology and services. In this way, the customers get the technology they want and simply transfer the revenue from one division within the wireline carrier to another within the same carrier's umbrella.

Looking for this shifting of revenues from one business unit to another is an important process when evaluating any communications company, and is particularly important with the wireline carriers. They may be approaching the most critical period in their independent existence as technology and regulatory changes threaten the very wireline connection that previously ensured their survival.

Wireless Companies

Anyone who watches television knows that the battle for wireless supremacy rages at full speed. This 1998 market of $33.1 billion is expected to grow to $50 billion in the year 2000, according to Standard & Poors (S&P). Market share rankings for wireless are a little unusual in that the POP (an acronym used to represent the total population to which a specific wireless provider can offer its services) is used as a measure of market share. This does not necessarily represent the total number of subscribers, which must be tracked separately.

Table 14.1 lists some of the major wireless suppliers and their POP/subscriber performance numbers as listed in a July 1999 S&P Industry Survey report on the wireless telecommunications industry This table is certainly a gross simplification of a complicated industry, but it does raise some important questions related to the evaluation of marketing and sales performance for a wireless carrier. For example, Bell Atlantic and AirTouch generate almost six times the revenue per POP as Nextel. Even AT&T Wireless is earning less than 1/3 the revenue per POP as AirTouch and Bell Atlantic. It is reasonable to want to know why there is such a large discrepancy and then decide for yourself whether this lower performance level by Nextel is a result of extenuating market conditions or internal management problems. Viewing this data over a length of time provides a trend line which may shed some light on the situation. Future competition will only increase, making it even more difficult for each of these companies to gain new customers.

Another trend line to evaluate is the penetration of subscribers to total POP for a given provider. This is really the equivalent of available market share for a provider. As the penetration starts to approach the maximum POP number you can fully expect for new customer revenues to decline and for revenues to be earned by increasing sales to the existing customers. The

Table 14.1 Major Wireless Companies: POP/Subscriber Performance

Provider	POPs (millions)	1998 Revenues (millions)	Revenue/ POP Ratio
AT&T Wireless (AWE)	314.6	$5,400	17.16
Vodafone-AirTouch (VOD)	64.3	$3,900	60.65
Bell Atlantic (BEL)	56.9	$3,700	65.03
Nextel Communications (NXTL)	165.3	$1,800	10.88

provider now moves from a growth market to a mature market, which typically translates into much lower future revenue growth rates.

This domestic U.S. industry segment is tracked as the Telecommunications (Cellular/Wireless) segment and includes companies such as AT&T Wireless (AWE), a tracking stock issued by AT&T in early 2000; Bell Atlantic (BEL); Vodafone Group PLC-Airtouch (VOD), which is planning to merge with Mannesman AG of Germany at the time of this writing; Nextel (NXTL); U.S. Cellular (USM); Sprint Corp. PCS Group (PCS); and other carriers. Betas for this group vary significantly between companies.

It is important to understand that a wireless provider pays a fee for the rights to a POP and the fee is determined on a per-POP basis. Extensive upfront costs are also incurred in setting up the initial equipment needed to provide service. These expenses must be amortized over a period of time, which represents a large fixed expense that must be paid down by the cellular company buying the POP license. A common measure of market valuation is obtained by dividing the market value of the company's outstanding shares by the total POP licenses owned.

New companies dedicated to simply providing wireless communication services have a difficult time showing any profit at all. When evaluating a target wireless company, a trend analysis tracking revenues per subscribers, expected new subscribers, and cost projections, with a hard look at future cash flows, would be a good idea. Anyone buying an existing wireless company that is not yet showing a profit must have deep enough pockets to fund the operation for a few years until a profit is earned. Conversely, the buyer must be sure that additional synergy exists between its current offering and that of the target company such that a profit can be shown in a shorter period of time than could be obtained by the target company on its own. For the strategic buyer, the purchase of an existing wireless company can provide an excellent opportunity to direct the buyer's company into a new, exciting, growing, and potentially very lucrative direction. The buyer should make sure that expectations are in line with industry profit and growth reality.

Data Communication Companies

While the wireline companies have a strong relationship with the customer regarding telephone and voice communications, the data communications companies have a strong relationship with customers with respect to their data networking needs. The technology has existed for years to combine voice and data over the same network. Unfortunately for the telephone companies, the disruption to their operational and regulatory environment caused by the divestiture of AT&T kept them from fully capitalizing on the rapid deployment of PCs into the business environment. A new data communications industry grew up during these postdivestiture periods of upheaval, and data networking companies now comprise a solid and respected industry in their own right.

It is helpful to separate the data communications industry into several different segments so that any company's position within the industry can be clearly understood. As part of this discussion, keep in mind that it has traditionally been possible to route data on the customer premises at high rates of speed, and that very high data transmission rates have been possible within the national telecommunications infrastructure for many years. The challenge has been, and still remains, with the implementation of high-speed connections between the customer's high-speed on-site network and the high-speed national telecommunications infrastructure. This need has become more obvious and critical as Internet usage increases.

The 1980s and 1990s were a time for increasing the speed and availability of local area network connections within the customer's premises while simultaneously decreasing costs. Companies like 3Com and Cabletron thrived on the LAN explosion. The 1990s saw the incredible rise of the Internet, along with a commensurate rise in the use of portable computers, so that people looked for ways to connect not only to the Internet but also back to their offices using the Internet as the data transport vehicle. Companies like Cisco Systems and Bay Networks came to rise during this dynamic period. Much consolidation has happened in this industry, with Bay Networks being acquired by Nortel, 3Com acquiring US Robotics, and much other such M&A activity. The next stage of evolution will likely involve increasing access speeds from the customer's premises to the backbone network, improving methods of managing these increasingly complicated networks, and increasing backbone network capacity while simultaneously reducing networking costs.

The rapid pace of change in the networking industry, combined with the belief that huge market growth is in the future, has led companies to purchase other companies with a special technology. This type of product and market expansion acquisition quickly gets the buying company into a new market segment without the hassles and risks associated with developing the products with internal resources. Cisco Systems has acquired over 50 companies since 1993 and shows no signs of backing off of its expansion-by-acquisition strategy, which appears to be working considering Cisco's financial performance and huge market valuation. Some think that Cisco Systems could become to data communications what Microsoft has become to the software industry.

The importance of product and company reliability in the data communications industry cannot be overstressed. While people would never have tolerated their business telephone being out of service for more than a few minutes, companies today have come to rely on their data networks as mission-critical aspects of their business. If the company is questionable or the product is unreliable, the buyer simply may not be willing to take a chance.

In the midst of all of this expansion and tumult we find new companies entering the marketplace, proving the validity of their approach, only to be purchased by another larger player. It is reasonable to assume that this business model will continue to flourish and that industry consolidation will continue. In short, it is not unreasonable to expect that the data networking industry will eventually settle down to a duel between networking provider titans such as Cisco, Lucent, and Motorola. Smaller companies will thrive in niche markets while the larger companies compete for the larger infrastructure contracts.

This group of companies is tracked in the Computers (Networking) group, and various peer groups are contained within the larger segment. Companies in this segment include Cisco Systems (CSCO), 3Com Corporation (COMS), Cabletron Systems (CS), and Network Appliance (NTAP); many other related companies are tracked in the Communications Equipment group. Companies in this group include JDS Uniphase (JDSU); Nortel Networks (NT); Lucent Technologies (LU); Fibercore Inc. (FBCE); and Tellabs, Inc. (TLAB), the Internet Networking Division of Motorola. Betas for this group also vary widely between companies.

The fairest way to evaluate a target company's financial performance is to compare the target's performance against that of another company within the same specific industry segment over a common period of time. Industry trends will affect both companies and clearly it is unfair to compare the performance of a Network Equipment Technologies to a Cisco if for no other reason than from an economy-of-scale perspective. If you see substantial deviation between the performance of the target and the performance of the comparison company, then you have highlighted areas for further investigation, which is what you are looking for in the first place. Since this industry is heavily public standards driven, it is difficult to have a proprietary technology for very long. De facto standards exist in this industry just as they do in others, with the Cisco way rapidly becoming the de facto standard.

Important Considerations

The following are items that should be considered as a supplement to the standard due diligence evaluation. They relate specifically to the industry and company type under investigation and should provide a much more complete picture of the target company in relation to its other industry-specific competitors.

Wireline Companies

If history is any measure of future actions, then the most likely buyer of a wireline company is another wireline company. Your target company just may fall into that category. The following is a list of considerations that should be added to any comprehensive due diligence program.

1. The regulatory impact of the acquisition must be considered when looking to purchase a wireline carrier such as an RBOC.

2. A close look at the target's current subscriber base and its trends over the last few years is a worthwhile exercise. You will likely find that revenues have shifted from one division of the company to another as new technology was introduced.

3. A profit analysis by division is also called for, because migration from one technology segment to another may look irrelevant on the consolidated financial statements but could be disquieting on the division level. This is particularly true if the primary purchase motivation is the performance of a specific division.

4. Check with the local public utility commissions of the states served by the target company to determine if there are any major pending actions against the company.

5. What are the company's service records with respect to repairing of lost service and the management of installations? What is the company's level of service with respect to incomplete, dropped, or blocked calls? Has this service level increased or decreased over time?

6. A thorough review of the company's past accounting practices with respect to depreciation of fixed assets is highly recommended. Regulated entities often were (and possibly still are) creative in their accounting practices. Revenues were often determined based on a fixed return on investment calculation with a maximum return, such as 12.5 percent, allowed as billed customer revenues. Assets were depreciated over a longer period of time and assets were purchased to increase the investment base, which translated into a raise for the company. Once the company was no longer regulated, the assets magically lost value through accelerated depreciation and every nickel spent on capital equipment had to be justified. Understanding the way that these past events affected the historical financial statements of the target company helps in understanding the basis for the numbers presented in the target's current financial statements.

7. How is the company positioned to provide enhanced digital services to its subscriber base? The good news here is that local subscribers recognize the name of their local wireline provider and are more prone to subscribe to a new service from their familiar provider than to sign up with an unknown. This can turn out to be very lucrative for anyone who properly manages that relationship.

8. What type of investment has the company made in higher-speed data networking technology such as fiber optics? Does the company currently offer any high speed data connection products to its subscribers such as ISDN, ADSL, or others?

9. Is the internal operation of the company handled by employees or has the process been outsourced to a third party? If it has been outsourced, what is the contractual relationship with this third party and what is that company's specific state of financial and operational health? What is that third party's performance track record?

10. Has any other major telecommunications services vendor chosen to target the target company's geographic and market area as its foray into offering subscriber products and services? If so, who is the company and what is the target company's competitive analysis of the threat? If not, is it likely to happen in the future, and who does the target see as the most likely company to initiate the threat?

Wireless Companies

The wireless industry has some unique attributes that can add to or subtract from the potential value of a target company. Consider these items in conjunction with the others required for a complete due diligence evaluation.

1. What is the company's POP and has it grown or shrunk over time?

2. What is the percentage of the POP that currently subscribes to the target company's service? Is this percentage growing or shrinking over time? Is this percentage approaching the maximum subscriber base as defined by the POP size? How much does it cost the target to add another subscriber (Cost per gross add)?

3. What are the revenues per subscriber as shown over time? Are they increasing or decreasing?

4. What technology is used by the provider? TDMA, CDMA, or analog? What are the target company's plans with respect to dealing with expected digital technology? Does the company plan to add any additional application-oriented services that increase the value of the wireless connection to the customer's portable unit?

5. Is any additional competition expected into the target company's market area, and how does the company intend to deal with this additional competition?

6. What percentage of the company's revenues are derived from paging services, and how does the company intend to deal with the high likelihood of paging services becoming obsolete as cellular costs continue to decrease?

7. What relationships does the target company have in place to handle roaming and long distance charges? What is the company's strategy for dealing with flat pricing for roaming, air time minutes, and long distance as offered by some competitors? What are the company's incollect/outcollect revenues and expenses, and how have they changed over time?

8. What are the company's operational statistics pertaining to incomplete calls, dropped calls, and the number of redial attempts? How have these statistics changed over time, and what is the company's strategy for improving these statistics?

9. Does the company directly own the FCC license or does it operate under a sublicense from another company? What are the terms of the agreement (in either case) and what is the likelihood of the agreements remaining in effect into the future? What type of licenses does the company have in its various markets?

10. What is the target company's coverage area and how many antenna sites does it have for that coverage area? How does this number of antennas compare with competitors in the same area? (Note: More antennas in a coverage area usually means better coverage for the same frequency range.) Does the target's system operate at 850 Mhz or 1900 Mhz?

11. How is the target set up for available telephone numbers that can be provided to its subscribers? Does it have enough numbers to meet expected demand or is there a potential problem looming on the horizon?

12. What is the company's customer retention ratio? It is always easier and less expensive to keep a customer than to find a new one. Plot the customer retention ratio over a period of time to see if it changes in either a positive or negative way. In either case, it will likely highlight other areas of investigation.

13. How is the company prepared to deal with the next generation of wireless technology appearing on the horizon? This is a highly dynamic industry full of creativity, growth potential, and drive. This combination always leads to unexpected advances and changes to which a successful player must adapt.

Data Communication Companies

The data communications industry is a rapidly changing one that requires a balance between adherence to industry standards and hard work to differentiate your company from others. Customer service, reliability, price, and speed are a few of the keys to success in this arena, and any prospective target company should be evaluated using these and the following points as a due diligence guideline, along with the other points mentioned throughout this book.

1. Do the company's products adhere to accepted standards? Are the standards U.S.-only standards or are they ones approved by the international standards committees? Are they proprietary standards that only apply to a limited portion of the market? Is that market strong enough to support the company and its future growth plans?

2. What is the company's track record regarding the release of a new product? Does the released product meet specifications or does it require a few design modification iterations before being deemed reliable enough for mission-critical application?

3. Is a substantial amount of retraining required for administrative personnel who are responsible for the installation, configuration, and maintenance of the product?

4. How does the company sell, install and service its products? How does this strategy compare with the company's direct competitors within its particular industry segment?

5. What are the growth prospects for the particular segment within which the target company participates? Is it waning due to industry saturation or technological change, or is it growing in response to real consumer demands?

6. What has been the company's percentage sales growth figures when compared with the industry's specific percentage market growth? If the company's percentage sales growth lags behind the industry, it may indicate a problem worthy of your attention. If the company leads the industry, percentage sales growth figures might indicate an area of strength that can be further exploited.

7. Who are the engineers within the company who understand the technology needed to squeeze the maximum amount of data transfer efficiency from a design? What is the company's relationship with these people, and what is the likelihood that they will remain as employees after the acquisition?

8. Who defines the product specifications for future products and what has been their success rate on past products? Did the products have the required feature set to meet customer needs, and did the product design deliver those features on time and within budget?

9. What is the company's strategy for dealing with the rapidly increasing data transmission speeds? Does the company currently have the expertise to design and market products that address this market need or must it look to supplement its resources in anticipation of success in that arena?

10. Does the company have plans in place for dealing with the evolving wireless communication industry, and what is its strategy for capitalizing on this upcoming trend?

Chapter Summary

The need for higher bandwidth and smaller, less expensive, more reliable network connections will always be with the telecommunications and data communications industry. Companies that choose to compete in this arena must be willing to frequently reinvent themselves and their technologies in response to these industry changes. Data and voice communications exist today in primarily digital format, which opens the door for increased integration of the two networks. Smaller firms often tend to develop technology that addresses a specific market need but often do not have the financial reserves needed to fully capitalize on that technology's potential. Acquisition of that company by a larger, more established firm works for both the buyer and the seller. The buyer acquires rapid entry into a new market segment and may acquire specialized design technology along with it. The seller gets a chance to see its products and technologies implemented quickly across an industry where otherwise the implementation may never have happened, or certainly would have taken a longer period of time. Time is a great enemy in the telecommunications industry when it comes to the introduction of a new technology product, because another newer technology is usually just around the corner.

The expected rapid expansion of the wireless communications market, in conjunction with the rapid expansion of the Internet, presents a unique business opportunity for the merging of data and voice that does not come along very often. The aware M&A professional can use this climate to his advantage and also to the benefit of the other party, whether buyer or seller.

15

Internet-Related Businesses

It is safe to say that no single business or technical phenomenon has had such a far-reaching effect on the daily lives of more people, more quickly, than the Internet. Given its pervasive nature in contemporary daily life, it is difficult to remember that the World Wide Web (WWW) has only been in existence since the early 1990s. Prior to this, the Internet was a tool used primarily by universities and research organizations for transferring data. There is no question that the evolution of the Internet and its applications will continue to drive new technology, product, and company creation, which also creates a fertile environment for M&A activity. Understanding the nuances of this industry is a must for every professional.

The intent of this chapter is not to present an overview of the Internet or WWW, or to evaluate the legitimacy of the various ongoing legal battles that surround this amazing phenomenon. The intent of the information presented in this chapter is to augment the standard due diligence and target selection procedures outlined elsewhere in this book with information that applies specifically to the Internet and its related business segments.

Industry Realities

This unique industry develops without many precedents, and thus requires a new mode of thinking. Trying to fit an Internet company into an existing business model mindset will likely lead to inaccurate assessments and may cause the buyer to misinterpret the real value provided by the target company. There are some analogies that do work with respect to understanding Internet companies and those will be presented as applicable.

1. No single entity owns the Internet, but many organizations work together to make it function.

2. The Internet started out as an essentially free information source, and much of this same mentality has been carried over into today's Internet environment. Attempts at changing this free approach are constantly being tested.

3. The general public no longer views the Internet as a "geek" domain and indeed views it as a consumer resource.

4. "Dot-com" has become an integral part of the American colloquial jargon. The 1999 Christmas season in Chicago even had a billboard sign proclaiming that "Santa Claus is dot-coming to town." Few of these companies are showing a positive net income, although they may exhibit extraordinary revenue growth rates.

5. Many companies involved in the "plumbing" area of the Internet, which is the infrastructure area of the Internet, have shown consistent double-digit growth rates with little slowdown expected. The incredible success of Cisco Systems is indicative of this group's opportunity.

6. A business must have some type of Internet presence or it is considered somewhat archaic. Business partners require an email address just as they require a fax machine. Not having either makes communication more difficult and may interfere with future business relationships.

7. People are becoming more comfortable performing financial transactions online, as indicated by the huge increase in the numbers of people performing online stock trades. Forrester Research of Cambridge, Massachusetts, estimates that in 2002, 30 percent of trades done by individual investors will be performed online for a total of $5 billion in commission fees. This is big business. The recent merger between Charles Schwab (a discount brokerage) and U.S. Trust Corporation (a wealth management firm) portends the future where individuals will be able to bank and manage stock investments through a single online point of contact. This online financial management strategy will become the norm instead of the exception in the future.

8. Security is one of the single most important issues facing the upcoming e-commerce industry. Consumers express concerns not only about the privacy of their financial information, such as credit card numbers, but also about personal information such as date of birth, children's names, address, and Social

Security numbers. Just as it took years for people to trust their ATM machine and electronic deposits, consumers will remain leery about online financial transactions until information security is proven reliable.

9. Given the immense technological complexity of the Internet, it is mandatory that it remain easy to operate from a user's perspective. It usually takes extensive planning and copious preparation to make the complex appear simple and reliable. Any company intent on working in the Internet arena must understand this reality.

10. A small company can appear as big as, or even bigger than, a large company simply by the quality of its Web site. A comprehensive, well-organized, informative, friendly, and attractive Web site speaks volumes to consumers who daily become more sophisticated and more demanding of the sites that they visit.

11. Web site visitors can be lost or gained in a moment. In a physical domain, the customer must at least walk down the street to another store. Online, the customer simply clicks a link or types in a URL and they are shopping at a competitor's site.

12. Customer service is critical, because the shopping experience is highly compressed when compared to a standard bricks-and-mortar shopping experience.

13. An estimated $5 billion to $13 billion was spent with online shopping in 1998, up from $1.4 billion in 1997. This still accounts for less than 1 percent of North American retail sales. The growth rate is evident here and there is plenty of room for gaining more online shoppers.

14. Consumers are constantly looking for higher-speed connections to the Internet that do not require a physical connection, such as those available through wireless communications. Connection prices continue to drop, with some internet service providers (ISPs) offering free connections.

15. Computer purchase price discounts are being offered to buyers who subscribe to an online access account for a specific period of time. This serves the double purpose of getting a lower-priced computer into the consumer's home while also signing them up for an online account. Customers do not change service providers without a reason to do so, which means that if this customer is kept happy, he could represent a regularly recurring revenue stream for years to come.

16. The government has traditionally chosen to allow the Internet to evolve in its own way as opposed to forcing it to conform to some type of governmental regulation. However, personal privacy and data security issues have recently

gained the government's attention, as have sales tax issues. Whether the temptation to interfere will be too great for politicians remains to be seen, but their influence should not be ignored.

17. Standard media companies such as Time-Warner are now merging with online companies such as America Online (AOL). This provides an online outlet for the media company's intellectual content while also providing expanded name recognition for America Online. AOL will offer Time-Warner's media content on its Web site; Warner Bros. retail outlet stores will now sell AOL subscriptions. This is a strategic merger of two large companies which redefines the playing field upon which the Internet game is played. Initial market reaction to the merger was profoundly negative, with AOL stock price dropping precipitously immediately after the announcement.

18. Online advertising dollars are moving from the portal sites to those that specialize in a particular market area. Companies that sell to audiophiles would rather spend online advertising dollars with a Web site that caters to audiophiles as opposed to a Web site that also sells automobiles. This type of advertising approach has traditionally applied to printed advertising and is now being adopted by online advertisers as well.

19. Market valuations applied to many of the "dot-com" companies are so high, especially for companies with negative earnings, that purchase of the companies is difficult to justify from a financial perspective. Mergers and acquisitions in this fetal industry must be justified on a strategic or operational basis as opposed to a financial one. Some question whether a stock-based purchase transaction negates these high target company valuations, and I tend to believe that paying a high price for a company, no matter how it is funded, is still paying too much and opens the buyer to excess risk should future performance not meet with expectations.

20. Explosive growth is the norm for the Internet, and there are no signs of this growth slowing in the near future. The United States leads the way with over 50 percent of the world's Internet users.

21. International Data Corporation (IDC) estimates that 101 million worldwide users accessed the Internet in 1997 and that this number rocketed to 159 million in 1998. This change represents a 58 percent annual growth rate.

22. 1999 estimates were that one-third of the American population is connected to the Internet. This leaves substantial room for domestic growth and enormous international growth potential. IDC estimates that 27 percent of households were online-enabled in 1998, up from 18 percent in 1997 and 13 percent in 1996.

23. The wide acceptance of the Internet and its associated standards presents a unique time in human history in that an accepted communication standard is available for nominal cost to every nationality. The technology is easy enough to use that rapid information dissemination is easily accomplished and for little expense.

24. People who frequent the Web find that their perceptions of time and space change in that a simple click can take the user to a Web location thousands of miles, and a complete culture, away. The world becomes a smaller place to those who frequent the Internet.

25. Internet technology must be separated from the services and benefits offered through using this technology. Although advanced and sophisticated technology must be in place to implement the Internet, the true business opportunities lie in the ability to provide useful services using the Internet as a delivery vehicle.

26. Data delivery bandwidth will continue to increase, while the cost of delivering that bandwidth will decrease. Incredible developments can be expected as high-speed bandwidth becomes accepted as the norm. More bandwidth is always good.

The Internet business segment is full of companies of all types and sizes. The companies listed here are all recognized names that stand the best possible chance of profiting from the Internet's growth, which implies that less-recognized companies may be in worse financial condition than those listed here. The year in which the company was founded is also given after the stock market symbol, which was not done in other chapters, simply to illustrate the overall dynamic nature of Internet companies.

This group of companies is tracked as the Computer (Software & Services) segment, with numerous peer subgroups. Companies that are members of this group include Amazon.com (AMZN; 1995), America Online (AOL; 1991), E*Trade Group (EGRP; 1994), Excite, Inc. (XCIT; 1995) and Yahoo, Inc. (YHOO, 1995). Betas for the companies in this group vary over a wide range. Because much of this group does not yet show a profit, their stock prices are subject to wild valuation swings.

Several well-known Internet companies still show a negative net income at the time of this writing, and others who make money show 3.5 percent to 12.6 percent net incomes. Although this net income range is acceptable for some industries, the Internet businesses are expected to perform at much higher levels since their investment appeal is low inventory, low cost of goods sold, and high profit margins. AOL has a dominant market share for its particular industry segment and still showed only a 3.5 percent profit margin in 1998. AOL does, however, report for ending 1998 $631 million in cash and another $930 million in other current assets. Many Internet companies show substantial current asset holdings, in all probability as a result of their successful initial public offerings. These companies are not likely to run out of money in the near term, but at some point they must show some type of profit or their high stock valuations may start to decline. A liquidity analysis is very important when dealing with companies showing negative earnings, as the "burn rate" at which the company uses cash to fund operations will eventually deplete cash reserves if the company does not show a profit.

The major point to understand about Internet companies is that they do not generally yet show a profit, and they are not usually expected to be profitable for several years into the future. In justifying a high stock valuation level, analysts must attach a large future revenue increase which is assumed to translate into earnings that can then be discounted back to the present time with a positive result. There would be no other reason to purchase the stock because the company is currently losing money.

Again, it is clear that the Internet is the high-growth industry for today's business environment. It is also clear, though, that the Internet spawns new industries, companies, and technologies at a rapid pace. What is true today may not be true in a few years, which makes the process of basing today's high valuations on large future gains suspect. If the future changes in a negative way, the present values could be a recipe for a negative investment return instead of a cash pump for future growth. The potential acquirer of an Internet company must consider the current stock valuation as a strategic, market, or product expansion investment and not as a financially justifiable investment. It is simply too difficult to financially justify the purchase without making assumptions that are highly speculative.

When financial performance is not a credible measure of performance, you must fall back on other criteria. The management team then becomes more important than it is with most other evaluations. Does the management team have a history of being able to adapt to changes in the environment, short as that history period may be for some of these stocks? Does it have an experienced board of directors and a seasoned management team with a proven track record from other business endeavors? Is there something unique about this particular company's technology that positively or negatively differentiates it from its competition? What have been the financial trends associated with this company's growth when compared to others in the same industry segment? These and other questions now become very important, and the subjective interpretation of the future will determine whether the investment is justified or not.

Important Considerations

In light of the unique and speculative nature of the Internet business climate, it is suggested that acquirers consider the following points in addition to those outlined throughout the rest of this book. Buying another company always includes a certain amount of inherent risk. Buying an Internet company takes that inherent risk to a much higher level, but not buying an Internet company might also portend your company's decline if one of your competitors makes an Internet company's technology work for them. This fast-paced world may leave your company far behind if you are not proactive with your Internet strategy.

1. What are your competitors doing with respect to the Internet? What will happen to your company if you do not adopt a sound Internet strategy? What market advantage would you gain if you adopted a valid Internet strategy before your competitors?

2. Does your target audience use the Internet as a communication medium? Would your customer relationships and account control increase with the use of a credible Internet strategy?

3. Is there synergy between your product offerings and the Internet as a delivery medium? Is it possible that your operational costs will decrease if your customers can be properly trained to interact with your company using the Internet as the backbone?

4. What type of Internet-related technology does the target company use? Is it proprietary technology or is it OEM'd through a third party company? If proprietary, who are the employees responsible for the technologies' successes, and what are these employees' relationships with the target company? If OEM'd, what is the relationship with the OEM and would it be impacted by your acquisition?

5. How does the target company earn its revenues at this time? Advertising? Licensing of software? Product sales? E-commerce? Data mining? Get a de-

tailed historical breakdown of revenues by source and evaluate the internally generated future revenue projections. Have the company's negative cash flow levels decreased from one reporting period to the next or is it progressively losing more money? What is the cause for either of these circumstances?

6. Analyze the information obtained from Step 5 above over a period of time to spot positive or negative trends in revenue generation. What were the reasons for these changes?

7. Take a detailed look at the management team. What is their track record with the current company and with previous other startup companies? How did they deal with highly dynamic environments? How will this team fit with the buyer's corporate culture?

8. What type of stock option program is in place for key employees? If you purchase the company, and cash out their options, will they remain motivated to drive the Internet portion of your acquired business to higher and better levels? Will they get restless and want to take their new money and start another startup company? What type of employment agreements are in place with key employees?

9. What is the target company's international strategy? Does it currently have any international presence, and is there a way for your company to assist with or benefit from that international Internet presence?

10. Is there any pending legislation that would either positively or negatively affect either the target company or your combined entity?

11. Have any of the target company's competitors been recently acquired, and by what types of companies? How were the deals structured, and how do those acquisitions affect your particular transaction?

12. Is this Internet company so unique that not purchasing it severely limits future possible acquisitions? Referring to the AOL/Time-Warner transaction, it is important to remember that there are only a few AOLs and Time-Warners out there. After they are gone, the selection gets substantially limited, as do the potential benefits.

13. How successful has the target company been at retaining employees? What has been the secret of that success? Was it simply a matter of offering them large stock options, or is there an employment climate that keeps them around? Can that climate be effectively transferred to the buyer's company?

14. Has the company introduced any new technology? What are its future technology enhancement plans? How do those plans compare with the competition, and how will they fit in with the buyer's future plans?

15. What is the company's status with respect to Internet security? Has it ever been successfully hacked, what was the damage done, and what has been done to ensure that a successful future hack is not possible? Is there any pending litigation as a result of a security violation?

Chapter Summary

Predicting the future is always a blend of historical analysis, educated guessing, and industry experience. Predictions in the Internet business segment also require a strong dose of faith in your educated guesses, because there is really not much historical precedent upon which to base assumptions. There is a natural inclination to fall back on the analysis tools that have served us well in the past, and I suggest that you use these as a starting point. But you should also clearly understand that the Internet business area is unprecedented in many ways and cannot be analyzed using traditional techniques.

The Internet transcends international boundaries as its natural birthright. It changes time and space such that a general consumer expects instantaneous access to information and businesses that are halfway around the world. It is expected that everyone will eventually be an Internet user and that information should be freely and readily available, and from any geographic location. That access should be fast, easily obtained, reliable, and inexpensive. This is a tall order for any industry, but an order that the Internet business segment as a whole must shoulder, and shoulder credibly. Otherwise, the incredibly high stock valuations currently placed on these companies' shares are simply not justified. And only history will separate the visionaries from those who got stuck in the "stone ages." (Refer to Chapter 5, "Financial Analysis Concepts." for additional information of valuing companies with low or negative earnings.) I do believe that every company intending to compete in the future must adopt some type of Internet strategy. However, this strategy should provide an enhancement to what the company has already done to become the success that it is today. We may some day see the arrival of technology that allows a vendor to ship a tractor to a buyer using an electronic connection link, but I don't expect that to happen in the near future.

I do, however, see intellectual property content being delivered over the Internet, whether it be books, software, music, or other forms of content that are easily digitized. Web sites already exist that provide this content. Imagine this: You purchase a software package from an online vendor, download the package to your PC, and access the user manuals electronically from an Internet Web site location. The entire transaction could be paid for using an electronic credit card transfer. In short, this entire transaction could happen instantaneously, online, and never involve the exchange of a physical component. This procedure is happening today and will become commonplace in the years ahead. If you are a company that has potential for this type of transaction you must aggressively be looking for ways to implement this technology into your corporate operation. If you don't do it, one of your competitors will, and then you will be playing catch-up instead of being the leader. Acquiring this technology and expertise through a company purchase may turn out to be the best possible means for providing this capability to your customers. Perhaps the acquisition can then be justified based on your company's revenue and earnings gains instead of those directly derived from the target company's operations. The buyer is much better prepared to analyze and project Internet technology impact on the buyer's own company than projecting the future of an entire industry. Under these circumstances, the future company-specific projections are more credible and require less "crystal-ball" forecasting, which reduces acquisition risk and increases your likelihood of having your acquisition expectations successfully met.

Acquiring a profitable firm is risky enough. Acquiring a company that does not yet show a profit but sports a high valuation adds another level of risk to the endeavor. All of the standard due diligence recommendations presented throughout this book should be applied first, and then a strong dose of Internet-specific investigation based on the recommendations from this chapter should be incorporated into the due diligence investigation. Through this due diligence combination, buyers should be able to ascertain major risks associated with the purchase and effectively evaluate the positive and negative potential impacts that the purchase will have on the buyer.

16

Preparing to Buy and Sell

Sellers want to obtain maximum dollar from their transaction, which is particularly true for the sellers of privately held companies. Buyers are looking for the best possible company and transaction that fits their M&A business objectives. Advance work done on the part of both buyers and sellers makes the likelihood of a successful transaction higher. This chapter presents a number of recommended actions that both buyers and sellers can take to best ensure that the transaction is optimized to the benefit of both parties.

Determine Your Buyer Type

Buyers fall into a few general categories, although transactions between large companies may involve multiple categories. The specific criteria that a buyer applies to a transaction is heavily dependent on that particular buyer's acquisition objectives. The more that a buyer and seller know about each other's driving motivations, the more likely they are to find the common ground that can become a consummated acquisition transaction. This section takes a look at the various buyer types and their dominant characteristics.

Product or Market Expansion Buyer

A major driving force for M&A activity is the buyer's need for product or market presence. Depending on the study you read, product or market expansion plays a role in between 50 percent to 70 percent or more of all acquisitions. A product or market expansion buyer is looking to quickly expand its product offerings, its market presence, or both. Quite often, this buyer is not looking to get into a new industry or technology but is simply looking to expand its reach and presence within its existing industry. Cisco Systems states that a common objective with many of its acquisitions is to broaden its product offering and market presence in a quicker time frame than could be accomplished with internal development efforts.

This type of transaction might include the purchase of a competitor (market expansion), an international company (also a market expansion), or a company that provides products that are an enhancement to those already offered by the buyer (product expansion.) A company that already sells conventional modems might purchase a company heavily into ISDN or ADSL technology as a way of expanding its product lines into those areas. This does not represent a strategic change for the buyer as much as it represents a market and product expansion of its existing operation. The risk associated with a product line or market expansion is less because the buyer is simply expanding in an industry that it already understands and has an established presence. Less risk is always good news, which is what makes this type of transaction so popular.

Competitor acquisition transactions are covered in more detail in Chapter 17, "Franchised and Competitor Transactions." Companies that own any substantial percentage of market share must consider the antitrust implications of a competitor purchase. In fact, some companies use this as a deal-stopper criteria, which may eliminate a competitor transaction before it even starts.

Strategic Buyer

The strategic buyer is looking for a way to round out his company's weaknesses or leverage its strengths through the strategic acquisition of another company. A typical strategic investment might involve the purchase of an Internet commerce technology development firm by a major conventional retail chain. The addition of the Internet commerce technology enables this major chain to strategically place itself on the Internet, possibly preempting some of its competition. By purchasing a technology supplier, the chain has locked up the technology, reducing the possible alternate technology vendors that the chain's competitors can use to get their own Internet commerce sites established.

I worked for Telenova, Inc. in the mid-1980s during the period of time that 20 percent of its stock was purchased by Wang Laboratories. Telenova designed and manufactured integrated data and voice switching systems and Wang was known as a provider of minicomputer systems, networks, and applications. An Wang, the founder of the company, believed that voice and data would eventually combine into a single network and was working to position Wang Laboratories as a single-source supplier of both technologies. Wang furthered this approach by its purchase of Intecom, another major telephone switching company.

We all considered this a strategic purchase at the time, because Wang's intention was to position itself in the telephone switching market while simultaneously leveraging its strength in the data processing and networking area. In addition, Wang had money, while Telenova was a startup company always in need of more funding. The ultimate goal of the strategic move was to use the voice and data networking backbone provided by the telephone switch as a basis for selling more data processing equipment. However, Wang Laboratories had little experience at selling voice communications equipment and a substantial cultural and technical education was involved in Wang Laboratories' making this transition.

Notice that a strategic purchase has a higher level of risk associated with it when compared to a product line or market expansion acquisition. Any strategic acquisition should be carefully considered for both its positive potential and also for its possible longer-term negative effects should the acquisition not work out as planned.

Assume that a company makes a strategic purchase and then has some level of success selling that technology to its customers. It could find itself with a mess on its hands should it later decide that this acquisition didn't work and exit the industry. Customers might resent the fact that they purchased this technology in large part because it came from a preferred vendor who is now telling them that what was originally presented in the sales calls is no longer applicable. This could have serious customer relations implications for the buyer, and for this reason alone strategic buyers are advised to enter into a strategic transaction with a clear understanding of its implications.

Bottom Fisher Buyer

Buy low, sell high. Sounds pretty easy, doesn't it? Making this philosophy work in practice is another matter altogether. A bottom fisher buyer is one who looks for and specializes in purchasing companies when that company can be purchased at a bargain price. This buyer is looking to purchase a company at a rock-bottom price, do some quick and visible modifications to the operation, and then resell it to someone else at a higher price.

A company with a low P/E ratio, price to book value, or price to EBIT/EBITDA ratio would look attractive to the bottom fisher buyer. Add a little cash to the equation and the bottom fishers will likely come knocking at your door. Quite often a bottom fisher buyer is a financial holding company that really does nothing else but buy, hold, and sell companies. This company might have its own "troubleshooting" team who swoop in on the recently purchased bargain company and aggressively turn it into a profitable business entity. Just as people look for structurally sound houses with no curb appeal as a "fixer-upper" on which they can make money, so does the bottom fisher look for basically sound companies that are currently selling at a bargain price. Once fixed up, the intention is to sell it for a profit.

There are all kinds of reasons that a company becomes bottom fisher bait. The industry itself might not be the investor darling it once was, or other industries could be showing a higher-than-expected return which pulls money out of less glamorous business segments. The company might have suffered a management change from which it has not recovered. Any or all of these possibilities could contribute to the devaluation of what would otherwise be a well-run and highly valued company. Look to the bottom fishers to find these companies.

Financial/Leveraged Buyout Buyer

The financial buyer is one looking to purchase a company simply on its financial merit alone. This buyer might think that the company is a solid purchase because it can be broken into smaller pieces and then resold for an overall profit. The buyer might want the acquisition so that the holding company's overall value is large enough to itself attract another buyer. A financial buyer might purchase the seller with the expressed intention of simply liquidating the company, deeming it more valuable liquidated than as an operating firm. The company's purchase price must be low and the company itself must already be in financial trouble for it to qualify for this type of transaction.

A leveraged buyout would be another type of financial buyer transaction. In this case, the buyer puts very little money down on the transaction and uses the assets of the company itself to fund the acquisition. In this way the buyer has little out-of-pocket expense and is in a position to take advantage of the increased profitability that comes from improved financial operation and higher debt. Higher debt leverage also means, however, that a decrease in sales revenue will more dramatically decrease net income and overall company value. Leverage works both for you and against you.

Window Shopper Buyer

Window shopper buyers, sometimes called "tire kickers," are the seller's worst time drain. These people have the look and feel of someone truly interested in buying when they are really only looking around. Even worse, the buyer may not realize that he or she is not really ready to buy and sincerely deceives all parties involved into thinking that he or she really will buy if the right deal comes along. Sellers should be particularly careful of competitors who express an interest in buying. A competitive window shopper might distract you from your primary business operation, might learn proprietary information, and never really be seriously interested in the purchase. This is not to say that a competitor is never a viable buyer, because that is clearly not the case. Sellers need to qualify a competitor's intentions a little more closely than those of a conventional buyer.

The major benefit to a window shopper is that he or she can learn about the operation of a number of companies in a way that would not normally be available. From this information, he or she may find ways to better run his or her own company and will likely recognize the exactly right deal when it comes along. The sellers who trained the window shopper along the way, for free, are the ones who really pay in this case.

Determine the Right Deal Size

We have all had times when our eyes are bigger than our stomachs. Although this may make for an uncomfortable evening, the experience of having taken on too much usually passes pretty quickly. Taking on an acquisition that is too large for the company, personnel, and personalities involved can leave a lingering headache that lasts far into the distant future. Making this maximum deal size determination early in the process enables the team to use this as a deal stopper/company filtering criteria. In this way the buyer only performs a detailed investigation on companies that meet the right price tag criteria.

Management Experience

Some people think that they can manage anything. Most of us, however, have a learning curve associated with our abilities to manage an organization. Shareholders are rarely willing to let someone learn effective management skills on their nickel. They want someone running an organization who is familiar with the requirements of any company the size of the one in which they own shares.

Managers also need to know their limitations. This is not to say that they shouldn't stretch their limits, but they should clearly understand the points where their personal experience may not be up to the requirements of the combined companies. Most executives will pass on an acquisition that pushes them past their own point of effectiveness, and rightfully so on most occasions. A successful track record always makes it easier to move to another company and usually to a better position. In light of this discussion, I suggest that the executive management team take a look at the maximum size organization that it could quickly jump up to without compromising existing management quality levels. Size may be determined by employees, revenues, or any other criteria that management deems applicable to their decision process. Remember that an acquisition adds revenues, expenses, employees, customers, vendors, and valuation on an almost overnight basis. Once acquired, it is up to the executive management team to make it work.

Managers who are uncomfortable making this determination in conjunction with their staff may consider the services of an outside management consultant. This person can work with the executives to determine the level at which the managers will be stressed but not broken. A little advanced, honest evaluation will keep you on the path to future success. That pays dividends for you, shareholders, employees, and your other business partners.

Buyer Risk Tolerance

No financial planner would recommend that you risk more money than you are willing to lose. The same advice applies to an acquisition. A high-risk acquisition that also requires that the buyer highly leverage itself to secure funding really puts the new entity into a "make-or-break" situation which may well be uncomfortable for all involved parties. Although it can be an adrenaline rush to bet the farm on an investment, it can also cause a lot of sleepless nights. Shareholders rarely like sleepless nights and may sing the praises of a risk-taker who succeeds, but will turn on and discharge that executive if a deal falls through and places the entire enterprise in jeopardy. All this leads to a very important question, the answer to which will vary from one company to the next: What is the level of risk to the buying company that shareholders can tolerate in acquiring another company?

You may find this a moot point because the financial covenants that the buyer has already agreed to will preclude the company taking too much risk. If the buyer is financially solvent and unconstrained by external covenants, it should still only make investments that it can live with. Betting the farm on a new acquisition is a last-ditch effort akin to spending your last dollar on a lottery ticket. Sure, you could win, but would you really bet your last dollar and your future livelihood on its coming true?

Legal Restrictions

Anytime that someone lends a company money, the lender will want to ensure that the borrower can repay the debt. Covenants, or specific agreements, are usually inserted in the financial documents requiring that the borrower keep its financial condition within certain specific parameters. Typical covenants would include keeping the current ratio above a certain level, such as 1.2, or keeping the debt-equity ratio below 2. Notice that these covenants are designed to ensure that the borrower has enough cash on hand to pay its bills and also has not incurred too much long-term debt for its equity level.

These covenants can be used as a backdoor way into calculating the financial parameters that the acquisition target must meet. Knowing the buyer's current financial condition, you can calculate the postacquisition debt, equity, and income parameters that must be met from the target company's side to ensure that these covenants are not violated. It is easier to perform these calculations when a specific company is targeted, but a general assessment is possible working backwards as suggested.

Affordability

Buying a company for more than the target's operations and the buyer's extra credit-carrying capacity can afford is rarely a sound financial move. Any downturn in the future performance of either company could put both in jeopardy. The initial question that buyers must address is the maximum affordable deal size. The maximum size is naturally dependent on the target company's financial and operational performance. The right combination of debt, equity, and earnings that make a deal viable requires initial calculations followed by detailed study. The various methods of funding a deal are presented in detail in Chapter 6, "Deal Types and Their Funding." Financial ratio analysis is presented in detail in Chapter 4, "Effectively Using Financial Ratios." Determining the synergistic effects of the acquisition is presented in detail in Chapter 7, "Strategic Synergy and Transaction Structures."

Here are a few general guidelines to help in making that maximum deal size assessment.

1. Issuing shares to fund the transaction divides the corporate earnings over more shares, which has the effect of decreasing the earnings per share. Decreased earnings per share usually translates into a lower share price, which rarely makes shareholders happy.

2. Look for ways to maintain earnings per share levels so that fully diluted calculations show share values remaining the same or even increasing.

3. Keep debt levels under those where your lenders, or investment industry advisors, would feel a decrease in creditworthiness would result. A drop in future earnings estimates usually precedes a drop in share price, once again an undesirable situation.

4. Make sure that the interest coverage ratio remains at a level consistent with the industry. If it gets too low, you might find analyst recommendations falling on the side of a decreased share price.

The major value generator for any acquisition transaction is usually the future success of the combined companies. Buyers must be able to show that taking on substantial debt or incurring other significant financial obligation in conjunction with the purchase of another company is warranted. Making that case so that investors concur is the art of salesmanship combined with solid financial analysis.

A Minimum Deal Size

A minimum deal size of 5 percent to 15 percent of the buyer's market capitalization is recommended by some analysts, based on the contention that a deal size of less than that is hardly worth the time and money spent on the acquisition process. I have a difficult time suggesting that a deal could be too small, especially for a strategic buyer. Suppose that you run a $500 million company that wants to buy a $1 million company (0.2 percent of buyer size) for strategic technology intellectual property rights reasons. If you can turn that $1 million investment into a $20 million division simply because you now are the exclusive owner of the technology rights, it seems like the $1 million is money well spent.

A financial buyer might well want to set a minimum deal size threshold simply to amortize the fixed deal costs over a larger acquisition value. To spend $100,000 purchasing a $500,000 company with the intention of turning the acquired company back into a profitable entity for resale seems a little extreme. After all, this scenario means that the buyer must recoup 20 percent of the purchase price ($100,000/$500,000) before it starts to recoup any of the price paid for the company itself. The right answer to this size question, as with most business problems, is, "It depends." It depends on the size of the buyer and the buyer's intended goals from the acquisition. It depends on the seller's financial condition and creditworthiness. It depends on the strategic nature of the transaction and the amount of strategic leverage the purchase can have on the buyer's operation.

If it makes long-term sense, then losing a little money in the short term may well be the right approach. On the other hand, if short-term profitability is a top priority, then increasing the deal size to the 5 percent or greater level provides a reasonable threshold under which valuation a deal should not be considered.

Determine the Deal-Stoppers

There is always a point beyond which a buyer or seller will not budge. Pushing beyond that point is not only counterproductive, it can alienate the party being pushed to the point that no further negotiations are possible. These deal-stoppers can be applied by both buyer and seller. The seller may have specific requirements associated with the sale and closely held corporations will likely have more deal-stoppers than publicly held corporations. Typical seller deal-stoppers include the requirement that all existing employees be retained for a period of time after the sale, that the company not be broken up for a period of time after the sale, a minimum purchase price under which the seller will not even consider an offer, and the requirement regarding the deal structure, such as all cash or all stock.

Learning about, and resolving, these deal-stoppers early in the transaction process makes it more likely that the buyer and seller can come to some type of final agreement. The real disappointment comes when the transaction has proceeded into the due diligence stage only to discover that a deal-stopper lurked in the wings. Buyers use deal-stopper issues as the filtering criteria for determining the target company to pursue. If the company is publicly held, the buyer may likely use the annual report to learn information that determines if a deal-stopper is present or not. Privately held companies reveal less information to the public, which makes determining the presence of a deal-stopper more difficult. In these cases, the deal-stoppers will require discussion between management of the two companies.

When determining deal stoppers, it is critical that you differentiate between "like to have" and "must-have" criteria. A "like" can be negotiated. A "must" is a mandatory requirement that, if not present, stops the acquisition process in its tracks and causes everyone to go home. Buyers determine their deal-stoppers based on the overall requirements of the acquisition and corporate culture. Here is a partial listing of buyer deal-stoppers:

1. The size of the transaction is too large or too small.

2. The company is not located in a geographically desirable area.

3. Seller products or services do not provide the expansion needed to meet the buyer's needs.

4. Litigation is pending against the company that could seriously erode valuation.

5. The seller is a union or nonunion company and will culturally or legally clash with the buyer.

6. Regulatory changes are in process that could put the company in a compromised position.

7. The seller is a competitor and the combination would draw attention from antitrust regulators.

From this list, it is evident that a deal-stopper is one that is really not easily modified to meet buyer criteria and has a dramatic impact on the transaction. A deal-stopper for one company may not be a deal-stopper for another.

A secondary level of problems can affect sellers, and early attention to these issues will make selling the company a faster and simpler process. Many of these items reside in the legal and financial management areas of the company's operation and are covered in greater detail in other sections of this chapter. It is sufficient to say that the more of these major administrative problems that a seller can eliminate before offering itself for sale, the less risky the transaction will appear to the buyer. The less risky the transaction appears, the higher the likely purchase price will be. For this reason alone, sellers should be motivated to aggressively find these problems and resolve them early in the process.

Protecting Shareholder Interests

The ultimate goal of every business decision must be to increase shareholder wealth. This is particularly true for publicly held companies and less true for closely held corporations that may have owner/managers with alternate agendas. A corporation must answer to its shareholders and a publicly traded company must do this every day as determined by the market share price. Actions that increase share price are always welcomed by shareholders, while those that decrease share price often meet with sharp criticism. In today's media-driven economy, this feedback is almost instantaneous.

A merger proposal by a major publicly traded company will be analyzed by several brokerage houses, who will gladly share their insights and opinions with CNBC or other media outlets. If the furor associated with an acquisition is substantial, management will have to make some type of public justification for the purchase. Proving that it increases shareholder wealth in either the near or reasonably distant future must be the bottom line of the justification message. More than one corporate executive has found himself on the receiving end of a shareholder class action suit simply because the shareholders felt that the executive had another agenda associated with the decision other than increasing shareholder wealth.

Sellers can help the publicly traded buyer by providing a wealth-increasing justification for the purchase. The buyer may not agree with all of the seller's assertions, but such justification will indicate that the seller understands the public buyer's side of the transaction. Buyers who are closely or privately held corporations have a lot more flexibility in their decision process. This type of buyer can assume that a purchase will not provide a positive return for a period of time into the future and not have to justify it to a faceless public. The deal cannot be scrutinized in detail by the media because the media will not typically have enough information to provide any meaningful analysis (although we all know that this often does not stop them). The result of this situation is that a seller with a marginal performance track record might find a more receptive audience with privately held corporate buyers or with publicly held buyers who have a proven success record of turning acquisitions into profitable ventures.

Systemizing Seller Processes

Sellers should recognize early on that the buyer is actually purchasing the future earning power of the selling company. The historical information is interesting as a way of gauging the reality of future performance projections. Ultimately, the seller must believe that the level of performance seen in the past will at least continue into the future or else future income streams are deemed more risky. The higher the risk, the higher the discount rate applied to future cash flows and the lower the resulting present value of the selling company.

Sellers must focus on minimizing perceived future buyer risk from the point at which the decision is made to sell the firm. Risk comes from uncertainty, which means that the seller can control perceived future risk by minimizing the level of uncertainty associated with seller business operation. This section takes a detailed look at many areas in which the seller can focus his attention to ensure that unnecessary risk is removed from the valuation equation.

Organizing the Financials

Your financial statements tell the buyer, financially, who you are. They reveal how money is spent, how income is related to expenses, and whether the company is making a reasonable return on the amount of capital invested in it. They tell a story about how money was invested in the company and what the investor return has been. If you think about it, they tell a potential buyer a lot about your business philosophy and how well you manage money. Publicly traded corporations must provide audited financial statements and an annual report. Managers of a publicly traded company understand the importance of treating the financial statements as a sales document. This section is more aimed at the manager of a privately held company that is looking to sell.

Every business manager knows that audited financial statements, in the United States, are prepared according to GAAP procedures and must comply with certain standards. This knowledge imparts a certain level of confidence on the part of the buyer's financial people. This confidence can be seriously injured if the buyer's accountants discover that some type of financial sleight-of-hand was performed. This realization immediately calls into question all other reported financial information. This level of undermined trust might then carry over into the entire due diligence process, or cost the seller the deal before it even starts. Creating a set of financial statements that accurately represent the seller's business situation while remaining GAAP compliant should be the goal of pre-sale financial statement preparation.

The Financials Are a Sales Document

Given the importance of the financial statements and the amount of attention they will receive, there is no question that they should be treated as a sales document. Everyone on the buyer's due diligence team will likely review the financial statement in one form or another. A set of audited accounting financial statements is a viable starting point for a company wanting to achieve top dollar, assuming that the cost of the audit does not offset its benefits. In some cases you are better served by having this audit done months before you must actually present financial statements to prospective buyers. In this way, error, discrepancies, and process corrections can be accomplished long before the sale process starts. Remember that someone is going to take a close look at how your company handles money. Make sure that they see a well-run machine that jealously monitors and accurately reports shareholder equity.

Don't be afraid to discuss information presentation with your accountant. If he understands your financial intentions, he might make recommendations on how the financial statements can meet your stated financial goals while still remaining in compliance with GAAP. As a final recommendation, have another unrelated accountant review your final financial statements. When done, ask the accountant to present you with a financial assessment of the company represented. What areas would he be most interested in? What aspects cause the most concern? What areas look great and indicate a well-run company? What recommendations would this second accountant make to the management of the company as a way to increase shareholder wealth?

Getting another unbiased view of the financial statements provides you with a preview of what to expect from a buyer's accounting staff.

Historical Income and Net Worth Reports

As stated earlier, the buyer is expecting to gain value from future performance expectations. Those expectations will, however, be compared against the past performance as a measure of feasibility. For this reason, the historical income statement, balance sheet, and cash flow information are all important to the sale process. This is particularly true if you expect the sale prices to be set as a multiple of earnings or EBIT/EBITDA. These values come from your historical financial statements. An increase in the EBIT as represented on the income statement has the effect of increasing the sale price if the price is set as a multiple of EBIT. An increase in earnings has the effect of raising the sale price if you expect the sale price to be determined as a multiple of reported earnings.

There isn't much you can do to present these values in a positive light if you start only a few months before offering the company for sale. You can, as an alternative, manage the company's operation on an ongoing basis such that the reported values have the effect of maximizing company value as seen by the buyer. Optimizing financial reporting so that they cater to the standard valuation techniques presented in Chapter 19, "Determining the Right Price," may increase the purchase price (valuation) without violating accounting reporting guidelines.

Creating Pro Forma Financial Reports

Someone is going to make a prediction about the seller's future performance prospects. It will either be the buyer, who wants the reports to be conservative in nature so that a lower purchase price is justified, or it will be the seller, who wants the future to look as optimistic as possible with the intention of garnering the highest possible sale price. A highly recognized method of valuation is through the discounted cash flow (DCF) analysis. This analysis uses future projections of cash flow into the company. These future estimated values are then discounted back to the present time using a discount factor set by any number of different criteria. It is typical for a discount factor to include a risk-free rate, a market return rate, and a factor that incorporates the amount of risk that an investor associates with a given company's performance. It might also represent a weighted average cost of capital (WACC) factor, which represents the estimated average financing cost to the buyer for funding the purchase through debt or equity.

In either case, the discount rate is applied to future cash flow projections. It is in the seller's best interest to spend time creating these reports as such and not leaving it to the buyer's discretion. Surely the buyer will create his own estimated projections but providing your own assessment sets a reasonableness range against which the buyer's estimates will be compared. Without your assessment the buyer's estimates stand alone and unchallenged.

Much of the sales process revolves around the selling of an idea. The pro forma financial statements provide that vehicle through which you can sell the buyer on the idea of the company's future performance abilities.

Additional Areas for Standardization

Throughout the organization the seller will discover areas that represent business processes that, although undocumented, work very well. These are the very areas that will concern the buyers as they perform their due diligence simply because these are areas that are likely dependent upon a person instead of a procedure. Should something happen to that person as part of the acquisition, or for any other reason, that procedure would be disrupted or lost with them.

If you look at this situation from the seller's perspective, you will realize that these areas should be standardized anyway. The loss of that one person would negatively affect the seller just as it would the buyer and is an unnecessary business liability. Here are a few areas to consider a review for standardization opportunities:

1. Engineering design and costing areas

2. Manufacturing processes, cost control, and purchasing

3. Quality control

4. Product specification creation and verification

5. Sales procedures

6. Financial policies and credit

7. Budgeting and expense tracking

8. Public and media relations

9. Customer service and postsale maintenance

10. Customer satisfaction assessment and reporting

11. Personnel policies

12. Other general operational areas

My intent here is not to make the seller's business life revolve around a set of arbitrary rules and regulations. In some environments, this could standardize the creative uniqueness out of the organization, which would clearly be counterproductive. It is only for the seller to understand that things that seller employees "just know" will not be perceived as readily transferable to the buyer. If these important procedures are not documented, then there is no firm way of verifying their existence other than to take the seller's word for it. You can imagine the discount rate that a buyer will apply to this type of information.

Whether your organization is for sale or not, standardization is a valid and valuable procedure for a company independent of its size. I have a client company with fewer than twenty employees who is now standardizing his internal operational procedures, realizing that he really cannot grow past his current level and maintain his quality standards without these procedures. Sellers win twice when implementing a standardization procedure. They win because their standard operation will likely run more efficiently and they win because the procedures increase value during the sales transaction.

Creating the Sales Prospectus

Sellers who want top dollar for their company will prepare a high-quality sales prospectus, or marketing brochure. This brochure is only given to a prospective buyer after they have met the initial buyer qualification criteria. This prospectus will take some time and effort to create. Sellers should think of is as marketing literature associated with the sale of a product which, in this case, is the company itself. This document is clearly intended as a sales document. It will contain many of the components of a sales proposal (see

Table 16.1 The Sections of the Sales Prospectus

Section	Objective
Investment Summary	Presents a one- to two-page overview of the investment and its expected returns.
General Company Overview	A top-level overview of the seller company. Basically presents the reasons why this is a company worth buying.
Overall Market Analysis	Presents an assessment of the overall industry and the company's relative position in that industry.
Marketing and Sales	A detailed discussion of the company's marketing and sales operation. Includes a discussion of customer base, products, services, and other pertinent aspects of the sales and marketing process.
Unique Assets and Properties	Presents unique processes, strategies, or intellectual properties that are transferred as part of the sale.
Management	An overview of key management personnel who will transfer with the sale.
Historical Financial Statements	Audited historical statements presenting company performance over the past three to five years.
Pro forma Financial Statements	Projected future pro forma financial statements that present the company's "guesstimate" of future overall financial performance.
Shareholder Information	A detailed breakdown of seller ownership and any information pertinent to the seller as relates to shareholder relationships and strategies.
Asking Price	The asking price for the company and any pertinent justification for the presented price.
Conclusion	A one- to two-page wrap-up of the prospectus that basically confirms the premise set out with the Investment Summary section.

Table 16.1), with the intended result being to entice the buyer to continue further with the purchase procedure.

Spending the time and money on the quality of the prospectus is time and money well spent by sellers and their advisors. This is a document that must stand alone in presenting the seller company to prospective buyers, and should reflect well on the seller. You and your company never get a second chance to make a first impression to prospective buyers.

The Need for Confidentiality

Perhaps the biggest liability that a seller incurs during the sale process is the unknown reaction of customers, vendors, competitors, and employees to the prospect of being sold. Better employees, not wanting to work for another management team, might immediately put their resumes on the market. Customers might choose to transfer a portion of their business that used to go to the seller to one of its competitors until the sale process finalizes and they know who they will deal with in the future. Vendors start to wonder if your business might go elsewhere simply because the new managers may require a shifting of those relationships.

These are all very realistic, and unwelcome, eventualities that are best avoided by simply keeping the possibility of a sale to yourself and a limited number of team members. Seller management should expect that the word will eventually leak out and that a formal statement will have to be made. Until that point in time, I strongly recommend that seller management do everything possible to keep the prospect of a sale a secret matter from everyone but key management team members, financial partners, and prospective buyers. Buyers should absolutely have to sign a nondisclosure document that clearly informs them of the need for secrecy.

Business brokers have ways of presenting a seller company such that the company remains "relatively" anonymous until a qualified buyer shows a sincere interest. At that point, the buyer is presented with the detailed prospectus. It would be a disappointment to go to all of this trouble to preserve the secrecy of the transaction only to find employees, friends, or neighbors talking about it at parties or over the Internet.

The military works with secret information on a "need-to-know" basis. This means that even if you have the proper level of security clearance, you are not presented with information unless you have a need to know. I suggest that sellers treat the fact that the company is for sale as a "need-to-know" level of importance item and jealously guard its secrecy. In fact, the military first determines if you can keep a secret before training soldiers to do the job associated with the secret information.

Perhaps team members should be selected first on their ability to keep a secret and secondly on their ability to make a contribution to the team. A few misplaced words could seriously erode the value of the transaction, potentially costing the seller millions of dollars in value or even the entire transaction. You can always apologize later to anyone who might have had their feelings hurt. You cannot always recover that key employee, customer, or buyer who was put off by having the prospect of a deal revealed before all parties were ready.

Working with Major Customers during the Sale Process

The buyers, at some point in the due diligence process, will want to talk with your major customers. This is a tricky time for the sellers and one best handled with any possible error being on the side of caution. This situation becomes particularly tricky if the buyer is a competitor. A member of the selling company management should first forewarn the customer about the buyer's interest in a meeting. In this way the seller can present the customer with the seller's reasons for selling so that there is no misunderstanding. It is also important that the seller convince the customer that business will continue as usual or even improve after the acquisition. This argument becomes more difficult each time that it must be presented for a new prospective buyer, so limiting the number of buyers or spreading the customer visits around to different customers is advised.

You may want to prepare your customers with likely questions that they will be asked as part of the meetings. Select customers, if possible, who will present your past and prospective future relationship in the best possible light. Remember that future revenue and income projections determine the present value (sale price) of the company. Statements by major customers regarding their future ordering plans are integral to those future revenue projections. Treat them as gold: They are as valuable.

Chapter Summary

Buyers and sellers must both take advance preparation steps to ensure that the sale/purchase process is as productive as possible. The requirements and objectives of publicly and privately held firms will differ simply due to the difference in shareholder relationships. Privately held companies have more flexibility because they do not have to answer to the general public and to analyst scrutiny. Publicly held companies, on the other hand, must pay heed to the public reaction to any announced sale or acquisition plans.

Sellers should take steps to create processes and procedures that facilitate the transfer of information from seller to buyer. Seller financial statements should be accurate and able to withstand the scrutiny of a formal audit without raising any material errors. The selling prospectus should be prepared with care to ensure that the company is presented in the best possible light. More than likely, prospective buyers will see the prospectus before they even meet with a company representative; as a result, the prospectus must stand on its own.

Buyers must have a clear understanding of their objectives with respect to the acquisition. Buyers will generally be motivated by product expansion, market expansion, strategic, or financial reasons. Independent of the motivations, buyer management must make sure that they do not take on a purchase that exceeds the skill sets of the management team or that puts the buyer in financial jeopardy. Having a sound business basis for making the acquisition is mandatory and will vary with the basic category that the buyer falls in. Determining minimum criteria for the transaction enables team members to filter out sellers who do not meet minimum requirements so that the most likely candidates can get the level of attention they deserve. Anything that could be seen by the buyer as a risk to that income should be minimized, or eliminated, if the seller wants to obtain the maximum price. Both buyers and sellers are served by uncovering any deal-stoppers early in the process to minimize the disclosure of confidential information and wasting time and money on a deal that has a low likelihood of completion.

17

Franchised and Competitor Transactions

Franchising in advanced technology areas has not really caught on except in a few areas, for reasons that will be discussed in this chapter. If you manage a company looking to expand its operation you may find that franchising is a viable alternative to either an IPO or outright sale as a fund-raising technique. A franchised organization may like what your company does and attempt to purchase your company as a way of enhancing the value that it provides to franchisees. Routing your products or technology through their established franchise network may make a very powerful business combination. Franchising basics are presented throughout this section for those with minimal prior exposure to franchised operations.

Competitor transactions are a completely different matter altogether. The likelihood of a competitor attempting to purchase your company is very real, and this type of transaction requires more caution than a standard purchase. More can be lost in a competitor transaction than with a conventional buyer transaction, especially if the competitor later chooses not to buy your company once due diligence is finished. This chapter takes a look at these two transaction types and makes recommendations regarding what can be done to minimize exposure in competitive situations. The information and steps presented in this chapter are intended as a supplement pertaining directly to franchise and competitive situations. The other evaluation, valuation, and due diligence recommendations presented throughout this book should be followed in addition to those presented in this chapter.

Selling To a Franchised Business

If you are considering selling to a franchise it is important that you qualify not only the franchiser but also the franchisee. The acquisition might be struck with the franchiser but the franchisees are the ones who will ultimately make your product successful through the franchised channel. You can almost think of this type of transaction as a "product line" or "market expansion" acquisition.

An Overview of Franchising

The franchiser is the parent company that develops and markets its product or services through the franchisees. There is one franchiser for an organization and many franchisees who bear the name of the franchiser. For example, RadioShack is the franchiser who then sells the franchisee the right to open a store with the RadioShack name.[1] In 1999 RadioShack had approximately 6903 store units, of which 1934 were franchisees and the remaining 4969 stores were company-owned. It promotes its RadioShack Select concept of placing a store within a store as a way of stimulating its expansion. The franchisee pays an initial franchise fee to RadioShack of $7,500, which gives the franchisee the right to use the RadioShack trademarked name, logo, and other protected entities. The franchiser will likely provide training and other assistance to the franchisee as part of the franchise fee. RadioShack provides seminars, training manuals, workshops, and a store operations manual as part of the franchise fee.

A royalty is then paid by the franchisee to the franchiser on an ongoing basis as long as the franchisee is in business. This royalty usually runs in the three percent to nine percent range, with some charging no royalty (such as RadioShack) and others charging a higher percent. RadioShack requires that any franchisee have at least $60,000 in capital to put into the local business in the form of equity capital. Notice that this setup enables RadioShack to sell its products through motivated local retail outlets without having to pay the high capital costs of setting up and manning the store. The local franchisee is responsible for the daily operation, with guidance from RadioShack along

[1] See Laverne Ludden, *Franchise Opportunities Handbook* (Indianapolis, IN: JIST Works, 1999).

the way, but particularly in the early stages. The primary benefits derived from franchising from the franchiser's perspective are:

1. The ability to expand rapidly without a large infusion of capital.
2. Local franchisee management is motivated because it is their own money, not the parent corporation's money, on the line.
3. Because money is raised without a sale of equity or debt, the franchiser gets to retain more control over its stock and keeps its debt load at a lower level.

The franchiser does, however, lose a great deal of control over the operation of the local franchisee outside of those items specifically stated in the franchise agreement. This may cause image problems for the company if the franchisees do not maintain the quality levels desired by the franchiser. The franchiser also gives up some profit margin by placing the franchisee distribution level between the franchiser and the final customer, but this is usually offset by the much larger number of stores using the franchiser's products or services along with the recurring royalties.

Franchisees often become resentful of the franchiser once the franchisee gets over the initial startup stages and starts making money. Six percent royalty payments is a lot of money to a company that may only have a percentage net profit before tax of 15 to 20 percent. Franchisees often sue their franchiser for lack of performance or other contractual violations simply as a way of getting out of, or reducing, the royalty payments.

Success breeds success, and franchisers should understand that a successful franchisee may later become a competitor. The franchiser trains the franchisee during his early business stages and helps him become successful. At that point, he may become a direct competitor or an indirect competitor in that he will himself become a franchiser. Franchising is typically oriented toward a process that has successfully shown itself repeatable. Franchisees purchase a known, proven business process when they sign the franchise agreement. The franchisees will also look to the franchiser to remain on top of the industry and provide the franchisees with the latest, most successful items that will keep the franchise name foremost in the consumers' mind. If the franchiser drops the ball on this very important point, it may find itself the recipient of a class action suit filed by franchisees. These are never a pretty sight.

In summary, franchisees are supposed to increase the credibility and brand name value of the franchiser's trademark and the franchiser is supposed to do what it takes to promote and improve the franchisee's likelihood of success. If either fails to maintain his end of this relationship, then the franchisee and franchiser are both in trouble.

Evaluating Franchisee Relationships

If you intend to sell your company to a franchiser so that your technology or products can be sold through the franchisee channels, you must take the time to qualify the relationship between the franchiser and its franchisee. This is the seller's due diligence responsibility. The evaluation becomes even more critical if the purchase transaction involves franchiser stock or a percentage of future royalties. The future success of your products and this franchise network is heavily based on the relationship between the franchiser and franchisees. A sour relationship may well sour your sales with it. Here are a few points to consider when evaluating this relationship:

1. What percentage of franchisees succeed or fail, and in what time frame after opening? What are the major reasons for success or failure? The franchiser should have this information readily available (or that tells you something right there about the franchiser).

2. Compare these failure rates with other franchised operations in the same industry. If higher, it certainly warrants asking why. If lower, then be pleased.

3. Is there any pending litigation between a franchisee and the franchiser? Expect that there is since that is almost always the case. Find out more about the specifics of the case(s) and determine if it is a class action suit brought by many of the franchisees or a few disgruntled owners.

4. What product or service areas have historically been the channel's most successful? How does the sale of this product or service technically compare with the sale process for your product or service? See Chapters 9 and 10 for more information on the personnel requirements related to technology sales. Is there a good synergy, or will selling your product be a stretch for the existing personnel?

5. What uniqueness does the franchiser offer that will make your offering more successful in the general market?

6. Are the royalties being paid on time? Are any of the franchisees seriously behind in their royalty payments, and what does the franchiser plan to do about it?

7. What is the rate of franchisee expansion? Has it sped up or slowed down in recent years (months)?

8. What is the franchiser's financial condition?

9. How has the acquisition of your company been sold to the other franchisees and what was their reaction?

This is by no means an exhaustive listing of due diligence topics that apply to a franchiser, but it should get you started in the direction of looking for those items that are significant to your transaction. It would be a shame to work hard to get your company to the point that it was solvent and doing well only to sell to a poorly managed, poorly financed franchiser who does a better job of running its media campaigns than it does its daily franchisee relations and operations. You may get your purchase price from the transaction but may not get the ultimate satisfaction of seeing your product or service ideas succeed in the postsale environment, which is often a very important aspect of the sale for private sellers.

Competitor Transactions

A competitor has just expressed an interest in your company. You know that a competitor is most likely to truly understand the value intrinsic to your company, but you also know that a competitor is going to want to investigate your operation. This is a very uncomfortable time for the seller and one not entered into lightly. This section takes a look at the various aspects of competitor transactions and some ways of protecting you and your company.

Special Considerations Due Competitors

How may times have you wondered just how your competitor did one business activity or another? Just how do they set their pricing points? Just who are their major customers and why did those customers choose them over you? What are their future product, service, and pricing plans? Companies have entire departments dedicated to nothing more than analyzing competitors and designing strategies to deal with their various anticipated future moves. The M&A process provides a way to short-circuit all of that research with a few weeks of open disclosure on the seller's part. Although unethical, it does happen that a competitor will offer to purchase a company simply to get an insider's look at the operation. Sellers must take steps to protect themselves when it comes to competitor transactions.

Competitors can use the due diligence information to:

1. Develop marketing campaigns that offset your future plans.

2. Develop products that contain a comparable, or better, feature set.

3. Deterministically price proposals and RFQs with confidence knowing your financial constraints.

4. Approach customers circuitously in such a way that it does not look like a violation of the nondisclosure agreement signed as part of the acquisition process.

5. Capitalize on proprietary production or development techniques in such a way which does not violate the legal protection provided yet improves their own technical operation.

6. Get to know personnel at your company as well as you do. Although frowned upon at least and possibly prohibited by an agreement, your employees may try to leave to go there, or the competitor may court them. Trying to enforce a legal agreement is sticky at best and could be disastrous on employee morale at worst.

This partial listing should be enough to make you nervous about competitor transactions. Imagine sitting in one of your major customer's offices with your major competitor being asked to explain why your customer should be willing to buy from your competitor? That one alone, for me, is enough to make every confidentiality, competitive, and territorial instinct kick into overdrive. A competitive transaction cannot be treated like any other. It is a product and market expansion acquisition attempt that might well be at your expense. Sellers who see competitive deals fall through after due diligence usually experience a mild panic when they realize the compromised position that their company now experiences with respect to that particular competitor. Erring on the side of caution with a competitor-buyer is better than indiscriminately revealing confidential information only to later have the transaction fall through. Future buyers may perceive the seller as being less valuable now that one of its major competitors knows extensive proprietary information about the seller's finances, customers, operations, and technology.

Are They Serious?

This is the first and most important question to ask yourself and them. "Are you serious about this purchase?" If, at this point, you don't believe them, you are really not obligated to proceed with the transaction. Make sure that your legal staff is in on the goodbye letter, but don't feel pressured into proceeding with due diligence when a competitor is involved. On the other hand, sending a competitor on his way simply because he is a competitor might also be sending your best buyer prospect away as well. There must be a way of protecting your company while still allowing the competitor to see enough to verify the company's value. Here are a few suggestions that might help you navigate this tricky course:

1. Spend a great deal of time qualifying the competitor's intentions prior to the signing of the letter of intent.

2. Try to ascertain the specific items of concern to the buyer. Remember that your competitor likely knows you and your company as well as you know their company. He or she also knows your industry and product lines. Some of your personnel may have even worked for this competitor at some point. They should be able to relay the areas of their primary concern.

3. Once you know the areas of concern, ask about the performance levels that the buyer would like to see to feel comfortable with the proposed price in the letter of intent. Try to get these in writing and ensure that the buyer's expectations will be in alignment with reality.

4. Include these performance or other due diligence levels in the letter of intent. In essence you are trying to get the buyer to agree to buy your company if these particular areas comply with the required performance levels. In this way, you may be able to limit the buyer's level of confidential information exposure while still providing them with the comfort needed to proceed with the purchase. Try to keep the criteria from being too restrictive or you might provide the buyer with an unintended out clause.

5. Make sure that employees have a clear understanding about information that is in-bounds and out-of-bounds from a due diligence perspective.

Any competitor must appreciate the risk that you will take in letting him into your organization. He will likely accept some level of restriction as long as it is not unreasonable. As the due diligence process evolves you may come to believe that the intentions are sincere and feel more open about revealing information. Remember that you cannot take back information that has already been relayed. You can, however, keep the information from being relayed to a competitor on a fishing mission simply by qualifying the competitor before the letter of intent is signed.

Competitor Customers

Competitor buyers, on the other hand, are trying to determine how much of your business will transfer to their business once the transaction is completed. This is once again tricky business on both sides because buyers don't want to reveal any unnecessary customer information either. That buyer also deserves to know the level of sales it can expect after the sale is final. They can't determine value until they see the customer list and you won't show the customer list until they agree to the intrinsic value. Here is a way to address this dilemma:

1. Make sure that specific customer performance criteria are included in the letter of intent.

2. Provide a listing of your major customers by company name only, without contact information provided.

3. Provide a breakdown of products and sales figures for the major customers, once again leaving off the customer contact name. If this is a contact that they already have, then there is nothing new provided other than these incremental sales, which they then get when the sale finalizes anyway. If they don't already have a contact at that account, you once again haven't really told them much other than that there is business to be had at that account, which they also already knew.

4. From these figures, along with an accountant statement regarding their reality, the buyer should be able to determine the level of incremental revenue it will obtain from the sale. Remember that the buyer will have special relationships with some of the same customers who are on your list. This relationship may be either positive or negative.

Using this incremental disclosure procedure enables you to inform the buyer without providing your entire recipe for marketing success.

Customer Feedback

If you are a buyer, you will likely want to talk with some of the target's major customers. The seller, on the other hand, won't want you talking to any of them for fear of losing their business should the acquisition deal not work out. Under these circumstances, something will likely have to give way. Perhaps the buyer agrees to only visit a few of the major accounts and signs a new nondisclosure with respect to that particular customer and for specific areas of the customer's business. The buyer is simply trying to determine the level of sales success and to qualify the customer relations. This should be possible on a sampling based on a few customers, chosen as agreed upon by both buyer and seller, and should not need a complete survey.

Just remember that the more of this due diligence that can be done anonymously, the safer it is for both buyer and seller. Should the buyer learn about a specific account and then a few months after a failed acquisition win that account from the seller, the seller might file a suit enjoining that particular customer's business relationship with the buyer until resolved. By that time, the customer will have moved on to another unrelated company and both buyer and seller will have lost that customer. Keeping it anonymous while pertinent is the safest way to handle customer information when dealing with a competitor. Should visits to customers be required, then make sure that a representative of both the buyer and seller are present at the meeting. It is also a really good idea to forewarn the customer about the meaning of the meeting and have them sign a nondisclosure as well. Neither buyer or seller wants any details released until both parties are ready.

Herfindahl-Hirschmann Index (HHI)

Antitrust issues must be considered with a competitor purchase. A rough estimate of the Justice Department's level of attention to the transaction is provided by the HHI. This index, when calculated before and after the proposed merger, sets a threshold by which you can estimate your transaction's level of antitrust exposure. Although the HHI is not the only standard for determination, based on the adoption of the 1992 Merger Guidelines, it still provides useful information regarding the change in industry concentration that results from a merger of two companies within the same industry. The intent of antitrust action is to ensure that competition remains active in the industry and that the consumer is not adversely affected by the merger.

The HHI is simply the mathematical sum of the square of all company market shares. This sounds more complicated than it really is. Assume that an industry has 6 companies each with an equal (16.67 percent) market share. The square for a single company would be $16.67 \times 16.67 = 277.89$. Summing this for all six companies provides a total of $6 \times 277.89 = 1667.34$. According to the HHI, this is a moderately concentrated industry. The thresholds are shown in the Table 17.1

Assume that two of these companies decide to merge, forming a single en-

Table 17.1 HHI Value Thresholds.

HHI Value	Guideline Assessment
Less than 1,000	Unconcentrated industry. No single company has a dominant position over others.
More than 1,000 and up to or equal to 1,800	Moderately concentrated. The level of competition is spread over a smaller number of firms, but no firm is assumed to have a dominant position.
Greater than 1,800	Highly concentrated. There is a possibility of a single company exercising excessive control over a market, diminishing competition, and potentially injuring customers.

tity that will have a joint market share of $2 \times 16.67 = 33.34$. The new HHI value is calculated as $33.34 \times 33.34 = 1,111.56$, plus $4 \times 277.89 = 1,111.56$, for a total HHI $= 2,223.12$. Notice that this value is clearly above the 1,800 threshold and highly likely to draw antitrust attention from the Justice Department. If this buyer and seller choose to move forward with the deal they should anticipate and prepare for some type of antitrust defense. The 1992 guidelines add several additional criteria that determine if a merger is anticompetitive.

1. Are there any anticompetitive effects arising from the merger?

2. Does the merger significantly increase market concentration? (See the HHI discussion.)

3. Can the anticompetitive effects be diminished by the entry of new competitors into the market? What are the barriers to entry for these competitors?

4. Are there efficiency gains obtained from the merger that offset any negative impact expected from the merger?

5. Would either merger party have ceased operation or exited the market if the merger did not take place? Are consumers better off with the merger than from a reduced number of companies in the market?

You can see from these guidelines that there is a lot of subjective language involved with determining if a deal is anticompetitive. As always when dealing with issues of this magnitude, find an experienced antitrust attorney to help you navigate these judicial waters.

Chapter Summary

Franchise and competitor transactions have their own special attributes. Buyers and sellers are advised to treat these two special transaction types as such. The value of a franchise-related transaction is heavily dependent on the relationship between the franchiser and its franchisees. A careful study of that relationship and plans for moving your product or service through the existing franchise network is warranted by any seller who is compensated based on future franchiser performance. This advice is applicable whether or not a purchase of licensing agreements is under investigation. If the seller's product or service is of an advanced technology nature, it is very important that the technology skill level of the franchisees be evaluated for their ability to adopt the skills needed to sell this more advanced technology.

Competitor transactions are full of areas where otherwise proprietary information can be revealed to a direct competitor. The best defense with this type of transaction is to spend a lot of time evaluating everyone's intentions and sincerity before signing the letter of intent and revealing information. Steps should also be taken to keep specific secret information as general as possible unless absolutely necessary and buyer intentions have been confirmed to seller satisfaction. Beware that the seller is not too defensive or he could scare away the most likely buyer who will see, and pay for, the intrinsic value of the seller's company. From the buyer's perspective, a purchase not only expands the buyer's market and product line but also eliminates a competitor, making this type of transaction potentially very attractive to a competitor.

Performing Due Diligence

The buyer has already covered a lot of acquisition ground before getting to the due diligence stage. This stage is likely the most time- and money-consuming portion of the M&A process and one not entered into lightly by either buyer or seller. Both buyer and seller will likely reveal confidential information to each other, sellers expose much of what makes the target company valuable, and buyers spend much time and money verifying the seller's claims. Often the due diligence team is chartered simply with finding items of negative synergy which drive down the final purchase price, and team compensation structures are established specifically to further this negative synergy discovery process.

This chapter takes a detailed look at the due diligence process and its management. Much of the information presented will refer to other chapters that covered the specific topic areas in more detail. The intention is to present an overview and general methodology that will minimize the likelihood of your becoming buried in details to the point that you leave the due diligence stage more confused than you were when starting. For purposes of illustration, BuyerCo is the company looking to make the purchase, SellerCo is the target company being considered for acquisition and the customer is the company that procures products or services from either the buying or selling firm.

Due Diligence Overview

Due diligence is simply a fancy term for "taking a detailed and systematic look" at a potential acquisition candidate. The diligence, or "attentive care, heedfulness" as defined by *American Heritage Dictionary,* is applied to the various components of the acquisition target, or seller. The intention of the entire process is to verify the validity of claims made by the seller or to corroborate assumptions made by the buyer. The ultimate goal of the process is to provide a level of confidence to the buyer about the values obtained with the acquisition.

When It Typically Happens

Due diligence takes place after a number of other steps have already been completed:

1. The proposed target company (SellerCo) has been selected, from a larger number of other potential targets, as the one most likely to meet BuyerCo's purchase criteria.

2. Initial meetings between buyer and seller have already taken place.

3. The buyer and seller agree that the buyer is willing to buy and the seller is willing to sell, as long as certain criteria have been met.

4. An initial purchase price has already been agreed upon as outlined in a letter of intent executed by both buyer and seller.

5. The terms for payment of the purchase price have also been outlined, subject to specific conditions outlined in the letter of intent.

6. A confidentiality agreement has already been signed by both buyer and seller.

7. SellerCo is usually required, by BuyerCo, to agree to a "no-shop" clause that precludes SellerCo from offering itself to other potential buyers for a specific period of time, usually 60 days or so. Risk to SellerCo is intrinsic to no-shop agreements, and they should only be agreed to when the buyer is proven to be serious and the deal is highly likely to go through. Sellers are also encouraged to keep this due diligence time frame to the shortest possible reasonable time, which can range from one month to six months depending on the deal size and other transaction-specific issues.

8. An agreement is set up regarding what respective fees will be paid, and who will pay them.

9. SellerCo must agree to provide BuyerCo with detailed, and unrestricted, access to all SellerCo records.

10. BuyerCo must feel that the due diligence process results are satisfactory or it has the right to withdraw from the deal. SellerCo will likely want a detailed definition of "satisfactory" before signing this clause.

11. BuyerCo demonstrates that it has the needed funding to execute the purchase. All needed legal, regulatory, or other agreements are in place such that the purchase can be finalized once the due diligence process is satisfactorily completed.

This listing is by no means exclusive of any other terms, conditions, or stipulations that SellerCo or BuyerCo can negotiate into the letter of intent. A meeting of the minds has already been established between buyer and seller before due diligence ever starts. This is a very important concept to retain. Due diligence is not a phase to enter into lightly. Buyer and seller should be in agreement that the deal should go through once the due diligence process turns out as expected.

The Need for Due Diligence

Some people act as though the purpose of the due diligence process is to catch the seller in any misrepresentations or lies. Although this can happen, the primary purposes of due diligence are:

1. To provide the buyer with a higher level of comfort with and exposure to the seller's operation. This process not only confirms buyer beliefs but also serves to highlight areas of misunderstanding between buyer and seller.

2. To provide a technique for the buyer to minimize the amount of risk associated with the purchase of a company. Risk can never be completely eliminated, but it can be minimized through an effective due diligence process so that the number of unexpected surprises is minimized.

3. To uncover unknown areas of synergy that simply might not have been visible from the general public's perspective.

4. To provide both seller and buyer personnel with a chance to work together in a project-oriented environment. Working together is the best way to determine if cultures can merge, and the due diligence process provides that opportunity in a relatively controlled, focused environment.

Just as you would take a used car to a mechanic for a checkup before finally making the purchase, so should you run your proposed acquisition target through a checkup just to make sure that there aren't any lingering problems that nobody was aware of, or simply overlooked. See the appendix for a starting list of due diligence areas of investigation.

What To Expect

The time frame required for due diligence will vary with the type of company involved. Typically, the buyer will want to spend as much time as possible looking into as many areas as possible. The seller will want the process over as quickly as possible because its personnel are disrupted from normal business activities while answering due diligence questions. Sellers will also strive to preserve secrecy by opening as few of its proprietary operational doors as possible. From the seller's perspective, every piece of information revealed to a buyer who ultimately does not purchase the seller is a piece of competitive information that could later be used against the seller. In addition, sellers will strive to present the company in the best possible light, which often implies freely offering information regarding areas of value while minimizing exposure to areas that may detract from the company's perceived value. This does not imply that sellers should be dishonest; however, a wise seller will only selectively offer negative information unless specifically requested by the buyer's due diligence team. This caution is particularly true when the buyer is a competitor. See Chapter 17, "Franchised and Competitor Transactions" for more information on this important subject.

Once the due diligence process begins, you will likely find the seller cordially cooperative at first and more open and cooperative as time goes on— to a point. At some point the seller will reach a tolerance threshold where they will contend that enough information was provided and the buyer should not need any more to make the final decision. At this point, the seller might even close off access to additional seller information until further discussions are completed. Does due diligence always come to this type of confrontational point? No. But it is not uncommon for the sellers to become irritated with the disruption associated with the due diligence process. SellerCo management might even start to feel that continual involvement in the due diligence process distracts SellerCo key personnel to the point that company operation is being impaired, which is to both BuyerCo's and SellerCo's disadvantage.

At first, certain buyers will look to either confirm or refute information that is believed true. As buyers dig deeper into SellerCo's operation, they will find additional information requiring additional research. It is possible that early due diligence efforts will uncover a deal-stopper that essentially brings the entire process to a halt, pending either further negotiations or a complete cessation of M&A discussions and activities. These discovered items are in addition to the deal-stoppers that should have already been resolved during the letter of intent stage.

Personalities will either mesh or conflict during the due diligence process. People will get to know each other, for better or worse. A deeper understanding of the successful likelihood of merging the two cultures will also unfold. As part of the due diligence assessment process, the intangible, personal aspects of the findings will be evaluated.

The Intended Result

The ultimate result of the due diligence process is to present, to the buyer's M&A team and management, a comprehensive assessment of the seller's overall operation that substantiates the seller's asking price. It will likely be in the form of a report that highlights the results from key discovery areas designated in the early phases of the M&A process. Also presented will be additional findings that provide information pertinent to the strategic, synergistic, operational and financial goals of the acquisition. Rarely is the report simply that "everything that we thought true was true." Instead it will include some matched initial expectations, some positive surprises, some negative surprises, and some things that turned out to be less optimistic than initially expected. In the final analysis, the due diligence report should present:

1. Areas where expectations were met.

2. Areas where expectations were exceeded.

3. Areas where expectations were found less than expected.

4. Problem areas uncovered that decrease value which can and typically will be used to negotiate a lower price from SellerCo.

5. Positive areas uncovered that increase value and are generally kept private to the buyer only.

6. Ways in which uncovered synergy can be exploited and are kept secret from SellerCo as part of the negotiations.

7. Valuation increases or decreases that should be applied to the original price negotiated with the letter of intent.

8. A final purchase price that is now based on the additional valuation items uncovered as part of the due diligence process.

9. A summary of whether, in the opinion of the due diligence team, the company "materially" meets the expectations in existence when the initial letter of intent was negotiated and signed.

Hopefully the due diligence process will simply confirm what the buyers already assumed to be true. It should be fully expected that due diligence will reveal things of a negative nature that detract from SellerCo's value. In fact, should due diligence not bring some negative aspects to the foreground, a careful look at the due diligence process itself would be justified. Sellers don't usually consciously try to mislead the buyer but will usually tend to take an optimistic view of SellerCo's value and future prospects. Presenting that optimistic perspective to a buyer who is basically pessimistic should cause some level of uncovered misunderstanding during the due diligence phases. Whether the inconsistencies are a result of deceit or of interpretation is a topic for the due diligence team to decide.

Aiding the Postacquisition Transition

One excellent byproduct of the due diligence process is the additional insight provided to the buyer regarding cultures, operations and other important SellerCo attributes. This additional information will be helpful in determining the specific steps involved with the handling of the postacquisition environment. A better understanding of SellerCo's personnel, processes, technologies, and overall culture may keep BuyerCo from causing unnecessary disruption or upset to SellerCo employees once the acquisition is finalized. Chapter 22, "After the Deal Closes," deals with postacquisition topics in more detail. Simply note that the detailed information obtained during the due diligence process should not be ignored when formulating postacquisition strategies and tactics. Initial integration tactics may turn out to be undesirable once more cultural, technical, or other factors are uncovered.

Managing the Overall Process

Managing the vast number of details that come from due diligence activities is an important part of the overall process. Data are obtained from the various investigations performed by the due diligence team. Turning that data into information that provides insight into the target company's health and value requires an ability to separate the material from nonmaterial.

Materiality and Its Importance

My sister-in-law gave me this advice when I embarked on my first trip to Europe in the early 1970s: "See everything." It turned out that the advice, although well intended, was a little cumbersome because seeing everything eventually turned into a mountain of overwhelming facts that did not translate into a greater understanding of my European hosts. I learned that by narrowing my attention to those areas of primary interest provided the time I needed to look deeper and learn more relevant information about the most salient areas. Due diligence is similar in a lot of ways. Investigating a company could take you into operational areas that, although interesting, might not really contribute to the ultimate goal of due diligence: determining and verifying the basic value being purchased.

Determining the important areas worthy of detailed investigation is an excellent starting point for any due diligence operation. It is always easier to find something, or dispel the existence of it, when you know what you are looking for. Spending the time at the very beginning to determine some threshold for determining information importance will make the process easier and more productive for everyone. I suggest that you designate some type of weighting system that attaches a level of priority to a specific area of investigation, such as A being "must determine" items, B being "nice to have" items, and C being "optional." It is also helpful to determine a weighting scale that designates the importance of an item to the overall value of the acquisition transaction from their highest to lowest materiality with respect to the project. "Critical" indicates an items deemed a deal-stopper. "High" indicates one with high potential value impact, either negative or positive. "Medium" indicates an item with nominal potential impact on value. "Low" indicates an item with a negligible possible impact on acquisition value but is nice to determine if time allows.

Here is the rationale behind the two weighting scales. Any project is comprised of tasks that require completion. Setting a priority to these items gives team participants the ability to determine the order in which items should be completed. The importance items indicate the discovered areas of operation that have an importance on the value of the acquisition. Likely the critical items will also be the A items listed at the beginning of the due diligence phase. As the project unfolds and additional information is discovered, other items will move into different levels of importance and priority on the list. This rating system provides a common framework within which the team, as a whole, can discuss items found and evaluate their impact.

The Due Diligence Team

Due diligence is a team operation that requires the coordinated efforts of engineers, accountants, lawyers, personnel management, business managers, marketing professionals, and others as needed. If the company must meet specific EPA requirements, the services of an environmental engineer would be retained. Should the company have extensive operations in a foreign country, an expert in that country would likely be added to the team. At a minimum, the team should include business managers familiar with the business requirements and intentions of the transaction. After all, if every legal, financial, and technical aspect of the deal is in place but the business goals are not met, then the deal is already starting at a deficiency. A recommended starting list due diligence team members is shown in Table 18.1.

Coordinating the activities of these various managers and working team members and collating their findings requires a dedicated effort. The due diligence process must evaluate areas in question, perform the evaluation within the required time frame, provide the required assessment valuations, and promote cooperation at the same time. Ideally, the team coordinator should create a team spirit in which discovered information is revealed to the entire team so that a coordinated assessment can be obtained.

Looking for Early Deal-Stoppers

Deal-stoppers, sometimes called "deal-killers," are those issues that, if not satisfactorily resolved, will stop the acquisition process with everyone going home alone. Obvious deal-stoppers from the seller's perspective would be finding out that the buyer cannot come up with the required funds, or the seller might strongly desire that the company not be broken up into smaller divisions for a minimum period of time after the sale is finalized, only to find out that the buyer's specific intention is to break up the seller immediately after purchase. Notice that this second issue is a deal-stopper from both sides in that the buyer may not want to buy if the breakup would not be publicly endorsed by the sellers and the seller would not want to sell if the intended breakup would be pursued by the buyer.

The major deal-stoppers will be determined by the buyer, and much of

Table 18.1 Due Diligence Team Members

Member/Business Area	Investigation Topics	Comments
Team Manager	Overall coordination	Coordinates team member activities. Keeps the project on track and on time. May also review the general business aspects of the deal.
Corporate Accountants	Financial statements, internal procedures, and future projections.	Determine the accuracy of information contained in the reported financial statements. Understand currently in-place accounting procedures. Evaluates financial assumptions tacit in future projections.
Corporate Lawyers	Legal structure, pending litigation, legal compliance with required statutes, ownership, and other legal matters of importance.	Qualifying the legal standing of the corporation is a critical first step. Additional ownership issues should be evaluated and clearly understood. EPA, union, or other legal issues should be reviewed and assessed.
Engineers	Evaluate engineering technology and management procedures.	Assess technical compliance of products. Evaluate development procedures for possible synergy. May require legal assistance in evaluating licensing agreements.
Manufacturing	Assess manufacturing technologies, reporting procedures, cost methods, and other pertinent attributes.	Looking for unique attributes that may provide synergy. Evaluating to determine efficiency and underlying philosophy.
Environmental	EPA compliance and other related issues.	Dependent on company type and really cannot be ignored in today's environment.
Marketing and Sales	Evaluate and understand sales and marketing policies and procedures. Assess customer relationships and future expectations.	Emphasis should be on evaluating today's operation as a means of determining the likelihood of future maintenance or improvement of performance.
Personnel/ Human Relations	Thoroughly understand existing personnel policies and procedures.	Evaluate areas where policies between buyer and seller may conflict and asses financial and legal aspects. May involve accounting and legal team members.
Executive Management	Other executive managers.	Looking for management synergy or areas of potential conflict. Hopefully will promote cooperation between both companies.

this determination can be done before the due diligence process even starts. In fact, the first stage of the due diligence process will focus on determining if any deal-stoppers are in place because finding one of them basically eliminates the need for any additional investigation. In fact, many deal-stoppers can be discovered before the acquisition process has proceeded even to the letter of intent stage.

Assume that BuyerCo's deal-stoppers include a minimum (maximum) revenues size, market capitalization, profitability, or ownership structure. Most of this historical information can be found from public sources where internally generated SellerCo projections will be found during due diligence. Finding deal-stoppers early is an important part of the due diligence process. It is futile to evaluate manufacturing processes if in-place seller legal requirements make the deal unattractive to the buyer. Assessing the legal requirements early to eliminate deal-stoppers saves other team members time and money. Here is a listing of possible SellerCo attributes that could or would be deal-stoppers:

- Projected sales revenues will fall under BuyerCo requirements.

- SellerCo profitability might be found to be under BuyerCo minimum requirements.

- SellerCo might have a sale price expectation that is unreasonable from BuyerCo's perspective.

- Litigation might be pending that was not publicly disclosed.

- Leasing arrangements for land, buildings, or equipment might preclude BuyerCo from pursuing required business strategies.

- SellerCo might be a union shop, while BuyerCo specifically precludes unions from its operations, or vice versa.

- Dissent between board members or majority stockholders might create a contentious environment that BuyerCo deems prohibitive.

- Intellectual property rights which are integral to valuation are found to be in legal dispute or owned by a silent partner who might not react favorably to BuyerCo ownership.

- Sales are concentrated in a few major customers instead of spread over a broader customer base.

- Private correspondence regarding pending regulatory changes reflect negatively on SellerCo's value.

BuyerCo deal-stoppers might also be subjective in nature. For example, BuyerCo may require that SellerCo be a "green" company; it must have an active program designed to promote environmentally friendly business activities. BuyerCo may require that SellerCo not have business ties to certain countries due to political, economic, or social reasons. BuyerCo or SellerCo can clearly define these criteria for themselves and terminate the acquisition process once noncompliance is discovered.

Most transactions attempt to find as many deal-stoppers as possible before the letter of intent is even signed. If you know that something is a deal-stopper, you are better served getting it on the table early and either negotiating an agreeable compromise and moving forward or agreeing that it is insurmountable and walking away before much money or energy is invested. A recommended way of dealing with deal-stoppers is to provide the other company in the transaction with a written and confidential listing of known deal-stoppers and ask them to address these items in an early executive meeting. In this way, a deal-stopper can be highlighted, discussed, and resolved between the management personnel most familiar with the topic and its business impact. This approach is particularly valuable when a publicly traded firm goes into play. Multiple companies may start bidding for its purchase, making timing critical. A lot of time cannot be spent investigating and the overall deal structure must be quickly determined along with salient information pertaining to financial statement and valuation issues.

Sometimes deal-stoppers are not brought up early on as a sales tactic on the part of either buyer or seller. The principle behind this approach is that once the other party understands the "real" value associated with the company, items that early on looked like deal-stoppers will drop from deal-stopper status to simply being major negotiating points. Only history can accurately determine which approach is right.

Typical Time Frames

The time frame that may pass from finding the acquisition target company and consummating a letter of intent may be as short as a few days or as long as a year or more. Once the letter is signed, the due diligence process is usually completed within a few months, and usually in less than two months.

The buyer might be familiar enough with the seller's operation that an extensive due diligence procedure is not required. This would be particularly true if BuyerCo and SellerCo are long-standing competitors in the same industry. Companies get to know their competitors pretty well, and likely know as much about their competitor's operation as their own. Under these circumstances, it is not atypical for BuyerCo to present SellerCo with a listing of issues that must be addressed before coming up with a final price for the letter of intent. The more detailed BuyerCo's understanding, the more specific the questions may be and the more accurately everyone's expectations can be established.

Using the Due Diligence Information

The purpose of the due diligence process is to decrease the amount of risk associated with the purchase of the target company. All actions, reports, and procedures should in some way contribute to achieving that purpose. Once the deal-stoppers have been determined, and satisfactorily resolved, it is then up to the team to evaluate those items deemed critical to the valuation of the target company. Tracking and reporting on these items is an important part of the due diligence process because the reports become the means through which the discovered information is relayed to the negotiating team. Creating a book in which all pertinent information is collated provides a simple, yet effective way of organizing, tabulating, and tracking discovered information. The next section takes a detailed look at the book, its structure, and its use.

Creating the Diligence Summary Book

Any major project can easily get out of hand if there is not an agreed-upon schedule with goals and deadlines attached. As the amount of information collected increases, the tracking, collation, and interpretation of that information becomes more difficult. In addition, information is revealed over time, and one set of findings might possibly contradict those found at either an earlier or later time. Ensuring that assessments are performed with the most accurate, current information available at the time is a mandatory aspect of the due diligence process. For this reason I recommend that a "book" be created that acts as a centralized information tracking tool. This book might be as simple as a three-ring binder or as complicated as a relational database complete with video files, Web links, and photographs. The level of sophistication is up to the due diligence team with the clear understanding that the due diligence process is designed to evaluate the target company, not the other way around.

STRUCTURED FORMAT

The book is a reference document and should be structured as such. It serves a few major purposes:

1. The book acts as a tickler file which better ensures that important items of investigation are covered.

2. The book enables another member of the team to reference information, findings, and assessments made by other team members delving into other areas.

3. It provides a written record of findings which can be referenced later as needed for either performance comparison or postacquisition integration purposes.

A structured format is recommended so that any member of the team can easily find sought-after information without having to deal with a custom format for each individual section.

REQUIRED SECTIONS

The book can be divided in any way that meets the objectives of the due diligence team and you may find that the following approach gets you started in developing the one right for your particular situation.

Phase I: Deal-stoppers. Table 18.2 is a listing of the various deal-stopper items that pertain to this particular acquisition. Particular attention should be paid to these items because a mistake on any deal-stopper will have serious repercussions later in the process. This information recording format enables an uninvolved person to review the status of each deal-stopper item and to understand its importance, its resolution, and the basis for the resolution. As the project proceeds into more detailed analysis, you might find it valuable to review these early pages to see if things once thought true are still accurate in light of additionally uncovered information. All deal-stopper items will have a Critical importance and an A priority if ranked according to the procedure outlined earlier.

Phase II: High-Value Impact Items. Items that have the highest likelihood of positively or negatively impacting the proposed valuation of the target company are next in line for evaluation. Remember that the team has a limited amount of time within which to perform its analysis, and you certainly want to ensure that the most important items are completed before any optional items are pursued.

Table 18.2 Deal-Stopper Assessment Information Pages

Subsection of the Deal-Stopper Page	Comments
Deal-Stopper Title	A reference name for the item.
Deal-Stopper Description	A more detailed description of the deal-stopper item.
Reason for Its Importance	A detailed description of the buyer's reason for considering this item a deal-stopper.
Status	Whether the deal-stopper is present, possible, or not present. *Present* means that it is an existent problem and requires resolution. *Possible* means that more information is needed to determine status. *Not present* means that it has been evaluated and found not to be an existent problem.
Resolution	How the issue was resolved.
Information Source	The source of information to determining the status of this deal-stopper item.
Date of Source Information	Date on which the information was received.
Responsible Team Member(s)	Team members involved and responsible for performing this assessment.

There are two ways to address this list of important items. Although they are not deal-stoppers, they are important items that affect valuation. Some items will appear on the due diligence project list for each acquisition candidate. Others, however, will appear or disappear depending on the candidate involved. Determining this listing is important to managing the entire process. Try this procedure for determining the items that appear on the High Importance, A or B priority list.

1. Segment the areas of research into well-defined section titles applicable to the investigation. Titles might include product compliance, customer base assessment, marketing strategy, pending litigation, and so on.

2. Add a few general items to each section that usually require investigation. Highest impact on valuation should be used as the inclusion criteria.

3. Have each team member add or delete items to each area of investigation, once again using highest order of valuation impact as the inclusion criteria.

4. Collate all responses into a single list and then select the top 10 to 15 items for each section and use these as the High Impact Items for investigation pur-

poses. These items will all have a High importance, A priority standing or it should not be on this list.

5. Attach a completion date to each item, along with the name of the team member ultimately responsible for its assessment completion.

6. Finally, rank and list these items in order of expected completion date so that you now have a standardized methodology for tracking major project point status and completion.

7. A detailed sheet should be completed for each action item similar to that listed in the deal-stopper section of the book, but with one important addition: Impact on purchase price valuation should be added to the reported information. Positive impact on valuation should be interpreted as an item that actually adds value to the transaction price, such as those experienced from synergy or those that operate more efficiently than initially expected. Neutral impact indicates that the area performs as expected and is already included in the price negotiated during the letter-of-intent phase. Negative impact assessment indicates that this area has a lower value than initially assessed and decreases the value to the buyer, and should be considered as a reason for decreasing the purchase price. A proposed increase or decrease in value should then be provided by the team member making the assessment.

8. All other items pertaining to the various operational areas under investigation should now be listed in their proper, respective category. Along with the item listing should be simple check marks and valuation reporting slots that indicate positive, neutral, or negative, along with a valuation change number. A detailed description is not required for noncritical items but a valuation estimate should be provided if applicable. Most items will likely receive a neutral assessment.

9. A running tally of net positive and negative valuation changes resulting from the due diligence operation should be provided at the end of book. A summary should also be included that indicates any high-importance items that require addressing by the negotiation/assessment team. Any single high-importance item will not, by itself, typically be a deal-stopper. But a combination of high-importance items might present a picture that, in totality, seriously undermines the attractiveness of the acquisition candidate.

PUTTING IT ONLINE

Performing these diligence reporting operations using conventional paper is functional, but does not necessarily take advantage of the myriad technologies currently in existence that can automate this process. A due diligence project is an excellent candidate for a groupware application. The tallying of the positive and negative valuation effects is a standard database/spreadsheet operation. Teams that undertake a number of due diligence projects should consider methods of automating the procedure. In this way, messages can be sent electronically between team members from remote locations with the project book always being current and available, online, to any team member.

Without question, security must be maintained for this book; you would not want anyone outside of the core team to have access to the information. But a person should not be on the team in the first place if you are concerned about their being able to keep the process and results a secret. The technology exists to assist with the automation of this process and the quick generation of summary reports and statistics. The larger the project, the shorter the time frame, and the more frequently due diligence is performed, the more viable an automated support system becomes.

General Tips for Better Success

Communication is the key to the management of any successful project and a due diligence project is no different. It is important that team members communicate with each other, especially in the high-importance areas that might have an impact on other areas of investigation. The regularity with which meetings, or conference calls, should occur is really a matter of internal choice, but I feel that a weekly meeting to review high-importance items or dramatic findings is appropriate. The team manager's job is to keep these meetings informative, lively, and not overly time-consuming. This is also a technique for keeping the project on track. It is amazing how effective team peer pressure can be in keeping people focused on completing their assigned tasks within the allotted time frame.

Distribution of meeting minutes should be provided on a strictly need-to-know basis, as incomplete or tersely reported information can be misinterpreted and cause unnecessary misunderstandings as part of the ongoing negotiations.

Areas Investigated

The value is in the details and the due diligence process is really about determining the status of the various details involved with the running of a thriving business. Some M&A professionals contend that due diligence should not be simply about creating lists and then checking off listed items until finished. I couldn't agree more. A list by itself does little more than take up paper space and human time. Using a list as a reference and coordination tool that keeps all team members working in a common direction and time frame is an excellent management tool. I suggest that you look at this listing of action items as a management tool that is as indispensable as your telephone when managing a large due diligence process.

Coopers and Lybrand provides a booklet that contains an excellent starting list of proposed due diligence action items related to various areas of investigation. This listing is available directly from Coopers and Lybrand as their "Checking Into an Acquisition Candidate" publication. It is also available in Joseph Morris' *Mergers and Acquisitions: Business Strategies for Accountants*. Neither of these listings divides out the high-importance items or places a priority and time frame for completion on each item. These are very important steps that contribute greatly toward keeping the project on track and on schedule. I do recommend that you review these lists and select those items applicable to your particular due diligence requirements, and then separate the items as outlined earlier in this chapter.

No single list will give you every item that should be reviewed for your particular situation, but it can act as a reminder of items that must be addressed as part of the process. Also, expect that the list will be a dynamic document in that items will be added as the process evolves. Information will present itself that will eliminate the need to research other areas, and information will pop up that places additional items on the list. Keep at it. Keep structured. Remain consistent and try to have some fun along the way. You are trying to formulate a huge puzzle while solving a mystery at the same time. Who doesn't like solving a great mystery?

Special Technology Areas of Investigation

Due diligence of a technology firm must take a hard look at the underlying technology of the target firm. After all, technology is what the target company sells, and if that technology or its products are flawed in any way it can have a dramatic impact on the company valuation. Using an engineer to evaluate engineering products and processes is the best way to get a credible assessment of the products and technologies involved. For this reason alone, having an engineer as an integral part of the due diligence team makes a lot of sense as both an advisor and an insurance policy. You wouldn't expect an engineer to perform a financial audit. Why would you want an accountant to perform a technology evaluation? This section takes a close look at some technology-specific areas deserving of a deeper investigation during the due diligence process.

PRIOR EMPLOYERS AND EMPLOYEES

Silicon Valley and the other technology areas have a mentality and temperament all their own. Many times I would attend a beer bust at my Silicon Valley employer only to have a neighboring firm's manager, who had crashed our party, offer me a job at his company. The history of Silicon Valley can be traced back to Fairchild. AMD owes its initial existence in large part to Intel. Silicon Graphics and so many other firms owe their start to Stanford University. The graphical user interface that made the Apple Macintosh so famous finds its roots at the Xerox Palo Alto Research Center. The core group of software engineers that created the Netscape browser all came from the same group that was transplanted to Silicon Valley from Urbana-Champaign, Illinois.

It is difficult to be in the high technology field for any length of time at all and not have worked with someone who worked with someone else who helped start one company or another. The implications of this shuttle employment temperament is that much expertise and experience gets transferred from one company to another, independent of the nondisclosure and noncompete clauses signed. It is also not uncommon for personality conflicts and cooperation to carry over from one company to another as managers leave one company to start their own. Some people contend that the heated rivalry between Intel and AMD is a result of the personalities of Andrew Grove, CEO of Intel, and Jerry Sanders, CEO of AMD.

Wang Laboratories made a name for itself by providing fully compliant SNA (Systems Network Architecture) products that transparently attached to a network using the SNA network standards but with products that did not come from IBM. Getting technical specifications would normally be tough for a company wanting to follow this strategy unless the company had a special relationship with IBM, which An Wang, the founder of Wang Laboratories, had. Wang was the largest single owner of IBM stock as a result of his selling his patented core computer memory technology to IBM. If you did not look deep enough, this little-known but very important strategic fact would go overlooked.

Technology due diligence should take a look at the background of existing key employees to get a better understanding of their backgrounds and existing industry contacts. Is it possible that the target company is using technology brought over from a prior company as part of its design and implementation processes? Is it possible that prior target company employees have left and gone to other companies, taking target company secrets with them? Could any of these personnel transfers either put the target company at a disadvantage or perhaps expose it to litigation as either the defendant or plaintiff? When knowledge is the asset of value, and that knowledge transfers to another company with an employee, any company must take a hard assessment look at areas of exposure. The due diligence team should do the same.

LICENSING AGREEMENTS

Technology licensing agreements should also be given a close inspection. These agreements are often sold in the early days of a company's life to help fund early expansion or to create multiple sources for products. Independent of the initial motivation for creating the licensing agreements, they now present other companies that have expertise with the very technology being purchased by the buyer. These agreements may have special provisions or clauses in them that change with ownership, time or external market conditions. Any buyer of a technology company should take a long legal look at licensing agreements that have either been offered by or purchased by the target company. You never know what is in these agreements until you look, and looking before you buy, instead of after, is always a safer approach.

Verification Of Technical Performance

It is one thing to develop a marketing brochure for a product and then develop the product. It is another altogether to develop a product that actually performs to the specifications outlined in the marketing brochure. At the risk of sounding cynical, it is not uncommon for a company to sell a product, knowingly or unknowingly, that does not meet 100 percent of its published specifications. Management might attempt to justify these actions by saying that the known defects do not materially affect the usefulness to the customer and that denying the customer the right to use the product is actually doing the customer a larger disservice. Independent of what people may think about this type of thing happening, I can assure you that it happens.

This is where the results of an independent testing lab, or at least an autonomous group within the target company, become highly valuable. Simply taking the design and production department's word that products perform as specified makes life easier but may not really add to the due diligence value. Expense usually prohibits testing of all products, but testing of those of paramount importance or those with specifically desired technology is very important. Larger buyers will often perform this analysis using their own internal testing services. Whether the products are spot-checked for manufacturing flaws, design flaws, or postshipment defects, this technological assessment of critical technologies and products must be performed. Otherwise, the products or services purchased might later be found defective and it will then be the buyer's responsibility to make things right again with customers.

Engineers can usually differentiate a sophisticated design from one that simply meets specifications. Part tolerances, design flexibility, line of code, logic flow, and component counts are several benchmarks used to differentiate a creative design from one that "meets expectations." Software designers often spend hours looking for the most efficient programming technique that addresses a specific logical requirement. Hardware designers will strive for designs that use the least restrictive component specifications, using the minimum number of components while still meeting the design objectives. Only another experienced engineer, or someone experienced with technical design, will recognize such unique design characteristics, which represent intrinsic engineering value that simply would not be obvious without a detailed engineering investigation.

Determining Value Components

More often than not, much of a company's value is hidden from public view. The success of an organization is usually a unique blending of its people, technology, inspiration, vision, opportunity, and drive. Making these varied components work in a way that creates success is an art as well as a science. Those who contribute to this piece of art may not be obvious at first glance. You can almost certainly assume that the power structure of an organization is not shown on its organizational chart.

Finding these valuable assets may take more time than expected. This asset might be a person rarely visible outside of his office. It might be a board member with a special relationship to another industry leader. It might be a member of the media who simply likes what the company does and takes every possible opportunity to promote the company's activities. These items do not show up on a balance sheet and may have a dramatic impact on the overall company value.

People of Special Value

It is common practice to address company management like they are the ones in power within the organization. While this is usually true, it may not be true when dealing with technology companies in particular. More than one successful company was spawned by the idea and effort of a few engineers who, using weekends and evenings, developed the initial prototypes of a product. This prototype might have been the catalyst for receiving the initial venture capital funding that got the company off of the ground. At this stage, the engineers and venture capital firm own shares of stock. The venture capital firm will likely ask that a professional management team be brought in to manage the business so that the engineers can continue designing. The management team may or may not have stock at this point, but clearly the largest ownership percentages are those of the engineers. If you are talking to the management about critical business ownership decisions, you may possibly be talking to the wrong people. Although these management people will influence the decisions made by the owners, the owners are the ones who will make the ultimate sell decision. Treating these invisible owners as irrelevant can be disastrous to the transaction's success, and it may alienate them to the point that future relationships with the company are not possible.

Always verify the ownership structure of a company before making any serious overtures at a purchase. Publicly traded companies must disclose their ownership structure as part of their SEC filings, but privately held companies can be a little more tricky. Take a look at the original corporate charter filings with the state and find the names of the original executive members who were listed at the time of incorporation. Look also at the employee roster at the target company. If you see these names, and do not have them in your meetings, you are likely making a mistake and should clarify these relationships before getting too far along in the process.

Patents

Technology companies get funded and thrive on proprietary technology that provides some type of legal patented protection. Depending on the level of product sophistication and industry, the patent might go unchallenged for years. Every patent has a legal life of 17 years, after which time it is no longer protected. Should a company be selling its patented technology as a special asset, it is wise to investigate the patent details, such as when it was issued, the level of protection, if it was contested, the person who is the original developer of the patented technology, and other pertinent information. Patent law is a specialized area in which it is wise to use the services of an experienced patent attorney when assessing patents or other intellectual property that is of a material value to the buyer and a major contributor to the purchase price.

International Due Diligence

This topic could fill a book on its own. It is sufficient to say that adding an international aspect to the due diligence process simply makes a complicated situation even more complicated. American and UK firms looking to apply their version of due diligence to a firm in another non–Anglo-Saxon country will likely find a few surprises along the way. Cultural differences between countries will make some of our own concerns irrelevant in their culture and vice versa. Not knowing the cultures and customs of your foreign target's country and people simply creates a breeding ground for misunderstandings that could otherwise have been avoided. Before you even start the due diligence process, you should make sure that this major step is one you are willing to take. In fact, you might determine that a more gradual introduction to the foreign country, its people, and the firm itself is more in everyone's best interest. Many firms start out international purchases with an alliance of some type that eventually can grow into a full acquisition.

If you are planning to purchase a foreign firm, start with these simple steps which will likely save you time, money, face, and a boatload of apologies:

1. Do some basic investigation about the country and culture into which you are planning to invest.

2. Find local legal counsel in the target's country and make this firm a part of your acquisition team. Make it clear to this firm that you expect them to help you avoid common cultural pitfalls.

3. Check with your accountants about any accounting procedures that may vary between the United States and the target country. A financial statement in their county may not be subject to the same interpretation and reporting guidelines as those generated in the United States.

4. Verify the import, export, and other trade laws that the United States and target country may have in place that either enhance of detract from this international business relationship.

5. Try to get a realistic level of the point where your version of due diligence will be viewed as intrusive, or even insulting, so that you make sure that this line is not unknowingly crossed. Misunderstandings are easier to remedy than something considered a blatant insult.

The time frame for completion of due diligence of an international firm should not be too tight, since unexpected stumbling blocks will appear.

Tread Lightly but Firmly

Remember at all times that the due diligence team members are guests on the target company's premises. It is not that the team members should be reticent to look in areas of material impact to the transaction; it is just that they should be diplomatic in how they go about it. This is particularly true if a postacquisition merger of cultures is intended. Making the target company's personnel upset with the buyer's personnel may not negate the transaction, but it could seriously impact the future success of the merged company. Tread lightly but firmly in working through the due diligence process and you may find your respect for them, and their respect for you, increasing throughout the process, which will definitely pay dividends in the future merged environment.

Chapter Summary

Due diligence is a process of discovery. Due diligence team members endeavor to verify what is assumed to be already known, look for undiscovered areas of risk or benefit that will be inherited by the buyer, and assist with the valuation process. The process may take from one to six months or more depending on the complexity of the transaction.

Due diligence is a complicated yet important process that is best not left to chance. A due diligence team will have to survey the important areas of the target company, determine their viability and impact on proposed price, and stay on schedule while still promoting a positive image about the buyer to the seller's personnel. Sellers are continually looking to convince buyers that the asking price is warranted by SellerCo's areas of value.

Advance planning is the key to a successful and informative due diligence process. Knowing the areas and people of key importance and understanding the ultimate intention of the acquisition and areas of primary concern enable the investigators to focus in on topics most important to the process. Technology must be evaluated to get an accurate picture of a seller's product, design, and services value to the buyer. Engineers experienced in the targeted technology areas should be used not only to verify product performance to specifications, but also to determine the design levels of expertise existent within the seller. The professional history of key personnel should also be determined as a way of understanding the various linkages that exist within SellerCo's personnel and other industry firms. The technology evaluation should also investigate licensing agreements and other intellectual property issues as a way of verifying underlying technological value.

There is a time limit within which a seller will tolerate the due diligence team and their questions. At some point, the time will expire and the acquisition team will need to decide if the offered price and conditions represent a solid value for the company being purchased. Making sure that they are as well informed as possible is the goal of the due diligence team. Keeping their eyes on that objective increases the likelihood of getting there while not alienating the seller in the process.

19

Determining the Right Price

At some point in any potentially successful M&A process an acquisition target will come along that requires analysis. All of the techniques discussed in this book come into play during this evaluation. The specifics of the evaluation are heavily dependent on the companies, time frame, and personalities involved. Having a generalized approach provides a solid starting point for understanding the way in which the various financial tools presented can be put to functional use.

This chapter is an extended example of the proposed acquisition of a company recently brought to the attention of a major technology services company interested in acquiring another technology services company that meets specific criteria. The buyer is BigTech and the proposed acquisition target will be evaluated in two forms. It will first be evaluated as PrivTech, which is a privately owned technology services company. It will then be evaluated as PubTech, which is the same basic set of company financials simply evaluated as a publicly held company.

A Target Appears on Your Scope

Martin Graves is the president of a major technology services company located in the United States. As one of his commitments to the board of directors, he wants to consummate an acquisition during this fiscal year. The purpose of this acquisition is to at least add a new or expanded technology skill set to the company, while ideally also opening up new markets. Being a technology services firm, Martin believes that an infusion of new talent with a different skill set will keep the entire organization from becoming stagnant. The deal must pass a set of deal-stopper criteria before it will even be considered.

1. Sales revenues must be over $10 million and less than $700 million.

2. The company must be a domestic company with no international ownership or licensing issues.

3. The company cannot be in any form of legal dispute with either the government or a group of stockholders.

4. The company should ideally be privately held, but you are also open to the right publicly held company deal.

5. The acquisition must at least be neutral with respect to earnings per share and ideally should increase earnings per share.

6. Pooling of interests accounting is desired but not required.

7. Prior management must be willing to integrate itself into the existing BigTech corporate culture. Relocation is optional and prior executive management would ideally remain in place for a minimum of two years after closing the deal.

8. The technology skill set should enhance those already offered by BigTech, and ideally the company should add new markets to BigTech's already existing skills.

9. The deal should be accomplished with an all-stock purchase.

10. No antitrust issues must come forward as a result of the purchase.

This set of criteria was provided to the internal acquisition team, which consists of Judy Mellon (accounting), Mike Ingram (marketing), Jack Nelson (engineering), and Mindy Wilson (operations). The team meets once a week to discuss the marketplace activities from the prior week and any possible candidates that have been brought to their attention from their various brokers and investment banker contacts.

Over 30 companies have been looked at this year and so far, none have met all 10 of the deal-stopper criteria. A business broker from San Francisco called Mindy one Monday to let her know about a company that he thinks meets BigTech's criteria. He asked if she would like to see a general overview of the company and she agreed.

Martin looked at the sheet and smiled. Finally, the team was evaluating a company with which no deal-stoppers immediately jumped off of the page. Granted, he did not know the name of the company; the sheet was delivered anonymously at this stage because the seller did not want it to be publicly known that they were for sale. The basic criteria was there and Mindy had confidence that the broker in San Francisco knew what they were looking for and would not have sent this deal BigTech's way if there wasn't a likely initial fit.

Martin signed the nondisclosure agreement, after having it quickly reviewed by legal counsel, who saw no problems. The broker said that the prospectus, or marketing book, would be overnighted to them. Perhaps this was the one. The broker said that the company's name was PrivTech and that they had an operation very similar to BigTech's except on a smaller scale. The owners definitely wanted to sell but were not in a hurry. They were also looking for the right buyer, and the broker thought that BigTech could be that company.

Getting the Prospectus

Five copies of the prospectus arrived by 10:00 AM Tuesday morning. One copy was kept by Martin and the others were passed to the team members in a 10:30 AM cursory meeting. Everyone was interested in PrivTech and they dug right into the prospectus after being clearly notified that a nondisclosure had been signed and secrecy was naturally very important. They agreed to meet again at 3:00 PM to discuss PrivTech after they had reviewed the prospectus. At this time, no other staff members were involved with the process. At the meeting each member in turn presented a 5- to 10-minute overview of their thoughts on PrivTech as an acquisition candidate. The net result of the presentation was as follows:

1. No deal-stoppers are obviously present with PrivTech.

2. They have sales of around $420 million, less than 10 percent of BigTech's revenues.

3. The company is around 15 years old. It has a good reputation as a solid technology services house, and specializes in esoteric client-server technology development aimed specifically at government installations.

4. The vast majority of their business comes from government accounts, with the military being a top customer.

5. Glenn Francis, the founder and CEO of PrivTech, is well-known in the industry as a hard-nosed businessman who loves and protects his company while still retaining a strong interest in the technology. He is even known to review software code on occasion.

6. PrivTech operates like a large startup in that employees are motivated through a bonus structure, and through excellent salaries with benefits, to make their customer happy. It is not unusual for managers to work evenings and weekends to achieve that goal.

7. Their sales have been erratic over the last few years, and net income was nearly zero only five years ago. Net income has remained positive, but its growth rate has fluctuated between negative and positive since then.

8. Part of PrivTech's sales growth has come from the acquisition of smaller firms, which were then integrated into the parent organization.

9. Glenn Francis is known to be a wealthy man who contributes generously to breast cancer research. He lost his wife three years ago to breast cancer.

Marketing, operations, accounting, and engineering had no major problems with investigating PrivTech for acquisition. Everything would be obviously based on a successful due diligence review of its operation. The summary consensus was that BigTech should pursue this company as a prospective acquisition candidate. The broker has asked that BigTech respond in a maximum of three days with a tentative offer of what they would be willing to pay for PrivTech along with any contingencies associated with that price. The ball fell into Judy's court. She smiled, knowing that the financial fun lay ahead.

Major Steps in the Process

Judy had been through this process before. She knew the basic sequence would remain the same, even though the particulars that would unfold would be different with PrivTech than with any other company she had investigated. She called Rodney Small, a consultant who previously worked for years as an investment banker. Rodney wasn't cheap, but he was an excellent resource to have around at a time like this. He asked that the financial pages be faxed to him as soon as possible. In that way he could look at them Tuesday night in preparation for his meeting with Judy at 9:00 AM Wednesday morning.

Before hanging up the phone, Judy and Rodney agreed on their basic approach:

1. First, determine PrivTech's value as a standalone company.

2. Determine the value of any obvious synergy between BigTech and PrivTech.

3. Determine the lower, medium, and upper price ranges for PrivTech in light of Steps 1 and 2.

4. Determine the earnings-per-share (EPS) impact of the stock-funded purchase based on the three prices obtained from Step 3.

Rodney arrived at 9:00 AM, coffee, calculator, computer, and dog-eared prospectus in hand. He took the floor to present his valuation calculations, presented in Table 19.1.

Relative Value Approach

Rodney thought that a good place to start with a valuation process was by comparing PrivTech with other similarly-sized deals that had occurred in the last 12 months. Fortunately, there was enough M&A activity going on to provide a listing of publicly traded companies that had revenues close to that of PrivTech and were in the same general industry. This activity is summarized in Table 19.2.

Rodney then showed the comparable type of calculations related to PrivTech. This analysis is presented in Table 19.3.

Just from looking at the P/E ratios for the various companies, Rodney noted that the price range for PrivTech shares fell in the $18.3 \times \$1.02 = \$18.66$ range up to $31.5 \times \$1.02 = \$32.13$ range. The average for the sample of comparable companies is $26.03 \times \$1.02 = \$26.55$. Based on these prices and 14.15 million as the number of outstanding shares, the following range of purchase prices shown in Table 19.4 can be calculated.

Calculating the market value for a private company is a little complicated. There is no established market value for the company. In fact, the market value is being set by this acquisition procedure, so it is required that an estimated market value be "backed into" from existing comparable transactions.

Table 19.1 BigTech/PrivTech Valuation Calculations

	BigTech		PrivTech	
Income Statement	USD°	Percent	USD°	Percent
Revenues	$7,660	100.00	$427.0	100.00
Cost of Services	$5,974	77.99	$356.0	83.37
Selling, G&A	$696	9.09	$39.0	9.13
Depreciation and Amortization	$445	5.81	$7.8	1.83
Interest Expense	$48	0.63	$0.467	0.11
Income Before Tax	$497	6.49	$23.7	5.56
Taxes @ 35%	$174	2.27	$9.3	2.18
Net Income	$323	4.22	$14.4	3.38

Balance Sheet	BigTech	PrivTech
Current Assets	$2,669	$131
Other Assets	$2,339	$93
Total Assets	$5,008	$224
Current Liabilities	$2,081	$53
Long-Term Liabilities	$527	$5
Total Liabilities	$2,608	$58
Shareholders' Equity	$2,400	$166
Liabilities + Equity	$5,008	$224

° All dollar values in millions.

Table 19.2 Relative Value of PrivTech-sized Companies

Company	Revenues (millions)	Compounded Annual 5-Year EPS Growth Rate	P/E Ratio	Price/ Book Value	Enterprise Value[1]/ EBIT
CompA	$235	11%	31.5	3.5	13.1
CompB	$368	2%	18.3	1.9	7.3
CompC	$587	7%	28.3	3.7	14.3
Average	$397	6.7%	26.03	3.03	11.57

[1] Enterprise value = company market value minus outstanding debt plus cash on hand.

Table 19.3 PrivTech Analysis

	USD
Revenues	$427
Net Income	$14.432
Outstanding Shares (millions)	14.15
EPS	$1.02
EBIT	$24.2
EBITDA	$32.0
Market Price	N/A
Market Valuation	N/A
Valuation/EBIT	N/A
P/E Ratio	N/A
D/E Ratio	0.03
Current Ratio	2.47
Interest	$0.467
Taxes	$9.301
Depreciation and Amortization	$7.8
Shareholder Equity	$166
Debt	$5
Current Assets	$131
Current Liabilities	$53

All values in millions except per share data.

The following sequence of equations shows how the market value can be calculated from the EBIT ratio established from prior purchases of publicly traded companies.

$$\text{enterprise value} = \text{equity market value (EMV)} - \text{debt} + \text{cash}$$

$$\text{EBIT ratio} = \frac{(\text{EMV} - \text{debt} + \text{cash})}{\text{EBIT}}$$

$$\text{EBIT ratio} \times \text{EBIT} + \text{debt} - \text{cash} = \text{EMV}$$

This means that knowing the EBIT ratio for prior transactions, the EBIT of PrivTech, along with the debt and cash position of PrivTech enables the cal-

Table 19.4 Purchase Price Ranges for PrivTech

P/E Ratio Comp Analysis	Low P/E Ratio	Average P/E Ratio	High P/E Ratio
PrivTech	$18.66	$26.55	$32.13
Purchase Price[1] (millions)	$264.12	$375.69	$454.64

[1] Based on 14.15 million outstanding shares that must be retired at the listed per-share price.

Table 19.5 Market Value Calculated from Comparable EBIT Ratios

	Low	Average	High
EV/EBIT Ratio	7.3	11.57	14.3
Debt	5	5	5
Cash	11.3	11.3	11.3
EBIT	24.2	24.2	24.2
Market Value (millions)	$170.36	$273.69	$339.76
Outstanding Shares	14.15	14.15	14.15
Price per Share	$12.04	$19.34	$24.01

culation of an estimated equity market value, which is an estimate of a viable purchase price. This is demonstrated in Table 19.5.

Assuming that the book value for PrivTech is its shareholder's equity, it is also possible to calculate a purchase price using the price to book value ratios provided by the comparable transactions as shown in Table 19.6.

At this point in time, there is quite a spread in the reasonable price that could be offered for this company. The possible prices calculated extend from a low of around $170 million to a high of around $614 million, with per-share prices extending from a low of $14.15 per share to as high as $43.41 per share. The reasonable price range for the initial offer using these models is somewhere in between.

Constant Dividend Growth Valuation

The Gordon Valuation Model can be used to estimate the price of a share of stock for a company that demonstrates a consistent annual increase in its dividend payments. In the case of PrivTech, all of its earnings will transfer to BigTech, which is similar to a 100 percent dividend payment. If a constant annual growth rate is assumed, then the Gordon Valuation Model provides a reasonable way of calculating the stock price for a share of PrivTech stock.

Table 19.6 Market Value Calculated from Price to Book Value Ratios

	Low	Average	High
Book Value Ratio	1.9	3.03	3.7
Book Value	$166.00	$166.00	$166.00
Value	$315.40	$502.98	$614.20
Outstanding Shares	14.15	14.15	14.15
Price per Share	$22.29	$35.55	$43.41

$$\text{share price} = \frac{D1}{k - g}$$

where D1 = the dividend at the end of the first year of ownership, k = the required rate of return for this investment based on comparable alternate investment options, and g = assumed consistent annual dividend growth rate.

The prospectus reveals that PrivTech has an erratic historical dividend increase rate, which means that the Gordon model provides only a marginally accurate look at estimated share pricing. The prospectus shows that PrivTech estimates earnings per share next year of $1.1 million (see Table 19.7). Judy knows that BigTech gets a 10 percent return on its other alternate investments. From this information, Rodney prepared a table showing the various share prices obtained from the Gordon model and the company valuations that would result.

Discounted Cash Flow Method

The final valuation of PrivTech that Rodney wanted to pursue used the discounted cash flow (DCF) method. He was aware of the criticisms surrounding the method: namely, that it was too dependent on the value selected for the discount rate, and also that one could select the right discount rate to match whatever one wanted in an analysis. He also knew that the DCF is the standard method of determining the present value of a future stream of incoming cash flows. For this reason, he performed the analysis.

The first place to start was with PrivTech's projected future cash flows. He then had to determine the proper discount rate to apply to these cash flows. He planned to insert a terminal value at the end of Year 5 that extended into the future with a compounded annual earnings rate increase of 4.5 percent because he didn't expect that the company could maintain a five percent or more compounded increase indefinitely. The discount

Table 19.7 Gordon Model Values for Varying Growth Rates

Variable	Low	Medium	High
D1	1.1	1.1	1.1
k	10.0%	10.0%	10.0%
g	4.5%	5.0%	6.0%
P	$20.00	$22.00	$27.50
Shares	14.15	14.15	14.15
Valuation (millions)	$283	$311	$389

Table 19.8 PrivTech Valuation Using Discounted Cash Flow Method

Year	Today	Year 1	Year 2	Year 3	Year 4	Year 5	Year 6	
Cash Flow		1.1	1.18	1.16	1.23	1.31	1.38	
DCF Values		1.1	1.18	1.16	1.23	21.88	20.57	
Stock par value	$16.46						Gordon	Assumed
DCF/CAPM							Terminal	Growth:
							Value	4.50%

rate, k (used at Judy's recommendation), was determined using the capital asset pricing model (CAPM). The risk free rate (Rf) was assumed at six percent, the going rate for the 10-year Treasury bond. The expected market return rate (Rm) was assumed to be 10 percent, and β was assumed to be 1.3, which was the average β for the other comparable companies used in the study.

Using these values, the discount rate was calculated as:

$$k = 6\% + 1.3 \times (10\% - 6\%) = 11.20\%$$

A table summarizing the calculations was created, and is shown here as Table 19.8.

Rodney and Judy thought that the terminal value should be based on a dividend at the end of Year 6 or 1.38, which corresponds to D1 in the Gordon Equation. The growth rate (g) was assumed as 4.5 percent, which yielded a terminal value for the end of Year 5 of 20.57. This value was added to the Year 5 ending earnings to total 21.88. This value, along with the other

Table 19.9 PrivTech Valuation Ranges

Method	Low	Medium	High
P/E Shares	$18.67	$26.55	$32.13
P/E Valuation (millions)	$264.12	$375.69	$454.64
EBIT Ratio Shares	$12.04	$19.34	$24.01
EBIT Ratio Valuation (millions)	$170.36	$273.69	$339.76
BV Share	$22.29	$35.55	$43.41
BV Ratio Valuation (millions)	$315.40	$502.98	$614.20
Gordon Share Price	$20.00	$22.00	$27.50
Gordon Valuation (millions)	$283	$311	$389
DCF Share Price	$16.46	$17.85	$23.66
DCF Valuation (millions)	$232.87	$252.52	$334.75
AVG Share	$17.89	$24.26	$30.14
AVG Valuation (millions)	$253.15	$343.18	$426.47

cash flows, was discounted back to Year 0 using the 11.2 percent CAPM discount rate. This analysis provides a DCF-generated share price of $16.46, which translates into a valuation price of $16.46 × 14.15M = $232.87M.

Both Rodney and Judy agreed that this seemed like a fairly conservative analysis and ran medium- and high-value assessment scenarios also. To create these assessments, they assumed a terminal value growth rate of 5.19 percent, which was the average of the last five years, and seven percent, which was roughly its increase rate without the negative year in Year 3. The 5.19 percent scenario creates a DCF share price of $17.85 and a valuation of $252.52 million. The seven percent scenario created a share price of $23.66 and a valuation of $334.75 million. Rodney noted, with a little amusement, that the lower and higher valuations vary by over $100 million. Only history would know which of the scenarios was accurate.

Summary of Valuation Findings

Judy insisted that at this point the various valuation calculations be consolidated into a single table, shown as Table 19.9. In this way she felt better able to get an idea about the various valuations and their validity with respect to PrivTech.

Judy was concerned about the wide spread and considered using a weighting scale for each of the scenarios, but simply suggested that the highest value and the lowest value be dropped from the analysis simply because they

Table 19.10 Valuation Averages Adjusted by Removing Highest and Lowest Values

	Low	Medium	High
Adjusted Average Valuation (millions)	$273.85	$343.18	$379.54

seemed so far from the other values. When new valuation averages were calculated dropping the very low $170.36 million and the very high $614.20 million, the low turned out to be as shown in Table 19.10. The spread between highest and lowest is still over $100 million, but it is less distracting than the average numbers contained in the first average calculations.

Technical Valuation Approach

Market technicians claim that all future events can be reasonably estimated from past performance. This includes looking for events such as trading volume and changes in macroeconomics forces such as interest rates, stock price support levels, P/E ratios, and other criteria. Because PrivTech is not a publicly traded company, it does not have a stock price history, which makes the technical valuation approach irrelevant.

Market Anticipation Approach

Rodney laughed as he started to talk about the reasons why he had ignored the market anticipation approach to valuation. He laughed because he knew the many times he had sat at home watching the local financial news channel and had heard an analyst explaining why a specific future event would, or would not, cause the stock price to change. Rodney knew the internals of his client companies and truly could not divine the future with the certainty of a newscaster. Judy agreed that the market anticipation approach might be applicable to a shareholder evaluating BigTech's stock trading trends, but would not be applicable to a valuation of PrivTech. The only caveat on this assumption would be in determining the expected BigTech stock price trends during the due diligence period. Those fluctuations could substantially increase or decrease the cost of buying PrivTech with an all-stock deal.

Setting the Recommended Price

Rodney and Judy knew that they had to come up with a price range for the company on its own. Here is the rationale they chose to follow:

1. The P/E valuation showed that the average price should be in the $340 million range. This was a privately held company, which generally does not command the same P/E ratio as a public company, with decreases of as much as 50 percent possible. PrivTech had $131 million in cash and $166 million in equity, so a price much lower than $340 million seemed too low.

2. The Gordon valuation showed a medium value of $311 million, still within the ballpark of the P/E valuation. This analysis did not assume the most optimistic earnings growth, but did assume a more conservative number.

3. The average valuation of all methods came in at around $340 million also.

They chose to submit a range to the rest of the committee. They recommended a lower range of $290 million, a medium range of $325 million, and an upper range maximum price of $380 million. This was still a $90 million spread and both had wanted to get it within a tighter range, but this was just the way that the numbers worked out. They assumed that issues would come up in due diligence that would change the value one way or the other.

Determining Possible Synergy

There appeared to be several areas where positive synergy could exist between BigTech and PrivTech. The hope of every buyer is that the economies associated with a larger company will assist the smaller company with its own margins. A few areas came immediately to mind as Rodney and Judy reviewed the financial statements.

1. Cost of services could feasibly be reduced from the 83.37 percent of revenues currently seen to the 77.99 percent experienced by BigTech. This results in a $23 million savings based on the current revenue levels, and an increase in net income of $15.9 million.

   Judy noted that this higher cost level may be due to the higher salaries PrivTech paid its employees. Dropping this cost might require a decrease in salaries, which could cost some of the key people BigTech is trying to transfer with the acquisition. Judy noted that this was an important due diligence area of investigation.

2. Feedback from marketing (Mike Ingram) indicated that synergy might also be possible in the revenue area. He felt that offering PrivTech's services through

the standard BigTech sales organization could result in as much as a five percent increase in PrivTech sales in the first year and sustained thereafter. He calculated that this translates into a $12.4 million increase in PrivTech revenues, which ultimately adds $419,000 to the net income.

Combining these two initial synergy effects totals a positive $16.32 million to the PrivTech net income figure, which adds $1.15 earnings per share to the future expected financial. Adding that to the 1.02 current earnings per share indicates that $2.17 EPS is feasible.

Calculating a valuation using the Gordon Valuation Model and a $2.17 EPS value, the overall valuations explode to between $558 million and $760 million. At this point, the difference between $320 million and $370 million looks pretty trivial, but Rodney knew that overly optimistic assessments of synergy were a major area for underproducing acquisitions. Including only the $419,000 incremental net income in the EPS calculations increases the first year ending EPS from $1.1 to $1.13. This change increases the Gordon valuation to between $290 million to $399 million. By negotiating on today's numbers and not including the synergy, BigTech could experience large cost decreases after merging that could make a PrivTech purchase at $340 million or so a real bargain.

Determining Earnings per Share Dilution Effects

The final stage of the process was to determine the impact on earnings per share by a stock purchase. BigTech's stock is currently trading at $61 per share. The addition of PrivTech to the BigTech company using pooling of interests will have minimal impact on BigTech's debt since PrivTech carries little debt on its own. This analysis is broken down in Table 19.11.

This analysis shows that BigTech could feasibly offer up to $417 million for PrivTech without taking a negative EPS impact. This provides the negotiating team with latitude over its offering price. In theory, any price lower than $417 million should increase the EPS, which helps convince investors that this acquisition makes financial sense. This was looking nothing but up from the financial side of things.

Table 19.11 EPS Dilution Analysis

	Low	Medium	High	Max
Current Trading Price	$61	$61	$61	$ 61
PrivTech Purchase Price (millions)	$290	$325	$380	$417
BigTech Shares Required (millions)	4.75	5.33	6.23	6.84
Existing BigTech Issued Shares (millions)	153.08	153.08	153.08	153.08
New Issued Shares Total (millions)	157.83	158.41	159.31	159.92
New Combined Earnings	$337.43	$337.43	$337.43	$337.43
New EPS	$2.14	$2.13	$2.12	$2.11
Premerger EPS	$2.11	$2.11	$2.11	$2.11
Change	$0.03	$0.02	$0.01	$0.00

The Initial Response

Martin Graves listened to the financial presentation from his accounting manager. She felt, as did Martin, that a reasonable price for PrivTech would be in the $340 million to $410 million range. He had thought that earlier in the day simply from an instinctual standpoint, and was pleased that his instincts seemed on track. The other team members found no other major flaws at this point and clearly were waiting to get into the due diligence phase. The ball was now in Martin's hands. He called his lawyers and asked them to join the meeting. They had to respond to the broker with a budgetary price range for the PrivTech purchase along with any required contingencies.

The point of this phase was simply to get to the next stage. That stage will involve formal, and likely some informal, discussions with PrivTech management in general, and with Glenn Francis, PrivTech CEO and founder, in particular. Everyone agreed that a price of $340 million would not be so low as to be insulting, and would serve the purpose of getting to the next stage. Martin thought about the number of prior deals that had not passed the deal-stopper stage and realized that he really liked what he knew about this company. He wanted to get a closer look and would not be eliminated at this stage. He would propose $355 million, along with the standard contingencies, as a safety margin just to ensure that they actually got to have real discussions.

Thursday, the broker called saying that PrivTech wanted to have further discussions, but that Martin should know that Glenn was looking for at least $400 million. Glenn knew a few things about BigTech, having "taken business from them for years" (in his own words), and was interested in further discussions which he requested to happen on Monday. Martin agreed.

Negotiating the Purchase Terms

Martin held a meeting of his acquisition staff to discuss the upcoming meeting with PrivTech. He wanted to develop a negotiating strategy that would not only get them access to PrivTech due diligence, but also finally get them PrivTech at the price, and with the terms, that BigTech wanted. After much discussion, these points seemed to be the most important:

1. BigTech could offer a price of up to $410 million without negative earnings per share impact, and that additional synergy could make the $410 million price a real bargain.

2. PrivTech brings $131 million in liquid assets with its purchase, and only $58 million in debt, which means that PrivTech is actually contributing $73 million (21%) of the purchase price in net cash.

3. PrivTech employees are fiercely dedicated to Glenn Francis, and this dedication has seemed to increase since the death of his wife. He was also known as being dedicated to his employees.

4. Everyone agreed that if Glenn did not transfer with the purchase, employees might start defecting to other companies.

5. Glenn might be a management problem because he has a reputation of being his own man.

6. Glenn appears to be financially well off. His interests of late have been in contributing to breast cancer research and awareness. He is 57 years old, financially secure, and ready to do something different.

7. Martin did not want to pay more than $390 million for the purchase but would go higher if needed. The higher price would be justified on the basis of expected future synergy returns.

8. The deal should close as quickly as possible. A deadline of two months from the date of the letter of intent was set.

9. Although PrivTech had a reputation for having a free-wheeling culture, it also had a reputation for integrity and fairness. BigTech was known as being financially conservative, but it also tried to promote creativity among its workers. All felt that any cultural issues could be worked out.

10. Everyone was keenly aware of the higher salaries and benefits paid to PrivTech employees than those paid to BigTech employees. On the other hand, BigTech offered more diversity of assignments than PrivTech, which is an enticement for programmers and other creative technology people.

That night, without telling any of his staff, Martin called Glenn to arrange a personal meeting, without staff, to "just get acquainted" before the meeting. Martin told his staff that he would meet them in San Francisco without telling them anything more. Glenn and Martin met for dinner at a restaurant of Glenn's choosing. Glenn insisted that Martin try a special $155 pinot noir wine that he really liked. They had a low-key conversation about personal interests, life in the Bay Area, Silicon Valley and its quirks, and the rapid rate of technological change. Glenn let Martin pick up the check.

Leaving out the detailed negotiations that occurred at the next day's meeting, I present the finally negotiated points:

1. BigTech would pay $360 million for PrivTech. The acquisition would become final at a special stockholders' meeting to be held two months from the date of this meeting.

2. The purchase would be funded completely with BigTech stock with a ratio of 0.4171 shares of BigTech stock issued for every one share of PrivTech. BigTech would issue 5.90 million new shares to finance the purchase. Big-Tech share price was assumed to be $61 per share, which represented the average of 15 randomly selected days out of the last 20 trading days.

3. BigTech agreed that all PrivTech employees would retain their current salary ranges for a one-year period, after which time they would begin assimilation into compliance with the BigTech personnel policies. Employee pay grades would be adjusted or future raises would be reduced with the intention of eventually bringing these employees into parity with other BigTech employees. They understood that some employees may choose to leave as the assimilation went into effect, but many would choose to stay due to the otherwise favorable BigTech working environment.

4. Glenn Francis would transfer to BigTech as the Chief Technology Officer while also working as the executive manager of a special Breast Cancer Re-

search and Awareness Foundation set up in honor of his late wife. BigTech agreed to let Glenn run the foundation as his primary activity and agreed to initially fund the foundation with a $15 million contribution.

5. Glenn would participate with any strategic and major tactical planning sessions. In addition, he would participate as needed to ensure a smooth transition of PrivTech's major customers.

6. All pricing was contingent upon the successful completion of the due diligence process. PrivTech agreed to extend every possible assistance during due diligence and to be open to reasonable renegotiation of price and terms based on discovered due diligence items.

7. The transaction is subject to the resolution of any related, although unexpected, antitrust issues that might be raised during the process.

8. Other pertinent legal points inserted by, and agreed to, by each side's legal personnel.

9. PrivTech agrees to reopen negotiations should the pooling of interests method not be allowed after further due diligence review.

10. Any key PrivTech employees with stock options over a certain, to be specified, threshold must remain employees of BigTech for at least a two-year period or forfeit their options. They may leave within that two-year period only after receiving written clearance from BigTech management. They hoped that this would pass legal review and both agreed that they wanted to provide employees with an incentive to remain with BigTech after the transaction completed.

As they left the meeting, Martin shook hands with Glenn, congratulating him on the prospective sale of his company and asked him to come to Chicago to visit their operation. Glenn thought that was a good idea. Dinner would be on him this time, he noted with a smile.

Dealing with the Public Stock Market

The process of evaluating a publicly traded company is very similar to that for a private company, with one major difference. The market price for a publicly traded stock is already set by the stock market. The shares are not in the hands of a single concentrated group of shareholders but are instead spread throughout the market in general.

This section takes an abbreviated look at the prior example using most of the existing financial assumptions, except that PrivTech is now a publicly traded company called PubTech and its shares are trading at $26 each at the time of the signing of the letter of intent. The relationship between Glenn Francis and his employees, their history, culture, and financial performance are identical. The only thing that changes in the scenario is that PubTech is now a publicly traded company with a market valuation of $26 × 14.15M = $367.9M. BigTech shares are assumed to be publicly trading at the previously set $61 per share. One share of PubTech stock would be exchanged for 0.4634 shares of BigTech stock. In essence, based on the current pricing, each share of PubTech is worth $28.26.

Martin understands that stock price fluctuations may affect the net price that PubTech shareholders receive once the actual share ratio is established. If BigTech stock price increased to $65 per share, PubTech shareholders will receive the equivalent of $30.12. PubTech shareholders are protected in that the BigTech share price would need to drop to $56.10 before PubTech shareholders started losing money based on the selected exchange ratio. Given BigTech's performance and its $\beta = 1$, this was an unlikely scenario in the current robust marketplace. Martin also noted that PubTech's P/E ratio is $26/1.02 = 25.5$, which compares favorably to BigTech's P/E of 28.91.

1. In this case, Martin offered to purchase the company for $400 million, using stock to fund the deal. The higher price represents approximately a 10 percent premium over the current market price, which is offered as an enticement for PubTech shareholders to accept the offer. Martin certainly did not want to get into a bidding war with another company for the ownership of PubTech.

2. Glenn, who owns a large portion of shares in PubTech, still comes on board as the Chief Technology Officer, but he now starts the foundation on his own. He still has an agreement with BigTech that he can split his time between foundation management and his BigTech responsibilities.

3. The attorneys add jargon related to renegotiating pricing terms in the event of radical shifts in stock prices, much to Martin's disappointment.

4. The process is a little more complex since the formal SEC filing requirements must be made.

The purchase of PubTech by BigTech appears to be a sound business move from both a market expansion, strategic, and financial perspective. Martin wished that all deals were as clearly defined as this one.

Valuation Procedures for New or Marginal Firms

Placing a valuation on a new firm or one that is not yet showing a profit (a marginal firm) requires a process similar to that outlined earlier with the PrivTech purchase. Only a few of the valuation procedures will apply, because any marginal firm has no realized positive cash flows to speak of.

1. The Gordon Valuation Model disappears because it requires a positive dividend to be applicable.

2. The DCF becomes less valuable. A marginal firm has a high discount rate resulting from its higher risk. Its cash flows are in the distant future. The double impact of a distant future cash flow with a high discount rate creates a very low present value. The analysis can be done, but the calculated price will be small, which is good for buyers and usually unacceptable to sellers.

3. The P/E ratio calculations also don't apply since the company does not show any earnings.

4. Conventional wisdom would lead one to conclude that valuation can really only be determined using the EBIT ratio and/or the book value ratio. This is not necessarily true, because companies without positive retained earnings are often valued for large amounts.

Notice the importance of comparable deals in valuing a marginal company. It is critical that research be done for the industry to determine the going pricing thresholds for the purchase of a company that is not yet showing a profit. Anyone who watches the technology business markets knows that investors place a high value on companies that do not show a profit. This seems confusing and for good reason. If the present value of a company is based on its discounted future cash flows, then the company must be assumed to show a profit at some point in the future. These future cash flows must be assumed or nobody would buy the stock. After all, why would someone recommend an investment in a company currently losing money that was not expected to earn money in the future?

If you notice the industries that experience high valuation for marginal performers, you will notice that they are ones with explosive future potential growth. These companies already enjoy a dominant market share in this explosive market. As the market grows, and dominance continues, the company's revenues must increase explosively too. The question, then, is whether the management team can turn that explosive revenue growth into explosive profits. If the marketplace believes that the right team is in place, then it will invest heavily today in anticipation of huge returns in the future. If the marketplace starts to get hesitant about this highly speculative combination, you will see the stock drop precipitously. After all, marginal companies are strictly selling the future and the current valuation of the future is strictly a matter of how we perceive it today.

Anyone involved in an M&A transaction involving a marginal firm should expect fairly rigorous negotiations. After all, the market price has not been set and every deal sets its own valuation price. Having access to the specific valuation procedures used for other similar transactions, in similar industries with similar financial considerations, provides a baseline from which participants can negotiate. There are numerous databases out there that provide this type of information for both public and private deals. Private information is more difficult to come by since the parties involved usually will not freely disclose the information. After all, they don't have to.

The basic advice for negotiating price for a firm that does not show a profit is this: determine a reasonable low and high valuation range based on the EBIT and book value ratios. Take a shot at a DCF with highly optimistic future projections and see if you can theoretically justify the ranged prices determined with the EBIT ratio analysis. Then, sell, sell, sell the future.

Chapter Summary

A lot of work is done in the short period of time between when a deal is brought to a buyer's attention and the signing of the letter of intent. Even more work is done during due diligence and the later transaction closing stages. It is important that buyers and sellers calculate a potential purchase price using a number of different techniques, as shown in this chapter. In this way, a range of acceptable prices can be determined. It should always be remembered that a low transaction price that eliminates postpurchase cooperation between buyer and seller management could seriously degrade the future value of the deal. Also remember that paying too much for a transaction, which sometimes happens in the heat of the moment, places the transaction at a serious financial disadvantage because its required future financial performance must be commensurately higher simply to provide the needed return on investment. Make sure that you get the right range for pricing, and then work on making the business aspects of the transaction coalesce into a strong, business-based acquisition transaction. A low price does not always make for good business, and neither does buying an expensive trophy division.

20

Making the Buy/Sell Decision

After all of the due diligence is finished, the legal manipulations are done, and the emotional changes stop, buyer and seller must make the final decision to finalize the transaction. Buyer must buy, or not. Seller must sell, or not. Any of these actions will have consequences that affect both buyer and seller. This chapter takes a look at the final stages to making the final buy/sell decision and also methods of dealing with a decision to back out of the transaction.

Assessing the Information

The more informed you are when making this buy/sell decision, the more confident you will later be that the decision was made for the right reasons. It is always easy to evaluate a past decision from some time in the future and to apply 20/20 hindsight to the decision making process. Managers making the decision in real time do not have this luxury. They must make their decision based on the knowledge and motivations present at the time of making the decision.

The due diligence process is designed to provide the decision makers with the best possible information at the time of decision making. This fact alone makes the due diligence process an indispensable part of the M&A cycle. Shortchanging the time, expertise, and money spent on due diligence is courting later disappointment.

Buyer Information Base

The buyer has a lot of information available at the time that the closing decision is made:

1. Deal-stoppers have been evaluated and eliminated.

2. Due diligence has reviewed major value points and indicated the status of that review.

3. Buyer management has met with seller management and now has a better feel about the personality and cultural mix.

4. Depending on the level of secrecy and firms involved, public reaction to the acquisition should be gauged by the general analyst community's assessment of the combination.

5. Areas of positive or negative synergy should have been uncovered that detract from or add to the value of the target company. These synergies make the initially agreed-upon purchase price as stated in the letter of intent either a bargain or too expensive, depending upon items found and their valuation.

6. Competitor reactions to the acquisition should be reported, letting you know more about the likely competitive actions stimulated by your acquisition.

7. You will also have a better idea about employee reaction to the proposed purchase. In fact, purchases often open opportunities for buyer employees, which always piques peoples' interest.

8. More will be known about the current market conditions. Changes are likely to have occurred over the weeks of the due diligence process.

9. Any contingencies related to the initial letter of intent should be known to be applicable or not applicable at this time.

In summary, unknown items that were of concern at the time of the letter of intent should now be known. Target company risks should have been assessed and valued at this point. Money should have been raised or stock sold to fund the purchase. Everything that needs to be known is now known and a decision must be made.

Executive Management Team Considerations

Postacquisition consolidation is addressed in detail in Chapter 22. But let me present a few facts from an article in the September/October 1998 issue of *Mergers and Acquisitions* magazine. The content of Alexandra Reed Lajoux and J. Fred Weston's article, "Do Deals Deliver on Postmerger Performance?", is particularly recommended to those of you who believe that the success or failure of an acquisition is based on price, price, and price alone.

1. The failure or success of an acquisition is relative to the expectations associated with the acquisition.

2. The most successful acquisitions ensure that a strategic and operational fit is viable, where the least successful acquisitions do neither.

3. The five most listed reasons for postmerger failure are: cultural incompatibility, clashing management styles and egos, inability to implement change, inability to forecast, and excessive optimism regarding positive synergy effects.

4. Research by Kenneth Smith found that postmerger improvements are not related to strategy or price but rather to improved postmerger management.

I do not fully agree with the final point in this list, because I clearly contend that strategy and price are important to any acquisition. I do, however, think that this point helps to reinforce the contention that postmerger management success is critical to the postsale success of the acquisition.

The management teams of the buyer and seller have learned a lot about each other over the course of the due diligence process. Hopefully you took my advice and got members of the executive management of both companies involved at various stages of the process. In this way everyone gets a personal perspective on the other company's personnel, policies, management styles, and levels of professionalism. At this point, a heart-to-heart about possible stumbling blocks that could seriously impede postacquisition cooperation between buyer and seller management is warranted. Buyer and seller are both better served by getting these issues on the table now instead of waiting a year or two after the deal is closed to raise complaints.

The success of the postmerger entity and its employees is heavily based on cooperation, team operation, and unified direction. An accurate assessment of the likelihood of this level of team cooperation happening in the postsale environment helps management determine the required steps needed to quickly deal with what is realistically expected.

Bottom-lining the Purchase

I suggest that, if due diligence did not turn up any major flaws and all deal-stoppers are still resolved, then you must rely on your initial motivation and strategy in finally deciding to purchase. The weight must fall on the side of making the purchase. Strategic doubts should have been dealt with before this process even started. Can you back out of the deal? Probably, but not without incurring some substantial financial and credibility costs in the process.

Once, while canoeing down the Russian River in California, we came across a group of teenagers jumping from a 30-foot high-bridge into the river. It looked like fun and from the river it didn't look that high. From the bridge, however, it looked like a long way down. My zeal for taking the plunge was now mixed with a large dose of fear. Just before jumping off, I got some sage advice from a 14-year-old who did this jump on a regular basis. "Once you leave the bridge, simply control the flight and landing. Otherwise you can get hurt pretty badly."

I submit to you that you jumped off the bridge when you signed the letter of intent along with its associated contingencies. If those contingencies are met and a reasonable price has been determined, then stopping the transaction this late in the process is a lot like trying to climb back onto the bridge after jumping. It usually is unsuccessful and can really cause a lot of damage when you land.

The bottom line is that the letter of intent is a legal agreement. Breaking that agreement without a material violation occurring is not only a breach of good faith but could also open you and the company up to litigation on the part of shareholders, investors, brokers, and the seller. Don't jump off the bridge if you are not ready. Don't sign the letter of intent unless you really mean it. After that point, control and enjoy the flight and the smooth entry. By the way, I hit the water just fine and learned an important lesson about commitment in the process.

Determining the Final Price

Due diligence will likely have turned up several valuation-related items that may affect the purchase price. Remember that valuations will be found that both add to and subtract from the letter of intent price. It is very possible that the pluses and minuses will simply offset each other. It is also possible that items that substantially decrease the value of the company might be uncovered and these may be useful for negotiating a lower purchase price. Positive synergy is rarely brought to the seller's attention so buyers are unlikely to want to negotiate a higher price.

The buyer should consider the impact of renewed pricing negotiations on the overall transaction. If the positives outweigh the negatives, then negotiating a lower purchase price might not be wise, especially if there are other potential buyers waiting for your deal to fall apart. If, on the other hand, due diligence raises serious value-degrading issues, then you are fully justified in bringing them up in final price negotiation. If the seller insists on a price that is too high based on due diligence information, then the buyer is completely justified in backing out of the deal and your lawyers should ensure that this option is available in the letter of intent. Using immaterial negative due diligence valuation information as a way of squeezing a lower price might win you this particular battle but might also cost you the postacquisition cooperation and teamwork battles that will eventually win you the war.

Remember that publicly traded buyer stock will vary in market value over the due diligence time frame. These fluctuations can dramatically impact the net price received by the seller on deals funded substantially with buyer stock. If the buyer stock increases in value, then the sellers will get an effectively higher purchase price for their shares. If the stock drops, sellers will get an effectively lower price for their shares when exchanged.

If little of material value in a negative way is uncovered from due diligence, then your final price is likely the one negotiated with the letter of intent. You might be allowed a little negotiating room if the buyer's stock market value rises substantially after the letter of intent is signed and negative due diligence items are discovered. In this scenario, the sellers expect to receive more for the company than they initially expected and may be willing to negotiate some negative valuation issues. It is always easier to give up something when you are already receiving more than you expected. If buyer stock drops, buyers should be wary of upsetting the transaction since the sellers are now receiving less for the company than expected and may be looking for a way out of the transaction.

Postacceptance Activities

Speed is of the essence when integrating two organizations in a postacquisition environment. Buyer and seller should immediately form transition-integration teams that will work together to make the process as seamless as possible. Details on this process are provided in Chapter 22.

Backing Out of the Deal

It is possible that buyer or seller might simply decide that this particular transaction is not right for them and back out of the deal. Although the impact on the buyer must be addressed, the impact on the seller can be substantial and requires a carefully planned program of damage control. In general, the best way to handle the fallout associated with the possibility of a deal falling apart is to downplay the deal when it is first announced. Saying something like "We are pleased to be in these negotiations and view the future potential very positively" acknowledges the deal, presents it as potentially positive, but does not attach an unnecessary amount of significance. Remember that you can say anything you want after the deal closes, but prudence is warranted before that.

Impact on Buyer

The impact on the buyer is heavily dependent on who backs out of the deal. If the buyer initiates the withdrawal, then the only real negative impacts are the time, personnel, and opportunity costs associated with the M&A process and a possible image issue relating to the buyer making poor business decisions. A strong company with a solid management history should have little problem in effectively dealing with these issues. If it happens too many times, however, the next prospective seller approached by the buyer will be more reluctant to consider the buyer as a viable candidate.

More extensive damage control might be required with shareholders and the media if the seller withdraws from the transaction. Damage control is particularly important if the buyer has already stated how important this acquisition is to the company and heavily emphasized future benefits. Now the buyer must somehow project the seller withdrawal as an event that does not dramatically negatively impact the buyer's future revenues and earnings prospects. These later statements may directly conflict with those made in the heat of acquisition fever, which could create a credibility problem for buyer management.

For this reason alone, buyer management often downplays the significance of an acquisition until after the transaction is finalized.

Impact on Seller

The major impact of an uncompleted transaction will generally fall on the sellers. Sellers have had the buyer's due diligence team walking through its organization, talking to its vendors, interviewing its customers and while simultaneously distracting the seller from its core business activities.

This section provides a listing of areas in which sellers should consider damage control activities. As always, the best defense against an incomplete deal is to prequalify the buyer before signing the letter of intent, to downplay the importance of the deal to the future of the company, and to keep it secret for as long as possible.

DEALING WITH LOW OFFERS

It is possible that a seller can go through the entire due diligence process and finally obtain a purchase price that is lower than that initially agreed upon in the letter of intent. After all, that is the purpose of the due diligence process from a buyer's perspective: to uncover items that detract from value that can be used to reduce the price and also decrease the risk associated with the purchase.

Sellers should be ready for a final price negotiation and understand their lowest price limit. Should the buyer come back with a firm offer that is substantially lower, then the seller must decide if he wants to accept the offer or walk away from the transaction. Walking away means that the seller has to start the due diligence process all over again with another buyer, assuming that there is another buyer in the wings. Should the deal fall apart, I suggest that both buyer and seller simply publicly state that the "deal fell apart over differences that could not be reconciled." Anything more than that is like listening to two people argue about their divorce. The discussion is not very productive, it is full of potentially damaging content, and it serves no purpose other than to impugn the other party. Everyone loses in this scenario. I suggest that buyers and sellers impress the importance of "need to know" secrecy to their respective staff members regarding the reasons for the transaction falling apart.

The Liabilities of Not Selling

Sellers have a number of different areas that may require attention once a deal falls apart. This section takes a look at the major ones and provides some recommendations for handling them.

HANDLING EMPLOYEE PERCEPTIONS

Technology companies are heavily dependent on their employee base. These are the people who create the intellectual property that drives the profit engine. These are the people who sell to customers, manufacture the products, and handle postsale problems. These are the people who, if they lose faith in their employer, can simply "do their jobs," which may be the first death knoll of a dynamic technology company. Retaining employees while also keeping them motivated is always a challenge in technology areas. This becomes particularly difficult if the employees see that the employer's management structure is changing and company ownership is now in question.

This may make no sense at all, but I have consistently found it to be true: Once a company is up for sale, work inside the company gets sidetracked. It is not that work stops. It is just that employees continually wonder about the status of the sale and how it will affect them. They wonder whether they should buy a piece of computer equipment they need, or whether they should close that next deal since they really don't know who will be servicing the customer after the sale.

Doubt often breeds indecision, and announcing the sale of a company creates doubt. Managers have to deal with this doubt and uncertainty or they may not only see a productivity slowdown, but also might find themselves losing some of their best employees to other companies. Here are a few things that management can do to get things back on track with respect to the terminated sale:

1. Have a meeting with key employees and managers discussing the lost sale. Explain as positively as possible what happened and why the deal fell through.

2. Answer any questions they may have as honestly and positively as possible. Remember that these people were kept in the dark once before about the sale and fear that you will keep them in the dark again. Recovering their trust is very important.

3. Ask if there are any areas of particular note that will be negatively affected by the announcement. If so, ask for recommendations on getting things back on track.

4. Announce your plans regarding the likelihood of a future sale of the business. If you expect interest from other potential buyers you should mention that at this time and ask for employee support.

5. Explain your reasons for wanting to sell the company and explain the time frame over which you are willing to wait for a deal to close. Private sellers should also explain that at some point you will take the company off of the market and get back to business.

6. Above all, you must get the employees motivated to return to business as usual. Reinforce the fact that the company is not in trouble and that it is still very much a going concern.

7. Hold a company-wide meeting to present information about the sale and why it was lost, in general terms. Refer employees to their local managers for any specific questions. Also let them know that any questions can be routed to the executive committee through their manager or by email.

8. Be seen around the company. This is particularly important for private, closely held corporations where a single owner might call the shots. People need to believe that you still believe in the business and the best way to show that is to be out there, visibly making the business work.

Employees primarily want job security. Secondly, they want to work for a company, and a boss, who deserves their trust and whose leadership they believe in. They must leave this meeting believing that they are secure on both counts or you might see the lingering effects of the lost sale for years to come.

HANDLING CUSTOMER AND VENDOR PERCEPTIONS

Hopefully your customers and vendors were shielded from the due diligence process and really are unaffected by the lost deal. It is likely, however, that the major customers and vendors were contacted as part of the due diligence process and require some additional explanation about the lost deal. Remember that it is always better for a customer to hear about something first from you and secondly from everyone else. If you are first, you have the ability to frame the reference against which all other stories are heard. Here is a recommended procedure that, if followed, will mitigate any customer fallout.

1. Create a listing of all due diligence contacted customers.

2. Create a story that accurately and positively presents the situation surrounding the lost deal. Keep the information as specifically vague as possible.

3. Train all sales and marketing people on this story so that it is presented in a consistent manner.

4. Schedule appointments in person with the major customers and by phone with others.

5. Do a follow-up with the marketing and sales force regarding customers' response to the meetings.

Customers, like employees, simply want to know that things in the future will be at least as consistent as they were before the lost deal. They are looking for assurances that the lost deal does not portend a lost company too. It is up to management and the seller's employees to reinstill and maintain customer confidence in the company. They had it before, or they would not today be a customer.

The same basis approach should be taken with vendors. The major vendors should get special attention since they are once again the ones likely contacted during due diligence. If upper management was involved in the due diligence meetings with customers and vendors, they should also be involved in these postdeal meetings with major customers and vendors. Otherwise, a bad taste may be left in their mouths regarding their participation in the earlier transaction. This ill feeling might keep them from being as cooperative the next time a prospective buyer comes along.

Basically, you win some and you lose some; this one just didn't work out. Most business people understand that fact and will take it in stride as long as you, your management, and your customer/vendor-related operation reflect that it is still just business as usual. If they feel any sense of desperation from the company, a series of very negative, and unwarranted, problems can come up which are much more difficult to solve than simply explaining a lost deal.

CANCELING A COMPETITOR TRANSACTION

A derailed competitor transaction presents its own unique set of circumstances that are worth investigating and correcting. The due diligence stage revealed a lot of information about your operation, customers, vendors, employees, products, financials, and other areas that would never normally be revealed to a competitor. That potential owner is now back to being your competitor, but with a much more comprehensive information base from which to compete. You are likely at a disadvantage compared to the position you were in before the transaction began.

A meeting should be called with all staff members to discuss the amount of otherwise proprietary information which was revealed to the would-be buyer. It is also worthwhile to discuss proprietary information that you might have received about your competition as part of the due diligence process. A brainstorming session should then be held to determine the worst possible scenario that could arise from the competition having this information. This same brainstorming session should discuss ways in which any competitor information can be used in the future. If there are major exposure areas, then action plans should be created to help mitigate any negative impact. If the exposure is uncomfortable but not really damaging, then I suggest that you simply get back to work.

A competitor acquisition carries a little more risk with it than a standard acquisition from a noncompetitor. But the competitor is a company very likely to appreciate the value contained within your company before anyone else. They understand your business almost as well as you do. Simply be careful with revealing unrequested information during due diligence and take steps after the deal sours to minimize negative impacts. This is particularly true with respect to major customers, who now know your competitor, who also now knows your customer. If you are not careful, that customer could become your competitor's customer, and you would have a difficult time proving that the nondisclosure agreement was violated in the process.

Trusting Your Instincts

No manager gets to an executive position without learning to trust his instincts. Simple problems can be analyzed and an optimal path chosen. The more complicated problems associated with top-level business management are often not accompanied by a clearly defined right choice. That is where your instincts come in.

The same is true in an M&A situation. When all of the data, financial reporting, presentations, and due diligence reporting in the world cannot shake an uneasy feeling, there is likely something in the transaction that was missed. Have your M&A staff take another look at the areas that you feel are instinctively off in some way. You and they are better served by either confirming or refuting your instinctual issues at this time instead of after the deal is closed.

What if, on the other hand, the numbers indicate that a deal is marginal at best and your instincts still indicate that you should move forward with the deal? You can still buy or sell, but you had better think up a good story for the shareholders, especially if the public response was muted at best.

Closing Up Shop Completely

It is very rare that a liquidated company is worth more than the company is as a going concern, so closing up a public company is a highly unlikely scenario. This is not, however, rare with a privately held company in which the owners no longer want to run the company, there is no likely successor, and the owners are already financially well off.

Liquidation may look like an easy way out, but it needs to be tempered with a dose of caution. This is not a process that happens overnight. Employees will not be happy with this process no matter how delicately you present it to them. They lose their jobs because the owners want to do something else. You could wind up with some very angry employees on your hands or even a lawsuit. Some privately held companies in this position consider an ESOP as a possible way out that not only serves the needs of the owners but also those of the employees and managers.

Management Buyout or Selling to an ESOP

An ESOP enables the company owner to sell the company while also providing his prior employees with a chance to profit from owning their own business. The owner may get some very attractive tax breaks along the way which may make the ESOP even more attractive. Refer to Chapter 6, "Deal Types and Their Funding," for more information about setting up an ESOP. This chapter is required reading for a well off, bored entrepreneur with a sizable company payroll and motivated employees.

A management buyout (MBO) is like an LBO except that the lead investment group is the company's own managers. They may pool some of their own money for the LBO down payment or they may bring in an outside investor to help with the required initial cash funding. The beauty of an LBO is that the owner once again may get a solid price for the company, his employees get a chance at running their own company, and the owners are no longer involved with the daily operation of the business.

In either case, the owner will likely find that an MBO or ESOP will not only provide him with larger proceeds from the sale of the company. It will also provide him with the satisfaction of knowing that the prior employees who helped him to create his own financially secure future now have the chance to do the same for themselves.

Chapter Summary

Eventually a time comes when the transaction turns either into a closed deal, or it terminates with everyone going on with their separate business lives. Making the required decisions may or may not be simple depending on the circumstances surrounding the transaction. Should the deal fall apart in its later stages, buyers and sellers will have damage control activities to perform with employees, customers, and vendors. The best way to minimize any damage from a failed acquisition is to minimize the amount of information provided at the time of the proposed acquisition announcement. Buyers and sellers must also candidly and promptly interact with affected people with the intention of restoring trust, ensuring uninterrupted business operations, and keeping the company ready for another potential buyer or target, depending on whether you are a buyer or seller.

21

Legal Considerations

Almost every business transaction involves a legal agreement (contract) of some type. The contract is actually the nexus that defines and connects all of the transaction's various aspects. It is a legal document that binds the performance of the parties involved. When the transaction involves a corporation, the fiduciary responsibilities of the company management with respect to their respective shareholders must be considered from both a moral and legal perspective. Specific legal regulations are in place to protect the rights of shareholders during merger and acquisition transactions. No deal can be considered binding if it falls outside of these legal requirements.

Legal considerations fall into a few basic categories: those related to the states in which the corporations are chartered, those relating to Securities and Exchange Commission (SEC) compliance, those relating to antitrust issues, and those related to contract law ensuring that a contract is a legally binding agreement for both buyer and seller. Antitrust issues are covered in Chapter 17, "Franchised and Competitor Transactions." Issues specifically relating to contract law are beyond the scope of this book, and the reader is urged to seek an excellent contract law reference for detailed coverage of this important legal area. This chapter takes a look at state and SEC requirements, with additional information pertaining to insider trading considerations and the roles of professionals in the M&A process. Readers should not treat this chapter as a legally definitive treatise on M&A legal activities, but more as a general legal primer covering issues pertinent to a company and its sale or purchase. Team members should completely familiarize themselves with the legal issues outlined in this chapter, because a breach of any major legal requirement may well undermine the overall acquisition transaction.

State Laws

Corporations are chartered by their respective states, and must comply with the corporation laws applicable to that state. Whether a company is publicly or privately traded, it must comply with the state laws. In general, these laws should not excessively restrict a transaction but the final M&A transaction will not be legal unless the required state filings cannot be successfully completed.

If the companies involved are sole proprietorships, then corporate requirements will not apply and the transaction will likely be fully outlined in the transaction documents themselves. In this case, extra care must be afforded the sale contract because it is the final determination of contract terms and buyer/seller agreements. In general, transactions of any major size will involve corporations, and such transactions are the primary focus of this chapter.

Regulatory Considerations

The Securities Act of 1933 was initially enacted to provide a legal framework within which companies, desiring to publicly trade stock, could outline their financial status to investors. The Exchange Act of 1934 created the Securities and Exchange Commission and outlined procedures for the transfer of shares. These two acts were passed with the intention of correcting perceived market deficiencies, which at the time many believed contributed to the 1929 stock market crash. Companies traded stock and acquired each other under these guidelines until 1968, when the Senate passed the Williams Act, which amended existing law to provide a framework for M&A activities. It is primarily the changes added from this act that prescribe the specific levels of disclosure and time frames associated with current publicly traded company M&A activities.

Prior to the enactment of the Williams Act, companies could place potentially unreasonable (short) time frames on shareholders for making decisions regarding the acceptance or rejection of a purchase offer. Information disclosure was inconsistent and substantially at the discretion of the companies involved, often putting the stockholder at a disadvantage. A major intent of the Williams Act was to standardize the M&A disclosure requirements so that investors could make informed decisions about their publicly traded shares during an acquisition. Table 21.1 shows various SEC filings and schedules which help a company comply with the Williams Act.

There are various other regulations, timings, and stipulations associated with a tender offer and its processes. For example, the tender offer is considered to start at 12:01 AM of the day that the tender offer is published, advertised, or from when the tender offer materials are delivered to the target company. The buyer then has five days within which to distribute the tender offer materials.

It is possible to change the tender offer after it is first announced, but specific procedures must be followed in making the change, which is really considered to be a new offer. Target shareholders are given 20 days to consider the new offer which, for example, might have been prompted by a higher tender offer price.

Target company shareholders receive a packet that includes an *offer to purchase,* which outlines the terms and conditions of the tender offer, and a *Letter of Transmittal,* which outlines the method for transferring shares from the target shareholder to the buyer. Once tendered, shareholders can withdraw their tendered shares if desired by submitting a *letter of withdrawal* along with a *signature guarantee* that verifies that the signature of the submitting party is that of the shareholder.

A competing tender offer sent to shareholders provides the target shareholders with 10 days to consider the new offer. If the termination of the 10-day competing offer consideration period falls within the 20 days associated with the original tender offer, then no time frame extension is provided. If the competing offer's 10-day consideration period falls after the initial 20-day tender offer consideration period, then the time is extended as needed to allow 10 days consideration of the competing offer.

Being in violation of any of the various steps and time frames will at best complicate the tender offer process and can completely nullify the offer. Should the target company suffer any financial or public damage from the ill-planned offer, litigation against the buyer could swiftly follow. It should be clear from this discussion that the SEC-related requirements are substantial and full of pitfalls for the uninitiated. For this reason, I strongly suggest that you always use the services of an attorney experienced with SEC filing requirements when actually tendering an offer when either buyer or seller are

Table 21.1 Various Common SEC Filings and Schedules

Schedule/Filing	Description and Purpose
Schedule 14D-1	Filed with the SEC by the buyer at the time of initiating a tender offer. Includes detailed information about the buyer, its source of funds, and reason for pursuing the transaction. Ten (10) copies must be filed with the SEC, a copy must be hand delivered to the target company's executive offices, a copy must be hand delivered to any and all other bidders for the target company, and a copy, along with a phone call, must be delivered to each exchange on which the target company's stock is traded.
Schedule 14D-9	Filed with the SEC by the target of the tender offer within 10 days of the tender offer commencement date. Indicates whether the target company accepts or rejects the offer and provides information about the target company itself that is similar to that provided by the buyer in Schedule 14D-1. A copy is filed with the SEC and copies must be sent to each exchange on which the target company's stock is traded.
Schedule 13D	Must be filed with the SEC by the acquiring firm within 10 days of acquiring five percent of another firm's outstanding stock. Six (6) copies are filed with the SEC. One additional copy must be sent by registered or certified mail to the executive offices of the target company.
Schedule 13G	Filed by shareholders who obtain more than five percent of a company's outstanding shares, but acquired no more than two percent in the prior 12-month period and do not intend to take control of the company. Must be filed with the SEC on February 14th of each year.
10K Filing	A required annual filing with the SEC by any corporation with more than 500 shareholders and over $2 million in assets. Must be filed within 90 days of the end of the company's fiscal year.
10Q Filing	Similar to a 10K except filed on a quarterly basis, within 45 days of the company's fiscal quarter end.
8K Filing	Filed by a company when any substantial change occurs that could materially affect an investor's decision to buy, sell, or hold that company's stock. Typical events that require an 8K filing include a change in accounting procedures, change in ownership, bankruptcy, change of director, and the sale or acquisition of more than 10 percent of the company's assets. Must be filed no later than 15 days from the occurrence of the triggering event.

publicly traded. You should also be aware that the regulated time frames and filings may impact competitor and shareholder reactions as you plan your specific acquisition tactics. It is important that buyers remember that they want target company shareholders to accept the tender offer and should make the entire tendering process as simple as possible for the shareholders.

Differentiating a Tender Offer from a Voluntary Acquisition

It might be valuable at this point to differentiate between a tender offer and a voluntary acquisition. The context of the two transactions is really very different and the filing requirements reflect the difference. A *voluntary acquisition* is one worked out between the management and board of directors of both the buying and selling companies. The two companies agree that the acquisition is in the best interest of both companies and agree to proceed, usually pending approval by the respective company shareholders. Notice that the transaction is really accomplished between the two companies and the shareholders are asked to go along with the judgment of their board members. A *tender offer,* instead, takes the acquisition offer directly to the shareholders of the target company and is usually pursued when negotiations with the target company's board of directors have not met with the buyer's acquisition goals. It is much simpler to merge the two companies when everyone agrees, as anyone who watched the Pfizer, American Home Products, and Warner-Lambert situation unfold would agree.

It is possible for the buying company to simply walk away from a target when the target's board is strongly against the acquisition. It is also possible for the buyer to believe that the shareholders will eventually realize that the buyer's offer is in the shareholder's interest if presented directly with the offer. The tender offer is then made directly to the shareholders, bypassing the target's management and board of directors. The buyer's expectation is that the target's shareholders will accept the highest offer even if their board or directors strongly urges the target shareholders to do otherwise. The target's board of directors can and often does take specific measures to ward off the tender offer, but there are specific boundaries which they cannot cross for fear of being found working against the interest of their shareholders, opening themselves up to future litigation against them or the company. The next section takes a closer look at board member responsibilities.

Board Member Responsibilities

A corporation's board of directors have the initial responsibility of evaluating the viability of any proposed buy, sell, or merger activities. Depending on the transaction type involved, the transaction may then require shareholder approval but a large level of trust is placed by shareholders into the hands of the board members. If the board strongly supports one position or another, the shareholders often simply go along either by explicit vote or by proxy voting.

Company board members must always make decisions based on their fiduciary responsibility to the shareholders in that their decisions must act in such a way that increases shareholder wealth. Although this sounds fairly clear-cut, the reality is that various transaction details are open to interpretation and what may increase wealth in the eyes of one person may undercut wealth in the eyes of another. Laws are in place that provide guidelines for reasonable levels of interpretation on the part of board members.

Business Judgment Rule

It is tacitly assumed that board members act in the best interest of shareholders. Any shareholder who believes that his best interests were not served by a board decision must prove that this fiduciary responsibility was improperly executed. This assumption of innocence enables board members to accept transactions that might on the surface appear to work to the detriment of shareholders.

Assume that two acquisition offers are presented to the target company's board. BuyerA proposes a purchase price of $90 per share all-cash and fully intends to break up and sell the company components after purchase. BuyerB proposes an $85 per share purchase price paid for using BuyerB stock in the form of a merger. The target company's operations will be consolidated into BuyerB's existing structure. The board believes that future synergy with BuyerB will likely increase seller shares to a value of $115 in a 12-month period with an even larger increase possible. Even though the initial sale price to BuyerA is higher, the board may well contend that BuyerB's offer is in the shareholders' best interest. The business judgment rule protects board members should they accept BuyerB's offer instead of BuyerA's.

As with most legal issues, nothing is ever quite this clear-cut and board decisions are no exception. The courts have been called upon to evaluate various board decisions and their assessments provide a little more guidance with respect to appropriate board member actions.

Revlon Duties—Not Taking Defense Too Far

Continuing with the previous example, board members of a target company may truly believe that the breaking up of the company by BuyerA is not in seller shareholders' best interest. To protect against a breakup of the company, the target's board can enact certain antitakeover defenses that seriously decrease the value of the target company to a prospective buyer. Should buyers still persist with the purchase attempts, the board members may find themselves in a position where the breakup of the company becomes unavoidable. Once this point is reached, further attempts to undermine target company value through the enactment of antitakeover tactics may well begin working to the detriment of the ultimate intention of preserving seller shareholder value. This is where the Revlon Duties decisions come into play.

The Delaware Supreme Court decided in the *Revlon, Inc. v. MacAndrews and Forbes Holdings* case that board members caught in the position outlined in the prior paragraph have a duty to shift their focus from one of antitakeover defense to that of getting the highest possible price possible for the company. The board can take any legal steps needed to get the highest possible price during negotiations; however, further actions that undermine seller shareholder value interests while trying to avoid a takeover could be legally actionable against the board members.

Buying Back Shares as a Takeover Defense

A target company that is in play may find it best to purchase its own shares as a way of circumventing an unwanted tender offer. Assume that BuyerA presents a tender offer of $85 per share when the current market price is $75 per share. Board members may believe that this price represents a low purchase price for the stock and may not believe that shareholder interests are served by accepting this $85 offered price. As a defense, the board may authorize a self-tender offer where the company offers to purchase shares at a higher price of $90 per share.

Delaware Supreme Court decisions made in the *Unocal v. Mesa Petro-*

leum case contended that such actions by board members are acceptable as long as the board has a reasonable belief that corporate policies were in danger and that the actions were made in reasonable proportion to the danger presented. Remember that shareholders always have the option of selling shares to their buyer of preference, but that most shareholders will choose the highest offered price.

Strategic Mergers Are Not Invitations To Bid

The courts made an important ruling related to the difference between a company agreeing to a strategic merger and one actively available for purchase with the court's assessment of the *Paramount Communications, Inc. v. Time, Inc.* case. In its ruling, the court determined that the friendly merger agreement between Time, Inc. and Warner Communications, Inc. was a strategic merger thought best by the boards of directors of both companies. This did not imply that Warner Communications, Inc. was for sale but instead meant that the board of directors had exercised their business judgment rule prerogative and agreed to merge with Time, Inc.

When Paramount Communications, Inc. attempted an unsolicited purchase of Warner Communications, Inc., which was refused by Warner, the court determined that this unwanted advance was not warranted since Warner Communications, Inc. was not for sale but simply pursuing a merger which it thought was its best business course. The good news about this ruling is that a company can enter into a strategic merger agreement and not necessarily expose itself to having to ward off unwanted suitors.

Merger Discussion Disclosure Issues

When two companies are discussing a possible merger, it is best to keep the entire process secret until a final agreement is reached. Should an officer of either company deny the existence of ongoing discussions it may be construed as misleading to shareholders who are making buy, sell, or hold decisions based on currently available market information. The stock markets are assumed by many as efficient in that the share price at any point in time represents a valuation that incorporates all information available at that time. If misleading information is included in that mix, then efficient market theory no longer applies and shares may become "improperly" priced.

If nobody asks, company officials are not required to tell. If asked, it is best to answer "no comment" to any question, because this is neither affirming nor denying that talks are going on. But expressly denying the existence of merger talks when they indeed are going on is a misrepresentation of the truth and will likely open the company, officers, and board members to a class action suit if shareholders later contend that they financially suffered due to this misrepresentation.

Dealing with Holdout Minority Stake Owners

There is the very real possibility that a successful tender offer will not enable the buyer to obtain 100 percent of the target company's shares. It would be tempting for those last uncommitted shareholders to negotiate a higher price for their shares given their now-strategic position in the transaction. However, the buyer is afforded some protection under these circumstances as determined by specific state law.

In general, once a buyer owns 90 percent of the target's stock it can adopt a merger resolution and basically merge the purchased company with the buyer's. This is sometimes called a "short-form" merger. Those remaining uncommitted shareholders will receive the same compensation as all other shareholders who accepted the tender offer, with a legal proviso. The uncommitted shareholders usually retain the right to have the courts determine an objective fair value for their shares should they feel that the tender price seriously undervalues their shares.

Insider Trading-Related Issues

Insider trading is an important issue to shareholders involved with operation of a company pursuing an M&A transaction. Insider trading laws are in effect to minimize the likelihood of a shareholder profiting from nonpublic transaction information prior to that information's release to the general public.

Imagine that you are a founder/manager of a company that is in the middle of an already-announced merger transaction. Also assume that this particular transaction has a possibility of being terminated by the Justice Department on an antitrust basis. Assume that the initial reaction by the stock market was favorable in that your company's stock rose 10 percent within a few days of the announcement. Finally, assume that you just found out that the Justice Department does indeed plan to open a full investigation into the transaction based on its initial contention that the deal would be bad for consumers and a violation of antitrust laws.

If you bought stock just before your company announced its intention to merge and enjoyed the run up of stock price after the merger public announcement, it would be really tempting to sell your stock before the Justice Department ruling becomes public knowledge, because you firmly believe that your stock will drop to a price even lower that your initial purchase price. If you act on this news and sell your stock before the public announcement, you are acting on insider information and could be found in violation of securities fraud laws. But what if you are not an employee or manager? What if you are a consultant or contractor working for the company? If you have proprietary information that is not available to the general public and you use this information in your trading activities, you may also be in violation of insider trading laws.

It used to be that the buyer or seller of stock had to have some type of fiduciary role within the company to be subject to insider trading stipulations. That is no longer the case. If you are exposed to privileged information and act on that information to your own gain, then you could find yourself guilty of insider trading. The short swing profit rule is designed to provide some type of objective guideline for what is acceptable trading for corporation insiders. The rule states that officers, directors, or owners of 10 percent or more of a company's stock cannot perform a sale followed by a purchase, or a purchase followed by a sale, within a six-month period of each other. The sale or purchase do not even need to be prompted with insider trading intention to subject the stockholder to penalties.

There is good news here for shareholder/employees, though. The courts found in the *SEC v. Pegram* decision that it was legal to decide to initiate a trade as part of a planned investment strategy that had nothing at all to do with insider information. Assume that an insider, in March, decides to sell a block of stock in September so that the money could be used to purchase stock in other companies, the intention being to diversify the shareholder's portfolio. Should the company suffer some type of financial setback in August of the same year that could not have been foreseen to the shareholder when the intention to sell was initially revealed in March, then the sale can occur without exposing the seller to insider trading or fraud issues. It is difficult for shareholder/owners to separate their personal finances from the success of their companies. The most direct way for shareholder/owners to benefit from their share-generated wealth is to sell some of their shares. These insider issues only apply to publicly traded companies because closely held company shares cannot be as readily transferred from one owner to another.

The Legal Obligations of Professionals

The manager of an M&A team is really managing a group of directed professionals. Team membership will change over the course of the acquisition depending on the issues at hand and level of target company familiarity. At some point the work of the business analysts, accountants, lawyers, engineers, and personnel department will come together to create a complete picture of the target company. The team manager's job is to make sure that this picture accurately reflects the realities of the target company as it is today and reasonably projects future value to the buyer. Understanding exactly what you can expect from team professionals is an important part of having them deliver the needed assessments. This section takes a closer look at the roles of accountants and lawyers.

Accountants

Financial analysis is an integral part of any acquisition because much of the valuation is based on historical and projected financial information. If the underlying information is not accurate, then it is difficult to accurately determine a purchase price. Managers truly appreciate a well-prepared, reliable set of financial records so that business decisions can be made on a solid financial information footing. The role of the accountant becomes important at this point. An accountant should be an integral part of the acquisition team and should be familiar with the buyer's business as well as the financial objectives for the acquisition. This may be obvious, but make sure that your accountant has some experience with merger and acquisition transactions and their many nuances.

Audits are a common starting place for any acquisition team accountant. Whether you accept the audited statements of the target company or have your accountants perform their own audit, it is critical that the financial assumptions be verified over a period of several years. You will also need financial reporting information for your own firm if Form 8K reporting is required. Have your accounting team initially review the audited records of the target company. Areas of particular interest involve revenue recognition, depreciation methods, inventory valuation, and accounts receivable. These business areas are critical to the operation of any company and a thorough understanding of the accounting procedures used in their valuation determination is instrumental to a complete understanding. Expect that the accountant report will contain caveats regarding inability to verify underlying information, the time frame limits over which the analysis applies, and others. Make sure that the report covers the periods of interest to you and the other business members of the acquisition team. A glowing or negative report that does not cover the business area or time frames of interest is of little business benefit even though it might be completely accurate from a GAAP perspective. It is customary to ask a CPA for a "comfort letter" that outlines various financial aspects of the acquisition. This letter may be requested by either buyer or seller if the transfer of stock is involved. The comfort letter has a specific format that should be available from your CPA.

An accountant will be able to provide you with tax advice regarding the transaction. This is particularly important if the seller or buyer is a privately held corporation. Your accounting team should also take a close look at the postacquisition challenges associated with integrating the two companies' accounting systems and procedures. This is an important part of the due diligence process that should not be shortchanged. The costs and disruption associated with data and system conversion, along with data verification, can be substantial. Having an accountant as an integral part of the acquisition team is recommended so that the accountant becomes well aware of the financial and business goals of the transaction. The accountant will be sensitive to any areas where provided information may be used or interpreted in such a way that exposes the accountant to later litigation. Contracted accounting firms will likely want an engagement letter that clearly defines their intended roles and the limits of their liability.

Lawyers

Lawyers are trained to make sure that a specific legal document contains all the necessary ingredients needed to make it legally binding. Lawyers are not, on the other hand, typically excellent business managers. That is your job and the lawyer is there to ensure that your business objectives are legally defined and executed in a binding agreement signed by all concerned parties. Have at least one attorney as an integral part of your due diligence process. This attorney must have experience with M&A negotiations and contracts as necessary background requirements.

Specialized attorneys are often brought in to review such important legal issues as intellectual property ownership, corporate entity legal standing with the state, ESOP structures, licensing agreements, employment agreements, and other legal aspects that are inherent to the value and later operation of the acquisition. These evaluations are often done early in the due diligence process, because a problem in any of these key legal areas may be a deal-stopper. Uncovering them early saves money that would otherwise have been spent in other due diligence areas. Some people use their lawyers to negotiate the actual transaction details with clear guidance from the acquisition team. Others prefer to work out the major points of a transaction between the primarily responsible persons on both the buyer and seller sides. Once decided, they hand the letter of understanding to the attorneys to work out the specific verbiage.

Either approach can be right depending on the circumstances. It is critical, however, that the documents being signed are thoroughly read and understood by the signing parties. This is particularly true when selling a privately held corporation using contracted legal services. The lawyer goes home with a check once the agreement is signed, but the buyer and seller must live with whatever is included in the finally signed agreement. Blaming a contractual mistake on the lawyers is no replacement for an agreement that clearly defines the actual intentions of buyer and seller.

Be clear with the attorney regarding your negotiation points. Keep notes of your conversations and create a correspondence log related to all legal communications. Set up ground rules for interaction between you and your attorney, between your attorney and the client, and your company's attorney and the other party's attorney. Remember that you control the business aspects of the transaction while your attorney makes sure that the contract language reflects your desired and agreed-upon arrangements.

Chapter Summary

M&A transactions place businesses, employees, shareholders, and managers in unique situations. Buying and selling a business is not a common occurrence for most corporations or company owners. The complexities associated with the sale of publicly traded companies are strict. It is important for the business M&A manager to understand that there are specific legal constraints within which all negotiations must transpire. If the persons involved with the M&A transaction are also shareholders, then another set of criteria is applied to determine if any traded shares are the result of insider information. Without some knowledge of these various legal areas a manager could unknowingly expose himself and his company to legal actions that could otherwise have been avoided.

Board members have a specific responsibility to act in ways that enhance shareholder value, but they also have certain protections with respect to how their responsibilities are executed. Due diligence team managers should also clearly understand what can and cannot be expected from professionals such as lawyers and accountants. The more clearly everyone on the team understands the objectives and limits of involvement, the more reasonably and efficiently the due diligence process will proceed.

This chapter was not designed to make you an expert in the various legal aspects associated with the purchase and sale of a publicly traded company. It is, however, designed to create an appreciation and understanding of the importance and complexities associated with an M&A transaction. You should make sure that the right people, with the right knowledge, are on hand to ensure that the transaction proceeds smoothly, legally, and profitably for all involved parties. Finally, you should make sure that your particular legal situation is evaluated by an attorney.

22

After the Deal Closes

Many studies indicate that a large part of the value associated with an acquisition lies in the methods of handling the postacquisition environment. Thinking that the deal is finished when the documents are signed is not atypical, but it certainly appears mistaken, just as selling a technical product and not providing postsale support is a mistake. This chapter investigates areas of consideration when developing an integration strategy and provides specific steps to get you started on the path of successful postacquisition integration.

General Posttransaction Issues

The types of actions covered in this chapter deal primarily with organizations choosing to integrate the acquired business into the buyer's already existing environment. There are times when this might not be best. These exceptions are covered in the next three sections with information presented throughout the remaining section generally applicable to all post transaction situations.

Acquire and Separate

If the acquisition was financially motivated with the intention of breaking up the purchased company after purchase, then working to integrate makes no sense at all. It is probably best to make your intentions known and to inform employees, vendors, investors, and others that you intend to split up the organization. Once you have determined the dividing lines, act promptly to make it happen. Indecision usually breeds inaction on the part of employees, and your entire acquired venture could stand still while you remain in indecision. That is costly and counterproductive.

Divesting

You might be divesting the company of one or more of its divisions. If this is the case, you must take steps to ensure that the soon-to-be standalone entity has the required overhead and other functions to operate as a totally separate unit. This is the reverse of acquisition merging; you are actually making sure that the unit that was previously merged can stand on its own when divested.

Acquire and Isolate

There is no requirement that a fully acquired company must be fully integrated into the financially merged company's operation. In fact, there are excellent times when operational integration is counterproductive.

Assume that the buyer is a large, highly structured company. The acquired company is highly entrepreneurial, highly creative, and proud of its dynamic energy. A large part of the value purchased with the acquisition was to capitalize on the creative by-products of this group. Making this group conform to the larger organization may, and likely will, undermine the very creativity that you purchased in the first place. Integrating the acquired company personnel into the larger company but allowing them to operate under a different, less restrictive, set of rules will likely engender resentment by the buyer's existing employees. This resentment might be aimed at both the acquired employees and also the managers who let this happen.

An alternate approach to integration is to leave the acquired company as a completely separate operational entity. It can still take advantage of the buyer's economy of scale opportunities such as advertising, benefits procurement, financing, and other areas that improve margins. When products or services are created, they can then be transferred to the larger organization for full marketing capitalization. Remember that the valuable asset purchased in this example was the creative energy of the target company's personnel and processes.

Transition Team

A transition team should be set up to handle the important decisions related to company integration. Many of the larger strategic issues related to the integration were likely worked out in the acquisition process itself. The transition team's job is to now take the steps needed to implement the directional changes deemed most desirable during the acquisition process. The team should have the ear of top management of both the buyer and seller, with top management attending meetings on occasion to simply demonstrate the importance that they place on the integration process.

The team should include members from both the buyer and seller company. The overall strategic goals of the integration should be clearly understood, along with the time frame for implementation. Members should align their actions so that every step taken brings a successful integration closer to being a reality. Other team members should be from operations, engineering, legal, personnel, marketing, sales, and finance. All team members may not be needed at each meeting and can be called in on an as-needed basis, but there should be a core management group whose single focus is the successful management of this integration process.

The team should clearly understand that things won't simply happen because they issue a memo to employees that it should. There may be resentment, contempt, boredom, apathy, or other emotions involved with the integration process on behalf of buyer and seller employees. The team must find a way to overcome integration obstacles. It must find ways to motivate employees to move on their own in the direction of integration. Memos or emails from the team to affected employees is a good idea. If affected employees feel that something positive is happening, they will be more likely to give the team and management the benefit of the doubt. If the integration is "done" and things are not as the employee expected, management may find that a previously confused employee will become disgruntled. See the later sections that cover communication for additional information on this important topic.

Timing Considerations

As mentioned earlier, the sooner you begin integration procedures, the better it typically is for everyone. This does not mean that an unplanned knee-jerk response is needed. It means that the transition team should have clear marching orders to start, and start now. People expect changes to occur immediately after an acquisition. They may not like the thought that change is coming, but they have accepted that as a fact of life associated with the purchase. Dragging your feet for weeks, or months, before making changes will allow employees to get back into their old mode of operation. When you later choose to make changes, you will likely find dissatisfied employees who resent being disrupted again.

Metaphorically speaking, I have always felt that getting all of one's wisdom teeth pulled at once may hurt a little more, but it is going to hurt whether the dentist pulls two teeth or all of them. Go through the pain once and get it over with: Get all teeth pulled. Similarly, plan the integration during the due diligence stages or immediately afterwards. Then, barring any legal restrictions to the contrary, get to work taking very specific actions while everyone is still disrupted as part of the purchase.

Involve Both Buyer and Seller

The seller's employees understand the seller's culture. The buyer's employees understand the buyer's culture. Any transition team must include members of both companies in a functional, contributory way to really optimize postpurchase returns. Some buyers feel that they know what is best for the seller and now that the seller's company is owned by the buyer, the buyer is going to make the seller function like the buyer feels it should. This type of unilateral mandate on the part of the buyer is almost always a mistake. It will most likely breed resentment on the part of the buyer's personnel. At best, it will likely create an environment in which the seller's personnel are polite, never overtly disrespectful, but inconspicuously undermining the buyer's integration intentions.

In the early 1980s Texas saw a huge influx of people from northern states such as Illinois, New York, and Ohio. These new people decided in many cases to "show" the Texans how things were done. When I moved to Texas in the late 1980s, I was lumped in with all the others who came from northern states. Although people were rarely directly impolite, they clearly had a closed ear to any recommendations from an outsider. One day, I saw a bumper sticker that shed light on my confusion. It read, "We don't care how you do it up north!" Not respecting the culture of either buyer or seller can create this type of animosity that will certainly cause loss of return on the acquisition investment. Involving both buyer and seller in the integration planning and implementation is a required first step when moving toward successful integration.

The Need for Communication

Effective communication is arguably the most important ingredient of an integration plan. The best personnel with the highest levels of commitment and motivation can be completely undermined by a poor communication process that keeps them from working in sync with each other. This communication does not need to be complicated in structure, but it needs to be consistent and sincere in its execution. Daily meetings in the first few weeks after the acquisition are probably warranted, and these meetings can move to every other day, then weekly and so forth, until they are no longer needed. Watch the team dynamics carefully. The cultural problems that you see come up between buyer and seller team members may well represent a microcosm of the larger problems to be solved later. If you can't solve them on the team level, you will probably not be very lucky on the production floor either.

Communication is a two-way street. Open communication should exist on the team and also between team members and employees. Set up a letter or email box to which employees can send comments, recommendations, or complaints. Make sure that employees know that no recrimination will be taken against people who write in and that all submissions will receive a reply. Consider posting an integration accomplishments history on a bulletin board, or internal Web location, so that employees can see how things are going. Provide a simple email link from the report so that employees can easily respond to the team with respect to a given reported item.

You might even want to go so far as to use some of the available groupware tools to create a survey where employees provide structured feedback on their perceptions regarding the levels of progress seen. Keeping track of these surveys should provide the team not only with valuable feedback, but also inform it as to when it is no longer needed. At some point the number of respondents will level out. The comments will become routinely the same and will likely come from the same people. In short, a status quo will be reached and the team will know that it is no longer needed to manage the integration. The problems that now exist are those of a completely integrated organization.

Legal Issues

Business life can be messy and complicated. The seller may have taken certain aspects of the operation for granted that now must be reassessed in light of the acquisition, as shown in Table 22.1. In addition, the transaction itself may have some lingering legal aspects that require attention in the postacquisition environment.

Making sure that all legal aspects of the transaction are covered is often not very glamorous, but it is important. If the legal foundation of the newly

Table 22.1 Last-Minute Legal Aspects—Postacquisition

Items	Possible Required Actions
Filing of IRS forms	Filing of the final 1099 and other related IRS-related forms.
Banking Accounts	These accounts should be closed with appropriate balances transferred to the buyer's accounts, as appropriate.
SEC Filings	All required SEC filings related to the transaction should be verified as filed and updated as needed.
Title Transfers	All associated assets and other titled filings must be updated to reflect the new ownership.
Material Violations of Acquisition Agreement	Should violations of the letter of intent or acquisition agreement occur, the proper legal filings must be made to secure the proper remedies.
Price Adjustments	Due diligence may uncover areas that will require a future assessment with respect to the purchase price. These are messy and should be avoided if at all possible.
Shared Assets or Services	Seller may have shared a building or service with another company. These relationships must be transferred to the buyer or renegotiated with prior coshare business.
As Needed By Counsel	The legal members of the transition team should create a listing of legal action items for tracking as part of the transition management process.

acquired relationship is not securely in place, then the entire future of the acquisition is in jeopardy.

Cultural Issues

Taking stock of cultural issues is not a trivial task but an important one that the personnel departments of both companies should undertake as a joint project. Table 22.2 is a partial listing of cultural areas that should be considered when determining the right way of handling future integrated activities. Remember that the seller may have ways of doing things from which the buyer can benefit, and vice versa. Keeping an open mind is the key to finding value when integrating cultures. Unless specified otherwise, assume that the table refers to both buyer and seller cultures.

Table 22.2 Cultural Transitions—Postacquisition

Item	Description and Comment
Management Communication	How does management communicate with employees? Is it written, oral, or in person? How is important news relayed?
Management Decision Making	How are major decisions made in the company? Do employees pay undue attention when specific events happen as indicators of major decisions being in process?
Cultural Activities	How does the company handle events such as birthdays, weddings, new babies, and others? Is there a company picnic or beer bust-like event that is an integral part of the culture?
Holidays and Shut Downs	What are the company holidays or plant shutdown periods? How do employees feel about these, and have they been asking for changes to this policy?
Union Status	How does the union fit in with the companies? Can union and nonunion employees be mixed in the same environment without engendering resentment on either party's behalf?
Overtime	Does each company have an explicit or tacit position on mandatory overtime or avoiding overtime completely?
Incidentals	What are the company positions on smaller items such as premium coffee, free snacks, cafeteria food, smoking, work hours reporting, dispute resolution and escalation, music at work, and others?

It is amazing how the simplest things can have far-reaching significance. Coffee, for example, is a regular source of comment. Assume that the seller used to provide its employees with a premium coffee as an unwritten benefit. The buyer has a reputation for streamlining costs whenever possible but has specifically agreed to not implement these cost-cutting policies with the seller's organization, which it intends to leave as a standalone, wholly owned business. A simple act like changing the coffee at the seller's site from premium to standard could be interpreted by employees as the first indication that the buyer eventually intends to renege on its agreement. More than once I have heard coffee brought up as an indicator of the management policies. Sensitivity to these simple issues can keep either buyer or seller from taking a simple action that could have far-reaching implications specifically because of the cultural environment within which it happened.

Management Issues

In the midst of the changes involved with the integration, it is important that management keep a clear, timely focus on resolving and preserving the major value areas. The key value areas will have been highlighted during due diligence and should be a primary focus of the transition team's project plan.

Sales and Marketing

Sales and marketing is primary to the integration process. A decrease in sales revenue on the part of either buyer or seller can have a serious impact not only on daily operations but will also impact the investment return received from the acquisition. This topic is so important that a special section is dedicated to its management and is presented later in this chapter.

Personnel

Redundancy is a fact of life with many mergers. Where the two separate entities once required multiple people to perform a function, only a smaller percentage of those people may be required in the postacquisition environment. This is a harsh fact of M&A life but a very real one nonetheless.

If downsizing of personnel on either the buyer or seller's side is required, then it should be treated in a respectful and courteous way. Treating downsized employees with anything less is unnecessary and will definitely be noticed by those employees that remain behind. In today's technology business climate, nobody can afford to lose key technology personnel. They are difficult and expensive to replace. Taking good care of those employees who must be downsized will reflect well on the company and better promote employee loyalty while performing what is always a difficult process.

Although I encourage you to act swiftly if downsizing is required, I also encourage you to be selective about who you let go. Letting people go because of their position on the organization chart could do tremendous damage due to cultural issues related to certain employees. Many long-standing employees may have power within an organization that has nothing to do with their job title. Treating that person poorly could create far-reaching consequences that could simply have been avoided with a little further study. Assisting downsized employees with interviewing techniques, outplacement assistance, job hunting, and retraining may ultimately turn out to be the least expensive way of letting people go. Make sure that personnel is involved with any downsizing decisions and that legal has been contacted with respect to potential litigation issues resulting from the downsizing. Downsizing is never a process to be entered into lightly, but it is one that should be done swiftly, surely, and in an informed way when finally started.

Tracking Actual-to-Projection Results

Some companies take the stand that once the integration starts, there is no longer any reason to track the two companies as separate entities. Their contention is that tracking the performance of the acquired entity, once integrated into the buyer's organization, adds complexity to what is already a difficult process. They may also contend that it distracts from the overall intent of postmerger integration, which is to treat the two entities as one.

The M&A team may have another perspective on things, however. Without feedback it is difficult to assess performance level. If the financial and operational results of the acquired company are not tracked against the objectives set out at acquisition, then the team has no way of determining if its acquisition process is working or not. Overall merged entity performance is the ultimate determining factor, but without separately breaking out the acquired company's performance there is no way of determining if the merged company performance changes were the result of the acquisition itself, resulting synergy, or some completely independent outside influence.

Whether the performance can be tracked or not will depend in large part on the tracking systems in place within the buyer's organization. Top management may not want to track the entity performance for political reasons. If the company, overall, does well but the acquisition underperforms then this information could be used against an executive who would otherwise get stellar marks. Why track something that could later have a negative political fallout? This is a question that each executive must answer personally.

Marketing Integration

An uninterrupted marketing and sales process is perhaps one of the most important aspects of acquired company integration. This process is often not handled well at all, and customers tend to take a "wait and see" attitude with respect to actual performance in the postacquisition environment. When the buyer is much larger than the seller, the buyer's customers will not react in any substantial way at all. But the seller's customers will wonder what the acquisition will do to their existing relationship with the seller. When the two merged entities are very large and of comparable size, then both buyer's and seller's customers will be interested and possibly concerned. This section investigates some important postacquisition items that may be applicable to your particular situation.

Brand Equity Expansion or Sacrifice

Seller and buyer both have their brands. These brands have a position in the customer's mind. That position may be positive or negative based on the customer's prior experience with the company offering these branded products or services. Combining companies presents a chance to restructure the offering of products and services under the various brand labels.

Assume, for example, that the seller has a great product but a terrible service network. Also assume that the buyer has a great service network that is nationally branded and respected. Saying that the seller's prior products are now serviced under the buyer's reputable brand will likely increase sales of the affected products while also increasing service revenues. This branding overlap can work both ways in that some seller products or services might sell better under the buyer's brand names while some of the buyer's products or services might sell better under the seller's brands. Acquisitions present a unique chance to restructure brands and products in such a way that optimizes value while retaining customer credibility. Don't forget that the companies themselves are brands and require some type of integration/synergy strategy.

Products and Services

Product and service integration typically happens in two stages: the short-term stage, in which immediate overlap and synergy is exploited, and the longer-term stage, in which cooperative product and service development is pursued. It is important that the marketing team develop a strategy that provides for both the short-term and long-term phases.

Short-term synergism includes the ability to easily sell one product when another is already committed for purchase by the customer. The ability to cross-sell additional product offerings can provide extensive short-term revenue opportunities. Long-term benefits require that the marketing and product management teams treat the two company's products and services as a single offering. Product consolidation and cross-pollination can create tremendous longer-term benefits as long as the teams managing the product specification process keep their eyes open for opportunities.

Sales and Marketing

An area of possible conflict in both the short- and longer-term time frame is the division of territory and product lines between salespeople. If the salespeople are confused, the customers will become confused and a confused customer is rarely a customer who buys. A thorough investigation of territories, products, customers, and quotas must be performed with the initial emphasis on keeping the sales machine working at its prior capacity. Joint sales calls may be possible depending on the cultures and products involved. Territory shifts in the middle of the business or buying cycle could be counterproductive and should be rigorously examined before implemented.

A careful examination should also be undertaken to ensure that the acquisition has not created a disincentive for salespeople to bring in orders. This is particularly true when buying a competitor whose salespeople are currently selling to the same customers with competitive products. If this situation is not handled properly and quickly, the salespeople who are now from the same company may still compete with each other for the customer's business. Customers may take advantage of this situation in the short term but will start to have concerns about this type of in-company competition if it continues for very long.

The longer-term perspective can include segmenting the products between different sales forces, consolidating products and services into a single sales force with smaller territories, or any number of other sales management approaches. Acquisitions present opportunities for enhancing the sales and marketing process. Ultimately the seller and buyer customer databases will likely be combined, so putting the database analysts to work on this integration earlier in the process will only make the later process smoother and less disruptive to personnel and customers.

Benefit Marketing/Selling Is the Key

As with everything else involved with successful technology marketing and sales, benefit selling is the real ticket to success. Marketing and sales should make a sincere and strong effort to ensure that buyer and seller customers are presented with the consistent message that the acquisition will benefit them. The marketing and sales effort must then back up this message with concrete actions that indicate to the customer that these benefits are already starting to happen and will only get better.

Technology customers arc pretty sophisticated. They will recognize the marketing message for what it is, and will also recognize the actions for what they are. If the actions support the message then the acquisition will be perceived as positive, with an enhanced customer relationship being the result. If the actions are not consistent with the message, credibility could be lost, which is usually expensive and time-consuming to recover.

Postsale/Purchase Debriefing

The acquisition process is constantly evolving with new analysis techniques and the rapid change of technology. The marketplace changes rapidly, and so does the speed with which information flows between organizations. An M&A process must change with the demands of the marketplace. The acquisition team should consider taking the following steps as a learning tool for working more effectively in the future.

1. How would you assess and improve on the finding of an acquisition candidate?

2. What was your opinion of the broker or other finder service used in the last acquisition? Would you trust or use this resource again?

3. How would you assess the effectiveness of the other outside professionals used on the acquisition? Would you recommend using them again?

4. Do you think that we got the target for a fair price? If not, what would have been a more fair price from your perspective? Explain your answer.

5. How was the letter of intent stage handled, and what would you recommend in the future to make it more effective?

6. How would you assess the due diligence stage, and what would you do in the future to make the process more effective?

7. Are you pleased with the legal services provided, and would you use them again in the future?

8. Did the postacquisition integration work out as planned? What could have been done to make that process more effective?

9. How would you assess the internal team communication achieved with the last transaction? What could be done to improve team internal communication and cooperation?

10. Is there any additional resource that should be added to the acquisition team? If so, what is it and why would you recommend its addition? Do you have any recommendations with respect to people or technology that could help in getting that resource included with the team?

This is not an exhaustive listing of possible topics for consideration, but it provides a basic framework around which you can determine the specific areas and questions of interest to you and the other team members. Only through this type of postacquisition evaluation can you derive continuing process improvement which will make all future acquisitions easier, more interesting, and more productive. Deals will always come along and you want to be ready when they do.

Chapter Summary

Any well-run organization will perform effective sales, marketing, financial, and operational analysis on a regular basis. These analyses are the basis of future strategic success. An acquisition presents a point in time where customers, employees, investors, the media, and others expect changes. This shift in expectations can provide the opportunity for buyer and seller to rearrange their operations in ways that otherwise may raise suspicion. As a result, it is important that seller and buyer management not treat an acquisition as "just any other time" since opportunities could be lost by not using this strategic shifting point to its full advantage.

It may best serve the future prospects of the postacquisition entity to merge, separate, divest, or isolate the operations and cultural aspects of buyer and seller companies. Choosing the optimal configuration requires a sensitivity to the companies and objectives involved with the acquisition. Any number of legal and cultural issues can create discord or opportunities for co-operation between buying and selling companies, depending on the handling of the situation by involved buyer and seller teams. If substantial changes are expected then prompt action is recommended so that affected personnel know quickly and the companies can move forward with minimal uncertainty.

Buyers are encouraged to perform a team debriefing after an acquisition is finalized. M&A due diligence and other processes should be evaluated, along with chosen methods for integrating the organizations. Team members may find that their duties should be reassigned to best capitalize on existing skill sets or areas of interest. Methods of evaluating the success of an acquisition should be developed and tracked into the reasonable future as a way of better designing methods for setting valid expectations. Above all, team members must remember that the value of an acquisition appears in future results that occur after the acquisition is finalized. Making sure that areas of value are preserved and capitalized on in the postacquisition environment is of paramount importance. Much of the value associated with a technology acquisition lies in the people acquired with the transaction, and losing those people may mean losing a large portion of the acquired value. For this reason alone, some buyers choose potential acquisition candidates using cultural compatibility as a critically important consideration.

Creativity is critical in rapidly changing technology fields. Companies don't create: People create. Disregarding the impact of an acquisition on key personnel may cause the exit of the most marketable employees, which seriously erodes the value of the acquired personnel assets. Financial analysis is an important part of the acquisition process, but care must also be given to ensure that the cultures and employees of value are not overlooked if a successful acquisition is desired.

Bibliography

Technology Investing

1. Murphy, Michael. *Every Investor's Guide to High-Tech Stocks and Mutual Funds.* New York: Broadway Books, 1999.

Financial Analysis and Accounting

1. Livingstone, John Leslie. *The Portable MBA in Finance and Accounting,* 2nd ed. New York: John Wiley and Sons, 1997.

2. Ramesh, K. S. Rao. *Financial Management, Concepts and Applications.* New York: Macmillan Publishing, 1987.

3. Sulock, Joseph M., and John S. Dunkelberg. *Cases in Financial Management,* 2nd ed. New York: John Wiley and Sons, 1997.

4. Welsch, Glenn A., and Daniel G. Short. *Fundamentals of Financial Accounting,* 5th ed. Homewood, IL: Irwin, 1987.

5. White, Gerald I., Ashwinpaul C. Sondhi, and Dov Fried. *The Analysis and Use of Financial Statements,* 2nd ed. New York: John Wiley and Sons, 1998.

Valuation

1. Copeland, Tom, Tim Koller, and Jack Murrin. *Valuation: Measuring and Managing the Value of Companies.* New York: John Wiley and Sons, 1995.

2. Damodaran, Aswath. *Damodaran on Valuation: Security Analysis for Investment and Corporate Finance.* New York: John Wiley and Sons, 1994.

3. Damodaran, Aswath. *Investment Valuation: Tools and Techniques for Determining the Value of Any Asset.* New York: John Wiley and Sons, 1996.

Strategic Issues

1. Aaker, David A. *Managing Brand Equity.* New York: Free Press, 1991.

2. Berringan, John, and Carl Finkenbeiner. *Segmentation Marketing: New Methods for Capturing Business Markets.* New York: HarperCollins Publishers, 1992.

3. Bruce, Margaret, and Birgit H. Jevnaker. *Management of Design Alliances: Sustaining Competitive Advantage.* West Sussex, UK: John Wiley and Sons, 1998.

4. Clemente, Mark N., and David S. Greenspan. *Winning at Mergers and Acquisitions: The Guide to Market-Focused Planning and Integration.* New York: John Wiley and Sons, 1998.

5. Ernst, David. *Collaborating to Compete: Using Strategic Alliances and Acquisitions in the Global Marketplace.* New York: John Wiley and Sons, 1993.

6. Martin, Michael J. C. *Managing Innovation and Entrepreneurship in Technology Based Firms.* New York: John Wiley and Sons, 1994.

7. Weinstein, Art. *Market Segmentation: Using Demographics, Psychographics, and Other Niche Marketing Techniques to Predict Customer Behavior.* Danvers, MA: Probus Publishing Company, 1994.

General M&A

1. Ernst & Young. *Mergers and Acquisitions: Back-to-Basics Techniques for the 90s,* 2nd ed. New York: John Wiley and Sons, 1994.

2. Gaughan, Patrick A. *Mergers, Acquisitions, and Corporate Restructuring,* 2nd ed. New York: John Wiley and Sons, 1999.

3. Hooke, Jeffrey C. *M&A: A Practical Guide to Doing the Deal.* New York: John Wiley and Sons, 1997.

4. Morris, Joseph M., et al. *Mergers and Acquisitions: Business Strategies for Accountants.* New York: John Wiley and Sons, 1995.

5. Paulson, Ed. *The Complete Idiot's Guide to Buying and Selling a Business.* Indianapolis: Alpha Books, 1999.

6. Rankine, Denzil. *A Practical Guide to Acquisitions: How to Increase Your Chances of Success.* West Sussex, UK: John Wiley and Sons, 1999.

7. Shea, Edward E. *The McGraw-Hill Guide to Acquiring and Divesting Businesses.* New York: McGraw-Hill Companies, 1999.

8. Sherman, Andrew J. *Mergers and Acquisitions from A to Z: Strategic and Practical Guidance for Small- and Middle-Market Buyers and Sellers.* New York: AMACOM, 1998.

9. West, Thomas L., and Jeffrey D. Jones, eds. *Mergers and Acquisitions Handbook for Small and Midsize Companies.* New York: John Wiley and Sons, 1997.

General Technology Company Histories

1. Dev Jager, Rama, and Rafael Ortiz. *In the Company of Giants: Candid Conversations with the Visionaries of the Digital Age.* New York: McGraw-Hill, 1997.

2. Jackson, Tim. *Inside Intel: Andy Grove and the Rise of the World's Most Powerful Chip Company*. New York: Penguin Putnam Inc., 1997.

3. Quittner, Joshua, and Michelle Slatalla. *Speeding the Net: The Inside Story of Netscape and How It Challenged Microsoft*. New York: Atlantic Monthly Press, 1998.

4. Swisher, Kara. *aol.com: How Steve Case Beat Bill Gates, Nailed the Netheads, and Made Millions in the War for the Web*. New York: Times Books, 1998.

Due Diligence Starting Checklist

DUE DILIGENCE GENERAL INVESTIGATION AREAS

General Background
  Buyer
    Contact Personnel
  Seller
    Contact Personnel
  Time Frame for Completion
  Buyer-Intended Objectives for Acquisition
Deal-Stoppers

AREAS OF INVESTIGATION

  Legal
    High-Impact Items
    Corporate Structure, Bylaws, Charter, etc.
    Ownership
    SEC Filings and Relationship
    Board of Directors
    Pending Litigation
    Intellectual Property Ownership

Regulatory Issues
Accounting and Finance
 High-Impact Items
 Past Accounting Procedures
 Verification of Financial Statements
 Internal Policies and Procedures
 Automation
 Auditing of Statements
 Publicly Traded Stock Performance
 Banking and Investor Relations
 Financial Structure
 In-Depth Ratio Analysis
 Forecasts
 Tax Situation
Research and Development Engineering
 High-Impact Items
 Internally Developed Technology
 Purchased Technology
 Unique Design Strategies and Techniques
 Adherence to Standards
 Independent Certification Testing (UL, CSA, etc.)
 Patent Review
 Key Engineering Developments and Personnel
 Verification of Product Performance to Specifications
 Design Verification Procedures
 New Technologies Under Development
 Success in Meeting Design Goals
 Research Alliances
Marketing and Sales
 High-Impact Items
 Customer Base Analysis
 Distribution Channel Analysis
 Product Definition Process
 Pricing and Demand Analysis
 Market Analysis
 Advertising and Promotion
 Regulatory Issues

Segmentation Analysis
Positioning
Future Strategies
Historical Trends by Product and Region
Personnel Review
Production
High-Impact Items
Manufacturing Locations
Yields and Performance
Proprietary Processes
Cost Breakdown by Product
Personnel
Union Issues
Environmental Impact Issues
Material Planning
Purchasing
Automation Levels
Human Resources
High-Impact Items
Policies
Retirement Plans
Benefit Package
Stock Options
Employee Contracts
Employee Turnover Rates
Pending Personnel-Related Litigation
Sources of Employees
Overall Cultural Assessment
Internet Usage
High-Impact Items
Internal Usage
External Usage
Technology in Use
Future Strategy
Management
High-Impact Items
Management Style

History of Executive Managers
Promotion Strategy
Corporate Culture Requirements
Overall Use of Technology (May warrant a dedicated section)
Reporting and Evaluation Procedures
Employee Development Policies

Index

Printed and bound by CPI Group (UK) Ltd, Croydon, CR0 4YY

16/04/2025

14658442-0008